MemoSur/MemoSouth
Memory, Commemoration and Trauma in Post-Dictatorship Argentina and Chile

Edited by
Adam Sharman
Milena Grass Kleiner
Anna Maria Lorusso
and
Sandra Savoini

Critical, Cultural and Communications Press
London
2017

MemoSur/MemoSouth: Memory, Commemoration and Trauma in Post-Dictatorship Argentina and Chile, edited by Adam Sharman, Milena Grass Kleiner, Anna Maria Lorusso and Sandra Savoini

Series: Studies in Post-Conflict Cultures, no. 10
Series Editor: Bernard McGuirk
The books in this series are refereed publications.

This volume forms part of the project *Memosur—A Lesson for Europe: Memory, Trauma and Reconciliation in Chile and Argentina*, funded by the European Commission, Marie Curie Actions – IRSES.

The rights of the editors to be identified as editors in this work have been asserted by them in accordance with the Copyrights, Designs and Patents Act, 1988.

Cover design by Hannibal.

Cover photograph, Pasaje Santa Catalina, Córdoba.
© Patrizia Violi, reproduced by permission.

Individual contributions © the contributors, 2017.

All unauthorised reproduction is hereby prohibited. This work is protected by law. It should not be duplicated or distributed, in whole or in part, in soft or hard copy, by any means whatsoever, without the prior and conditional permission of the Publisher, CCC Press.

First published in Great Britain by Critical, Cultural and Communications Press, London, 2017.

All rights reserved.

ISBN 9781905510504

Contents

Introduction: MemoSouth — A Note for Europe 7
Adam Sharman

The Politics of Memory

Disappearance, Mourning and the Politics of Memory 35
Patrizia Violi

The Politics of Remembering and Forgetting in the Argentine Education System 56
Daniel Filmus

"Who Needs Identity?": Disappearances and Appearances in Argentina — The Abuelas de la Plaza de Mayo 73
Cristina Demaria

How to Live after Loss?: Aparecida, Reparation and Collective Pleasures in Post-Dictatorial Argentina 93
Cecilia Sosa

The Museum and the Archive: Detention and Denunciation

Beyond the Walls: Campo de la Ribera (Argentina) and Villa Grimaldi (Chile) in the Urban and Social Fabric 115
José Manuel Rodríguez Amieva and Milena Grass Kleiner

Tracing Memory: A Semiotic Analysis of the Museum of Córdoba Provincial Memory Archive 147
Paola Sozzi

Live to Tell 164
Norma Fatala

The Closet, the Terror, the Archive: Confession and Testimony in LGBT Memories of Argentine State Terrorism 181
Daniele Salerno

Loathe Thy Neighbour: State-Led Violence and Popular Involvement in Franco's Spain and Argentina's Last Dictatorship   195
Daniel Oviedo Silva

Falklands-Malvinas

Traumas, Memories and Identity Processes   219
María Teresa Dalmasso

More Than 30 Years after the Malvinas: War in Film and on Television   236
Sandra Savoini

Returning: The Journey to the Islands in Contemporary Narratives about the Malvinas   249
Alicia Vaggione

Minefield/Campo Minado: A Veteran in the Theatre of War   261
Mike Seear

Staging

Foreign Plays and Repertoire in the Teatro de Ensayo de la Universidad Católica de Chile during the Dictatorship (1973-1989): Constructing a Canonical Interpretation   281
Andrea Pelegrí Kristić

Chronotopes of Truth and Memory in Post-Coup Chilean Theatre   298
Andrés Kalawski

Claudia Di Girólamo and Rodrigo Pérez's Aquí están*: Little Resistances in the Context of the Fortieth Anniversary Commemoration of the Military Coup in Chile*   314
María José Contreras Lorenzini

Scripts and Projections

Opposition to the Pinochet Regime: Two Movies for Two Kinds of Memory   333
Anna Maria Lorusso

Monstrosity and the (Re)Creation of Argentine History: An Analysis of La asombrosa excursión de Zamba   348
Sebastián Gastaldi

On the Use and Abuse of History in Post-Dictatorship Argentine Documentary   359
Adam Sharman

Figurations of Memory in Stories by Children of the Revolutionaries   375
Pampa Arán

"Why Did They Take Down the Pictures?": Conspicuous Absences and "La Historia de Algo Más" in Roberto Bolaño's Estrella distante   389
Rui Gonçalves Miranda

Notes on Contributors   410

Index   417

Introduction
MemoSouth — A Note for Europe

Adam Sharman

The Project and the Period

The essays in this volume have their beginnings in a project called *Memosur—A Lesson for Europe: Memory, Trauma and Reconciliation in Chile and Argentina*. The project involved institutions from four countries: Argentina, Chile, Italy and the UK.[1] The task was to bring together, whether in travelling or hosting, expertise (not only academic) from the fields of memory, post-conflict and post-traumatic studies, and to train that expertise on the post-dictatorship periods of Argentina and Chile. *Memosur* may be translated as Memosouth. The project and the book treat of southern memory—memory from South America and memory of South America, it being understood that "memory" has become a metonym for memory of dictatorship.

The name *Memosur* is a play on at least two names from South America: *Cono Sur* and *Mercosur*. The geographical area at the tip of South America is known as *el Cono Sur*, the Southern Cone, and the sub-regional trade area established in 1991 between Argentina, Brazil, Paraguay, Uruguay and Venezuela is called *Mercosur*, short for *Mercado Común del Sur*, Southern Common Market or (why not?) SouthMart. The project name's gesture towards the larger region is a reminder that the 1970s' Argentine and Chilean dictatorships that form the subject-matter of this book were, though of course absolutely singular in their particular configurations, by no means unique. Brazil, Uruguay, Paraguay and Bolivia all had the experience of dictatorship. Indeed, it is a matter of historical record that Brazil, in 1964, was the first in the region to "disappear"

---

[1] Funded by Marie Curie Actions—IRSES, European Commission, the project involved the Alma Mater Studiorum—Università di Bologna, the University of Nottingham, the Universidad Nacional de Córdoba, and the Pontificia Universidad Católica de Chile. The editors and all the participants in the Memosur project would like to express their gratitude to Marie Curie Actions. Thanks also go to Jeremy Lawrance, Bernard McGuirk and Gareth Stockey for their participation in the project; and to Cecilia Sosa, Bernard McGuirk and Mac Daly for their help in the preparation of this volume.

people, in that premeditated practice of state terror captured in language by the strange use of the transitive. In Gustavo Germano's photographic exhibition-installation, *Ausencias/Ausências* (Absences), he juxtaposes an original, usually family photograph taken in Argentina and dated mostly at some time in the 1970s with one taken by him in the same spot and with many of the same people in the 2000s.[2] Only in each of the updated photographs there is someone missing, or perhaps more than one person absent. The thing about the Brazilian photographs is that many of the originals date from the 1960s. The second point about the bigger picture is that the Southern Cone military regimes did not act alone, but were generally supported by the USA at a time when Cold War considerations were absolutely determining in Washington's foreign policy calculations.[3]

Argentina and Chile also had their particular histories. Political instability in Argentina stretching back to the first in a long line of twentieth-century *coups d'état* in September 1930 appears to have led to what Argentine social scientist Guillermo O'Donnell calls "mass praetorianism". According to O'Donnell (2002), as the century developed and the military coups piled up, powerful interest groups in the country, who all shared a belief in modernization but who all had a slightly different modernization in mind, got used to making aggressive sectoral demands that would frequently rely for their success on the backing of the armed forces, since they were the ones who exercised greatest power over the presidency. "The threats of a coup d'état were very real, and any government that valued its survival could not afford to ignore them [...] Norms tended to be transformed into naked power strategies. All those sectors that were capable of using the strategy of formulating threats against the government did so, for to be more threatening than the other sectors was the most effective means available to each sector for the attainment of its demands" (O'Donnell 2002: 402). If the general political instability had to be temporarily stabilized and a sector's interests served by yet another military intervention, then so be it. Politics thus became mass praetorianism. One of the lessons from the South, then, is

---

[2] **http://www.gustavogermano.com/gallery/ausencias/**.
[3] For a commanding history of and meditation on the phenomenon of the dictatorships, see Alain Rouquié (1987).

Introduction

that a Manichaean view of dictatorship has to be rethought. According to O'Donnell, many sectors of Argentine society (not just the conservative Catholic right, and not just the tarot card-dealing López Rega) had become accustomed to demanding, or at the very least half-expecting, military intervention. A former guerrilla fighter, remembering the political and economic chaos that preceded the coup of March 1976, recollects that he and many of his comrades shared the view that could be found in many walks of Argentine life: anyone in the Casa Rosada, the Presidential palace, apart from "that woman" (*esa mujer* being Isabel Perón, who had succeeded Perón when he died) (in Blaustein 1995). We don't care how you get her out… As though, incidentally, and after 46 years of military intervention, "that woman" was the problem.[4]

Chile was different. Long fêted as one of the most stable democracies on the subcontinent (though it too had known military rule in the twentieth century), the democratic tradition was abruptly interrupted by the Pinochet coup of 1973, at a time of political and economic turmoil in the country. The elected socialist Popular Unity government was toppled and its president, Salvador Allende, killed. The military took over the universities, persecuted organized labour, and dismantled the political system. As in Argentina, "subversives" were identified and pursued.[5] The Valech Report, compiled after the dictatorship had gone, and revised in 2011, put the number of torture centres operating in Chile during the Pinochet dictatorship at 1,132; in Argentina there were 340. As the state terror unfolded and the number of disappeared grew in both countries, a few groups of citizens managed to make their demands heard. In Chile the Association of the Relatives of the Disappeared, formed mainly by women, drew attention to the fate of the disappeared. In Argentina, from 1977, it was the Mothers and Grandmothers of the Plaza de Mayo.

The return to democracy was different in each case. In Argentina, the junta's policy of deindustrialization had left

---

[4] The phrase "that woman" (*esa mujer*) also traditionally refers to Eva Perón. For a biting assessment of Argentine machismo of the time, see V. S. Naipaul (1981).
[5] As both Fatala and Sozzi point out in this volume, the phenomenon of the disappeared in Argentina began with abduction, detention and torture before the 1976 coup.

the country unable to repay its huge foreign debt. But it is defeat on the Falklands-Malvinas that brings the demise of military rule. In Chile, it is a brokered transition which hands back political power to elected politicians, but the *ancien régime* remains a powerful force in the background. This continued influence was due in part to the dictatorship's perceived competence in economic affairs, the Pinochet regime, assisted by the so-called Chicago Boys, having steered the country to an economic prosperity of sorts, at the expense of a large foreign debt, by following an identifiably neoliberal economic programme. Still, after over seventeen years of dictatorship, Patricio Aylwin becomes president of Chile in March 1990.

Against a backdrop of economic ruin, the post-dictatorship period in Argentina is marked early on by the publication in 1984 of *Nunca más*, the official report into state terrorism and the fate of the *desaparecidos*. Attending the first Trial of the Juntas, the great Argentine writer, Jorge Luis Borges (1985), writes of his shock not so much at hearing of the atrocities committed by the military, but at hearing the unwitting banalization of trauma, the "routine of his hell" (*la rutina de su infierno*), in the language of a victim who stood before the court to testify. Culture makes its own contribution to the inquiry into the past, with María Luisa Bemberg's *Camila* (1984) speaking about late twentieth-century Argentina without ever speaking about late twentieth-century Argentina (strictly speaking, the film is about the nineteenth century) and Oscar-winning historical melodramas such as Luis Puenzo's *La historia oficial*, about a history teacher who is, in effect, taught the recent history of her country by, among others, her pupils.[6] After the first trials, President Alfonsín takes a strategic decision to push for laws that would place limits on the prosecution of the military—sacrificing justice to prevent the country from further tearing itself apart. In 1986 comes the law that sounds so terminally grammatical in English, the so-called Full Stop Law (*punto final* in Spanish means both "full-stop", that is, the punctuation mark, and "final point" or "cut-off point", in the sense of the chronological marker after which no further accusations would be acted on). And then, in

---

[6] See Triquell (2016) for an overview of post-dictatorship Argentine cinema.

Introduction

1987, comes the Law of Due Obedience, designed to place similar limits on the category of persons who could reasonably be held responsible. In 1990, in the name of "national reconciliation", a new president, President Carlos Menem, pardons most of the military personnel who had been convicted in the 1980s.

In Chile meanwhile, President Aylwin creates a South Africa-style National Commission for Truth and Reconciliation to investigate violations of human rights by the state. Two reports lay out the extent and apparatus of state terrorism and the fate of the missing, the Rettig Report and, later, the Valech Report.[7] Chile opts for a "politics of consensus" (Nelly Richard in Kalawski in this volume) to navigate its way back to a functioning post-dictatorship democratic order. The country's strong export economy had never ceased to get its wine and apples onto supermarket shelves in the developed nations. By 2010, it had become the first South American country to join the OECD. From roughly 2000, Chile witnesses a shift in its politics of memory. Debates on the country's human rights record and experiences of repression under the dictatorship begin to gain ground and to be sanctioned by the state itself. The period sees the establishment of the Museum of Memory and Human Rights in 2010, inaugurated by President Michelle Bachelet, the country's first female president, and the conversion of former detention and torture centres into peace parks and sites of memory.

From 2001, Argentine produce struggled to find its way onto domestic, let alone foreign, supermarket shelves. Having experienced the debt crisis of the 1980s, as the military government played Argentine roulette with the dollar exchange rate (Rock 1987: 373), the Menem years promised an explosion of modernizing reforms. However, come 2001 the country was plunged into profound economic crisis. After an interregnum of indecision, the Peronist leader, Néstor Kirchner, was elected president. *Kirchnerismo* (which includes the work of Kirchner's wife, Cristina Fernández de Kirchner, who succeeded him in office) brought about a rebuilding of the economy, a rebooting of the judicial system,

---

[7] See the documentary by Patricio Guzmán, *El botón de nácar (The Pearl Button)* (2015) for a moving, poetic account of one of the common fates of the Chilean disappeared.

and a mobilization of civil society. The impunity laws were declared unconstitutional, trials of military personnel resumed, former spaces of torture and detention were resignified as memory museums, and the state began to organize memory. An endeavour simultaneously necessary and not without its problems. As Norma Fatala says in this volume, the Kirchner government's decision to specify the start-date of state terrorism as the March 1976 coup, and not before, had the effect of eliding the responsibility which politicians, union leaders, regular police and para-police organizations had for repression long before that time.

In 2006, the publishing house Eudeba re-edited *Nunca más*. With a new prologue. The original prologue, from 1984, was thought to have spawned the "theory of the two demons". Seemingly traceable to remarks by former president Raúl Alfonsín (Crenzel 2013: 6), the theory, if indeed it ever was a theory as such, appeared to maintain that what had happened in Argentina in the 1970s was the result of two equally demonic forces: state terrorism, on the one hand, and revolutionary armed struggle, on the other. The 1984 prologue appeared to sanction this view, that is to say, that the fight was between two equally diabolical excrescences and that the rest of Argentine society was the innocent victim. The new edition set out to challenge that view. The 2006 version of *Nunca más* updated the details of the deaths and detentions of the dictatorship period and added a new prologue.[8] The original prologue remained, but was followed by a new one. The new prologue argued that the theory of the two demons that was advanced, it seemed, by the original was invalid: that the two sides were wholly unequal in the forces they could muster (the state clearly superior). The government had stepped in to supplement the interpretation of the country's recent past. Ten years later, in May 2016, barely five months after having taken office, and to mark the fortieth anniversary of the coup of 24 March 1976, the new government of Mauricio Macri produced a new edition of *Nunca más*. The new edition suppressed the 2006 prologue.

By 2016, Argentina and Chile had firmly entered the time of anniversaries—of the Pinochet coup, of the Falklands-

---

[8] The prologue's author was Eduardo Luis Duhalde. See Dandan (2016) for an overview of the debate from 1984 to 2016.

Introduction

Malvinas war, of the March 1976 coup. But, especially in Argentina with the policy reversals of President Macri (see Filmus and Sosa, in this volume), the politics of memory and commemoration were fissile and disputed.[9] How to commemorate? How to make public space for memory without it becoming state memory? How to teach trauma? Should one even teach trauma? What ethical responsibilities do the older generations who experienced dictatorship have to younger generations? And what responsibility do younger generations have towards the older generation when they "receive", as one says so trustingly, memories of trauma?" Have we, in this respect, really understood the consequences of what Aleida Assmann (cited by Contreras in this volume) says, apparently with such equanimity?:

> Social memory does not change gradually but undergoes a perceptible shift after periods of around 30 years when a new generation enters into offices and takes over public responsibility. Together with its public presence, the new generation will authorize its own vision of history. The change of generations is paramount for the reconstruction of societal memory and the renewal of cultural creativity.

The point is that the dictatorships ran from 1973-1989 (Chile) and from 1976-1983 (Argentina). But we are in 2017. Forty years or more have gone by since the coups and a little under forty since the high watermark of the most violent repression. New generations are remembering. Contested, imperilled even by recent government attempts to redefine the politics of memory, there is nevertheless a new sociability of mourning (see Violi, Demaria and Sosa in this volume), in which those who were not directly affected by violence could, as Cecilia Sosa puts it in her essay, adopt grief as a personal commitment to a new way of being together. This contested politics of friendship, if we may call it thus, involves, though is not reducible to, a new sociability, in which new generations and new social movements (feminist and LGBT) queer the pitch of the conventional rituals of mourning (one

---

[9] For an English-language insight into the decision by Argentina's Supreme Court to commute the sentences of those found guilty of torture, see Goñi (2017).

is not supposed to dance at funerals...) and open up the possibility of a politics of affect; and a new thinking, one of whose intellectual sources is Gilles Deleuze's work on desire, and which is not content with the traditional Enlightenment categories of thought, what Deleuze called "state philosophy" (the subject, consciousness, ideology, belief), preferring to think that not everything passes by way of a libido-less reason. Not without its blind spots and the articles of faith characteristic of any school, movement, trend or tradition, the new politics of memory, which, as we write, some fear are becoming an old politics of memory, nevertheless present a clear challenge to traditional approaches to the subject.

Such approaches to memory, commemoration and trauma have become more complicated since the dictatorships of the 1970s and 1980s for another, allied reason. The new social movements are powered by social media. The rise of electronic technologies has made it easier for us to "remember" events we never experienced firsthand, for human memory to access and store traces of an unimaginable number of experiences and an unimaginable amount of data from the past, traumatic or otherwise. Memory, which has always had its mnemonic devices, its technological appendages, archives and apparatuses, is now even more inseparable from *tēchnē*—from technology narrowly defined, but also, more expansively defined, from art, artifice and craft, and thus from the mediations of museums, memory sites, film, television, theatre, narrative fiction and the archive. The essays that follow will touch on just some of these technologies as they address matters of memory, commemoration and trauma in post-dictatorship Argentina and Chile.

The Essays
We have divided the book into five parts. The first part deals with the politics of memory and the disappeared. How are the Southern Cone states and their citizens to remember, commemorate and indeed teach the past? The section opens with Patrizia Violi's study of the phenomenon of the disappeared, taking her cue principally from Argentina but also from Chile. How does society mourn when there is no body? How does grieving interact with memory and politics? Disappearance profoundly alters the normal dynamics of life

Introduction

and death. Funeral rituals mark the natural ending of life. With disappearances, this order also disappears. Those who remain are left unable to work through the long process of mourning, whose purpose, Violi notes, is the separation from the dead and the reestablishment of a precise border between life and death. Funerary rituals also bind together private and public dimensions of grieving; they socialize mourning. Violi's hypothesis is that the impossibility of performing the usual rituals of mourning that occurs with *desaparecidos* has produced alternative rituals, which have helped to construct an extended "community of mourning", in Cecilia Sosa's phrase, and to hone a new politics of memory which transforms private memories into a public fight for justice and democracy. Mourning signs become *transformative devices* that act as semiotic shifters between different, but not mutually exclusive frames—private grief versus collective forms of political action. The result, perhaps *the* lesson for Europe from the South, is that a new landscape of memory is possible: a landscape that reimagines the nation and the beyond of the nation through photographs, images, art exhibitions, sites of memory and counter-memory. These and other manifestations become the public stage where mourning, memorialization and political action meet. As Violi says, apropos of the Mothers of Plaza de Mayo in 1977 (it is easy to forget: they began to gather deep into the most murderous phase of the dictatorship), "in the beginning there were photographs".

Daniel Filmus, an academic and politician heavily involved in the recent Fernández de Kirchner government, considers the question not of what lessons should be learned from the dictatorship, but the more immediate question of what lessons should be taught in Argentina's schools. What should the education system teach the next generations about the dictatorship and the disappeared? Arguing that the country's education system had traditionally, and deliberately, "forgotten" whole areas of history and experience, strictly in accordance with the interests of the dominant classes, he suggests that the dictatorship of 1976 took this a step further: it "disappeared" authors, texts and entire subjects from the curriculum just as it was disappearing individuals it regarded as threatening the social order. The return to democracy reinstated certain things, but it was not until the Kirchner-Fernández governments that bold changes were introduced. Schools, it was decided, should transmit the traumatic events of the recent past; not just teach them in instrumental fashion but impart the experience that lay behind them. Pointing up two risks, that of rendering remembering mechanical, such that it invites only forgetting, and that of prescribing memory as an unquestionable legacy, the piece ends with a third risk, the risk, in the author's view, currently being run by the new government of President Macri, elected in 2015: that of reinstating a politics—and a schooling—of forgetting.

Cristina Demaria engages with the work of the Abuelas or Grandmothers of the Plaza de Mayo, whose goal has been to find and return the estimated five hundred children abducted from detainees-*desaparecidos* by the Argentine dictatorship. The Abuelas justify their search in the name of the *right to identity*. Examining the Abuelas' website, visual testimonies from the series *Historias con identidad* (2012) by grandchildren restored to their original family, and two graphic short stories from *Historietas por la identidad* (2015), Demaria registers the insistence with which the Abuelas have moved the question of identity back onto the pre-modern terrain of biology, nature, genetics. Isn't identity, as post-structuralists and semioticians have told us, always discursively constructed (one isn't born "a general", one becomes one...)? The question is: what happens when these children, who, in Demaria's phrase, have been "disappeared" alive, are found? Exploring the differences between male and female found grandchildren (the men tend to appropriate their new name/self more readily than the women), she remarks on the emblematic case of Victoria Montenegro, whose "adoptive" father killed her actual father, and whose ideology she had embraced until the moment of epiphany of the "I am happy to have found myself" (as opposed to the "I am happy to have found that my self is more complex than I thought"). The figure characterizing such stories is that of a *real* identity buried beneath the lies of the apparent one—as though everything up to that point in life was *unreal*, i.e. had not happened. For Demaria, what this intractably complex matter shows is that memory does not belong exclusively to the subject, but that the memory of what one has lived merges with collective forms of memory, living on as a strange archive hosted in the body, an "intra-bodies memory" that lies between individual and social bodies,

Introduction

processes and objects.

Cecilia Sosa pursues the question of the disappeared in Argentina, asking whether we can learn anything from experiences of suffering. Analyzing *Aparecida* (Appeared) (2015), Marta Dillon's account of the discovery in 2011 of her missing mother's remains in a mass grave, she explores the possibility of an experience of loss in which the past is not simply obliterated, but rather worked through in unconventional ways. Sosa turns to the "affective turn", apprehending the text not just as cognitive form but as a *body* which is able to touch, move and *affect* us. *Aparecida* helps us to read the intensities of a particular moment in Argentina's process of mourning, for Dillon's book is embedded in the Kirchner years, which involved a particular way of *being* and *doing* with others. The new way of mourning, Sosa says, involved those who were not directly affected by violence and yet who adopted grief as a political commitment. Formerly (see Demaria above), only those related by blood to the missing had the authority to demand justice. The Kirchner period changed that. Adopting loss as a *state* matter, it challenged the unspoken entanglement between bloodline victims and truth, which had marked Argentina's human rights landscape for more than 30 years. The multitudes that took part in memorials embodied a non-biological conception of kinship, creating affective ties beyond blood. It is a generational affair: H.I.J.O.S. succeed Madres, but avoid positioning themselves "in an endless childhood". And it is a feminist, queer affair. *Aparecida* marks the time of the new social movements, of a new sociability able to take pleasure (dare one say it?) in mourning. Argentina's experience of trauma allows us to glimpse, Sosa suggests, an ethics that does not reside in individual subjects as atomistic silos, but rather in the collective ties of a new political family. Is this the lesson for Europe (and beyond)?

The second part of the volume covers detention centres, museums or sites of memory established in former detention centres, and accusatory practices in and beyond the walls of such centres. It begins with the odd-man-and-woman out: a lengthy comparative piece by two authors that brings together the two countries under scrutiny. José Manuel Rodríguez Amieva and Milena Grass Kleiner embark on a comparative study of two former detention centres, or Covert Centres of Detention, Torture and Execution, as they have become known, Campo de la Ribera in Córdoba, Argentina and the Cuartel Terranova/Villa Grimaldi in Santiago, Chile. State-sponsored violence, they assert, is a highly structured organism that can only work by virtue of the connections between the armed forces, secret organs of repression, civilian political and economic powers, and foreign powers. The final link in the chain, however, is "an insidious civilian tolerance [...] which, whether out of complacency or fear, allows it to operate". Challenging the view that the centres were utterly aberrant, the piece reinserts them into their respective urban contexts, suggesting that, even at the height of the repressive period, they maintained relations with the neighbouring community. In fact, it was precisely because of such relations that they could, after the dictators had gone, be turned into memory sites, often at the insistence of local people. The study explores the reconversion and resignification of these places following the return to democratic rule and in light of a new architecture of memory. Such sites come up against the impossibility of there ever being a memory degree zero, some kind of natural, neutral way of constructing in bricks and mortar a place of remembrance. Competing interests vie for architectural and narrative control in their attempts to recreate a coherent account of the past. But the sites exhibit the contradictions, the aesthetic and ethical tensions between original features, recreations to scale and new artefacts, that is, between different forms and perspectives that make for complex, eclectic places that overwhelm.

Paola Sozzi examines the museum of the Córdoba Provincial Memory Archive in Argentina, which during the 1970s functioned as a secret detention and torture centre. The museum's sombre mission nowadays is to bear witness to the truth of the terrible events that happened there, laying down a Theseus's thread of memory by means of a complex and intertwined spatial system in which "traces" tell a story about the past and make it "seem real". That is to say, images and objects in the museum function quite literally as traces of the past, recalling in their very materiality the concreteness of the disappeared bodies with which they once came into physical contact. The museum, Sozzi suggests, breaks the barrier between domestic space and public space and refuses a heroic narrative of the victims, proposing instead a representation of their everyday lives. The Memory

Introduction

Archive is a register of objects; but it is also a subjective experience. Everything passes through the materiality of things: objects are traces of the past presence of another body that is now absent, and hence cry out "I am real", at the same time as they establish an eerie experience of proximity to that body through the materiality that stands before us.

With Norma Fatala we move to a consideration of narratives of survivors of the clandestine detention centres in Argentina. Her contribution registers, above all, the multiple nuances of survival, most apparent in the different status given to different prisoners. Even a terrorist state had to account for legal prisoners, whereas the *desaparecidos* had no "entity", as the dictator Jorge Videla infamously, albeit correctly, put it. The actions of certain survivors are far from clear, some who were considered traitors by former comrades turning out to have saved tens of lives. Collecting information about their captors was the only possible means of reversal for human beings subjected to the almost total power of others. As Fatala says, information becomes the gift which survivors would bring back from their descent into hell. Nevertheless, living to tell the tale of thousands is not an easy task. While self-justification may play a role in the discourse of the returning subjects, giving testimony not only fulfils an ethical imperative, but in it the intensity of personal feelings provides us with some kind of measure of the irreconcilable nature of the crimes. However, if survivors' testimonies are invaluable, they may have a negative impact on collective memory when politicized. Survivors proclaim themselves not only the memory of genocide, but also, and all too readily, the memory of defeat. In order to demonstrate the military's aberrant quality, and to justify their own survival, they reproduce the effects of terror and risk suggesting that no alternative form of politics is possible.

Daniele Salerno revisits the Provincial Memory Archive of Córdoba studied by Paola Sozzi, this time to explore the under-studied topic of LGBT people (one knows progress has been made when it is not necessary to spell out the acronym). He analyzes a small corpus of interviews from the Oral History Archive that detail repression of LGBT people before, during and after the Argentine dictatorship (the "perpetrator" of sexual repression, he remarks, is not only the dictatorship). The analysis points up the unsettling fact that the archive is a complex enunciative device which, through the life story interview, throws up the paradox that questions now asked of the interviewees overlap with the interrogation to which they were subjected in the same place decades ago. In a certain sense, they are once again called upon to "confess" their sexuality. Second time around, however, the interview-confession allows interviewees to reconfigure their own subjectivity and to gain political agency. The detention centre that was once the place of human rights violations becomes a place for the struggle for human rights. But, Salerno cautions, the reconstruction of political agency is not straightforward. The case-studies analyzed show a tendency on the part of some LGBT people to deploy the human rights organizations' trope of "restoring victims' humanity", but at the expense of their *politicality*, if we may put it thus. In other words, they were guilty of *being*, not of doing.

Daniel Oviedo Silva gives us a lesson from Europe. Examining the delicate matter of citizens' collaboration with dictatorship, he compares the Argentine dictatorship with the Civil War and post-war periods in Spain. Collaboration classically occurs through accusatory practices, a state's intelligence services obtaining from prisoners who have cracked under duress, but also from intra-community denunciations, the information for its abductions. In Spain, the Nationalist advance and the elimination of Republican enemies were assisted by information provided by neighbours and municipal corporations. Later, under Francoism, the population's collaboration proved decisive in military justice, the principal channel for most of the "legal" repression. In Argentina, collaboration passed through institutional channels: letting agencies, schools, universities, companies. But research into the Spanish case highlights something more unsettling, namely, the community level: the neighbourhood, kinship or patronage-based denunciation networks. In both cases, personal grievances sat alongside political motives; the relationship between collaboration and coercion was hard to disentangle; and collaboration hastened the erosion of previous social relations and the imposition of new forms of social control that would shape the respective new national communities.

The third part of the book turns to the Falklands/Malvinas War of 1982, or, more specifically, to the

Introduction

question of how the war, its dead and its survivors are remembered and commemorated. María Teresa Dalmasso opens the section, examining what she calls Argentina's commemoration-compulsion. Training a sociosemiotic gaze on the print media during the twenty-fifth and thirtieth anniversaries of the Malvinas War, she argues that Argentina is stuck in a passional fabric of melancholy and anger, two variants of a frustration born of the country's "destiny-neurosis" (we are supposed to be great, why aren't we great?). Commemorations are but the visible sign of an incomplete national work of mourning from which angry-melancholic dissidences constantly irrupt and in which memory has a tendency to sink into the political. The Malvinas/Falklands anniversaries are one such vector. The shared conviction in an Argentine territorial identity that has been instilled at school and internalized as a painful wound makes it difficult for people to detach themselves from the passional relation to the islands; and suddenly memory becomes politics (becomes forgetting) as tragic continuities are constructed between, on the one hand, the behaviour of the military during the dictatorship (what it did to "subversives"), and, on the other, its behaviour during the wars (what it did to its own conscripts). Everything happens, in the affective intensity of commemorations, as though there had been no widespread passional investment, no mass gatherings and no flag-wavings, in support of a war driven by the same military that had thrown conscript-aged young people ("subversives") into mass graves.

Sandra Savoini explores Argentine audiovisual production about the Falklands/Malvinas war. The process of *de-Malvinification* of the country after the defeat resulted in a general veil of silence drawn over the subject of the war, one of the exceptions being audiovisual production at anniversary moments. However, the early films, such as Bebe Kamín's *Los chicos de la guerra* (Our Boys at War) (1984), projected the self-exculpatory view widely held at the time, Argentine society preferring to construe its own soldiers (*los chicos*, the boys, in the film) as victims of their own officers and, by analogy, to construe society and soldiers as victims of military dictatorship. In short, the responsibility of the community before, during and after the armed conflict was erased. The word "Malvinas" itself gradually comes, then, to stand in for a traumatic experience, the meaning of which obstructs other possible ways of understanding the territory. With the arrival of the Kirchner government, the "Malvinas question", Savoini argues, began to be reframed, with an increasing questioning of the role of society and of the Argentine state, on view in the television drama *Combatientes* (Combatants) (2013). Closely related to other areas of memory production, audiovisual productions such as *Malvinas—30 miradas* (Malvinas—30 Views) (2014) allow us to understand memories as historical devices of power-knowledge that produce what can be said and shown, the analysis of memories on screen allowing us to grasp the fundamentally semiotic construction of reality.

Alicia Vaggione explores a documentary film, *La forma exacta de las islas* (The Exact Shape of the Islands) (2012) by Edgardo Dieleke and Daniel Casabé, based on the work of Julieta Vitullo, and a chronicle, *Fantasmas de Malvinas. Un libro de viajes* (Malvinas Ghosts: A Book of Travels) (2008) by historian Federico Lorenz, that feature return journeys to the Malvinas in the 2000s. The journey enables a return of sorts to the past by means of questions about the present, questions triggered by an unsettling wandering through landscape. The journey interacts with time, interrupting stagnant meanings about the past, and allowing a war veteran to shake off a way of thinking about the islands that has remained frozen since the time of the war, in favour of new perspectives that come from the recording of experience. This experience of journey, Vaggione suggests, affords a perception of time that is neither linear nor chronological, but rather intensive and purely emotional. Moreover, this experience and this time are connected to that which comes back as a ghost, that which cannot be overridden by memory. The film and the book insist on building a memory made up of multiple ways of reading the war experience and of seeing the island territory located at the end of the world. The journey, with its objects of memory, may also be a vector that allows for the processing of other unique—uniquely female, uniquely maternal—experiences of loss.

Mike Seear served in the British army in the Falklands/Malvinas war. Here he details an artistic re-staging of the war. Seear describes Lola Arias' production of *Minefield/Campo Minado*, the first stage play about the 1982 conflict and whose cast, crucially, featured only veterans of

Introduction

the war. Seear tells of his own part in helping to recruit one of the key members of the cast, a former Gurkha (Seear had been the 1st Battalion, 7th Duke of Edinburgh's Own Gurkha Rifles Operations and Training Officer). The myth of the bloodthirsty Gurkha had been strong in Argentina at the time of the war and remained potent years later. Here, finally, was a Gurkha in the flesh: quietly spoken and mild-mannered. The play strove to express not only the experience of war, but the often traumatic work of memory—the work of memory, precisely, as minefield; in Seear's words, a "treacherous terrain that needs to be crossed with care and might prove explosive". Through the veil of black humour and the casual attitude characteristic of combatants, the play captures a shared traumatic battlefield experience, reenacted in a simulated on-stage therapy session. For the ex-combatant performers, the play brings about combat veteran unity and reconciliation; for the non-combatant civilian spectators, the final scene produces a cathartic ambush that is an ambush of catharsis.

The fourth part of the book takes up the theme of performance, of the performing or staging of memory through theatre, in theatre, and in the theatricalization, if we may put it thus, of public space. The three essays in this section all focus on Chile. Andrea Pelegrí Kristić argues that histories of the theatre in Chile have traditionally viewed the repertoire of the Teatro de Ensayo de la Universidad Católica (TEUC) between 1973 and 1989—a repertoire dominated by foreign and/or classic plays—as proof of a wish to subvert censorship and surreptitiously speak about the political situation, that is, the Pinochet dictatorship. She suggests that the resistance attributed to some of the TEUC's programming may be a figment of historiographical imagination. As far back as the 1930s, the future founders of university theatres in the country sought to renew the performing arts in Chile by following the precepts of European art theatres. Foreign actors and playwrights, driven to the Americas by the World Wars, shaped the country's university theatres. Their primary objective was to universalize classical and modern plays that had a clear high aesthetic. That meant foreign plays. Such a repertoire ignores comedies, national productions, children's theatre, or other contemporary foreign works. While the promotion of a certain highbrow artistic style may have modernized the

Chilean stage, Pelegrí Kristić suggests, it was now the scholars who dictated the rules. More to the point, when the dictatorship arrives, the TEUC's turn towards foreign and/or classic plays does not look quite like the unambivalent gesture of resistance that historiography would have us believe it to be.

Andrés Kalawski continues the story of Chilean theatre, analyzing how torture and the disappeared were represented on stage between 1985 and 2011, that is, from the back end of the dictatorship to well into the democratic period. Theatre, he maintains, is an X-ray of the collective imaginary of an era, supplying a fictional correlation of what is happening in real life. Analyzing six productions, he considers whether the findings of the Rettig and Valech Reports regarding the dictatorship's crimes had an impact on dramatic writing and the performance of plays. He concludes that they did, that the reports moved the debate on from denunciation to the representation of what cannot be represented (Rodrigo Pérez's *Cuerpo* [2005]), and on to the possibility of understanding the past and of seeking justice. How, then, were the violations represented? And the disappeared? In 1985, in Ramón Griffero's *Cinema Utopía*, the concept that people had been disappeared could only appear as science fiction. In 1986, in Griffero's *99 La Morgue*, torture could be shown on a stage representing a morgue. This was theatre as recognition of and for those who had suffered repression. By 1995, and Griffero's *Río Abajo*, something had changed. *Río Abajo* brought justice on stage. While government pardons had left torturers free from punishment, on stage they were not so lucky. By 2000, and Andrés Pérez's *La Huida*, Kalawski argues, public debate regarding human rights not only allowed for the staging of personal experiences of repression but also looked to take the dictatorship down a peg by suggesting that even its methods of extermination, such as the practice of disappearing people, were "ancient history" (you are derivative even in your evil). Finally, by 2011, and Guillermo Calderón's *Villa + Discurso*, the audience ceases to play the role of passive spectators, and becomes instead part of the document/monument/social drama which the play presents. The play is about the conversion of the Cuartel Terranova detention centre, where a prisoner named Michelle Bachelet was held, into the Villa Grimaldi Peace Park, which was

Introduction

inaugurated in 2010 by the country's first female president, Michelle Bachelet.

María José Contreras Lorenzini continues the theme of the staged collapsing of the boundaries between art and life. She examines a well-known art/memory project that was developed to commemorate the fortieth anniversary of the Chilean coup. Claudia Di Girólamo and Rodrigo Pérez's *Aquí están* begins with a reading of testimonies provided by relatives of *desaparecidos*, moves to children's drawings of the missing, and ends with public readings of testimonies by well-known actors. On the one hand, *Aquí están* naïvely presents the testimonies as if they were the direct recounting of reality, and thereby dissimulates the mediations that characterize each and every collective construction of memory (in this case, the work of adult relatives, research assistants, famous actors). On the other hand, it precisely draws attention to the proliferation of layers of mediation that are combined in the mobilization of memories. And insofar as children are involved in the process, the performance not only foregrounds the question of how the younger generation understands the dictatorship, but also points up the creative process (it has been called postmemory) by which the past is flitered not just by multiple mediators from the older generation but by the imagination of the new one, now turned into agents of memory. In so doing, Contreras argues, the project points towards an alternative work of commemoration: not the official museumification of memory (bronze statues, stone plinths), but the creative intimacy of inter-subjective interactions producing a dynamic and multiple collective memory.

The final part of the book covers film, documentary, fiction and television. Anna Maria Lorusso studies a Chilean television series, *Los archivos del cardenal* (2011), and a Chilean cinema documentary, *Habeas corpus* (2015), that deal with an organ of the Catholic Church, the Vicaria de la Solidaridad, that tried to denounce the dictatorship's crimes and provide succour to its victims. The TV series has nothing "real" in it and yet has such a mimetic force—not least in the detail of its historical reconstructions—that it elevates itself, as Lorusso puts it, to the *status of document*. So much so that the last episode, screened live in the nation's Museum of Memory and Human Rights, became a genuine political action. The documentary film, in contrast, and despite real witnesses and documents, is punctuated by fictional interludes that suspend realism and mark a retreat from reality. The series is aesthetically conventional and yet its memory of the dictatorship presents examples of those who have risked their lives to oppose the regime, exempla that are timeless and universally applicable. As such, the series offers a "model script for dictatorship and resistance", while the more experimental documentary offers the suspension of all schemes. With its "dramatic realism" and belief in the referential efficacy of fiction, *Los archivos del cardenal* cuts deep into Chilean life. With its "traumatic realism" and mistrust of the possibilities of representing reality, *Habeas corpus* blocks the connection to social and political life. In the first, a *historia magistra vitae*; in the second, the subjective time of a tortuous mental experience struggling with the question of how—or even whether—to speak of trauma.

Sebastián Gastaldi analyzes a different genre of television programme, asking what kind of historical memory is legitimized in a children's TV series that deals with the Argentine dictatorship. Traumatic events are by nature strictly impossible to represent, certain forms of violence by nature beyond representation. And yet, Gastaldi suggests, these are the very forms that demand to be turned into discourse. What, then, is the dominant pathos of the TV series? What passions does it invite and how does it inflame them? The value judgements revealed in the series point towards stable, officially sanctioned equivalences: what is beautiful is good, what is ugly is bad. The series adheres to the discursive rules of classical taste, which entails a no less traditional treatment of monstrosity—monstrosity as that which is horrible and fascinating at the same time. The function of monstrosity in discourse is to crystallize a society's deepest fears. How does this pedagogical children's cartoon construct monstrosity? The on-screen dictators who pass before children's eyes are positioned as the antithesis of Hannah Arendt's theory of the banality of evil. Where Eichmann was, rather than a monster, a technician who took a series of decisions whose outcome was monstrous, these animated dictators, Gastaldi concludes, appear *essentially monstrous*, according to the logic of a fight between good and evil which means that the children can sleep easy in their beds, and those in Argentine society given to Manichaeism rest easy too.

Introduction

Adam Sharman addresses the relationship between history and memory through the vehicle of documentary film in Argentina. His question is whether there is a radical break in post-dictatorship Argentine documentary filmmaking between an older generation's "classical" view of history and a younger generation's postmodern "postmemory" view. As test cases, he takes two emblematic films that deal with the armed revolutionary groups of the 1970s, David Blaustein's *Cazadores de utopías* (1995) and Nicolás Prividera's documentary *M* (2007). On questions of history and generations, Nietzsche, he claims, remains our surest guide. If, in the older film by the generation of the *guerrilla*, witnesses' memories of Peronist militancy, armed and unarmed, are ordered into something resembling a classical historical narrative, in order to account for what their generation did, and in order that they have their say at a moment when few seemed interested in listening, the film also has critical elements that do not belong to the world of objective history-telling. In contrast, the much more formally experimental and questioning *M*, which charts siblings' search to discover what happened to their disappeared mother, like many probably abducted from the union stronghold that was the INTA, the National Institute for Agricultural Technology, films the younger generation filming the older generation, that is to say, draws attention to the creative appropriation of memory by a later generation. However, in the midst of this postmemory performance there is a strange reversal. The newcomer, Prividera, becomes the rationalist historicist—too many memories, he says, and not enough history—while the older generation become the relativists. What is called "postmemory", Sharman suggests, still has some explaining to do.

Pampa Arán examines three novels, published between 2011 and 2012, by Argentine writers living abroad, Patricio Pron, Ernesto Semán and Laura Alcoba, all of whom are the children of former militants. The corpus is composed of novels that form an "aesthetic of ruins" opposed to the fascist aesthetic of monuments. How does a subject reconstruct the distant political behaviour of their parents from their own present? Arán explores a series of chronotopes, condensed space-time figures, used by the writers to represent that memory construction. In Pron, it is the figure of the hole—the hole of depression, but also the dark hole of memory itself which the novelist must continue to stare into as a duty to the children of the missing. In Semán's novel, the ghost of the murdered father, based on Semán's own Cuba-trained, Maoist intellectual militant father kidnapped in 1978, bookends the novel. His son (in life and in fiction) recreates the story using the chronotope of The Island to capture the father in his state of martyrdom under interrogation and torture in the clandestine camp. Is it possible to reach the truth of memory, Arán asks? The chronotope of The Island makes sense as a historical truth that does not admit oblivion, but that does not remain in the past as a static place. In Alcoba's novel, the chronotope is again the island, but this time the island as revolutionary isolation-insulation (*a-islamiento*), not just a place but an experience—the initiation-experience of guerrilla training in Cuba of those who would be her parents. All three children-authors seek their own identity by delving into the reconstruction of their family history, where they find a complex, unnerving time and a blurring of the boundaries between the biographical and the autobiographical.

Rui Gonçalves Miranda brings the volume to a close. He begins with Maxim Gorky's meditation on the "indefinably unsettling" effect of absence on the cinema screen once the projector is turned off. He considers this "spectral" effect of cinema—the absent images that yet somehow remain, that cannot be forgotten—as a cypher for Chilean writer Roberto Bolaño's practice in his novel *Estrella distante* (Distant Star) about a shadowy, sinister figure in the Chilean airforce during the dictatorship. Aside from its cinematic techniques, the novel's allusions to cinema provide an image based notion of memory and a hint as to what is *not* there (we surmise: torture, violence, repression...). Cinema plays a decisive role in the novel, not because of what it can show, but because of its "indefinably unsettling" way of not showing. Coinciding with Argentine writer Ricardo Piglia's theses on the short story, Bolaño tells two stories: one in the foreground, another secretly encoded in the gaps of the first and built around the unsaid, the merely implied. The epic or tragic moments of history are, then, precisely what *Estrella distante* does not approach directly. Bolaño shows reticence, decorum even, in respect of the incommunicable experience of trauma, of that which must not be forgotten—and which must consequently be the object of memory and commemoration, repeatedly, always—but which cannot be clearly remembered. Beyond memory and commemoration there is always "something else".

Some who speak about trauma, such as Roberto Bolaño, often leave unsaid the words (*dictatorship*, *torture*...) that are their central preoccupation, out of a sense of respect, we surmise, for traumatic things that it is strictly impossible to represent fully, much less faithfully. In 1980, that is, at the height of the Southern Cone dictatorships, Argentine writer Ricardo Piglia (1941-2017) published one of the great books of the dictatorship, *Respiración artificial* (Artificial Respiration). The novel spends much of the first half dealing with a singular earlier moment of Argentine history, the 1850s, and the greater part of the second charting the alcohol-lubricated literary-philosophical discussion between two characters as they wait for an uncle/friend (who never appears). Dictatorship, torture and the disappeared are not, strictly speaking, spoken of. And yet there is not a single word from the earlier epistolary fragments or the later literary-philosophical debate that is not suffused with the experience of dictatorship. In the final analysis, Renzi and Tardewski's gentle but probing dialogue winds its way towards the German (Kantian) word *Humanität*, humanity. However, the characters only get to *Humanität* via the Humanities—via a long, digressive, respectful but never respectable Socratic dialogue on *and out of* philosophy, literature and history. It is another iteration of the debate between arms and letters. Unlike the poetics of the indirect so poignantly handled by a Bolaño or a Piglia (or a Bemberg), we have been less circumspect, more direct, and doubtless more academic, in naming the subjects with which this volume deals. This artlessness, which cannot be divorced from a certain academic commodification of memory, will, it is hoped, be made up for, *d'après* Renzi and Tardewski, by the calibre of the analysis of the experience of post-dictatorship.

The Translations
All the essays in the volume are in English, with quotations, or snippets of quotations, from the original Spanish sources wherever it was considered appropriate. We have provided in parentheses English equivalents for some of the institutions, laws, common terms or phrases that mark out

these memory debates as peculiarly Argentine or Chilean, but have spared the reader's patience by not doing so each and every time such a name, term or phrase is repeated. Readers will notice the number of references made to Córdoba in Argentina and Santiago in Chile: this is explained by the institutions that took part in the project and by the wish to make good use of local knowledge. Local knowledge does not, however, solve everything. Not least problems of translation. Aside from the habitual difficulties posed by translation, we note two of particular relevance. The ways in which Chilean and Argentine Spanish use *denuncia* as a noun and *denunciar* as a verb do not map neatly onto the English *denunciation* or *denounce* or *accusation* or *accuse*. In Spanish, one can go to a police station to *denunciar* a neighbour for playing his radio too loud; in English this might be translated, innocuously, as "to make a complaint" or, at most, "to report someone". But if the year is 1976 and the place Córdoba or Santiago, *denunciar* may be rendered, more chillingly, as "to inform on", "to denounce (to the authorities)" or "to betray". We have more often than not, however, kept variations of the English *denounce* simply to allow its etymological Spanish twin to be heard in the background. The word *Malvinas* is similarly fraught. At times we have opted for "the Falklands", as the islands are known to English-speakers; at others, we have gone for the diplomatic "Falklands-Malvinas"; but at other times we have chosen to keep the word "Malvinas" as it is. It is not that to make an Argentine academic say "Falklands" on every second line would be to sign them up to the (long gone) British Empire; it is rather, as Sandra Savoini says in this volume, that the word "Malvinas", the very sound of the word "*M-a-l-v-i-n-a-s*", touches an Argentine chord that gets utterly lost in translation.

Unless otherwise indicated, all translations have been revised by Adam Sharman.

References
Bergman, C. (1984). *Camila*. Audiovisual production. Argentina.
Blaustein, D. (1995). *Cazadores de utopías*. Audiovisual production. **www.youtube.com/watch?v= 7vRydH _dAvY**.
Bolaño, R. (2004). *Distant star* (trans. C. Andrews).

London: The Harvill Press.

Borges, J. L. (1985). Lunes, 22 de julio de 1985. *El País*. **http://elpais.com/diario/1985/08/10/opinion/492472809_850215.html**

Crenzel, E. (2013). El prólogo del *Nunca más* y la teoría de los dos demonios: Reflexiones sobre una representación de la violencia política en la Argentina. *Contenciosa*, 1(1), 1-20. **https://ecaths1.s3. amazonaws.com/ …/721173452.CRENZEL.Prologue.**

Dandan, A. (2016). De vuelta a los dos demonios. *Página/12*, 12 June. **www.pagina12.com.ar/diario/elpais/1-301566-2016-06-12.html**, accessed 15 July 2016.

Germano, G. (2007) Ausencias/Ausências. Online photographic exhibition-installation. **www.gustavogermano.com/gallery/ausencias/**.

Goñi, N. (2017). Fury in Argentina over ruling that could see human rights abusers walk free. At **www.theguardian.com/world/2017/may/04/argentina-supreme-court-human-rights**, accessed 11 May 2017.

Guzmán, P. (2015). *El botón de nácar*. Audiovisual production.

Naipaul, V. S. (1981). *The return of Eva Perón with The killings in Trinidad*. Harmondsworth: Penguin Books.

O'Donnell, G. (2002). Modernization and military coups. In G. Nouzeilles & G. Montaldo (eds.), *The Argentine reader: History, culture, politics*. Durham and London: Duke University Press, pp. 399-420.

Piglia, R. (1990). *Respiración artificial*. 3rd ed. Buenos Aires: Editorial Sudamericana.

Rock, D. (1987). *Argentina 1516-1987: From Spanish colonization to Alfonsín*. Berkeley: University of California Press.

Rouquié, A. (1987). *The military and the state in Latin America.* Berkeley: University of California Press.

Triquell, X. (2016). Configuraciones de la violencia de estado en el cine argentino post-dictadura. In D. Araujo, E. Moretin, & V. Rei-Baptista (eds.), *Ditaduras Revisitadas (Revisiting Dictatorships)*. Universidade do Algarve: Edicões CIAC. E-book, **https://drive.google.com/file/d/0B2f45zL8GWTRGt3ckNuQmJSUUU/view**

The Politics of Memory

Disappearance, Mourning and the Politics of Memory

Patrizia Violi

Disappearance

The ferocious military dictatorships that seized power in Chile and Argentina in the 1970s both shared one particular feature: they were heavily based on the disappearance of their victims: of their material bodies, together with any potential traces of their arrest and detention, and indeed, of their very existence.

The aim of this study is to examine the political, cultural and symbolic consequences of this mass phenomenon, as well as the different forms of mourning and working through this gave rise to in a "wounded society". Indeed, each disappearance not only produced a "wounded family" (Sosa 2011), it also affected the whole body of a society in many complex ways. My specific goal here is to highlight the interplay of grieving, both private and public, with memory and politics, and analyze how the work of mourning has been redefined as a form of political action. Because of the limitations of the present essay, my analysis will mainly focus on the case of Argentina; although the disappearance of prisoners was also practised in Chile, the extension of the phenomenon was much wider in Argentina. Here the official number of disappeared has been estimated at around 30,000 persons, thrown alive into the sea or buried in anonymous common tombs, and its symbolic relevance acquired a dominant role in democratic and anti-military discourses.

Disappearance means not only the elimination of material bodies, but also the impossibility for relatives and friends to know what happened to their loved ones. A double cancellation is here at work, both on the level of physical evidence and on the level of knowledge, with the effect of producing a pervasive uncertainty in the people who remain, and who are unable to obtain any kind of certainty, however painful it may be.

Even names were disappeared, producing "a disorder in relation of proper names", as Sosa (2014a: 63) observed. From the philosophy of language, we know that proper names have a specific status as rigid designators (Kripke 1972), pointing to one specific individual only, and operating as highly singularizing linguistic devices. But the military, disappearing thousands of bodies from the public sphere, also cancelled their names as well. To cope with that lack, a highly generic term had to be used: *desaparecidos*, a term that refers to the whole of this undefined category, and not to specific individuals. The relatives did not even have a title to describe their own situation, the usual categories in use being inappropriate for their status. They were not widows, or orphans, but husbands, wives, children or parents *of a desaparecido* or *desaparecida*. The category of *desaparecido* becomes in this way the form of enunciation for a whole field of beliefs, practices and symbolic actions, a different system of classification, both at the individual and collective levels.

Disappearance is a highly complex and multilayered device that can be read on different levels and according to different perspectives, as Pilar Calveiro (1998) has shown in her seminal work, a general device that was the basis for the logic of *El Proceso* (the Process of National Reorganization), as the dictatorship was called by the military. In the first place it is obviously the most radical way to eliminate all witnesses who might testify to the crimes committed by the military. However, disappearance is more than a power device to hide the less presentable aspects and contents of an infamous regime, it is also a control device to generate terror: not knowing what happened and what is going to happen produces a diffuse feeling of incertitude, fear, suspicion and mistrust on which state terrorism was based.

In a sense, disappearance began before the victims' death, before the cancellation of their bodies and traces, with the attempt to annihilate their humanity and identity. Prisoners disappeared for the external world, but disappeared also, in another way, inside the clandestine centres: detention and torture centres were first of all places of the psycho-physical deconstruction of individual identity. What disappeared was, at the deepest level, all forms of differences: differences between individuals and differences between their possible different behaviours. Death or survival was to a large extent casual: it was reported by survivors that military personnel often claimed that they were like gods with power over life and death, which was completely independent of what prisoners might or might not do. No heroes and no betrayers, only people deprived of their differences and their deepest humanity. We can see here at work the most subtle functioning of the disappearance device, with precisely the disappearance of all forms of diversity and difference, and at the very end, the disappearance of any possible sense, given that meaning is rooted in differences.

Mourning and its Ritual
First and foremost disappearance altered the normal dynamics of death and life. Under usual circumstances, life has a cycle, and even when a violent death occurs, funerals, ceremonies and burials represent the natural ending of life. But when people disappear without leaving any trace, this order too disappears, and people are left without the cultural and symbolic structures to come to terms with death. In normal circumstances, funerary rituals and all forms of taking care of dead bodies are a crucial part of mourning, and fulfil two important main functions.

First of all they mark a precise separation between life and death. The working through of a loss is a long process that takes different stages, but whose final aim is the separation from the dead and the reestablishment of a precise border between life and death. Physical separation is the first step: cemeteries are precisely places of a threshold separating the living from the dead, spatial borders between the city, a space of activity and businesses, and a sacred space of a different order (remembering that the etymology of *sacred* is "separated"). All practices of taking care of dead bodies, washing and recomposing them, burying them in a distant and "other" space, are indispensable premises for those who remain to continue living, a first fundamental step in the long and painful process of the working through. Burying the dead is merely a way to fix the place for the living.

Cemeteries are not only physical spaces; they are first of all psychological spaces, spaces of an external threshold that becomes internalized. Without a psychological localization of the encounter with death, the border between life and death cannot be established and life cannot start again. Dead bodies play a crucial role in this passage: after having been taken care of, they need to be moved out of sight of the living, buried in a place where rituals of remembering can take place, but where the remains are not visible. The barrier between life and death implies also a different visibility regime between being able to see (which is the regime for living people), and not having to see, which is what characterizes our relationships with the dead.

Funerary rituals do not only help in making possible the separation between life and death, they also have another important role, which is that of establishing a link between private and public dimensions of grieving. Mourning is never an exclusively individual process; although it is certainly a painful work which each individual has to do by herself, it is always inscribed at the same time into a social and collective dimension. Funeral rituals have a mediating function between the private and the public sphere, and they allow us to transfer individual working through into a collectively shared context that in some way supports and helps this painful elaboration. Such rituals are typically shared by the whole community of relatives, friends, neighbours; in small places it is quite common for the whole village to take part in the religious rites that accompany the burial. The collective and social character of celebrations is marked by a series of practices and external signs, from the dress code of the mourning period, in our world signified by the colour black, to the authorized leave from work for certain periods, or the abstention from public amusements—at least in traditional environments. All these habits can be seen as forms of the socializing of mourning, making it visible and inscribing private loss into a public, collective dimension. Grief is not a completely private situation but, as Judith Butler has observed, "furnishes a sense of political community of a complex order" (Butler 2004: 22).

If on the one hand funerary rituals fulfil important functions for the living, both of separation from death and of inscription into a social dimension of mourning, on the other they have also a role with respect to the dead, giving them a social identity. Such rituals stabilize, so to speak, the identity of the dead in a form which is recognized and shared by the community: a socially recognized body as opposed to an anonymous body without identity and name.

It is worth noting that all these intertwined social and symbolic functions can only be accomplished in the presence of the dead body: they all depend on and revolve around this unsettling entity which is, and at the same time is not any more, the person we knew. It is only the dead body, in a way, that can enunciate death and make it real.

The question, then, is: what happens, both at the

individual and collective levels, when the body is missing?[1] It is well known that the lack of the body and the impossibility of performing any form of care and ritual renders more difficult and slow the working through of the loss. No burials, no rituals, no graves are possible in these cases,[2] and new symbolic forms of collective ceremonies have to be created; for example, in the case of a shipwreck, the throwing of flowers into the sea where the boat disappeared.

But, in the case of the state terrorism we are considering here, something even more frightening happens: it is not only the body that is missed, but also all knowledge about the destiny of the victim is to be cancelled. The erasure of both the body and the possibility of finding out what happened to it prevents the incorporation of the victim within those who remain. How can one elaborate the loss of those who no longer exist, not because they died but because they are missing, together with all traces of their very existence after they were kidnapped? The *desaparecidos* are neither alive nor dead, haunting ghosts preventing any working through.[3]

Another important element that qualifies the notion of disappearance is the very particular experience of temporality that it implies. Using here the linguistic category of aspect, we can say that death is generally an event that is both punctual and terminative, something that happens at a very precise moment, ending life with a very clear cut. Under normal circumstances, life and death have very precise temporary borders and delimitations.[4] Mourning too—at least

---

[1] On the ritual dimension of the Madres de la Plaza de Mayo's actions, see also Demaria & Lorusso (2012).
[2] See on this point Schmucler (1996).
[3] As Ludmila da Silva Catela (2014) has documented in her extended study of the relatives of the *desaparecidos*, feelings of uncertainty, doubt, disbeliefs and loneliness characterize the experience of those who remain. Interviews with various relatives of disappeared people have shown that it generally took many years before they would admit to themselves that their loved ones were not going to come back and had certainly been killed.
[4] It could be objected that this is not always the case: today there are more and more common undecidable cases between life and death, where people are not dead, but cannot be considered fully alive either. The difficulties, also legal, of dealing with such situations are, in a way, indirect evidence of the "natural" punctuality of death under normal circumstances.

in the public forms I discussed earlier as a recognized and socially shared code of behaviours, practices and even dress habits—has precisely defined temporal borders with their own endings.

Disappearance has no borders, no ending, no time: only its beginning is temporally marked at the moment a person is taken away, but in that moment nobody could know that he or she is going to disappear. This also alters the relationship between the public and private dimensions of mourning: normally, funerals are a public, and shared, time of grieving, followed by private forms of elaboration of loss. But what happens when traditional funerary rituals are not possible and the disappearance of somebody remains as an open wound, an irreparable wound that cannot have any public reparation? What kind of semiotic practices can be brought into play to elaborate such a loss? What alternative forms of mourning can be activated, and with what social and political consequences?

The Political Function of Memory
My hypothesis is that the impossibility of performing the usual rituals of mourning has forced alternative forms and rituals, and these alternative forms have contributed in an essential way to the construction of an extended "community of mourning",[5] as well as to the growth of a political function of memory, transforming private memories into a public and political fight for justice, truth and democracy. In the aftermath of military dictatorships, the extended phenomenon of disappearance has redefined the working through as a political and forward-looking issue, highlighting the intertwining of grieving, memory and politics. The non-closure of mourning, impossible to accomplish until the certainty of death and the material evidence of the body is attained, paradoxically became one important propulsive force for political activism, democracy and justice. Where disappearance has made traditional forms of mourning impossible, it has, on the other hand, opened up a symbolic space for different paths of action.

But who were the main actors of such a process, or, in semiotic terms, who covered the actantial role of Addresser, setting the structure of Destination? From the very

---

[5] On the community of mourning, see also Sosa (2014b).

beginning, the agency of these actions was mainly driven by the *afectados* (affected people), to use the expression of Elizabeth Jelin (1994; 2008), those who have suffered through their immediate relatives, the Madres, the Abuelas, the H.I.J.O.S., all defining themselves through a family relationship with the *desaparecidos*. These groups were the main subjects of a reaction and a protest against the military, which, if it at the beginning mainly took the form of an inquiry into the disappeared relatives—at least as far as the Mothers were concerned—soon assumed a very clear and precise political profile. Acting as Addresser, they configured the frame of Destination, triggering the action and establishing the system of values.

An extended debate has taken place in the last years about such a phenomenon,[6] described as a familialistic monopoly of pain, and which, according to some scholars, soon became a monopoly of memory and a form of power, naturalizing trauma into a biological normativity and restraining its resonance from extending to wider sectors of society. I will not discuss here in detail this specific question, but only indicate some elements that might make the picture more complex than it might appear at a first sight. Although it is certainly true that the evocation of a bloodline played an essential role in the politics of human rights associations in post-dictatorship Argentina, a more detailed analysis might reveal other aspects, opening up to other, alternative, readings, as has been shown by Cecilia Sosa's work (2011; 2014).

Moreover, it should be noted that the naturalization of a human rights discourse within a family-oriented interpretative framework was not only due to the associations of relatives, as the state also played a crucial role in it. Probably the most important step in that direction was the law of economic reparation for the victims (1994) that, as Vecchioli (2005) claims, transformed a kinship tie into a legal figure, thus making the disappeared almost into an exclusive and "private" property of their family.

Familialistic discourse has a long tradition in Argentine society. Military personnel, too, were used to referring to the idea of the family as the "basic cell of the nation", assuming for themselves the role of the strong father. A familialistic

---

[6] See Jelin (1994; 2008), Taylor (1997), Longoni (2010).

isotopy imbued with male paternalism crosses Argentine political imagery both during the dictatorship and then during the democratic government, suggesting continuity between the familial military's narrative and the language of democratic government and human rights movements.[7]

However, a paradox lies in this picture, since the actual idea of family evoked by the relatives' association does not really fit into the traditional one. "Although they all evoke conventional family titles, the *Madres*, *Abuelas*, *Familiares* and *H.I.J.O.S* have all created affective arrangements that do not correspond to the nuclear family model" (Sosa 2014a: 15). If we consider, for example, the Madres, certainly the most important and famous of these associations, we can see that the family image they depict is quite an unusual one. First of all there are no fathers in the picture here but only mothers, and thus the "basic cell" of the family appears to have been deconstructed. Moreover, if on the one hand the movement assumed the thematic role of mother as a basic feature of its identity, a move which could be read in an implicit continuity with the traditional Catholic imagery of the Virgin Mary, on the other it opens up a new, non-traditional and transversal politics of feminine solidarity that goes well beyond the traditional family nucleus.

Probably, it would be correct to say that both readings to some extent coexist and are in a dialectical tension with each other: certainly the human rights associations of relatives started from an undeniable bloodline that was also used by the government itself to manage a familialistic privatization of victimhood. At the same time, however, they spread into society, making public, and political, what at the beginning was "just" the search for the disappeared loved ones. In this way loss did not remain confined to the private grief of the family, but opened up for collective political activism, creating also new forms of sociality and "public intimacy", to use Sosa's words. Although the *vexata quaestio* of familialism in Argentine society is not the object of this present work, it is however indirectly addressed here: according to my reading, alternative forms of mourning gave raise to, and became part of, an extended social awareness in the whole of society, overcoming bloodline ties and forcing

---

[7] See on this point also the contribution of Cristina Demaria in this volume.

the thresholds of the private elaboration of grief.

As a consequence, different subject-positions became possible, besides the affected subjects of victims' relatives: a much-varied category of "implicated" subjects (Rotheberg 2014) who might have been very differently positioned in the violent system of state terrorism. In this way the classical binary opposition of victim-perpetrator becomes deconstructed, giving way to a set of more nuanced positions: sympathizers on both sides, survivors, bystanders with different degrees of implication, and so on.

The spreading of new forms of social boundaries and political engagement grew out of the re-semanticization of the traditional repertoire of funerary practices and images, giving them new and unforeseen meanings. Traditional signs of mourning, generally linked to private expressions of grief, become in this way re-signified, acquiring a new public and political dimension, while at the same time maintaining some traces of their original signification of funerary rituals. Mourning signs can be seen, in this context, as *transformative devices* acting as semiotic shifters between different frames—private grief on the one hand, and collective forms of political actions on the other—that do not exclude one another but remain in an unstable balance. It is worth noting that these frames have a pluri-dimensional configuration: they are at one and the same time conceptual, embedding different forms of sense; emotional, conveying different affects; and pragmatic, implying different kinds of actions and practices.

A peculiar semiotic tension between different values is achieved in this way: death and life, private and public, tradition and innovation, personal grieving and public activism intertwine in what can be seen as a paradoxical, yet very creative, legacy of the disappeared.

A new landscape of memory takes shape, a landscape that redesigns the geography of the territory through photographs, images, art exhibitions, sites, places of memory and counter-memory, together with different practices ranging from commemorations to *escraches* to artistic performances and even juridical trials and testimonies: all these different manifestations become the public stage where mourning, memorialization and political action meet.

It would not seem very productive, however, to classify

the semiotic objects that are part of the memory landscape in today's Argentina according to their different expressive substances, separating, for example, photos and images from sites, memorials or practices. In reality all these elements merge together: places of memory, or counter-memory, are often the scene of commemorations or demonstrations, involving in their turn the use of photographs, and so on. We are in the presence of real syncretic semiotic objects, whose meaning is the result of the interaction of different semiotic systems. In what follows we will give some analytical examples of these peculiar semiotic configurations, focusing especially on the persistence of elements of mourning rituals and their transformation into public forms of memory.

In post-dictatorship Argentina, landscapes of memory are spaces of hybridization, where private forms of mourning give new meanings to public space, and, in their turn, public actions became essential components of personal workings through. A double semiotic transformation takes place in these cases, paralleling a shift between private and public sphere: private gestures acquire a political meaning of denouncement, while public spaces and acts of commemoration play the role of an impossible burial ceremony. The very same gesture, the very same place is thus deconstructed into its original sense and re-semanticized into a new form that does not belong to either the private or the public sphere, but rather is an unheard-of combination of both.

From Mourning to Political Action
In the beginning there were photographs. When in 1977 a small group of Mothers started their silent manifestations walking around in a circle in the Plaza de Mayo, each was carrying a photo of their disappeared children. At that stage these photographs were primarily indexical signs of recognition: the photos represented the features of the specific persons who had been abducted and could be useful to trace these missing persons if somebody recognized them. Semiotically, the photos had an individualizing, singular character, to designate one individual, as metonymic identification devices. This character, however, changed over time, according to the various transformations of the political situation during the post-dictatorship, a period far from being

politically homogeneous as the definite description used to refer to it seems to suggest.

During the 1980s, the Madres movement opened up to the idea of socializing maternity (*socializar la maternidad*), which implied a generalization of the individual kinship tie into a collective shared motherhood with a strong social and political connotation. As a consequence, the use of photos during the Mothers' demonstrations changed accordingly: photos did not appear any more in a significant number, instead more often large posters without pictures on them were used, with only the name and the date of disappearance, followed by a big question mark.[8] Use of the disappeared photos was the object of a big debate among relatives' associations: "To use or not to use photos, how to use them, label them with the name and the disappearance date or not, were always issues of discussion and negotiation among the relatives of the disappeared" (da Silva Catela 2014: 141, my translation).

What is certain is that, in today's Argentina, one of the most striking features of what I would define as a landscape of traumatic memory is the pervasive presence in the territory of photos of the disappeared.[9] Painted on the wall at the ESMA, exhibited in university spaces, covering entire walls at sites of memory and archives, the visages of young women and young men, mostly in their twenties, look at us from everywhere, sometimes smiling, sometimes with the serious gaze of an ID photo.

Over the years, photos have become different semiotic objects, changing their meaning and function. If at the beginning they were first and foremost indices pointing to the disappeared,[10] over time they acquired more and more often the role of *symbolic icons*. If in the former case they are images of a specific individual and generally labelled with the name and date of disappearance, as is the case in the photos of architecture students still exhibited in the main hall of the University in Buenos Aires (fig. 1), in the latter case they allude to the generic category acquiring a strong symbolic

---

[8] For more reference to these data, see da Silva Catela (2014: 141; 2015).
[9] On the use of photographs, see, among others, da Silva Catela (2009) and Longoni (2010).
[10] For the indexical function of photos, see Barthes (1980).

character, as happens with the images reproduced in stencil on the walls of the ex-military buildings at ESMA, which do not have any precise indications about their referents (fig. 2).

Fig. 1

Fig. 2.

Disappearance, Mourning and the Politics of Memory

Quite often, however, they have both functions at the same time, as is the case in the Córdoba Archive.[11] Here individual photos of young disappeared cover entire walls of the archive, producing a somewhat choral meaning effect (fig. 3).

Fig. 3

Moreover, every Thursday large reproductions of the photos are displayed in the street where the Archive, a former police station and detention centre, is located (fig. 4), where they assume yet other functions: a commemoration, a way of marking the territory, a form of street performance that addresses the community, and so on.

In all of these usages we can retrace a common echo of a funerary dimension: photos are intrinsically related to death, as Roland Barthes so convincingly argued. At the same time evidence of past existence and actual loss, we put them on tombs and give them a special place in our houses.

Even when photos were polemically used to reverse their funerary meaning, as when the Mothers used them to advocate the reappearance of their children in the famous slogan *Aparición con vida* (Return them Alive), they still alluded to death. This rhetorical inversion was a common strategy in the communication of the Madres: we can read in this way also the white scarf (*pañuelo*) they put on their heads, which, if on the one hand it reminded us of babies' nappies, on the other hand it contrasted, in a sort of ideal opposition, with black, the traditional colour of mourning.

---

[11] For an analysis of the Córdoba Archive, see the contribution of Sozzi in this volume.

MemoSur/MemoSouth

Fig. 4

Besides photos, other forms of iconic evocations of the disappeared spread into the urban Argentine landscapes, subverting the boundaries between mourning and political action. Amongst them the *Siluetazo*, silhouettes made in white paper that started appearing in many Argentine cities after 1983, with the return of democracy, during public demonstrations.[12] The "natural" size of the silhouettes, as big as a real human body, together with the name and the date of the disappearance written on the white paper, while making more abstract and less individualized the iconic representation, reinforced at the same time the substitutive function of the silhouettes in the place of the missing bodies. If, on the one hand, such a substitution evoked, in a strong and almost literal way, a funerary ceremony, on the other it was always performed during public and collective acts of protest, thus overlapping boundaries between forms of mourning and political actions, private grief and public memory. In the same vein, the more traditional forms of street art and graffiti reproducing images of *desaparecidos*, very common today in Argentine cities, constitute as many inscriptions in the urban landscape of shared signs of mourning re-signified as forms of political protest.[13]

In a way, it could be said that entire cities were transformed into places of inscription of voluntary and involuntary memory of the dead. As Vincent Druliolle observed: "In societies like Argentina, the past left wounds, political projects, and other traces as ghostly presences in the urban landscape that some groups want to bring back to light (and life)" (Druliolle 2011: 35). The urban space of cities is thus turned into a public sphere where private work of mourning is redefined as political, and the memory of past grieving as forward-looking engagement.

In contemporary Argentine landscapes—but the same is also true of Chile—spatial inscriptions of memory have many various and different forms, some official and institutionalized, some spontaneous and alternative. Trauma sites (Violi 2014) such as ESMA in Buenos Aires, la Perla, Campo de la Ribera, the Archive of Memory in Córdoba, museums such as the one in Rosario, spaces of memory like

---

[12] On the *Siluetazo*, see Bruzzone and Longoni (2008).
[13] On street art in Argentina, see Kozak (2004). On the use of street art as form of political communication, see Chafee (1993).

the Parque de la Memoria in Buenos Aires, stand alongside endless counter-places disseminated everywhere. Among them the various ex-clandestine detention and torture centres spread throughout the territory, and not all reconfigured as official sites, but often spontaneously transformed into local "micro-memory" projects by neighbourhood associations, or the *baldosas*, memorial plaques with the names of the disappeared, placed in the *barrios* where they lived.

It is impossible here to account for all these places, analyze them or even attempt a complete inventory.[14] For the purpose of my current argument it will be enough to point out how all these territorial marks are at one and the same time symbolic funerary monuments and places of public memory, redefining the work of mourning as political. From this point of view, there is no opposition between micro- and macro-projects, between official memories and *pequeñas memorias* (small memories), as Estela Schindel (2006) defined local memories. As Druliolle (2011: 31) pointed out, the picture cannot be reduced to any simplified dichotomy, but is rather "one of a complex network of crisscrossing issues about the understanding of remembering and its places—functions, forms, sites".

So much so, since places are not endowed with fixed and pre-given meanings, but acquire their sense from actions and practices that are there performed. It is precisely observing some of the practices linked to all places of memory that the meanings of remembering and the functions they perform became more evident, in their intertwining of mourning and political action. For example, it is quite common to see, at various memory sites, fresh flowers left by relatives close to the photo, or the name, of their beloved disappeared. I witnessed this both at the Córdoba Archive (fig. 5) and along the wall of names at the Parque de la Memoria in Buenos Aires. This is an obvious form of traditional mourning, generally confined to cemeteries or, sometimes, to places where accidents happened. To perform the same act in a public space produces an interesting effect of transformation since it

---

[14] For further references, see: Druliolle (2011), Draper (2012), Andermann (2012a; 2012b), Violi (2014), de Silva Catela (2015), Hite (2015), Conte (2015).

short-circuits two different semiotic fields: the funerary world of the cemetery with its private acts of mourning and the public space of documentation, a space of testimony and political engagement. Private forms of mourning enter into public space, acting as transformation devices and re-semanticizing it; in this way a third space is symbolically construed, a space which is neither private nor completely public, but brings with itself traces of both worlds. The impossibility of performing funerary rituals in cemeteries, under normal circumstances the places devoted to that, produces a transfer of semantic features of mourning into spaces dedicated to documentation and memory that become too, in their turn, places of public shared mourning for the whole community.

Many practices in post-dictatorship Argentina share similar double readings, from flowers left close to photographs at memory sites, to the act of planting a tree in the place where somebody was abducted by the military, to commemorations that often appear to substitute for funerals that will never take place. Even completely different practices, such as the cooking sessions organized by Hebe de Bonafini at ESMA, kept something of the convivial meals traditionally held after a funerary ceremony.

The overall meaning of such places is transformed in a stratified and multidirectional way: at the same time sites of memory, witnesses of past traumatic history, places of private mourning, spaces for political actions, they exceed the dimension of simple historical archives or monuments to become affective architectures, archives of feelings.

At the Parque de la Memoria in Buenos Aires such an intersection is even more evident: the inauguration ceremony acquired the sense of a funerary ritual, with the presence of many disappeared relatives, and even more so, the placing of the statue made by Claudia Fontes, representing Pablo, an adolescent born the same year as the artist, abducted with his mother when he was fourteen and who never appeared again. His figure was meticulously reconstructed by the artist, and his statue, looking toward the river, stands in the water as a symbolic tomb.

But maybe more than anything else, the inescapable link between mourning, grief and political testimony is the choice of some Madres, who wanted their own funeral ceremonies to be performed at the Parque de la Memoria, where their ashes were dispersed into the river, to finally join their forever lost children.

Fig. 5

References

Andermann, J. (2012a). Returning to the site of horror: On the reclaiming of clandestine concentration camps in Argentina. *Theory, Culture & Society*, 29(1), 76–98.

Andermann, J. (2012b) Expanded fields: Postdictatorship and the landscape. *Journal of Latin American Cultural Studies*, 21(1), 165–187.

Barthes, R. (1980). *La chambre claire. Note sur la photographie*. Paris: Gallimard-Seuil.

Bruzzone, G. & Longoni, A. (eds). (2008). *El siluetazo*. Buenos Aires: Adriana Hidalgo Editora.

Butler, J. (2004). *Precarious life: The powers of mourning and violence*. London and New York: Verso.

Calveiro, P. (1998). *Poder y desaparición. Los campos de concentración en Argentina*. Buenos Aires: Colihue.

Chafee, L. G. (1993). *Political protest and street art: Popular tools for democratization in Hispanic countries*. Westport: Greenwood Press.

Conte, G. (2015). A topography of memory: Reconstructing the architectures of terror in the Argentine dictatorship. *Memory Studies*, 8(1), 86–101.

da Silva Catela, L. (2009). Lo invisible revelado. El uso de fotografías como (re)presentación de la desaparición de personas en Argentina. In C. Feld & J. Stites Mor (eds.), *El pasado que miramos. Memoria e imagen ante la historia reciente*. Buenos Aires: Paidós.

da Silva Catela, L. (2014). *No habrá flores en la tumba del pasado. La experiencia de reconstrucción del mundo de los familiares de desaparecidos*. Buenos Aires: Ediciones Al Margen.

da Silva Catela, L. (2015). Staged memories: Conflicts and tensions in Argentine public memory sites. *Memory Studies*, 8 (I), 9-21.

Demaria, C., & Lorusso, A. M. (2012). A ritual to deal with an unspeakable trauma: The case of the Mothers of the Plaza de Mayo. *Lexia Rivista di semiotica*, 11-12, Torino, 327-356.

Draper, S. (2012). *Afterlives of confinement: Spatial transitions in postdictatorship Latin America*. Pittsburgh, PA: University of Pittsburgh Press.

Druliolle, V. (2011). Remembering and its places in postdictatorship Argentina. In F. Lessa & V. Druliolle (eds.), *The memory of state terrorism in the Southern*

Cone: Argentina, Chile, Uruguay. Basingstoke: Palgrave Macmillan, pp. 15-41.

Hite, K. (2015). Empathic unsettlement and the outsider within Argentine spaces of memory. *Memory Studies*, 8(1), 38–48.

Jelin, E. (1994). The politics of memory: The human rights movements and the construction of democracy in Argentina. *Latin American Perspectives*, 21(2), 38-58.

Jelin, E. (2008). Victims, relatives, and citizen in Argentina: Whose voice is legitimate enough?. In R. A. Wilson & R. D. Brown (eds.), *Humanitarianism and suffering: The mobilization of empathy.* Cambridge: Cambridge University Press.

Kozak, C. (2004). *Contra la pared. Sobre graffitis, pintadas y otras intervenciones urbanas.* Buenos Aires: Libros del Rojas.

Kripke, S. (1972). Naming and necessity. In G. Harman & D. Davidson (eds.), *Semantics of natural language.* Reidel: Dorddrecht.

Longoni, A. (2010). Fotos y siluetas: Dos estrategias en la representación de los desaparecidos. In E. Crenzel (ed.), *Los desaparecidos en la Argentina. Memorias, representaciones e ideas (1983-2008).* Buenos Aires: Biblos.

Rothberg, M. (2014). Trauma theory, implicated subjects and the question of Israel/Palestine. **http://profession.commons.mla.org/2014/05/02/traumatheory-implicated-subjects-and-the-question-of-israel/palestine**

Schindel, E. (2006). Las pequeñas memorias y el paisaje cotidiano: Cartografias del recuerdo en Buenos Aires y Berlin. In C. Macón (ed.), *Trabajos de la memoria. Arte y ciudad en la postdictatura Argentina.* Buenos Aires: Ladosur.

Schmucler, H. (1996). "Ni siquiera un rostro donde la muerte hubiera podido estampar su sello" (reflexiones sobre los desaparecidos y la memoria). *Revista Pensamiento de los Confines*, 3, 9-12.

Sosa, C. (2011). Queering acts of mourning in the aftermath of Argentina's dictatorship: The Mothers of Plaza de Mayo and *Los Rubios*. In F. Lessa and V. Druliolle (eds.), *The memory of state terrorism in the Southern Cone: Argentina, Chile, Uruguay.* Basingstoke:

Palgrave Macmillan, pp. 63-85.

Sosa, C. (2014a). *Queering acts of mourning in the aftermath of Argentina's dictatorship: The performances of blood*. Woodbridge: Tamesis.

Sosa, C. (2014b). Viral affiliations: Facebook, queer kinship and the memory of the disappeared in contemporary Argentina. In L. A. Freeman, B. Nienass, & R. Daniell (eds.), *Silence, screen and spectacle: Rethinking collective memory in the age of information and new media*. New York and Oxford: Berghahn Books, pp. 77-94.

Taylor, D. (1997). *Disappearing acts: Spectacles of gender and nationalism in Argentina's Dirty War*. Durham, NC: Duke University Press.

Vecchioli, V. (2005). La nación como familia: Metáforas políticas en el movimiento argentino por los derechos humanos. In S. Frederic & G. Soprano (eds.), *Cultura y política en etnografías sobre la Argentina*. Buenos Aires: Universidad Nacional de Quilmes.

Violi, P. (2014). *Paesaggi della memoria. Il trauma, lo spazio, la storia*. Milan: Bompiani.

The Politics of Remembering and Forgetting in the Argentine Education System

Daniel Filmus

> "The question is," said Alice, "whether you can make words mean so little."
>
> "The question is," said Humpty Dumpty, "who is to be master—that's all."
>
> Lewis Carroll

There is a considerable degree of consensus as to one of the principal roles of education systems, namely, that of transmitting from generation to generation the culture of a given society. Such a consensus, however, does not extend to the characteristics pertaining to this process of transmission nor to the social and political functions implied thereby.

For those brought up in the classical tradition of the sociology of education that arose with E. Durkheim (1991), the culture transmitted through the school system responds to cohesive ideals that allow people to live together in democratic society. These values allow coexistence and mutual respect between citizens on the basis of a general consensus regarding the norms and values that are to govern a society. The said consensus depends on a "neutral" code that, in time, corresponds to a given community and a determinate moment in history. Such a perspective is sustained by the conviction that there exists in the state, and by right, a "national spirit" made up of a collective consciousness which, through state action, must be imparted by schooling to each new generation for it to be fully integrated into society.

A more critical sociology of education, in contrast, conceives of society as non-existent as an organic whole. The social structure is sustained by a profound inequality in the distribution of economic, political and cultural resources. In this model, the contexts and practices of education are never "neutral" and never correspond with some "collective consciousness". They are the result of the dominance of some groups over others, expressed, amongst other ways, through cultural domination. From such a standpoint, the principal purpose of education is to transmit, as legitimate and universal, the culture of dominant groups, which is but one part of culture and therefore *relative* and *arbitrary* (Bourdieu & Passerón 1977; Althusser 1974). From the traditional perspective, both pedagogy and the role of the teacher are directed at unleashing a centripetal force of integration and social cohesion. For a critical-reproductivist sociology, however, the teacher delivers legitimacy, arising from his or her pedagogical actions, to the curricular contexts imposed by the dominant class or group, a part or a slice of culture but also a guarantee of reproducing social inequalities.

Remembering and forgetting, or what is present and absent in the pedagogical design and practice of the curriculum, depends, in Durkheimian terms, on what *society* considers it necessary to include in the intergenerational transmission of culture for the maintenance of order and social integration. From this perspective, the transmission of culture is destined to leave no room for critique but rather to recreate adult mandates. Its objective is the acceptance of an unquestionable legacy (Birgin 2016). In contrast, a critical perspective emphasizes the never neutral political character of the selection of merely a part of the culture and history to be transmitted and, of course, the form to be adopted in this transmission. The strength to be gained by the legitimizing of an unjust social order will depend, in the main, on the capacity of the dominant groups to naturalize, or to attribute some objectivity to, a range of contents and values only sustainable as the defence of their own interests. Thus, critical analysis will detect in instances of "forgetting", in the gaps left in the schooling process, one of the keys to opening up the teaching devices deployed to add symbolic force to the intention of perpetuating the material inequalities of society. Seen thus, it is possible to propose that the reason for the absence from the schooling environment of the history and values of subaltern groups in society (women, native peoples, workers, etc.) and of central social processes or traumatic facts—such as wars and genocides—is not a matter of chance or simply "forgetting". The recent history of Argentina is a clear example of such a tension between remembering and forgetting in the schooling environment, forever linked to the confrontation of vested interests and a politics of antagonisms.

The "Forgotten Ones" in the Argentine Education System

From its earliest phases, the Argentine education system has had as its main objective the integration of a highly heterogeneous population into a Nation and a State under the leadership of a very small section of society that represented the interests of the great landowners and of those who monopolized commerce with the colonial power of the time, the United Kingdom. It was thus that, at the end of the nineteenth century, a strongly exclusivist model in economics and politics, allowing for no mass access to property, participation in politics or upward social mobility, was determined to develop, from the construction of a neutral education system, the ideal mechanism for integrating and modernizing society. In order to achieve this objective, a national curriculum was designed and deployed to exclude from its content and practice an important part of the history, social processes and values involving the great majority of the nation, in particular the original peoples of the land. The construction of the Argentine nation was carried out upon the basis of a Europe-centred culture that marginalized from the school process both the early inhabitants and the popular sectors of society. Without any room for doubt, however, it was the military dictatorship that governed the country between 1976 and 1983 that took to the most aberrant and unusual extremes the censoring of schooling's contents and materials. The disappearances of individuals that occurred as part of the repressive mechanism of government had as its counterpart the "disappearance" of authors, texts and even school subjects (for example, the prohibition of modern mathematics, set theory and sociology) from the education system. Conscious of the role of education in the development of critical individuals, the military government murdered, persecuted, "disappeared", imprisoned or forced into exile a very great number of teachers. The level of sophistication with which the dictatorship imposed its censorship in schools had no precedents. The swathing prohibition of authors, texts and school subjects was accompanied by an even more efficient system of control: permanent self-censorship. Many teachers chose to exclude from teaching even things that had not been explicitly prescribed, for fear of suffering repression (Filmus & Frigerio 1988).

Remembering and Forgetting in Argentine Education

Democracy Is Recovered. But Is Memory?
The dictatorship attempted by every possible means to ensure that its actions, particularly in the realm of state terrorism and of its role in the Malvinas conflict, were not revised by the nascent democracy. The "ordered" withdrawal—not by a popular uprising—of the Armed Forces from government generated the conditions by which the military meant to control and tutor the political system over a long period.

The process by which education was democratized, in accordance with what took place throughout the whole country, was not straightforward. The opening up of democracy meant that the grave violations of human rights and state terrorism committed during the dictatorship became public knowledge and that the demands for those guilty to be judged, until then limited only to the organizations of the Mothers and Grandmothers of the Plaza de Mayo and other human rights institutions, eventually multiplied. The government of Raúl Alfonsín took up these demands as its own and as soon as it came to power created a special commission made up of well-known personalities from within Argentine culture to investigate the atrocities committed during the dictatorship. The Comisión Nacional sobre la Desaparición de Personas (National Commission on the Disappearance of Persons) published its naked and profound version of events in an emblematic text for Argentine democracy entitled *Nunca más* (1984). At the same time, the government took the decision to implement a characteristically memorable trial that culminated in the condemnation of the members of the Military Juntas that controlled the government from 1976 to 1983. The first two years of democratic administration were accompanied in the system of education by the overturning of repressive norms, the elimination of explicit censorship, and the opening up of participatory initiatives in the schools sector. Further, the period saw a gradual inclusion of subjects excluded in the preceding years. Programmes of study and curriculum designs underwent changes and began to include content linked to the crimes committed by state terrorism and to the need for the total enforcement of human rights.

The processes of democratization of public institutions and of the judging of those guilty of state terrorism began to be questioned by sectors of the Armed Forces. Permanent military uprisings against the constitutional order gained their "compensation" through the sanction and application of the Full Stop (1986) and Due Obedience (1987) (*Punto Final* and *Obediencia Debida*) laws and the pardoning of those who had been found guilty (1989). These measures caused the ending of the trials and established the basis of granting impunity to those responsible for genocide. In the education system this process meant a regression in the development in schools of the teaching of "traumatic" subjects and the return to self-censoring. Once again in Argentina there ensued yet another period of "forgetting" of the most painful facts of the country's recent past.

Under the headings of "reconciliation" and "national unity" the possibility that justice might reign was simply diluted. Paraphrasing Yosef Yerushalmi (1998), who, in his book *Los usos del olvido* (*The Uses of Forgetting*), claimed that probably the opposite term to "forgetting" was not "remembering" but "justice", it is possible to suggest that the lack of justice in Argentina was intended to produce a blanket of forgetting. In the education system, the institutionalization of not allowing teaching on the processes of state terrorism and the Malvinas conflict was confirmed in the Federal Education Legislation voted for in 1992. Amongst the obligatory contents that the education system had to deliver in schools such problematic subjects were not included.

The idea that issues to do with trauma ought not to be brought to attention nor be part of transmitting culture in schools was extended to at least two other dramatic incidents experienced by the country in the 1990s, namely, the most important terrorist attacks which Argentina has suffered in its whole history, the attacks on the Israeli Embassy (1992) and on the Asociación Mutual Israelita Argentina (AMIA) (1994), in which perished, respectively, twenty-two and eighty-five victims. This period, which combined impunity for genocide, the politics of "forgetting" of human rights and the predominance of a neoliberal economic model, ended in the worst manner imaginable. The taking to the streets of the population, with the cry of "que se vayan todos" (all of them must go), provoked the resignation of President Fernando de la Rúa in 2001. The repression of this popular uprising caused fifty deaths and unleashed a political crisis that only began to be resolved with the coming to the Presidency of the Nation of Néstor Kirchner, who won the April 2003 elections.

Argentina Recovers Memory and Seeks Truth and Justice

The government that came to power on 25 May 2003 drastically changed the politics of human rights that had prevailed in the preceding years. In his inaugural address to Parliament, the new president declared that the central axis of his political programme would be that of achieving Memory, Truth and Justice, and proclaimed the legitimacy of the fight against impunity led by the Mothers and Grandmothers of the Plaza de Mayo. Within months, in August 2003, the National Congress approved the project, put forward by the Executive, to repeal the laws of Punto Final and Obediencia Debida. The attempts to throw a blanket of forgetting over the crimes committed were buried under the claim for justice firmly held and advanced by the various human rights organizations.

Two years later, the Supreme Court of Justice declared both these laws unconstitutional, an act which triggered the trials of military and civilian perpetrators of the politics of state terrorism during the period of the dictatorship that had ruled the country from 1976 to 1983. A decade after the start of the trials, more than 2,200 members of the military had been indicted, of which 660 were found guilty and some 851 were still in the process of being tried.

The Challenge to the Education System in the Transition of Memory

When the new government established the fight for memory, truth and justice as official state policy, the Ministry of Education had to take up the challenge of recovering the work undertaken at the outset of the new period of democracy and extending the measures taken to transmit what had happened during the most traumatic periods of Argentine history.

The challenges faced by the heads of the Ministry of Education and the teams of teachers tasked with the implementation of the policy were by no means easy, given that a broad debate on the issue had been unleashed in society as a whole as well as in the education system itself. In brief, the debate turned on these axes: a) Ought schools to transmit the traumatic events of the recent past? b) How to change legislation to the effect that these subjects be taught in all schools throughout the country? c) How to guarantee that such a transmission of the facts of history not be reduced to a mere "mechanical reproduction of memory"? In respect of the first question, the Ministry of Education decided to take up the social mandate that had been installed in 2003 and to work towards the education system's being able to develop again the conditions that had enabled it to transmit to new generations the memory of traumatic situations that were in the distant past but, in some cases, very close to the present... situations that had often involved exclusion, suffering and death. Thus, schools had to assume the responsibility for working in the classroom with matters of genocides, wars, and acts of terrorism that had moved, and continue to move, deeply, the conscience of the citizens of Argentina. And, so, education is recovering one of its principal objectives. As Theodor Adorno writes (1998), "The pathos (the passion) for schooling, its moral seriousness, stems from the fact that it alone can work immediately, if one takes notice of it, in overcoming barbarity on the part of humanity... I am referring to the extremes, the mad prejudice, the repression, genocide and torture, about which there can be not the least doubt". This perspective, profoundly humanist, stands in counterpoint to the view that the task of education is supposedly neutral, because it stresses the political role of schooling. Yet it does not achieve this aim in a partisan fashion. To stress the political role of and in teaching implies trusting in the capacity of citizens to be brought up with a critical awareness. Citizens ready to avoid the repetition of history and to stop both the rise of dictatorships and the violation of human rights. In support of such a political commitment on the part of school, Inés Dussel (2001) has proposed that:

> The transmission of the memory of historic trauma shares the dilemmas of all cultural transmission and of all pedagogical activity, their ethical paradoxes and their political tensions, but it has characteristics that distinguish it from other modes of transmission. In the transmission of memory, it is human suffering that occupies the central and definitive role. Symptomatic of history, these traumatic events carry with them the very limits of representation, the crisis of truth and justice, obliging us to take sides, to explore the politics of transmission.

Remembering and Forgetting in Argentine Education

Yet the debate is not uniquely centred on the different views *vis à vis* the past and the ways of transmitting that legacy (Hassoun 1996), but on the implications that said history sheds upon the present. Each one of these traumatic processes, beginning to be included in the curriculum's design and in the schooling practice, weighs upon the decisions made in the present. As Jorge Luis Borges proposed in a prologue of 1968, "history is not a cold museum; it is the secret trap out of which we are formed, that of time itself. In today are our yesterdays". It is not possible to introduce into the classroom content referring to the devastating consequences of conquest and colonization for the native peoples without debating the manner in which, today, discrimination and cultural domination are expressed and operated upon the inheritors of those peoples. The problem of migration, so present on the public agenda today, is also affected by this discussion. To become conscious of the genocides committed during the military dictatorship obliges teachers and pupils to tackle issues of the day, such as the need to advance in the passing of judgements on those civilians and military personnel guilty of violations of human rights, or the permanent search of identity on the part of children born in captivity and subsequently stolen. The debate on the Malvinas conflict not only needs, as in the case of state terrorism, to be part of the process of judging those responsible for sending to their deaths hundreds of young men and for the violation of the human rights of the soldiers who fought there, but also implies opening further the discussion regarding an unjust international order that allows the United Kingdom to continue usurping a part of Argentine territory after more than 180 years.

Forgetting, or the non-presence of such topics as these in the classroom, exempts the school from the need to locate these facts as part of the pedagogical process and of the intergenerational transmission of culture, distancing the very conflict that invites a reconsideration of that transmission. For to consider that conflict only as a question of past history, without including its implications in and for the present, is a relatively comfortable alternative, thereby suggesting commitment to the project of those who only aspire to fulfil the merest formalities of what is to be expected of "modern" educational programmes. From within the Ministry of Education charged with implementing educational policy from 2003 onwards there arose a different view, one that would link past, present and future.

The second of the aforementioned challenges was limited to the need to ensure that the curricular contents be included in the study programmes of the whole country and, for that objective to be achieved, such contents had to be included in the new National Education Law, in a specific clause that put the obligation to teach these topics at every level of the education system. The debates over the new law took place throughout 2006. More than four million students, teachers and parents participated in this process, along with thousands of community organizations, churches, trade unions, chambers of commerce, universities, graduate associations, etc. Support for the inclusion of topics linked to recent memory and "traumatic" contents was of such magnitude that it halted all resistance in the National Congress, and inclusion was passed by a clear (nearly unanimous) majority in both chambers (Filmus & Kaplan 2012). Thus, article 92 of the National Education Law (No. 26,026) included the stipulation that for all provinces of the nation the following contents be applied in common:

- The exercise and construction of collective memory of the historical and political process that broke the constitutional order and ended by installing State terrorism; with the objective of generating amongst students reflections and democratic feelings and the defence of the Rule of Law and the full application of human rights in accordance with that principle outlined by Law No. 26,061;
- The case for the recuperation of our Islands, the Malvinas, the South Georgias and South Sandwich, in accordance with the principle outlined in the First Transitory Disposition of the National Constitution;
- The acknowledgement of the cultural diversity of indigenous peoples and their rights, in accordance with article 54 of the current law.

In respect of those who participated in acts linked to state terrorism, Law 26,206 (Article 70) is applicable in prohibiting them from carrying out any teaching role.

Thus, the law prescribes concrete mechanisms in order that painful, controversial and complex facts of history and

Argentine reality be not only incorporated as teaching material but also absorbed into the everyday reality of classroom experience and the construction of a different future.

To this point, we have emphasized the importance of schooling in the irrefutable commitment to transmit fully the history and culture of the country without excluding the dramatic and painful processes of the past and present. We have also summarized some of the legislative mechanisms that underpin and lend "obligatory" character to this transmission. At this juncture we wish to make clear that these processes are necessary but not sufficient for the education system to enhance its task of an effective and total incorporation of social memory into the new generations. The capacity for resistance of schools and practitioners in addressing such complex topics is habitually shown through the mechanizing and formalizing of the methods of transmitting memory. In other words, the school can transmit the experiences of suffering or horror by way of "teaching the memory of memory", ending up by producing "forgetting." Perhaps for that reason there has been and continues to be the most important challenge in tackling the scholarly task of transmitting traumatic experiences: the need to structure a teaching plan that, intensively, might put the new generations into contact not only with the facts and the contents of memory, but also with the sensations, dramas, sufferings, dreams and illusions of those who lived through them. To transmit the past as do traditional museums or as just some archaeological remains is a form of assuring that it stays stuck in its time and that it "does not loose its demons onto the present" (Dussel 2001). In his novel *The Name of the Rose*, Umberto Eco puts into the mouth of William, the monk who is searching for the truth, a fascinating reflexion on libraries. Speaking to his disciple, Adso, he asserts that a library can provide humanity with all the knowledge that men and women have ever produced, or just the contrary. As is the case with the library in the novel's setting, it can serve to enclose and to ensure that humanity never come into contact with its manuscripts. The art of keeping documents also implies hiding them away (Dussel 2001). A similar phenomenon may be observed in the culture transmitted by schools, which have their own logic, agents and particular cultures. The strategy of formally incorporating certain contents into curriculum designs and subject programmes may also imply that they never reach their intended recipients alive, being conceived of as the mere reproduction of memory. For this reason, it is necessary to complement a politics of inclusion of memory in the school environment with the essential development of pedagogies that ensure that the process of transition itself does not turn into some fixed, dead content but, in contrast, is transformed into a tool designed to establish contact with knowledge, feelings and legacies that focus activities in the present inseparably from constructing the future.

If there is a clear risk in the formalizing or rendering mechanical of a remembering that invites only forgetting, another challenge involved in the transition of memory is its being reproduced as an unquestionable legacy (Birgin 2006). The perspective from which the Ministry of Education introduced the memory programmes was sustained by the idea proposed by Hassoun (1996) regarding what might be considered a "successful transmission". Such would be whatever "offered to the receiver a space of freedom and a base from which to abandon (the past) in order (the better) to rediscover it". As pointed out by Merieu (1998), the transmission of this type of knowledge and awareness cannot be achieved mechanically: "it cannot be conceived as some duplication of the same, as implicit in many forms of teaching. It presupposes a reconstruction, on the part of the subject, of knowledge and awareness that it must inscribe in both that project and in those perceived as contributing to its development." The aim of our teaching task is to provide for new generations both knowledge of social and historical processes and a feeling for them; the pains and the horrors, dreams and hopes through which we have travelled. But if we are to achieve the "successful transmission" suggested by Hassoun, we must also create conditions whereby—with such awareness and feelings—the new generations might decide to travel paths very different to those we have travelled ourselves (Birgin 2016). The meeting point between generations implied in the educational process will surely include new perspectives, new questions posed by those who enter the space of memory for the first time. A successful transmission, if achieved, becomes a process of permanent recreation, depending on the continuing development of the critical faculties of the protagonists involved. This right to question, to re-elaborate upon our legacy, of course includes the right to forget or deny; but now as a right rather than as a result of that absence that imposes the emptiness produced by the lack of memory.

At this point, it is necessary to emphasize that the only possible strategy for incorporating this point of view is through the actions of the teachers involved. Experience shows that no transformation can arrive in the classroom if it is not supported by the willingness to change on the part of teachers and professors. Therefore, the first challenge in counting on them as fundamental to the introduction of these topics into the schooling experience is to invite them to be part of the development of the proposed strategies of inclusion in the programmes of memory and education.

A further and key consideration is the multiplicity of technical and audiovisual support systems available today that allow the transmission of memory through a range of multimedia productions. The setting up of the educational television channel *Encuentro* and of the children's channel *PakaPaka* has become an essential tool for reaching nationwide, with film and television materials, teacher training and access to pupils and students as well as extending contact with the country's communities as a whole. It is also the case that schools have been approached through the arts. Works from the theatre, cinema, literature, exhibitions of the plastic arts, amongst other media, have been privileged instruments in bringing students closer to situations that were very difficult to broach from traditional teaching perspectives and strategies.

By Way of Epilogue: New Winds of Forgetting Are Blowing

Some year and a half after the coming to power of the government of Mauricio Macri, it is possible to state that national politics pitched at recovering social memory and keeping alive the task of guarding human rights have altered profoundly. The new authorities have decided to go into reverse gear on the road taken by the state in respect of the claims of Memory, Truth, and Justice. The great social consensus regarding the politics of human rights achieved by the previous administration has made more difficult the official intention of reversing them quickly. But what has already begun is a strong media campaign that tends to delegitimize the struggle of human rights organizations and to accuse the former government of opportunism. As far as the criminal trials are concerned, there has been a clear attempt to slow down the process, home detention has been ordered for many of the accused and condemned and there has been a questioning of those judges who adopted a strong line against the genocide of the dictatorship. Furthermore, state support has been withdrawn from such human rights organizations as the Mothers and Grandmothers of the Plaza de Mayo. As for the campaign of delegitimizing appeals for justice, the present government has tried to advance in different directions. In every case, there has been a tendency to question memory itself. The Minister of Culture of the City of Buenos Aires, Darío Lopérfido, has questioned the emblematic number of 30,000 victims of forced disappearances and has argued that this figure was artificially inflated so that more families might claim the compensation to which they were legally entitled. Over and above that, as Adorno (1998) reminds us, when it comes to genocide, "to point to statistical figures or indeed to haggle over them is already unworthy of being human", and the aim of Darío Lopérfido has been to undermine the authority of human rights organizations. The Director of National Customs and Excise, Juan José Gómez Centurión, an ex-military officer who rose up against democracy during the government of Raúl Alfonsín, has thrown into question the sentences passed in the trials of the Military Juntas. He has argued that the actions of the dictatorship were not attributable to a premeditated plan for the extermination of citizens and the disappearance of babies. He has returned to toy with the theory that the violations of human rights were "excesses" the responsibility for which can be ascribed to certain members of the Armed Forces. For its part, attempting to contribute to "forgetting", the government has decreed, ignoring the existing laws, that the public holidays marking the dictatorship (24 March) and rendering homage to the fallen of the Malvinas conflict (2 April) could be moved to other dates. The ensuing fight culminated in the resignation of the Minister of Culture, the Director of Customs and Excise had to rectify his position publicly, and the government also had to take a step back in its attempt to change the date for remembering the dictatorship and the Malvinas victims.

Remembering and Forgetting in Argentine Education

In the case of the Malvinas issue, the intention to "forget" began on the very first day of the new government. President Mauricio Macri became the first ever democratically elected president not to mention the demand for dialogue with the United Kingdom over the sovereignty of the Islands in the traditional address which, in Parliament, establishes the new incumbent's mandate. Yet this glaring omission also revealed the wish to relativize the importance of the said demand for negotiation for the Argentine people in bilateral meetings that had already taken place with British authorities as, no less, with multilateral organizations. In a sort of metaphor for the official attempt to remove this subject from the national and international agenda, the Malvinas islands were "forgotten", or left out, in the design of the map of Argentina produced by the Ministry of Social Development. As for the rights of indigenous peoples, policies also underwent a profound transformation. The new government vindicated those who had committed genocide against the native populations in order to grab their lands. The Minister of Education, Esteban Bullrich (2016), maintained in his speech that Argentina is facing "a new desert campaign, not with sword but through education" (*La Nación*, 16 September 2016). The Minister brought upon himself the opprobrium of broad sectors of society, in particular certain Argentine intellectuals who declared publicly that "it is our right and our duty to demand that education not be left in charge of someone who has vindicated a crime against humanity, both literally and metaphorically" (in Rodríguez 2016).

The politics that are fomenting "forgetting" have had corresponding effects in the education system. The new Minister of Education has questioned all national programmes directed at transmitting in schools the social memory of our people and human rights. Thus, the nation has undergone the cancellation, dismantling, or reduction to a minimum of programmes directed at recording state terrorism, the recovery of identity of the sons and daughters of those who disappeared under the dictatorship, the maintenance of claims to sovereignty over the Malvinas and the implementation of the right to sex education. Particularly grave has been a watering down of policy in the sphere of Intercultural Bilingual Education, given that the National Ministry has been structurally deprived of support for provincial action in this issue. But the aims of government authorities nationally have been to go much further in stopping the function of schooling in respect of transmitting the processes and the traumatic facts that can recuperate memory historically absent from the classroom. Such an objective is but one of the dimensions of a project that is pitched at preventing schools from carrying forward their capacity to develop critical thinking amongst their pupils and students. This is how the authorities have expressed their policies: the Cabinet Minister Marcos Peña (2016) has stated that "critical thinking taken to extremes has caused great damage to education [...] to maintain a critical thinking leads at the end of the day to the loss of the axis of what is truth" (*Clarín*, 9 December 2016). The advisor to the President, Alejandro Rozitchner (2016), has gone further when referring to the role of schools: "critical thinking is a negative value being taught in the nation's schools [...] teachers enjoy saying that they wish their pupils to develop critical thinking as if the most important thing were to be attentive to the traps and pitfalls of society [...]. Enthusiasm and the wish to live are more important than critical thinking and objectivity" (*La Nación*, 20 December 2016).

All these statements are evidence of what is the ultimate aim of those who propose that "forgetting" return to reign over our schools. To educate young people who lack the capacity to look critically and from their own perspectives at society and, therefore, neither to try nor even intend to transform it. This stance does not only confront educational policies implemented in the previous period. It also questions the very foundations of the role of education. As Jean Piaget (1980) affirmed, one of the principal objectives of education is "to form minds capable of exercising critique, so that they can test for themselves whatever is presented to them and not accept it simply as that". Only thus will it be possible "not to repeat what other generations have done: to form creative individuals who are inventive, who are discoverers".

Winds of "forgetting" are blowing across Argentina and through its schools. The arm-wrestling between remembering and forgetting is not over and done with, for it is fought over on a daily basis in our classrooms. We trust that the permanent memory of our people, of its teachers and students, fortified by the politics and policies of transmission conducted over the last decade, will prevent this wind from being turned into a storm capable of blowing away and destroying the imperative of "Nunca más"/"Never again" that has risen up from within our history.

Translated by Bernard McGuirk

References

Adorno, T. (1988). *Educación para la emancipación. Conferencias y conversaciones con Hellmut Becker (1959-1969)* (ed. G. Kadelbach). Madrid: Ediciones Morata S.L.

Althusser, L. (1974). *Ideología e aparelhos ideológicos de Estado*. Lisboa: Presença.

Birgin, A. (2006). La apuesta por la igualdad de la enseñanza. Unpublished paper. Encuentro Regional del Programa Integral para la Igualdad Educativa. Bariloche.

Birgin, A. (2016). El trabajo de enseñar, entre el pasado y el futuro. Unpublished paper. Buenos Aires.

Bourdieu, P., & Passeron, J. C. (1977). *La reproducción. Elementos para una teoría del sistema de enseñanza*. Barcelona: Laia Ed.

Bullrich, E. (2016). Esteban Bullrich: Esta es la nueva Campaña del Desierto, pero no con la espada sino con la educación. *La Nación*, 16 September. **www.lanacion.com.ar/1938454-esteban-bullrich-esta-es-la-nueva-campana-del-desierto-pero-no-con-la-espada-sino-con-la-educacion**.

Durkheim, E. (1991). La educación, su naturaleza y su papel. In P. Natorp, J. Dewey & E. Durkheim (eds.), *Teoría de la educación y sociedad*. Buenos Aires: CEAL.

Dussel, I. (2001). La transmisión de la historia reciente. Reflexiones pedagógicas sobre el arte de la memoria. In *Memorias en presente. Identidad y transmisión en la Argentina posgenocidio*. Buenos Aires: Grupo Editorial Norma.

Filmus, D. (1988). Democratización de la educación: Procesos y perspectivas. In D. Filmus & G. Frigerio (eds.), *Educación, autoritarismo y democracia*. Buenos Aires, Miño y Dávila Ed.

Filmus, D. (1996). *Estado, sociedad y educación en la argentina de fin de siglo. Proceso y desafíos*. Buenos Aires: Ed Troquel.

Filmus, D., & Kaplan, C. (2012). *Educar para una sociedad más justa. Debates y desafíos de la Ley de Educación Nacional*. Buenos Aires: Aguilar.

Hassoun, J. (1996). *Los contrabandistas de la memoria*. Buenos Aires: Ed. de la Flor.

Meirieu, P. (1998). *Frankenstein educador*. Barcelona: Laertes.

Peña, M. (2016). Marcos Peña: "El pensamiento crítico le ha hecho mucho daño a la Argentina". *Clarín*, 9 December. **www.laopiniondetandil.com.ar/2016/12/09/marcos-pena-el-pensamiento-critico-le-ha-hecho-mucho-dano-a-la-argentina/**.

Piaget, J. (1980). *Psicología y pedagogía*. Barcelona: Ariel.

Rodríguez, C. (2016). Los repudios a la "campaña" de Bullrich. *Página 12*, 18 September. **www.pagina12.com.ar/diario/elpais/1-309683-2016-09-18.html**.

Rozitchner, A. (2016). Alejandro Rozitchner: "El pensamiento crítico es un valor negativo". *La Nación*, 20 December. **www.lanacion.com.ar/1968830-alejandro-rozitchner-el-pensamiento-critico-es-un-valor-negativo**.

Yerushalmi, Y. H., *et al.* (1998). *Los usos del olvido. Comunicaciones al Coloquio de Royaumont*. Buenos Aires: Nueva Visión.

"Who Needs Identity?": Disappearances and Appearances in Argentina — The Abuelas de la Plaza de Mayo

Cristina Demaria

> Who is called on to disappear? A little bit of everyone... It is a question of slow poisoning, a delayed psychic bomb. Identity is changed, it becomes hypnotized.
> Philippe Sollers
> (in Gordon 1997)

> Dudas sobre tu identitad? Vos podes ser uno de los nietos que estamos buscando... [Do you doubt your identity? You may be one of the grandchildren we are looking for...]
> Abuelas de la Plaza de Mayo website

> Disappearance is an exemplary instance in which the boundaries of rational and irrational, fact and fiction, subjectivity and objectivity, person and system, force and effect... knowing and not knowing... are constit-utively unstable. Nothing characterizes a terroristic society where the state, in the name of patriarchal, nationalist, Christian capit-alism, is disappearing people more than haunting.
> Avery Gordon

The Abuelas, the Right to Identity, and the Transmission of Memory: Preliminary Questions

The following pages are but a very provisional outcome of an intellectual and emotional struggle with the work and the history of the Abuelas de la Plaza de Mayo (the Grandmothers of the Plaza de Mayo), a non-governmental organization created in October 1977, whose main goal has been that of locating and returning to their legitimate families the five hundred children which the last Argentine dictatorship stole from their soon-to-be-disappeared mothers and fathers.

In these past forty years, the search (*la búsqueda*) of the Abuelas has been justified in the name of *the rights to identity,* or better, the right to find a real identity for all the supposedly living yet disappeared children, with all the material, biological, discursive, individual and collective, epistemological and political ramifications which such a statement entails. However, what are the meanings and the risks, or, on the contrary, the advantages, of practices of memory-building that need identity not as an effect, but as a *cause,* as the main object of value? In other words, what are the characteristics of memory practices and testimonies that survive on a very particular acceptation of what it means to "have" an identity? And how, at the same time, do these values and meanings imply a particular reconfiguration of the very identity of memory, its politics and commemoration practices, along with the agencies of its cultural, social and juridical actors?

I do not have a definitive answer to the above questions; nor do I have a precise argument to articulate and, eventually, demonstrate: how can one have any ultimate say on such a great trauma as that of losing a pregnant daughter and, consequently, her child? Or of discovering that—as actually happened in more than one case—the person you have been calling father for more than twenty years is the one who actually killed your biological father? That you are not the person, and the name, you thought yourself to be? Reality here surpasses any possible fiction, and the past never stands still to be judged. Hence, this short essay is a work in progress that, from a socio- and cultural semiotic perspective, attempts to interrogate the ambivalent expression "rights to identity" (*derechos a la identidad*) and what it means to speak of, and to represent, a memory in construction which stems from stories of, and with, identity. Where, and in relation to what network of problems, does the irreducibility of the concept of identity emerge?

In order to begin meditating on the Abuelas' own identity, along with their work with and for identity, a telling way is to look at how they introduce themselves and their mission on their institutional website, whose archival imagination and imagery is what I shall use as the repository of their way of addressing, and their discourse on, disappearances and re-appearances in Argentina's on-going post-dictatorship period. A period, however, that, no matter what the three Kirchner governments did in the field of human rights and memory politics, has produced a present in which the very use of the expression "state terrorism" is still not always so "embedded"[1] in the majority of the populace. Here is how the Abuelas describe themselves:

> In 1977 we began our struggle with the claim for the restitution of 13 children. As of August 2004, over 400 children have been recorded as missing. However, we know that there are approximately 500 kidnapped children. In many cases, their relatives did not declare such kidnappings, either due to their ignorance that it was possible to do so or because they did not know that the mothers were pregnant at the time of their disappearance.
>
> *Our demand is concrete: that the children who were kidnapped as a method of political repression be restored to their legitimate families.*[2]

Some of the main detention centres that operated during the *guerra sucia*, such as the ESMA, Campo de Mayo and Pozo de Banfield, functioned, also, as *maternidades clandestinas* (clandestine maternity wards), working with lists of detained couples waiting for babies. Around five hundred children have been appropriated as *botín de guerra* (war booty)[3] by what the Abuelas call the "forces of

---

[1] This is, of course, an opinion and not a "fact". Argentine people are still very much divided on this matter. Nevertheless, I have heard it many times during my stays in Argentina, and it has emerged frequently in the many fruitful discussions with Córdoba colleagues. In particular, I refer to a seminar held in Bologna by Norma Fatala during her secondment there (October 2015): see her essay in this volume.

[2] My italics. This is an extract from the English version of the Abuelas' website: https://abuelas.org.ar/idiomas/english/history.htm (accessed 28 August 2016).

[3] There is a documentary entitled, precisely, *Botín de guerra* (War Booty) directed by David Blaustein (Argentina, 2000), which gives an interesting perspective on this subject and on the Abuelas'

oppression" mobilized by what they label as not only a military, but also a civic dictatorship. Some of these children were directly given to army and military families; others have been abandoned in orphanages as NN (*ningún nombre*, or, person unknown) or have been sold to the highest or most convenient bidder. In each and every case, "they annihilated their identities and they deprived them of the possibility to live with their legitimate family, they deprived them of their rights and of their freedom".[4] These children, in short, have been "disappeared" alive, while their parents vanished under the wheels of the Argentine killing machine: they were given a different name and, in most cases, were never told that they had been adopted, since their "new" parents had been registered as their biological ones. Yet, thanks to the demands and the search of their grandmothers, their presence has been haunting Argentine society for the past forty years.[5]

I shall return to these "facts" and accusations expressed by the Abuelas, along with the ghosts they call for. First, however, both facts and ghosts need to be located within a broader, complex, multifaceted and, certainly, burdensome debate.

In the attempt to interpret the ways in which the Abuelas de la Plaza de Mayo deal with the re-appearance of their stolen grandchildren, it is indeed the much used and abused concept of identity in relation to the "actors" of memory in Argentina which emerges with all its entangled effects and affects. In other words, one has to take into account the strategies and the discourse that have been characterizing those collective actors whom Elizabeth Jelin (2002) has called "memory entrepreneurs" and their identities. Actors are here meant in a multi-layered cultural and semiotic sense, according to which they might display, and be characterized by, numerous elements, from specific thematic roles, to actantial positions and structures of

---

struggle. See www.youtube.com/watch?v=zVfOiNPZnk4.

[4] See the note above: this quotation is taken from the same page of the Abuelas' website.

[5] In response to the demands of the Abuelas, the Argentine government established, in 1993, the public body of the Comisión Nacional por el Derecho a la Identidad (CONADI). It coordinates the Genetic Data Bank that stores the genetic maps of all families that have disappeared children.

destination. What does it mean to call oneself Abuelas or Madres?[6] In other words, what does it imply to play with very powerful and layered gendered thematic roles? Or, indeed, to inhabit a search assuming the role of active subjects with a concrete and simple goal, giving their grandchildren back or, better, restoring their identity by reincorporating each returned subject into the social fabric to which he belonged "before" (cf. Gatti 2012)? From a narrative point of view, the Abuelas have always had a very recognizable actantial position which stemmed from a structure of destination that establishes their rights and, most of all, their values: truth, justice, freedom and *identity* vs lies, pardons (the amnesty and the Ley del Punto Final [Full Stop Law]), silences.

These actors, or rather actresses, and their agencies are but an extreme case of the power of the figure of yet another thematic and pathemic role, that of the *afectado/a directo/a* (directly affected) and his/her individual and collective narratives of suffering and abuse, in itself a structure of destination. First identified with the direct relatives of victims of state repression (the Madres, and then the voice of the Abuelas, along with the H.I.J.O.S. and the Herman@s), from 2003 on the label *afectado/a directo/a* has also included the survivors of the clandestine detention centres and the militants and political activists of the 1970s, occupying the public stage thirty years after the *golpe* (coup). Thus, the very notion of truth, the legitimacy and the authority to speak, even the very ownership of the topic of the memory of those years, has been inscribed in the *afectados'* personal direct experience, and, when it comes to the Abuelas, in a genetic bond, as the section of their website entitled "The grandmother and genetics" declares:

---

[6] Much has already been said on the use by the Madres and the Abuelas of the figure of the maternal, and on how the performance of this role acted as a very effective weapon against Argentina's fascist rhetoric of the *Patria* (Fatherland), the *familia* (family) and, in general, women's and mothers', and mothers' of mothers, place within the discourse of the nation. Here I shall not expand on this deeply problematic topic, which is also discussed by Patrizia Violi in this volume. I shall just mention very briefly the problem of *familismo* (familialism) in its relation to the question of identity, since it would take another essay to deepen this entangled matter: see Demaria & Lorusso (2012).

Hardly had the search begun when las Abuelas confronted the problem of identifying their grandchildren and urged the international scientific community to develop ways of doing so, and thus began the "índice de abuelidad"... which was 99.99% certain to determine parenthood, and therefore the Courts had to accept it as proof.[7]

The "index of grandparenthood", elaborated with the help of the American scientist Mary Louise King in the very year that marked the end of the dictatorship (1983), introduced "the biological"—DNA—into the claims of the social and cultural body of post-dictatorship Argentina, as Gabriel Giorgi (2014) comments:

> "The military wanted to appropriate the children, but they could not get hold of the genes": this statement made by Nora Cortina as a reaction to the "recovery" of Estela Carlotto's niece illustrates the central place which the biological occupies within the many Argentine variations of and on the discourse of human rights; in the very political imagination of a democracy that is built around "el nunca más".[8]

The very idea of Argentine memory transmission, whose strength and borders have been traced by this "familialism" (*familismo*), has long implied, paradoxically, the exclusion of other social actors and voices from the public debate on the meaning of the past and on the more general politics of memory.

Despite the ever-growing criticism of this *familismo*, and the recent surfacing of alternative ways of mourning and remembering (see Sosa 2014), the Abuelas do represent not only a very particular case of the many conjugations of identity and memory, but also of the possible predicaments of postmemory, along with the issue of whether a political struggle such as theirs is able to transform the subjectivity of "familial" grief into a broader historical, and collective, context; or, rather, into peculiar processes of transmission

---

[7] My translation. This is part of the Abuelas' presentation on the website that does not have an English translation: see the website reference above.
[8] My translation. This is an online article.

and commemoration centred on the figure of identity.

Indeed, the Abuelas' case poses quite a challenge to the very concept of postmemory. As Marianne Hirsch indicates, postmemory is not to be defined exclusively by "familial inheritance and transmission of cultural trauma" (Hirsch 2001: 9; see also Hirsch 2012); "moreover, it does not need to be strictly an identity position" (10). On the contrary, it could represent an inter-subjective transgenerational space of remembrance, able to trigger forms of "*retrospective witnessing by adoption*" (10; italics in the original). Surely the claim for identity and the whole "labour" of the Abuelas goes beyond individual restitutions, a fact proved by the significant number of documents, testimonies, films, documentaries, etc., that have been produced in order to reach a broader audience and, as we shall see (cf. paragraph two), claim that their fight for the right to identity is a universal one. However, with this in mind, what forms of identification, adoption, and projection are at stake in what Gabriel Gatti (2012: 361) defines as a "narrative of meaning" based on genetics and family, whereby identity "has been moved onto an almost pre-modern plane, that of the biological roots of being: with the Abuelas, identity is equivalent to nature, and nature is equivalent to genetics"? More generally, how are the affective relations to these victims mobilized and constituted in contemporary Argentine culture? In other words, can the Abuelas' case be revealing of the ways in which "memory can play a key role in processes of change and transition because it is itself flexible and has a transformative quality... it transforms knowledge in processes of continuous appropriation" (Assmann and Shortt 2011: 3). What exactly is transformed by the memories of the Abuelas and their *nietos* (grandchildren)? Which parts of the memory of the *desaparecidos* (the parents who have never been found), the living disappeared (those who have not yet been found) and of the re-appeared become "plastic": or, rather, keep on haunting whatever representations are being "circulated and received within a specific cultural frame and political constellation" (3)? Playing with Assmann and Shortt's proposal, I am here referring to the way in which the act of disappearing is also a way of controlling the imagination and the meaning of death, within an everyday life charged with a phantom reality which—even if one doubts whether it could ever be contained in one *form* of identity—the Abuelas are struggling to render visible or, at least, to turn its constitutive absence into something evident (but not *evidence*).

Stories of, and with, Identity

Following a brief meditation on the very category of identity in relation to memory, my interrogation will now move to the analysis of one of the many forms of textuality produced and sponsored by the Abuelas to promote their cause nationally and internationally. Among the impressive number of documents and texts that are available on their website and on YouTube, I have selected what I believe to be a significant example which promotes the rights to identity by presenting the direct testimonies of the returned grandchildren and of "Hijos" with still missing brothers or sisters, as in the visual testimonies of the series *Historias con identidad* (CIPE, Argentina, 2012). I will then conclude this study by incorporating two graphic short stories edited by and for the Abuelas in *Historietas por la identidad* (2015).[9]

To browse not only the Abuelas' website and its archive, but also its ramifications on the web, one is confronted with a bombardment of the term "identity", identity of, as, with and for. We find the above-mentioned graphic short stories, video-interviews and documentaries, but also the *Teatro por la identidad*, the *Televisión por la identidad*, the *Sport por la identidad*. The very term identity, though, is never explained but rather projected as the right to know "who one really is", a right towards which every subject is constantly aiming, within an extended time forever, and paradoxically, frozen in this process of searching, and waiting, for an appearance. But how can we view this kind of identity; or, better, how might we, as analysts, interpret it? What of its construction, its "scope", the need for it?

To attempt an answer, I shall juxtapose several quotations which I believe useful to reflect on the idea of identity and its relationship with memories and traumas. Here is what Stuart Hall (1996: 2) says in an essay not by

---

[9] This book is the result of an exhibition of thirty-five graphic short stories now published by the National Library of Argentina. It can be downloaded for free from the Abuelas' website: www.abuelas.org.ar/archivos/archivoGaleria/HistorietasIdentidad.pdf.

Identity and the Abuelas de la Plaza de Mayo

chance called *Who needs identity?*:

> Identity is an idea that cannot be thought in the old way, but without which certain key questions cannot be thought at all... *And where, and in relation to what set of problems, does the irreducibility of the concept, identity, emerge?*

What set of problems indeed? Might it be in relation to violence and deception, in relation to ghosts? If this is the case, how can we think of identity outside its post-structuralist status "under erasure", when identity has been previously erased? Or, rather, outside the semiotic conception of the representations of identity, of subjectivity and otherness as always discursively constructed? From a semiotic point of view, this construction implies a complex set of relations, and could never be thought of as a fact given once and for all. It is always, as Patrizia Violi (2007: 193) suggests, "a place of continuous reconfigurations and transformations, a place of conflicts and tensions, as of partial and negotiable stipulations". Nevertheless, the relations it implies, as well as the negotiations it entails, are questions that recur and return, especially when it comes to the intertwining of agency, politics and trauma, as Alan Meek (2010: 34) underlines:

> Traumatic experience becomes the basis for collective identification in response to the waning of earlier articulation of national and ethnic identities.... Fantasizing history as trauma both reveals and obscures what is at stake in contemporary articulations of identity.

And the fantasizing of history as trauma becomes even more problematic once we look at the highly fragmented and polarized Argentine post-dictatorial memory politics and at its very identity, within which the politics of the Abuelas fall.

Here we encounter, also, the elusive category of post-dictatorship, that is, the diversity of a period including: the transition to democracy, amnesties, the deepening of neoliberalism, economic collapse, increased social polarization between Buenos Aires and the rest of Argentina, human rights trials, ten Presidencies, those of the Kirchners legitimizing the right not only to identity but also to memory; a process that, unfortunately, is now being reversed by President Macri and his supporters.

However, it might be that one conception of identity (as a value) does not completely exclude the other (as a process), depending on where and with which levers of pertinence and relevance we position ourselves. On the one hand, the identity of the Abuelas is but an on-going process of transformation and game of negotiation that depends on the different phases of Argentine post-dictatorship and its political constellation. On the other hand, it is a process within which the returned grandchildren struggle to recuperate a position whereby identity is an object of value, a set of meanings in relation both to their lived past and to a new transmitted past to be incorporated into their own lives. Identity is here a process and a set of values, an embodied semiotic construction that points to scattered and multiple temporalities and forces, to ghosts that will never stop haunting.

This ambivalence becomes evident once we look at how these identities are narrated and the process of their acquisition described by some of the re-appeared, that is, once we listen to the voices of the "resurrected" (as one returned *nieto* called himself)[10] and to those of the resurrecting grandmothers. On the Abuelas' website "multimedia" section called *Nietos, historias con identidad*, we find archived eighty-four short testimonial clips of forty-two "found" or, better, "returned" grandchildren (for each of them there are two clips of approximately three minutes 50 seconds); coupled with eighteen similar video interviews called *búsqueda* (search), where sometimes a grandmother, at other times a brother or a sister of a still-not-appeared grandchild, tells us for whom, of which parents, and in the name of what, he/she is still searching; and five more short video clips belonging to a mini-series within the series on "La labor de las Abuelas" (The Grandmothers' Work).[11] The chronology and also the chronotope are here reversed and

---

[10] See the documentary film on the Abuelas' website and on YouTube, *Quién soy yo?*, by Estela Bravo (Argentina, 2007), at www.abuelas.org.ar/video-galeria/quien-soy-yo-140.
[11] These videos can be found on the Abuelas' multimedia archive at www.abuelas.org.ar/galeria-videos/nietos-historias-con-identidad-4; they are also available on YouTube.

re-framed: from the testimonies of those who now bear her/his real identity, to the ones calling for the still missing, up to the group of women that made it all happen.

Each of these three kinds of audiovisual testimony, and each case they present, results in a mosaic which juxtaposes and aggregates different images of a story that repeats itself and varies, as in the TV format of the series, introducing the recurrent collective subjects/actors of these *histories with identities*: the living ones that re-appeared, along with their disappeared parents; and those who have looked, or are still looking, for the missing ones. Within the same plot—who were the parents, how have they been taken away, and how has the *nieto* (grandson) or *nieta* (granddaughter) been found?—what changes are the names, the bodies, and who is captured in the pictures; sometimes the emotions that punctuate the testimony.

What does not change in each of these altogether more than one hundred clips is the same paratext that frames them, an introduction and an ending of several animated frames accompanied by the stentorian voice-over of the journalist Víctor Hugo Morales,[12] who announces, from a detached and objectifying suspended time and place of enunciation, the universalizing claim of the Abuelas: "In October 1977, a group of women began an individual search that has now become a symbol for the whole of humanity. More than one hundred returned grandchildren, *two generations that did not disappear*" (my italics). There are, indeed, those who are alive: a returned generation that has been re-born thanks to the Abuelas. These statements are followed by the emphatic enunciation of the title of the series: *Grandchildren, histories with identity*, and by the introduction of the *nieto* or *nieta* to whom the single video is dedicated: "here is that of Victoria Montenegro"; a cut, and we enter the recorded text, the space and time of the story of Victoria Montenegro, Victoria Donda, and many others. In the case of the videos that present an on-going search, Morales introduces the person to whom the search belongs,

---

[12] Víctor Hugo Morales is an extremely well known Argentine journalist who, besides using his voice for these interviews/testimonies, hosted a very popular TV programme in which he interviewed the Abuelas and the *nietos* every time one of them re-appeared. He acts as the accepted and legitimate male public television voice of the Abuelas.

as if the *búsqueda* is in itself an object: "here is the search for... *a search in the name of justice, truth and person*". Again, here we find collective transcendental values coupled with the singular, or, rather, with the person as a value in herself. The same voice-over accompanies us throughout the rest of the clip, a typical authoritative voice of the genre of the classic documentaries that *explains* the images, anchoring their meaning. At the end of every short clip, with the same tone and timbre, Víctor Hugo Morales concludes reaffirming:

> *A history with identity. A country that persists in the search for truth. Hundreds of identities are still abducted. If you were born between 1975 and 1980 and you do not feel at ease with what you are supposed to be, approach the Abuelas de la Plaza de Mayo.*

The individual is thus rendered collective, the Abuelas and the grandchildren becoming a whole country looking for truth, and at the same time individualized, along with the very essence of all the stories of the world: *le manque* that initiates every narrative; yet a *manque* that can be partially solved if "you" who have doubts go to the Abuelas. *Historias con identidad* ends with the direct interpellation of a ghost which is not haunting, but which is here hunted.

What strikes one the most about this series of clips is not only the almost invasive presence of this male voice—why not a female voice speaking for, or as if, or as one of the Abuelas? Is it also because legitimacy always appears as male?—but also the homogeneity of the plastic and figurative composition of the visual register: a rather neutral light-coloured (yellow, light blue, pink circles and stripes) graphic background, on which pictures and video footage are contained in round frames (for the photographs of the disappeared) or square frames (for video of the period of the dictatorship); the camera moving as if in a travelling shot from left to right, that is, following a linear strip and thus moving us along in time, as in a travel journey towards restored, or yet to be restored, identity (and truth and justice). In between such fastidiously constructed graphic and visual frames, the interspersed tales of the grandchildren are as much homogenized, presenting several prevalent thematic and pathemic semantic redundancies (isothopies) which can be divided according to the gender of the speaking subject.

Many a male witness, while expressing the pain and the fear of re-appearing, principally affirms the strength they gained from the certainty of a now available re-settled destiny. The figure, the image characterizing their stories, is that of a *real* identity buried deep down in the apparent one, hidden by the lies of their previous lives, yet ready to re-emerge. The body here becomes the re-constructed living, albeit hidden, trace: the body as a sign yet to be read, yet to receive the right code to interpret it. The only missing act, the performance of the conjunction with the real name, is described as an act that does bring the subject to its actual completion. These histories thus abound in claims such as: "I have always wanted to be called Juan" (the name given by the biological parents); "I became a musician like my father"; "I tend to walk with my hands crossed behind my back, as my mother used to do"; "I was way taller than everybody else in the family, as my biological father was"; up until "I have always known I did not belong to that family" or, worse, "my *padre de crianza* [adoptive father] used to abuse me and hit me all the time".

In stories told mainly by women, the fear and the pain which they share with their male counterparts are parts of a tale in which there is more space for confusion, and for the memories of an initial rejection of the "new identity", for the desire to escape from it, to deny it; in short, for the witnessing of a much longer and more difficult process of appropriation of their new name/self. The emblematic case is that of the now Victoria (previously called María Sol) Montenegro, whose *padre de crianza* killed her actual father, and whose first reaction was—in her own words—that of "great shame, the shame of being a daughter of subversion",[13] not even of subversives; along with the deep fear of losing the love of her father, whom she adored, and whose ideology she had, until then, totally embraced. The pain of which these women speak is of the kind expressed by Paula Logares, a pain that will never go away, "since you find a family but you do not find your mum and dad, and this is the deepest grief";[14] and not only will you not meet them,

---

[13] Quotation translated from the video available at **www.abuelas.org.ar/video-galeria/victoria-montenegro-de-40**.

[14] See previous footnote. Video available at **www.abuelas.**

and see their eyes only by looking at pictures but, most of the time, you learn of them only once you are older than them: you have survived their entire lives. However, the closing sequence of these women's "confessions" is always positive and optimistic, since, in the end, "I am happy to have found myself", "to have conquered my liberty and my freedom", or, "to have my life back".

It goes without saying that during the three minutes these clips last there is no time for the travails and the painful itinerary that each of these women and men must have faced. In other longer visual testimonies of about thirty minutes each, such as *Acá estamos* (of which there are so far ten "chapters"),[15] the stories told show much more complex narrative paths. Yet, even when the message is less institutionalized, the story of the reappeared is being re-interpreted, temporalized and spatialized through a sad "before" and a difficult yet joyful "after" in which—to go back to Victoria Montenegro's story—there appear to exist two distinct subjectivities: in the past when only María Sol existed—says her husband—her life was marked by a relative solitude and by a constant lack of real purpose vis-à-vis the future; the present, on the contrary, is a place-time where Victoria is a person full of strength, enthusiasm and friends. A similar case is that of the now Marcos Suárez[16] who "before" was a fat, rather violent and lost drug addict; but "after", having lost twenty pounds, has found a large, loving family and, most of all, self-esteem. The old "me" seems worth leaving behind, in an effort of re-semanticization and re-valorization of one's self which creates a history of linear and clear transformation (*a history with identity*), a history that creates bridges and continuities between the before and the after, one that is certainly easier to deal with, and to tell

---

org.ar/video-galeria/paula-logares-de-134.
[15] I am here adding to the corpora of the clips *Historias con identidad* a few fragments of the longer interviews edited in the video project *Acá estamos* sponsored by the Abuelas. On the Abuelas' website archive only one "chapter" is available, at **www.abuelas.org.ar/seccion/buscar?needle=aca+estamos**. All the other chapters are available on YouTube.
[16] See **www.youtube.com/watch?v=fYFzIlUjTBc** (for Montenegro) and **www.youtube.com/watch?v=WJwJGIIyQFE** (for Suárez).

to the world. With the one exception of Victoria Donda,[17] who in her "history with identity" says immediately: "I am the same person I have always been; I am just one. I have always been Victoria, even if I did not know it", the re-appeared seems truly to be a re-born.

  The re-appearance is thus always told as a saving transformation, one meant to speak to the still missing ones, as Víctor Hugo Morales has made clear, those to whom, in the last minute of the last clip of the whole series (in the micro-series dedicated to the work of the Abuelas), Sonia Torres—head of the Abuelas' office in Córdoba—speaks directly, prompting them "not to worry, do not be afraid, come to us: we are not only decrepit women, there are young ones ready to help you and welcome you". This kind of narrative is immediately as public as it is personal, the identity at stake a process and an object intertwined with the genetic, the cultural and the political. And this is even more powerful because it is first and foremost fuelled by the "re-apropriados", one's own identity narrative re-construction: *quién soy yo [ahora]*? The square brackets being my addition, since they never figure in the Abuelas' *búsqueda*.

To Conclude: From the *Who Am I?* to the *Are You There?*

And can you see me? The text I shall briefly mention in conclusion is one of the last sponsored by the Abuelas: a

---

[17] Victoria Donda's story is a rather troubling one: her father had been disappeared with the help of his own brother, who was at the time one of the most powerful officers in the ESMA, where Victoria was born and then "given" to a close friend of her uncle. There is a very moving documentary that tells her story: *Victoria* (directed by Adrián Jaime in 2008, and available on YouTube at **www.youtube.com/watch?v=QHrgjvqs5ps**). The reason why her story is particularly interesting is because Victoria not only started to show left-wing and human rights-oriented tendencies from a young age, but became in 2008, and still is, a member of the Argentine parliament. She is a well-known public figure besides being a *nieta*. However, her political interests and demands brought her into conflict with several of Cristina Kirchner's now past government positions; she is now, as the Córdoba Abuelas told me, a person "with whom they have disagreements". Her interview, however, is still available on the Abuelas' website at **www.abuelas.org.ar/galeria-audios/radio-x-la-identidad-4**.

book of *Historietas* not with, but for identity, since their addressees are the still missing ones. The preface of the book, signed by Horacio González (2015: VII; my translation), thus presents the work of graphic novelists who attempted to translate into cartoons the stories of thirty-five on-going searches:

> *Historietas por la identidad*, somehow, continues to work through histories in which absence is an everyday deep pain, further trapped within a total lack of knowledge [...]. Yet cartoons and graphic novels have always been related to the need to confirm that there is a justice for humankind [*los hombres* in the original], and made by humankind [again *los hombres* in the original]. Each artist here solves in her/his own way the dilemma the *búsqueda* represents, along with what any new conjunction of a new name with a life deprived or its destiny implies.

And here are two examples:

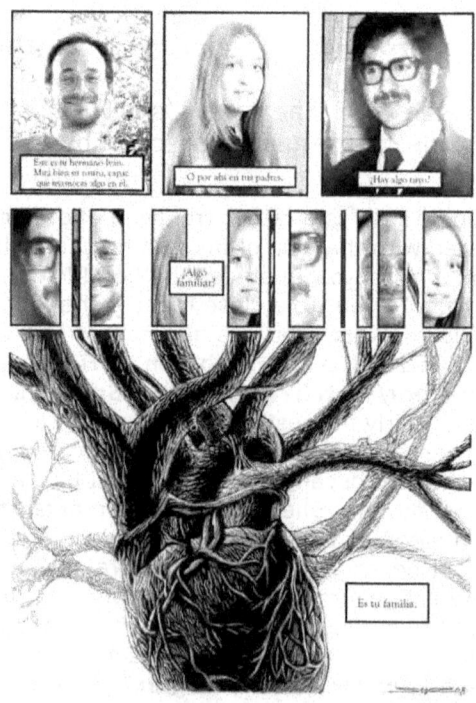

Identity and the Abuelas de la Plaza de Mayo

Via the use of photographs, "repossessing what has been taken away... as if by a diabolical magic act", these drawings incorporate photographs abrading: "This face is mine... and I have a right to find it" (Agosín 1989: 94).

These *historietas* are very simple texts, with a short written introduction that gives details of the family of the person who is being looked for. However, whether the first-person narrator coincides with the secondary witness who is composing the story (as in the first example: "This is your family: I am introducing it to you"); or, as in the second example, with the voices of the brothers/*afectados directos* ("This is our family. Can you see it?"), it is the use of the direct interpellation through the family pictures that prevails, having the power, as Avery Gordon reminds us, "to give people an imaginary possession of an unreal past or present [...] the photograph of the dead subversive serves this purpose because although the picture may distort [...] there is always a presumption that something exists, or did exist which is like what's in the picture" (Gordon 1997: 105). Or will exist, I would add, since this could be your face too. The photograph that summons the missing presence of a *desaparecido*, together with that of the living brother or sister, "registers the double edge of haunting: the singularity of the loss [...] the particular trouble the ghost is making for me; and the sociality of those abstract but compelling forces flashing now (and then) in the light of day, the organized trouble the system is experiencing" (105).

Gabriel Giorgi (2014) claims that the labour of the Abuelas, of which the texts presented here are but a very limited example, has resulted in a powerful reconfiguration of memory. In this non-coincidence of the body and the present with one-self, there emerges a memory that does not belong exclusively to the subject and its conscience. The memory of what one has lived and experienced merges with the collective forms of memory, the stories through which "we, Argentines, remember violence, the killing and the deaths, the *desapariciones*, justice and injustice" (see Giorgi 2014; my translation). The one promoted by the Abuelas would then be a "material memory", a biological archive which, of course, has to be culturally and socially activated and given meaning and relevance by institutional subjects and imagined communities; yet it is one that insists on, persists on its own terms. It is an archive which is hosted in the body, and which expands the ways in which what we come to know inscribes itself in the present, in the very texture of reality. A memory that has its own time, which is neither that of the *I*, nor that of the social, but that of the *entre-cuerpos*, the intra-bodies.

To return to Stuart Hall's quotation, is *this* kind of intra-bodies memory, a memory that lies in between individual and social bodies, between processes and objects, in between what constitutes a subject and the very process that ends up constituting it, in short, in between different politics of memory and individual traumatic wounds, a way to think again of, and with, identity? And does this imply that we have to embrace a "weak ontology"? That is to say, a way of thinking that is not only focused on the abstract study of the nature of being, but also on the beliefs underlining our ideas about "existence" that influence the ordinary and everyday relations we have with ourselves, with others, and with the world: "Ontological commitments in this sense are thus entangled with questions of identity and history, with how we articulate the meaning of our lives, both individually and collectively" (Coole & Frost 2010: 5). The genetic bond and identity as something to have and possess is indeed part of a set of relations, affects, forces, intensities, and ghosts: all elements that define different regimes of truth and forms of life, showing how any memory hosts different temporalities and, in the cases examined here, how a disappearance is real only when it is apparitional, "there in that moment of affective recognition that is distinctive to haunting" (Gordon 1997: 102).

References

Agosín, M. (1998). *An absence of shadows*. New York: White Pine Press.

Assmann, A., & Shortt, L. (2012). Memory and political change: Introduction. In A. Assmann & L. Shortt (eds.), *Memory and political change*. Basingstoke: Palgrave Macmillan, pp. 1-14.

Coole, D. & Frost, S. (2010). Introducing the new materialisms. In D. Coole & S. Frost (eds.), *New materialisms: Ontology, agencies, politics*. Durham: Duke University Press, pp. 1-43.

Demaria, C., & Lorusso, A. M. (2012). A ritual to deal with an unspeakable trauma: The case of the Mothers of the Plaza de Mayo. *Lexia Rivista di semiotica*, 11-12, Torino, 327-356.

Gatti, G. (2012). Imposing identity against social catastrophes: The strategies of (re)generation of meaning of the Abuelas de Plaza de Mayo (Argentina). *Bulletin of Latin American Research*, 31(3), 352-365.

Giorgi, G. (2014). Genética marcada. *Informe Escaleno*, 17 October, **www.informeescaleno.com.ar/ index.php?s=articulos&id=269**.

Gordon, A. (1997). *Ghostly matters: Haunting and the sociological imagination*. Minneapolis: University of Minnesota Press.

Hall, S. (1996). Who needs identity? In S. Hall & P. Du Gay (eds.), *Questions of identity*. Thousand Oaks: Sage, pp. 1-17. (Originally published 1986.)

Hirsch, M. (2001). Surviving images: Holocaust, photographs and the work of postmemory. *The Yale Journal of Criticism*, 14(1), 5-37.

Hirsch, M. (2012). *The generation of postmemory: Writing and visual culture after the Holocaust*. New York:

Columbia University Press.

Jenin, E. (2002). *Los trabajos de la memoria*. Madrid: Siglo XXI de España Editores.

Meek, A. (2010). *Trauma and media: Theories, histories and images.* New York and London: Routledge.

Sosa, C. (2014). *Queering acts of mourning in the aftermath of Argentina's dictatorship.* Woodbridge: Boydell & Brewer.

Violi, P. (2007). Remembering the future: The construction of gendered identity and diversity in the Balkans. In C. Goh & B. McGuirk (eds.), *Happiness and post-conflict*. Nottingham: Critical, Cultural and Communications Press, pp. 189-200.

How to Live after Loss?: *Aparecida*, Reparation and Collective Pleasures in Post-Dictatorial Argentina

Cecilia Sosa

Introduction: A Lesson to be Learned?

What is to be learned from traumatic pasts? Can experiences of suffering teach us something about the future? Drawing upon the process that opened up in Argentina after a military regime of terror caused some 30,000 citizens to vanish, infamously known as *los desaparecidos* (the disappeared), I would like to show how different ways of dealing with trauma in the absence of bodies might shed light on different experiences of reparation. I am particularly interested in the idea of "affective reparation" (Eng 2010: 196), since it points towards experiences of loss in which the past is not lost but "worked through" in creative and non-normative ways. In this respect, I propose that a consideration of Argentina's aftermath of trauma might help to delineate the grounds of an ethics that does not rely on individual subjects but rather on the collective ties which have emerged in response to loss. Ultimately, the question that drives what follows is how to illuminate alternative forms of being together in further landscapes affected by trauma and loss. Can the particular ways of contesting violence in post-dictatorial Argentina function as appealing *lessons* in transnational scenarios?

In the introduction to *Specters of Marx* (1994), Jacques Derrida is captivated by a problem: How to learn to live? He reflects that this is not a lesson that one learns from life, or that is thought through in life. Rather, it is something that comes from the dead, or better from the borders between life and death. "Only from the other and by death. In any case from the other at the edge of life", he writes (Derrida 1994: xviii). Here, I would like to consider this problem in the context of contemporary Argentina. Almost 40 years after the end of terror, with no bodies to be mourned, the traces of the traumatic past still haunt the lives of the living. In the aftermath of violence, Derrida's queries about potential lessons on how to live delineate an undoubtedly poignant issue. In 1979, at the height of the military terror, the infamous Military Junta leader Jorge Rafael Videla provided a definition of a disappeared person: "As long as he remains so, I'd say the disappeared is an unknown, as long as he's disappeared he can't be given special treatment, because he has no entity. He's neither dead nor alive... he's disappeared", he argued during a press conference at the Casa Rosada (*Télam*).[1] In a terrifying manner, viewed in retrospect, the Military Junta leader's definition seems to echo Derrida's thoughts. To some extent, the disappeared have been assumed as being caught in a sort of limbo, an infertile terrain that falls beyond the margins of the human. This particular territory could be named, after the meditations of Judith Butler in *Frames of War: When Is Life Grievable* (2009), as an *ungrievable* zone, where bodies do not deserve the right to be mourned as such. Remarkably, Butler also argued that the specific territory between life and death was the realm of kinship (2000). Drawing upon Derrida's and Butler's insights, I would like to propose that Argentina's aftermath of violence also offers the possibility of learning how to live collectively after loss. If so, it is precisely because the experience of terror has managed to challenge the boundaries of kinship while creating affective ties beyond blood.

In order to unpack this intricate set of questions, I propose to focus on *Aparecida* (Appeared) (2015), the autobiographical book written by the journalist Marta Dillon. The book eludes conventional definitions: it could stand as a *memoir*, a novel, a passionate and even playful chronicle, or even as poetry. In any case, *Aparecida* tells the story of Dillon's mother, Marta Taboada, kidnapped in 1976 and whose fate remained unknown for decades. Thirty-five years later, her remains were recovered. The title of the book signposts a transition: it names the transition from being "an unknown", as Videla was keen to say, to a different form of material reality. I suggest that in this process there was something to be learned. Moreover, I propose that a seemingly minor text can have something to say in relation to kinship, mourning and pleasure, not only in the context of contemporary Argentina but also in broader scenarios affected by loss. I suspect that Dillon's book might help illuminate a more inclusive politics of grief for expanded

---

[1] "Le diré que frente al desaparecido en tanto éste como tal, es una incógnita, mientras sea desaparecido no puede tener tratamiento especial, porque no tiene entidad. No está muerto ni vivo... está desaparecido."

scenarios. Drawing upon Derrida's impulse, I shall let a *disappeared/reappeared* body weave my thoughts.

Aparecida: A Body/Text

Fig. 1: Book cover of *Aparecida* (2015) by Marta Dillon

What are bodies able to do? And texts? Since the so-called "affective turn", an increasing number of authors, coming from the Humanities, the Social Sciences, Feminist and Queer studies, have proposed to approach cultural texts as forms of "cultural practices" (Ahmed 2004) or "expressive culture" (Labanyi 2010: 229-230). This approach involves reading literary texts not from the perspective of representation but rather as *bodies* that are able to touch us, hurt us, seduce us; and ultimately *affect* us. Gilles Deleuze (2004: 151) has already argued that a body does not define itself for its form or even as a singular subject, but rather "for the affections of those who are capable". Taking this invitation on board, I would like to approach *Aparecida* as a particular body/text that can help us to read the intensities of a specific space and time within Argentina's process of mourning; this is the so-called phase of the Kirchner years, the period initiated in 2003 by President Néstor Kirchner and continued under the administration of his wife and widow, Cristina Fernández de Kirchner, until December 2015. What are the intensities that a body can arouse when it makes its way back from the past? What are the circulations of anxieties and rhythms that a set of bones might generate? Thus, my proposal is to read *Aparecida* to examine the politics of memory delineated in a political epoch as powerful as it is controversial. Ultimately, it means reading a book in terms of the intensities of which it is capable while trying to capture the "forms of meaning that are not restricted to the cognitive" (Labanyi 2010: 230).

Marta Taboada was a teacher, lawyer, and activist in the *Frente Revolucionario 17 de octubre*, a Peronist guerrilla group popular in the 1970s. In October 1976, Taboada was kidnapped from her home. In August 2011, her remains were found in a mass grave. As far as the Argentine Forensic Anthropology Team could establish, she had been buried alongside other members of the FR17 who had been killed on a corner of the Buenos Aires suburbs, in a false clash with the military forces. "It was a death with no epic on a dark neighbourhood corner where no one dared to open the windows" [una muerte sin épica en una esquina oscura de un barrio donde nadie se atrevió a abrir las ventanas], writes Dillon (2015: 148).

In any case, *Aparecida* is not only an autobiographical book that testifies to more than 35 years of searching by a feminist-writer-journalist-daughter. Rather, it shows how an epoch digs up its own past, dialogues with it and makes of it its most intimate and precious treasure. From the very first pages, Dillon argues that the disappearance of her mother did not belong to her entirely. Rather, Marta Taboada's "return" was also part of "something bigger" (17). More than a personal recovery, her mother became *cosa pública* (a public thing) (Dillon 2015: 197). *Aparecida* can be thought of as a public treasure, a body/text that also *does* things. For instance, it delineated the affective cartography of a period, in which anonymous bystanders were also invited to share in grief. In this sense, *Aparecida* can be read as an initiatory passage and also as a process of "affective reparation", which signals an operation of mourning which is as carnal as poetic: the return of a body to a community.

A New Stage in the Process of Mourning

Aparecida is a dated text. It was only during the political period that started in 2003 that the experience of loss became visible in a new and undisguised manner. Dillon's book is embedded in the public culture of the Kirchner years, an era that involved a particular way of *being* and *doing* with others, and in which bodies recover the pleasure of being together.[2] It was also a period in which the past was rewritten and in which many of the symbols that were apparently buried reappeared; like Marta Taboada's body. During that time, grief became both a right and an official duty. This fusion, perhaps oxymoronic, entailed risks and discomforts.

Shortly after taking office, President Kirchner announced: "We are the children of the Mothers and Grandmothers of the Plaza de Mayo".[3] Self-invested as the figure of the son, the President showed how the lineage of the loss did not belong entirely to the "direct victims"—that is, the relatives of the disappeared—but rather could also be inhabited by those who were not directly affected by violence and yet adopted grief as a personal and collective commitment. In a furtive manner, the unspoken entanglement between bloodline victims and truth, which had marked the first decades of democracy, was challenged.

---

[2] This could be witnessed in the massive demonstrations on the anniversary of the military coup on 24 March every year, the celebrations of the Bicentenary of the May Revolution in 2010, the impressive mourning rituals in the wake of Néstor Kirchner's death that same year, as well as the demonstrations in support of Cristina Fernández de Kirchner, which continued as an expression of solidarity and resistance even after the official party was defeated by a right-wing economic coalition, led by businessman Mauricio Macri, in December 2015.

[3] This was part of Kirchner's inaugural speech before the United Nations General Assembly on 25 September 2003. See **www.cfkargentina.com/address-by-nestor-kirchner-at-un-general-assembly-2003/**, accessed 7 March 2017.

Kinship emerged as a brand new political tie.

Kirchner's unexpected death in October 2010 created an unusual momentum in the public affairs of the country. Two disparate experiences of mourning eventually intersected. While the government's detractors furtively celebrated indoors, a multitude of supporters cried in the streets, and spontaneously took over Plaza de Mayo to bid farewell to their leader. Thousands of youngsters with apparently no previous political background occupied the front of the scene to pay homage to the public man who had made them "discover the pleasure of politics", as they expressed it.[4] During the communal and highly theatrical procession, the current president and widow, Fernández de Kirchner, received the support of hundreds of mourners who became, somehow, an extended family in grief. The relatives' associations led the mourning rituals. The Mothers brought their scarves to cover the grave. "También era nuestro hijo" [He was also our son], they said, evoking Kirchner's inaugural speech. "Huérfanos otra vez" [Orphans once again], wailed the Children of the Disappeared. "Era nuestro segundo padre" [He was our second father], claimed the young Kirchnerists (*Página/12* 2010).

During those days of sorrow, Kirchner's statement in his inaugural speech acquired an expanded political significance. The mourning rituals showed how the notion of kinship in play did not correspond any longer to that of a traditional family. Rather, a self-fashioned and, to some extent, also joyful community in mourning managed to make visible the unconventional affiliations that have emerged in response to grief. The multitudes that were part of the memorials embodied a non-biological conception of kinship. This expanded family in loss, which had been formed in response to the military violence, already circulated throughout Argentine society through different unarticulated forms. Kirchner's death managed to render it visible.

Mourning ultimately empowered individual trajectories. By the time Dillon was writing her book, her partner was Albertina Carri, a talented filmmaker whose parents were

---

[4] Kirchner's death also marked the first public incursion of *La Cámpora* onto the public scene, a mainly youth movement within the official party that made a cult of the former president's remembrance. See Nassau & Scarpinealli (2011).

also kidnapped and murdered during the dictatorship. Together, Dillon and Carri have a son, Furio. Before Kirchner's death, Dillon writes: "Albertina y yo nos sumamos como *hijas* a las endechas desafinadas por la muerte del líder, el presidente que había reivindicado parte de la generación masacrada" [Albertina and I joined as *daughters* in the out-of-tune dirges for the leader's death, the president who had vindicated part of the butchered generation] (Dillon 2015: 97; my emphasis). To some extent, *Aparecida* embodies a queer, insurgent voice for Argentina's upcoming times. In what follows, I shall explore how this transformation was possible.

A Community beyond Blood

In the wake of terror, the network of organizations created by the victims adopted the form of a peculiar family: mothers, grandmothers, relatives, children and siblings of the "disappeared" conformed to what I have referred to as a "wounded family" (Sosa 2011a, 2013, 2014). All these kin-organizations evoked their biological ties to the missing to make their claims for justice. This particular overlap between kinship ties and groups of victims has marked the human rights landscape in the country. For more than 30 years the evocation of a community of blood functioned as the main instrument of political intervention. Seemingly, only those related by blood to the missing had the authority to demand justice. This misleading overlap between truth and lineage staged a fundamental paradox, which absented from the public scene those who had not been directly touched by violence, and ultimately imposed the status of the injured as the condition of sharing. The Kirchner period changed those furtive rules. By adopting loss as a question of state, it made room for new narratives that opened the experience of loss to new bystanders.

There is a surreptitious promise underpinning Marta Dillon's book. The promise is framed by Hélène Cixous' voice that inaugurates the book: "Quiero ver con mis ojos la desaparición. Lo intolerable es que la muerte no tenga lugar, que me sea sustraída. Que no pueda vivirla, tomarla en mis brazos, gozar sobre su boca del último suspiro" [I want to see disappearance with my own eyes. What is intolerable is that death has no place; that it has been subtracted from me. I want to experience it, hold it in my arms, enjoy the last breath on its mouth] (my translation). "Enjoy its last breath": as I will further develop, there is an experience of death that reclaims a certain pleasure.

Indeed, the absence of bodies had defined the work of most human rights associations in Argentina for decades. To such an extent that it was perceived as "intolerable" that the Madres brandish the slogan "Return them Alive" (*Aparición con vida*; literally, "Appearance with Life") in the late 1970s. Since then, the recovery of the material bodies emerged as an objective for most of the relatives' groups. Although the finding of the first mass graves in the early 80s dismissed the chances of recovering the disappeared alive, the Madres' "Return them Alive" tagline remained as a sort of Derridian "impossible claim" which fuelled a common horizon of the struggle for justice. In fact, the "live appearance" could be read as a form of stubborn affection which managed to make linear temporalities disjointed, and shaped the interstices of the politics of grieving for the past 40 years. During the Kirchner period, however, the feeling of "subtraction" started to be repaired. Not only the so-called "laws of impunity" were ruled to be unconstitutional by the Supreme Court of Justice on 14 June 2005, but also pardons were rescinded.[5] New trials against military personnel recommenced in 2006 and continue today.[6] In addition, the anniversary of the 1976 coup on 24 March was declared a bank holiday and National Day of Memory, and former detention camps were re-opened as spaces of memory. Moreover, during this period, as Cixous' statement anticipates, the experience of loss started demanding some sort of joy. Only in such a context could Marta Taboada's ceremony of reburial taste so much like a strange form of victory.

A Genealogy under Construction
In *Las formas comunes. Animalidad, cultura, biopolítica*, Gabriel Giorgi analyzes how the bio-politics that operated during Argentina's dictatorship tried to make the disappeared

---

[5] In 1986 and 1987 the Full Stop and Due Obedience laws put an end to most prosecutions of military personnel. In 1990, President Carlos Menem "forgave" most of the military officers who had already been condemned.

[6] Almost 1,500 military personnel are involved in cases across the country, as reported by Argentina's NGO, Centro de Estudios Legales y Sociales (CELS).

body a form of legal and historical evidence. Giorgi (2014: 198) argues that the military regime attempted to destroy "the bonds of that body with the community". As he writes, the scenes of abduction and forced disappearance that took place during state terrorism featured the production of "corpses without community" (*cuerpos sin comunidad*). The process not only recalls similar experiences of terror experienced in the Southern Cone as part of the Plan Condor initiative but also establishes dialogues with different events of disappearance and terror worldwide.

When the Anthropological Forensic Team announced the discovery of Marta Taboada's remains, Dillon still referred to the process as something that was alive, not quite something taking place in the present but rather a sort of continuum with no clear beginning or end. She refers to this process by using the gerund form *-ing*. "Now it was clear, Mum *is coming* back" (2015: 188; my emphasis). The use of the *-ing* allows the readers to experience the resonance of a process that is not finite but ongoing. What is being named, then, is a process of affective reparation that made that re-appearance possible.

Marta Taboada's remains are certainly interrogated by blood: there are genetic and forensic tests, which provide a belated time of death.[7] Yet Dillon makes clear that the body that finally reappears overflows biological certainty. It is a body that has been released from a strictly family economy. Marta Taboada returns not only for a daughter but also it "reappears" in the name of a wider community, which was configured in relation to those bodies that were made to disappear. In this sense, *Aparecida* appoints a community that goes beyond biological ties.

In the acknowledgements, Dillon dedicates *Aparecida* to her brothers ("Santiago", "Andrés" and "Juan"), and also mentions Marta Taboada's grandchildren, who had no opportunity to know her. Interestingly, Dillon also dedicates her book to those "quienes vengan llegando a inscribirse en esta genealogía, a tomar su palabra" [who are coming to join

---

[7] The Abuelas organization has also relied on genetics in their search for the new-born babies who were taken from their captive parents immediately after birth. A test enabled them to establish the "true identity" of the children with one generation missing.

this genealogy, to take its word]. This is a forthcoming genealogy that names a cast of extended heirs who are not limited to any traditional family. On the contrary, the book ultimately addresses "those who are coming", where the -*ing* form again highlights an on-going process of transmission—and even of contagion—which takes place in the present. It is to this genealogy "under construction", to this lineage beyond blood, that the book is finally dedicated. Thus, *Aparecida* unravels the affective landscape of a period in which bodies (and texts) reveal their capacity to bring this community to life.

The invitation to Taboada's funeral names a loose and heterogeneous collective of friends and activists. "Lo que quiero es que vengan todos" [I want all of you to come] (Dillon 2015: 153). Her call was heeded. The mother, grandmother, greatgrandmother, sister, friend, lover, *compañera* was re-buried in an ecstatic ceremony of victorious drums, music and flowers.

Memory in Flesh

Marta Dillon's book departs from what has been considered a point of arrival: the discovery of the remains. Right there, *Aparecida* confronts its readers with a morbid, uncanny insistence before the extreme materiality of those findings. The set of bones, which was buried as NN (*ningún nombre*, "no name" or person unknown) and recovered under Marta Taboada's name, is exhaustively described and examined. A feeling of discomfort eventually emerges in front of "una mandíbula loca" [a crazy jaw] (33) or "una cadera zigzagueante" [a zigzagging hipbone] (57), which through consecutive pages are assessed with impertinent detail. The five pieces of skeleton form a legacy difficult to archive. They speak about something activated, fully charged, almost in the flesh. In this manner, *Aparecida* delineates a way of conceiving of the body in which the boundaries between life and death, the organic and inorganic, and even between culture and nature are threatened. Dillon's book points towards a zone of uncertain potentialities that delineates a type of memory that waits at the antipodes of representation. Against memorial gestures, *Aparecida* reconstructs a spectacle of matter that is anchored in a practice; a work of mourning that takes place in the present.

Loss, Reparation and Collective Pleasures in *Aparecida*

Fig. 2: Montage part of the photo essay *Arqueología de la Ausencia* (1998-2000), by Lucila Quieto.
Marta Dillon poses in front of a photo showing her mother, Marta Taboada, holding her when she was a baby.
Photograph courtesy of the artist.

More than 40 years after the military coup, a book carrying the story of a disappeared woman begins to grasp the gravity of an absence, which seemed to have been subtracted from the word "disappeared". In doing so, it offers a way of re-politicizing the matter. *Aparecida* contributes to completing a floating sense, as if the very inscription of the word *desaparecido*s had finally been anchored and incarnated—never more literally—in five pieces of bone. While ostensibly focusing on a singular absence, *Aparecida* sheds light on a process that has been written in the plural. Dillon's book functions as an affective force that moves a singular body beyond itself, suggesting the extent to which a body is "always more-than-one" (Manning 2010: 123). It ultimately demonstrates why there have never been heavier bodies than those of the *disappeared*. This embodied memory in flesh and bone also stands as a quirky *lesson* from Argentina, which can be transferred to other landscapes marked by loss.

Pleasures in Mourning

As already anticipated, the Kirchner years signposted a time in which the experience of mourning claimed a certain pleasure. As Butler (2004: 22) argues, in the act of grief "something about who we are is revealed, something that delineates the ties we have to others, that shows us that these ties constitute what we are". Dillon's book reveals the ambiguous borders on which grief flows from the private to the collective. By countersigning the figure of the injured daughter, *Aparecida* battles at the threshold of kinship, the precise terrain on which blood gives way to more fluid and irregular affiliations. While conceiving her mother as "a public thing", Dillon introduces a sense of vulnerability that is not merely personal but political. In this sense, *Aparecida* shows how affect—anger, but also empowerment and joy—can also forge an alternative sense of community.

Far from sinking into despair or melancholy, Dillon's book resonates as a furious cry of victory. Navigating the end of a cycle, *Aparecida* proudly proclaims the secret desires that were hidden in mourning. It demonstrates how grief can also potentially announce forms of exhilaration, effervescence and empowerment. In doing so, it offers a rich example for investigating the entanglement between mourning, kinship and new forms of collective pleasure.

As Dillon recalls, the recovery of her mother's remains overlapped with her wedding with Albertina Carri, director of *Los rubios* (2003). The radiation of conflicting intensities, which tied a wedding to a burial, finds the brides getting rid of conventional wedding outfits. Like twisted versions of "cancan dancers" or "dominatrices with black rubber bras", they opt for dark clothes. Dillon writes: "Esas éramos más nosotras, más lascivas, más dispuestas a usar el luto para bailar clavando los tacos sobre el dolor, obligándolo a aullar de alegría" [That was more like us, more lascivious, aiming to use mourning to dance and nail highheels into the pain, forcing it to howl with joy] (96). Readers are faced with this provocative, almost oxymoronic image, in which "mourning is forced to howl with joy": I propose that this brilliant figure might be expressive of a poignant, radical and illuminated operation that took place throughout Argentina's last decade, a rhetorical figure that becomes expressive of the affective atmosphere embedded in the Kirchner years. However, it is necessary to investigate first how this tradition was initiated.

A Process of Transference

It was during Kirchnerism that the bereavement jargon of the victims emerged with new intensity. In the previous decades, humour functioned as a sort of "guilty pleasure", a protected and secret treasure among the youngest members of the "wounded family", the Children of the Disappeared. Since the mid-1990s, the descendants gathered in H.I.J.O.S.[8] While continuing the Madres tradition, the question of how to honour the name of the missing already involved a spectral relation to the past: the organization of the descendants not only assumed a backwards fidelity to their missing parents, but also positioned their members in an endless childhood. In any case, H.I.J.O.S. provided its members with an affective life-world that functioned as a new political family. Being part of the group not only included joining demonstrations and public assemblies, but also parties, camping and journeys. Friendship, politics and sex were tied together. Expelled from conventional structures of kinship, the descendants managed to recreate alternative social ties: the organization functioned as a "family of choice".

At the same time, unspoken distinctions cut across the group. As I have reported elsewhere, these hierarchies were mostly related to the extent to which each member had been affected by state violence (Sosa 2014). The differential levels of infliction installed a regime of ranks inside the group: the more one had been affected by violence, the more "privileged" the status one gained inside the organization. Personal status tended to increase in the cases of well-known disappeared parents. Those who had many disappeared relatives were known as the ones who had *sangre azul* (blue blood).

The discovery of this mischievous internal slang was a turning point during my fieldwork. The ubiquitous code that dramatically defined blood in connection to loss made me aware of a particular sense of humour that had emerged inside the group to respond to loss. It was a dark spirit of the comical, always flirting with death. This particular humour

---

[8] H.I.J.O.S. is an acronym that means "children" in Spanish. "H.I.J.O.S. por la Igualdad y la Justicia contra el Olvido y el Silencio" (Children for Equality and Justice, against Forgetting and Silence).

was also animated by a restrictive idea of "us": "Because we suffered, we are entitled to laugh" was the unspoken code. By the mid-1990s, humour functioned as a platform for the descendants to cope with parental absence. It enabled them to mourn through the contagious properties of joy. Yet the only ones entitled to make jokes were the true "orphans". By then, being a direct victim was a sort of strange "privilege".

The period 2003 to 2015 brought new tensions to the memory struggle. If at the beginning of the cycle the "wounded family" received Kirchner's presidential blessing, the same period also promoted more controversial narratives that challenged the official duty to remember while encouraging wider audiences to share in grief. Usually relying on playful and ironic imaginaries, the production of the younger generations brought to light new vocabularies and images, which offered empowering and non-victimizing accounts of trauma.

In 2003, Carri's autobiographical film *Los rubios* inaugurated a playful turn that would be the hallmark of the period. She did not only portray her disappeared parents through animated toy figures, but also replaced her own figure with an actor. The end of the film features the whole documentary team walking off into the sunset. They all wear blond wigs on their heads. The wigs showed how mourning could eventually be transferrable. During the Kirchner period, a thrilling list of descendants' productions continued to displace the steady family romance.[9] In his wild autobiographical novella, *Los topos* (2008), Félix Bruzzone, another disobedient son, offers a love story between a descendant of the disappeared and Maira, a transvestite sex worker. Through the character of Maira, who is suspected of being the protagonist's abducted sibling, Bruzzone brings to light a new constellation of desires to "transvest" the purity of the "wounded family". Moreover, in her *Diario de una princesa montonera, 110% verdad* (2012), Mariana Eva Pérez, with both parents missing, pokes fun at the Kirchernist

---

[9] For instance, the collective exhibition *Familias Q'Heridas* (2011, Jorgelina Molina Planas, Ana Adjiman, María Guiffra and Victoria Grigera), all daughters of the disappeared; the exhibition *Huachos* (Orpans) (2011), created by an artistic branch of H.I.J.O.S., who described themselves as "orphans scientifically produced by state genocide acts"; and *Filiación* (Filiations) (2013), Lucila Quieto's photographic collection.

"progressive" politics of memory, depicting the period as "the Disneyland des Droits de l'Homme" (Pérez 2012). Conversely, other contemporaries not "directly affected" by violence, have also followed on this non-normative path.[10] From multiple sides, traditional bloodline ties were estranged, mocked, and even subverted. This process of counter-signature can also be perceived as a mode of transitioning into more expanded forms of kinship (Sosa 2012: 221–33). In all these productions, dark humour was not only a privilege of the victims, but a secret tool to get new audiences involved. Moreover, within these displaced narratives, grief also became a furtive form of "coming out" for the wider society. To some extent, black humour might be considered as a fugitive gift offered to transnational landscapes affected by loss.

The *Guachx* Inheritance and the Feminist Turn

By the end of the Kirchner period, *humor guacho* (orphan humour) experienced another shift. The search for new forms of affiliation also included a feminist, queer turn. *Aparecida* introduces a crucial turn to give a non-normative account of the missing. It sheds light on an incisive and visceral form of feminist humour. In this novel turn, affect works as the "psychic glue", to use David Eng's (2010: 192) expression, a sort of mediation between language and identity, fantasies and history, subjects and subjectivities. It delineates a territory located in between life and death, which explicitly looks for alternative forms of kinship. This progressive feminist tone inevitably attaches memory to a gendered body.

"Nuestra fiesta se hizo un deber, una necesidad" [Our party became a duty, a necessity] (97), Dillon writes in relation to her wedding. *Aparecida* stands as a bloc of sensations that shows the extent to which mourning, pain and pleasure can be secretly entangled. On the eve of her mother's funeral, Dillon (188) laughs: "Nos reímos. Nos íbamos a reír a carcajadas toda la noche. Desde que el

---

[10] I have analyzed the cross-dressing characters of Lola Arias' theatrical production *Mi vida después* (My Life After) (2009) as a gripping example of the "non-affected" position (see Sosa 2012: 221–33). In *Cómo enterrar a un padre desaparecido* (2012), Sebastián Hacher, a writer with no missing relatives, adopts the voice of a daughter to find her missing father.

entierro tenía fecha, mi cuerpo era la caja de resonancia de unas risas cristalinas que sonaban a cada rato como perlas sueltas de un collar cayendo por una escalera de mármol interminable" [We laughed. We were going to laugh out loud all night. Since we had a date for the funeral, my body was the soundboard of a crystalline laughter that sounded every few minutes like loose pearls on a necklace falling down an endless marble staircase]. This disturbing, uncomfortable laughter speaks about an embodied legacy that largely exceeds Dillon's book. It speaks about a collective laughter in which the traces of the descendant's black humour re-emerge under the orders of an *ad hoc* sisterhood of female friends, ready to act as "wake planners" (187) for Taboada's funeral, and for any body recovered from the limbo of disappearance. Only within this expanded female network that draws upon a shared loss does it become possible to organize "a funeral postponed like a party" (153). To some extent, it could be argued that Taboada's funeral was the last party celebrated by the Kirchner period.

With Pride and Joy
In December 2015, the state's role of protagonist in the process of mourning had an official end. A new government led by businessman Mauricio Macri and a "CEO cabinet" took power (*Télam* 2015).[11] In the new conservative period, the expanded community in mourning came under threat. While 150,000 job cuts were registered in public administration, human rights dependencies were squeezed and asphyxiated by the lack of budget, the indigenous activist leader Milagro Sala was detained, becoming "la primera presa política" [the first political prisoner] of Macri's government (*Página/12*, 2016). In this regressive context, it was not surprising that a public servant denied the number of disappeared.[12] The

---

[11] President Macri's cabinet has been mostly composed of former executives from private banks and global corporations, including Shell and HSBC.
[12] I am referring to the then Buenos Aires Secretary of Culture, Darío Lopérfido, who had to be removed from his post. Macri himself questioned the long-accepted human rights position on the disappeared. In an interview with *Buzzfeed* he stated: "No sé si son 30 mil o 9 mil, es una discusión que no tiene sentido" [I don't know if it's 30,000 or 9,000, it's a discussion that makes no sense] (see **www.youtube.com/watch?v=YC8q0SHvJ4U**).

fiery reaction did not sound like mere support for some sacred numerical convention. Rather, it showed how the weight of a number had become synonymous with struggle.

The constraints imposed by the neo-conservative cycle seditioned a feminist-non-normative irruption. In the post-2015 period, the narratives of mourning associated with the dictatorship past intersected with a critical anti-patriarchal feminist wave, establishing new urgencies and a new intensity.[13] *Aparecida* foretasted this entanglement. It showed how loss could also promote alternative affiliations beyond blood. In so doing, it exposed how memory is not tied to the fixed temporality of duty but rather to untidy narratives that begin time and again with uncertain experiences of body-to-body transmission. Against official politics of remembering, *Aparecida* envisioned a forthcoming culture of mourning, where grief and pleasure were knotted together.

Although the conservative cycle threatened the expanded affiliations that had emerged in the 2003-2015 period, the process of transference of grief continued resonating, open to unexpected iterations and displacements. The current cross-fertilization between memory struggles and the recent feminst irruption also envisions alternative ways of inhabiting the future.[14] An appealing idea of *Matria* (Motherland) seems to be emerging.[15] Somehow, *Aparecida* anticipated this alternative form of feminist power: it imagined "a tribe of *cacicas* [female leaders]" (Dillon 2015: 205), a sisterhood of female friends in which a shared mourning acts as a main resonance box. This illusion, maybe this fiction, also included a politics

---

[13] The feminist tradition dates back more than a century in the country but has recently been re-energized by the formation of younger groups, including *Ni una menos*, a feminist organization of which Marta Dillon was one of the founding members.
[14] The new feminist wave participated in national and regional gatherings, "los encuentros", mostly linked to the *Ni una menos* organization.
[15] On 19 November 2016, more than 250,000 women took over the streets of Buenos Aires demanding "the end of patriarchy". On March 8, 2017, the local feminist movement took the initiative in a National Women's Strike, which included 44 countries. **www.facebook.com/events/1043905282422378/permalink/1098350346977871/**.

of memory for the generations to come. After all, as Derrida (1994: xx) argues, a non-normative politics of memory will impose further questions for a time that has not yet arrived. In the new context, *Aparecida* becomes a ritual text, almost a wild prayer for the future. In some sense, it has become a body-text that fights not to be archived, as it already functions as a space of memory. While moving beyond melancholia, *Aparecida* reminds us of the power of affect to build communities after loss. With blood but also with laughter, forcing pain "to howl with joy". Perhaps, this might be the most unattainable *lesson* from Argentina.

References

Ahmed, S. (2004). *The cultural politics of emotion*. London: Routledge.

Arias, L. (2009). *Mi vida después*. Audiovisual production. Argentina.

Butler, J. (2000). *Antigone's claim: Kinship between life and death*. New York: Columbia University Press.

Butler, J. (2004). *Precarious life: The powers of mourning and violence*. London and New York: Verso.

Butler, J. (2009). *Frames of war: When is life grievable?* London and New York: Verso.

Carri, A. (2003). *Los rubios*. Audiovisual production. Argentina.

Clough, P. (2010). Afterword: The future of affect studies. *Body & Society*, 16, 222-230.

Deleuze, G. (2004). *Spinoza. Filosofía práctica*. Buenos Aires: Tusquets Editores.

Derrida, J. (1994). *Specters of Marx: The state of the debt, the work of mourning and the New International* (trans. P. Kamuf). New York and London: Routledge.

Dillon, M. (2015). *Aparecida*. Buenos Aires: Sudamericana.

Eng, D. (2010). *The feeling of kinship: Queer liberalism and the racialization of intimacy*. Durham, NC and London: Duke University Press.

Giorgi, G. (2014). *Formas comunes. Animalidad, cultura, biopolítica*. Buenos Aires: Eterna Cadencia.

Hacher, S. (2012). *Cómo enterrar a un padre desaparecido*. Buenos Aires: Marea Editorial.

Labanyi, J. (2010). Doing things: Emotion, affect, and materiality. *Journal of Spanish Cultural Studies*, 11(3-4), 223-233.

Manning, E. (2010). Always more than one: The collectivity

of a life. *Body & Society*, 16(1), 117–127.

Massumi, B. (1995). The autonomy of affect. *Cultural Critique* 31(II, Autumn), 83–109.

Nassau, J., & Scarpinealli, L. (2011). Los jóvenes K conquistaron la plaza. *La Nación.* 21 October. At **www.lanacion.com.ar/1319685-los-jovenes-k-conquistaron-la-plaza**, accessed 12 November 2016.

Página/12. (2010). Con la compañía de los pañuelos. 29 October. **www.pagina12.com.ar/diario/elpais/1-155907-2010-10-29.html**, accessed 7 March 2017.

Página/12. (2016). Marcha a Plaza de Mayo por Milagro Sala. 18 January. At **www.pagina12.com.ar/diario/ultimas/20-290576-2016-01-18.html**, accessed 18 January 2016.

Perez, M. (2012). *Diario de una princesa montonera. 110% verdad.* Buenos Aires: Capital Intelectual.

Sosa, C. (2011a). Queering acts of mourning in the aftermath of Argentina's dictatorship: The Mothers of Plaza de Mayo and *Los Rubios* (2003). In V. Druliolle & F. Lessa (eds.), *The memory of state terrorism in the Southern Cone: Argentina, Chile, and Uruguay*, pp. 63–85. New York: Palgrave Macmillan.

Sosa, C. (2011b). On mothers and spiders: A face-to-face encounter with Argentina's mourning. *Memory Studies*, 4(3), 63-72.

Sosa, C. (2013). Humour and the descendants of the disappeared: Countersigning bloodline affiliations in post-dictatorial Argentina. *Journal of Romance Studies*, 13(3), 75–87.

Sosa, C. (2014). *Queering acts of mourning in the aftermath of Argentina's dictatorship: The performances of blood.* Tamesis Books: London.

Sosa, C. (2015). Affect, memory and the blue jumper: Queer languages of loss in Argentina's aftermath of violence. *Subjectivity*, 8, 358–381.

Télam. (2013). Videla en 1979: No está muerto ni vivo… está desaparecido. 17 May. At **www.lavoz.com.ar/noticias/politica/videla-1979-no-esta-muerto-ni-vivo-esta-desaparecido**, accessed 7 March 2017.

Télam. (2015). Macri presentará un gabinete plagado de representantes de grandes empresas. 7 December. At **www.telam.com.ar/notas/201512/129347-macri-gabinete-empresarios-ex-ceo-y-gerentes-de-grandes-empresas.html**, accessed 11 January 2017.

The Museum and the Archive: Detention and Denunciation

Beyond the Walls: Campo de la Ribera (Argentina) and Villa Grimaldi (Chile) in the Urban and Social Fabric

José Manuel Rodríguez Amieva and Milena Grass Kleiner

Introduction

The sites of torture and murder stand as mute witnesses. They bring us back time and again, in the surreptitious hope that they will disclose their secrets. We go on pilgrimages to these ominous, ghostly places burdened by grief, seeking some trace of those who vanished, some knowledge of how they drew their final breaths, because we are convinced that—violated and tortured—they felt more alone than ever just before they died. The pact of silence within the armed forces has closed off intractably any chance of reconstructing their deaths or of finding their remains. As a result, the ovens of Lonquén at their zenith, the mine pits, the sea, the desert, the river estuaries have become vast and uncertain graveyards where we keep on searching for them.

In neighbourhoods at the very centre of the city, a few other torture and extermination centres have been identified, restored, and signposted. Each of these places of remembrance tends to be quite different, since the type of memorial is usually determined by those who erect it, that is, by victims or the families of victims. The approach tends to combine attesting to the atrocities committed in the past with the construction of a future society based on respect for human rights as a guarantee against their violation in the future.

During the Pinochet Dictatorship, there were 1,132 torture centres operating in Chile,[1] either on the property of the armed forces or on civilian property that had either been confiscated or leased. According to the report of the Argentine National Missing Persons Commission (CONADEP), there were 340 clandestine detention centres in Argentina during the country's last military dictatorship. In general, most of the investigations into those places of horror have tended to deal with their internal workings. Patrizia Violi (2012) has pointed out that places of remembrance undergo several different kinds of transformation, ranging from

---

[1] Cf. the Valech Commission (**www.indh.cl/informacion-comision-valech**).

keeping the site as intact as it was when abandoned, to subjecting it to varying degrees of modification. Clearly, the physical state of the detention centres, which might range from buildings in exactly the same condition as they were when used by state forces—such as Campo de la Ribera in Córdoba, Argentina—to annihilated buildings—such as the Cuartel Terranova/Villa Grimaldi in Santiago, Chile—through every other intermediate state of ruin, would favour certain memorial policies over others. However, the decision as to whether to preserve the site by displaying every vestige of the crimes committed therein or by replacing them with metaphorical or allegorical features ends up having a very different impact on visitors. Some see the horrors as a moral example and method of prevention, so that state violence never be repeated, while others see a symbolic memorial which seeks to mend the social fabric as a step towards reconciliation. Whatever the decision, memorial sites were disconnected places, singularities in the urban fabric; yet, when fully operational, they formed part of an extensive, interconnected, comprehensive and dynamic network. State-sponsored violence is a highly-structured organism that only achieves maximum efficiency by virtue of the connections between the different branches of the armed forces and the *ad hoc* secret organs of repression, the civilian political and economic powers that support it, and the foreign institutions that collaborate with and uphold its domination, and, finally, by virtue of an insidious civilian tolerance, hidden and cynical, which, whether out of complacency or fear, allows it to operate. The movement of vehicles with abducted persons, the constant comings and goings from those houses—where loud music blared out suddenly at all hours and suspicious-looking characters lurked, where strange activities, from besieged houses under surveillance, were observed by neighbours—were tolerated despite the suspicion they aroused.

The aim of this study is to reassess two former torture and execution centres from a broader, more comprehensive perspective, a perspective that breaks down the physical and metaphorical walls built to maintain the perception that they were "aberrant" places, and visualizes them through the lens of their logistical urban grid operations. In the first section, we present the various uses to which Campo de la Ribera in Córdoba has been put, emphasizing the relations between the detention centre and the neighbouring community that prompted its transformation into a memory site. In the second, Villa Grimaldi in Santiago is approached from the perspective of the various narratives and diverse artefacts that have been built into and around it since it was recovered by human rights organizations. Finally, in the conclusion, we assess the commonalities of these two places that function as lurid devices in the state machinery devoted to surveillance and punishment, before becoming memory sites consecrated to the prevention of state terrorism.

Campo de la Ribera Memorial Park in Córdoba, Argentina

> Ribera means margin, border, edge. The place where the city ends and the plain [*la pampa*] begins. A particularly interesting place from which to study the horizon. (Marchetti 2010)

Campo de la Ribera, located northeast of the city of Córdoba in Argentina, started out as a military detention centre in 1945. After three decades, it became in December 1975 the headquarters of the Liberators of America Command, a group established to combat "subversion", made up of members of the Argentine army as well as provincial police from the province of Córdoba, federal police and civilian collaborators. This unit would specialize in the kidnapping, torture and execution of citizens suspected of participating in revolutionary political activities, its methodology of terror an anticipation of the *coup d'état* of 24 March 1976 (Garbero & Liponetzky 2012).

Campo de la Ribera would function as a Covert Centre of Detention, Torture and Execution (known by its Spanish acronym CCDTyE) until June 1978. On learning of a proposed inspection visit to Argentina that year by the International Red Cross, which had decided to investigate reports of human rights violations by the incumbent government, the military command managed to return the place to normal and re-establish the old Military Prison. In its three years of operation as a Covert Centre, it is estimated that Campo de la Ribera handled over 4,000 detainees, of whom over 100 are still missing (Garbero & Liponetzky 2012).

Fig. 1: Part of the exterior of the Covert Centre of Detention, Torture and Execution, restored to the appearance of the façade during the dictatorship. See **www.apm.gov.ar/clr/sitio-histórico**.

In 1986, Campo de la Ribera would finally stop housing inmates of the Military Prison. The site would remain abandoned until 1989. It was not until then that the Governor of the Province of Córdoba would take over the property with the intention of establishing a school there. The building would be refurbished in keeping with its new role:

> However, notwithstanding its being revamped into an educational institution, the building would retain some of its former features. Despite the changes carried out by the army and subsequent refurbishments to adapt it for school use, some potent vestiges of the horrors that occurred there remained, such as the hooks that hung from the patio, where the detainees were chained and later shot, as per some testimonials, or the huge vats where the system of underwater torture was perpetrated. (Dowd & Cambra 2015)

In 2004, the residents of the area began to petition for the school to be moved to new premises and Campo de la Ribera transformed into a place of remembrance. Two years later, in March 2006, the legislative assembly of the province of Córdoba unanimously passed the "Commemoration Decree" that established the creation of the Commission and the Provincial Memory Archive, and decreed the preservation of the places where Covert Centres of Detention, Torture and Execution used to operate. Within the framework of this decree, the Florencio Escardo Technical College was transferred in 2009 to a new building situated 150 metres away from the former school building (Córdoba Provincial Memory Archive 2015). Finally, thanks to the combined efforts of the community, neighbourhood organizations—chief among them, the La Quita Social Network—and human rights entities, the Campo de la Ribera Memorial Park was inaugurated in 2010 on 24 March, the date of the last military coup in Argentina (Dowd & Cambra 2015). Since its inauguration, the Memorial Park has offered guided tours to the old installations and free courses on the events of the last dictatorship. The establishment also has a museum dedicated to the memory of the missing persons, a public library, and a computer room, and has been the site of several fairs promoting workers' cooperatives and exhibitions of artists' collections (Córdoba Provincial Memory Archive 2015).

Fig. 2: Panoramic view from the interior courtyard of Campo de la Ribera Memorial Park. See
www.apm.gov.ar/em/estructura-represiva-estatal-en-córdoba

The foregoing could be regarded as a brief historical outline of Campo de la Ribera. The chronological history, however, makes little sense without considering the spatial location of the former Military Prison and without invoking the memory of the factors that confer significance on the past. Remembrance establishes the places and commemoration converts them into communal spaces. Inversely and correlatively, as Paul Ricoeur (2013: 88) warned, memories populate the memorial like a palace, they inhabit and define it, transforming it into a memorial of objects, of other subjects, of situations which unite them in a shared narrative.

The chronotopic coordinates of an event are defined by the meaning various subjects give to it. Thus, it becomes obvious that the spatial location of Campo de la Ribera is no coincidence: it lies on the outskirts of the city of Córdoba, in the vicinity of slum areas disregarded by urban planning policies, yet sufficiently close to enable rapid access from the city centre—optimal connectivity with the Córdoba Police Department of Information (D2), gateway to the circuit of detention, torture and execution—but sufficiently isolated to act as a receptacle for the elements rejected by Headquarters, those facets of itself the city chooses to ignore or conceal. Thus was it possible that the occurrences at Campo de la Ribera could have gone unremarked by residents of the city's centre. However, they could not have failed to be observed by the populations of the so-called Fifth Allotment (the Maldonado, Müller and San Vicente quarters) who were presented daily with evidence of what transpired there.

Fig. 3: Satellite image showing The Pearl, D2 and Campo de la Ribera. See **www.apm.gov.ar/em/estructura-represiva-estatal-en-córdoba**

The inhabitants of the area, the neighbours in the vicinity, in fact the whole community, lived alongside the terrifying signs of the arrests, torture and secret burials.

Campo de la Ribera and Villa Grimaldi

These memories outside the detention centres have largely been omitted from the official reports of the last dictatorship: the resounding cries of the victims, the clamouring defence of the accused, the stupefaction of broad segments of the population trying to decipher the reason for the events they could hardly make sense of.

The official version of events of the period from 1976 to 1983 is multifaceted: with the return to democracy in 1983, Raúl Alfonsín set up the National Commission on the Disappearance of Persons (known by its Spanish acronym, CONADEP), charged with investigating the kidnappings, tortures, executions and disappearances of civilians at the hands of the de facto government. This would culminate in the conviction of the three military juntas and guerrilla leaders accused of violating human rights; subsequently, the Laws of Due Obedience and Full Stop would be passed, as a form of compromise between the democratic state authorities and the armed forces.

The Menem government introduced neo-liberal pardons and amnesties throughout the 1990s. Subsequently, on 24 March 2004—following the economic and institutional crisis that would result in the resignation of Fernando de la Rúa— President Néstor Kirchner ordered that the portraits of the dictators Videla and Bignone be taken down from the Hall of Honour of the Military Academy in El Palomar; it was a symbolic act that would later be recognized as the beginning of a phase of revisionism of the official version in terms of action on state terrorism. The Kirchner government would then go on to lobby for the repeal of the Laws of Due Obedience and Full Stop; these decrees would later be overturned by the Supreme Court, enabling cases to be reopened and bringing many oppressors to trial—to date, there have been 1,886 prosecutions and 250 convictions (CESL 2015). Finally, to return to the topic of the present study, it was declared that more than thirty former Covert Centres in each province as well as nationwide would be transformed into places of remembrance. This clamour of measures, marches and counter-marches, and the struggle around official recognition of the crimes committed drew general attention to the stories of the victims, torturers and eyewitnesses, relegating to the background the whispers of the communities who had had to live with the daily collateral effects of terror.

Despite being overlooked in the general account of events, the recollections of the eyewitnesses and indirect victims of state terrorism have survived by being passed on through other channels: "When the official record does not consider the experiences of its citizens, it is the recollections of the protagonists in the story that keep the memory of what happened alive. These memories, excluded from the official versions, inhabit other places, take on other guises, circulating as fables or legends, kept as family secrets, sometimes remaining in the domain of the unspeakable, becoming fears or inconclusive silences" (Marchetti 2010: 23). Campo de la Ribera has been the scene of innumerable occurrences and incidents: memories that are still alive in the minds of the people who lived nearby. The grounds of the Military Prison used to be used by adults as a recreation park, and children in the area once gathered to play under the trees. The presence of a military enclave in the neighbourhood would not have been problematic or perceived as dangerous, until the Liberators of America Unit took over the premises. The following testimonial is taken from the book *The Story that Gave Birth to Us: Memories of State Terrorism in the Community*, in which the reversal in Community-Campo de la Ribera relations is reconstructed clearly:

> Before the coup of 1976, people lived normally alongside the military, and many girls married soldiers and had families; everyone could move around the area in peace, and every day the indigent of the community would go to get their free coffees from the soldiers. After the coup, the zone was sealed off from the community and closed to traffic, and the military lost contact with the people.
> At night, tanks could be heard on the streets, and many times we were surprised, stopped and searched, asked to show our papers or taken off the bus. We were questioned and many of us were detained for no apparent reason. Patrols checked our houses over and over, and sometimes conducted house searches. We often saw trucks transporting blindfolded people during the day and night, being taken to the prison. At night, you could hear the shots and screams: secretly we all knew that they were killing and torturing people there,

but nobody dared say anything because the few who spoke out disappeared and that would be the last we would ever see of them. We lived in constant fear, because the soldiers kept a permanent watch over the whole community; they were right on your doorstep and they searched you every time you went in or out. (Baldo *et al.* 2011: 82)

The strategic location of Campo de la Ribera on the outskirts of the city of Córdoba, its optimal distance between connectivity and invisibility, has already been pointed out. No less significant is its location in the Fifth Quarter, a stone's throw from the Saint Vincent Cemetery. As was mentioned earlier, the Police Information Department (D2) in the city centre was the gateway to the circuit of detention, torture and extermination. Eventually, the bodies would usually disappear in the mass graves of the Saint Vincent Cemetery. Once again, this connection could have gone unnoticed by the inhabitants of the city's centre, but not so by people in the vicinity, who were confronted daily with the evidence of military activity:

The toughest memories I have of that time... the people I used to see in those trucks... when I jumped up into a truck, because sometimes we were thrown a piece of bread or a bun from those trucks, since we were used to begging from the soldiers... Many times, when we got up on those trucks to beg, when we lifted the canvas we would see that there were a lot of hooded people inside, with black bags over their heads and their fingers tied with wire. We could see this because we used to hang off the backs of the trucks, and by the time the soldiers had chased us away and taken us down, we had already seen everything. There were people on the floors of the trucks too; and another thing that shocked me was that sometimes our paths used to cross—we were very naïve kids, so to speak— we would go to the back of the Saint Vincent Cemetery, and we would see the trucks coming in with many boxes, trucks full of coffins of dead people. (Baldo *et al.* 2011: 84)

The impact of the signs of terror on this community did not end with the end of the junta. With the return of democracy, two archaeological excavations were carried out at the Saint Vincent Cemetery, to look for the human remains of the missing. The first was carried out in 1984 by the cemetery personnel themselves using mechanical diggers, taking no precautions either in the recovery of the remains or in the scientific treatment of the evidence. The outcome of these excavations was the destruction of a mass grave with countless human skeletons, which would soon after be sent to the cemetery crematorium by order of the city council (Olmo & Salado Puerto 2008). It goes without saying that the political conditions were not yet right for a reliable investigation into the crimes of the de facto government, and that what was supposed to have the objective of making the evidence of what had happened clear, served as the subterfuge to destroy any trace—following the distinction made by Eliseo Verón (1993:129) according to which discursive traces result from the meaning accorded to marks on any signifying material.

Fig. 4: Image of the mass graves exhumed in Saint Vincent Cemetery. See: **www.lavoz.com.ar/Córdoba/ terrorismo-estado-capitulo-Córdoba**

In 2003, the exhumations recommenced, this time in a climate of cooperation between the various human rights organizations, the judiciary, the police and governmental bodies. The Argentine Forensic Anthropology Team (EAAF) would lead the investigation this time, supported by specialists from the National University of Córdoba. On this

Campo de la Ribera and Villa Grimaldi

occasion, the skeletal remains of 123 individuals were recovered and analyzed, with over half of the cases showing clear evidence of violent death, particularly multiple gunshot wounds. Thanks to archaeological-forensic techniques, the remains of seventeen victims of state terrorism have already been identified. The progress in this investigation contributed in turn to keeping the memory of what had happened alive, producing incessant discoveries that were then broadcast by the media: the most recent being the discovery of the identity of one of the missing persons in Saint Vincent Cemetery on 12 February 2015 (Simo 2015).

Another source of recollections about the crimes of the incumbent government would be brought to light in the period between 1990 and 2009 when the installations of Campo de la Ribera were rehabilitated to house the Canónigo Piñero Primary School and the Florencio Escardo Technical College. The education community would then coexist with the signs of torture, detention, execution by firing squad, and disappearances. Consider the following fragment of an interview carried out by Florencia Marchetti (2010) to former students of IPEM 133 Florencio Escardo. Their testimonies demonstrate how individual memory is constructed by resorting to the memories of those closest to us—"those people who are important to us and to whom we are important", according to Paul Ricoeur (2003: 171), attributing to them a specific mnemonic function—on the one hand, limiting their testimony to details recounted by relatives or neighbours in the community; and, on the other, realizing how the physical evidence of objects that remained also functions to stimulate the imagination and trigger new memories and stories about what went on:

> T: When I changed schools, I hadn't a clue, and then I found out about it all. It wasn't until I was in fourth year, my grandfather felt he could tell me that it used to be a secret detention centre, but I was too young, so I didn't pay much attention. Later, when it started to sink in, I wanted to know more about what had happened and what hadn't. We kids used to say that when we walked about the classrooms we were treading on dead people... that ghosts walked in the night... there were lots of stories, of noises, screams... many of the neighbours were saying that they really

did hear screams, it didn't seem to be mere gossip, it seems there really were screams in the night... many people who lived near the school ... but we didn't know whether to believe them or not because we hadn't been there when it happened... and if we'd heard them we'd have been terrified.

Then they went to that lady and asked her if it was true that she'd heard noises and they were told that, yes, it was true... that they used to hear cries that sounded more like women and infants, in the area you see there where the library is, in that area there were the... they called them the ones in solitary confinement, the loudest cries of all came from there...

M: In the bathrooms that used to be the cells.
T. In the bathrooms, yes, the cells. Solitary, that area is called.
F: Were you in school before the building was remodelled?
T: No, I wasn't, I came in right after it'd been changed.
M: I was.
F: Do you remember anything?
M: Yes, I remember my first year at school, that there was an area where the dining room is now, there we were all assembled, and you could see solder-marks of bars along the whole wall, painted over in white, and I remember the headmistress saying, "Don't be afraid, nothing's wrong, no ghosts of the dead, or anything like that, are going to appear." So, we just looked at each other, you know... and then we started to notice that, in the bathrooms, there was a small window on the back wall in each bathroom, and we decided to peep through, and we saw some little blue doors and on the other side it said "cells". The guys wanted to go in to see what was there. The truth is that it was ugly and not very well painted at all. Later, they began to renovate it, fix it up, bit by bit. (Marchetti 2010: 23)

The Florencia Escardo Technical College was, until it was transferred to its current premises in 2009, the source of many historical and mythical recollections, as well as the focus of a dispute around the use and abuse of the places

Campo de la Ribera and Villa Grimaldi

where the crimes of the last dictatorship had been perpetrated. The community organization "La Mazamorra" would denounce the dual purpose—efficient to say the least—in a statement on the occasion of the inauguration of the Memorial Park (in 2010) around the prior use of the premises as an educational establishment: on the one hand, the token concealment of the vestiges of the clandestine detentions and tortures carried out there, managing to erase the past or consign it to oblivion; and, on the other hand, the petty-minded government authorities who tried to ameliorate the deficiency of amenities in the poorer, more marginalized communities without too much effort or investment. Double concealment/discrimination, in fact: from the remnants of an ominous past that questions the present, and from the impoverished slums of the present, compelled to live amidst the scars of a past that is not acknowledged—physically or symbolically—in the collective memory. As Garbero and Liponetzky (2012: 182) put it: "Up to 2009, the Florencio Escardo College occupied those horrific premises, demonstrating clearly that the policy of oblivion was to silence, erase or conceal the marks of state terrorism suffered in this country." Ironically, therefore, the politics of oblivion would, through the same manoeuvre, fall both on those in the Fifth Allotment who had disappeared in the past and on those who were marginalized in the present.

Fig. 5: View of the interior courtyard of the Covert Centre of Detention, Torture and Execution from one of the cells. See **www.apm.gov.ar/clr/museo-de-sitio**

However, far from focusing on the state and on its countless failings, we are more interested, in keeping with the challenge of the missing persons from the past, in highlighting the power of marginalized communities today. For the whole process that begins with the reclaiming of the premises of an education institution, up to the inauguration of the Campo de la Ribera Memorial Park, was driven by the communities of the Fifth Allotment.

Whilst incumbent governments sought to forget, or pretended to forget, the communities of the Fifth Allotment—and especially the neighbourhood of Maldonado in the vicinity of the former Centre of Detention, Torture and Execution—remembered and demanded remembrance. In 2009, the new premises of the Florencio Escardo College were opened and, finally, the Memorial Park was inaugurated in 2010. It was from 2004 that "the community in the environs of Campo de la Ribera started to demand that educational establishments be housed in suitable buildings, and that the former Detention Centre be converted to a place of remembrance, initiating a struggle by the community that was channelled through the social network of the Fifth Allotment" (Garbero & Liponetzky 2012: 182).

The active participation of the people in the area would be the determining factor in the creation of the Campo de la Ribera Memorial Park for the Promotion and Defence of Human Rights. All that remains, finally, is to examine the activities subsequent to its inauguration, the actual link with the community in the vicinity of this memorial, the conditions that would make it possible for a continued and renewed involvement with the community. Will Campo de la Ribera become a community meeting-place in our time? Will the establishment of this place as a memorial, governed by official remembrance policy, allow for the existence and pervasion of local memory? What kind of relationships will be established with individual/unique memory, not subordinate to the global memory instituted by the state? Examination of the elements of narrative outside the hegemonic discourse implies elucidating at the same time the various relationships of affinity, tension or contradiction between the central institutions and the peripheral communities. The narrative generated and the practices of significance—semiosis and hysteresis, according to Marc Angenot's (2010) distinction—with reference to Campo de la Ribera Memorial Park offer a problematic node that is especially fruitful, if the aim is to find the basic relationship between local community remembrance and the tendency of officialdom to establish a socio-global memory.

Villa Grimaldi Peace Park, Santiago

Neither Villa Grimaldi nor the Cuartel Terranova exists anymore. They hold a symbolic place as the epitome of horror, representing all the detention centres and torture sites set up throughout the country during that period. They embody the extremes of which humanity is capable.[2] The Villa Grimaldi Peace Park (www.villagrimaldi.cl) has been raised on the same site, on the almost unrecognizable ruins of the stately home defiled by state violence.

The main house had been built at the beginning of the twentieth century (Salazar 2013)[3] as the administrative centre of the José Arrieta country estate, which is today the municipality of Peñalolen in Santiago, Chile. In 1964, the

---

[2] The first comprehensive study of the site by the Chilean historian Gabriel Salazar identifies five factors that made the Cuartel Terranova so instrumental within the apparatus of repression: "firstly, it was the command centre for the so-called 'second period' of military repression, characterized not so much by the massive detentions carried out randomly during the 'first period' (in which the National Stadium, and other such sites functioned as detention and torture centres) but by more selective detentions, carried out by commands that utilized 'intelligence analysis' and methods of torture designed to destroy secret groups of enemy organizations, cell by cell, with systematic efficiency (Salazar 2013: 107); secondly, it was the headquarters of the Metropolitan Intelligence Brigade (BIM), the operative branch of the DINA; thirdly, the highest-ranking officers of the DINA were stationed there; fourthly, and atypically, "all these officers participated personally (except for Krassnoff, who only gave orders) in the torture of the detainees" (109); and fifthly, perhaps due to this emblematic quality, the "Villa Grimaldi had the dubious honour of being the grounds upon which the Supreme Court of the Chilean Republic charged retired General, Augusto Pinochet Ugarte on 4 October 2006, on 23 counts of torture and 36 counts of kidnapping carried out in the Villa Grimaldi" (110).
[3] Although this is the official information on the Peace Park website, both Michael Lazzara (2007) and Germán Marín (2008) indicate that Villa Grimaldi was built in the mid-nineteenth century.

property was acquired by Emilio Vasallo Rojas, who named the place Villa Grimaldi due to his perception of its similarity to an Italian stately villa surrounded by well-cared-for gardens, water fountains, and sculptures. The house then turned into a meeting place for the Chilean intelligentsia, after which it became a discotheque.

On 14 September 1973, the Villa was seized and later that same year handed over to the National Intelligence Directorate (DINA), which had acquired possession by applying political pressure on its original owner, and the place was converted into a Centre of Detention, Torture and Execution. Approximately 4,500 prisoners of both sexes passed through the Cuartel Terranova, as it was subsequently renamed by the intelligence forces. Eighteen of these detainees were executed and 211 remain categorized to this day as missing. After 1978, the barracks were dismantled gradually and finally abandoned in 1980 (fig. 6). The site was then sold to a construction company owned by the brother-in-law of General Hugo Salas Wenzel, the last director of the National Intelligence Centre (CNI, the organization which replaced DINA in 1977). Finally, in 1989, all the installations were razed to the ground and demolished (fig. 7). A housing community that would generate real estate business was erected in its place, obliterating the signs of all the violations of human rights perpetrated there.

Fig. 6: Villa Grimaldi torture centre. Photo taken on the shoulders of journalist Marcela Otero (Kena Lorenzini, 1983). See: **www.archivomuseodelamemoria.cl/ index.php/88152;isad**

Campo de la Ribera and Villa Grimaldi

In order to avoid the complete obliteration of the Covert Centre of Torture, Detention and Execution, the Permanent Assembly for Human Rights of Peñalolén and La Reina initiated a campaign to denounce the facts and to recover Villa Grimaldi. Their objective was to see the site transformed into a "memorial dedicated to remembrance and the promotion of human rights" (www.villagrimaldi.cl). Once the project was signed into law by the House of Representatives, the land was expropriated by the state and handed over to the community on 10 December 1994. This new phase of the project was finalized on 22 March 1997 with the inauguration of the Villa Grimaldi Peace Park. Since that time, the site remains open to the public and operates as a historical curator to conserve memories of the recent past, as well as promoting a culture of respect for human rights.

Fig. 7: Recovery of Villa Grimaldi by civil society (Muñoz 2015). See: **www.revistapuntodefuga.com/?p=2006**

When the site was handed over to the Villa Grimaldi Peace Park Corporation, it had to decide on its approach to the memorial project. Robert Merino, a former member of the Board of Directors of the Corporation, recalls the tense debate:[4]

---

[4] Chilean director and playwright Guillermo Calderón raises the issue in his play *Villa* (2012), placing it within the debate over the

in 1991/1992, there was a clash over the very different visualizations for the sites of torture and execution... London 38, José Domingo Cañas, the Venda Sexy... the whole spectrum of the political left-wing... and then we had to testify before the Rettig Commission. There, we recorded key eyewitness statements of our experiences as survivors able to tell about the treatment of the detainees and the missing victims [...]. The restoration of Cuartel Terranova was important to us [...]. We scaled the walls of Villa Grimaldi three times looking for relics and taking photos; in those days, the military were in charge of security... one of the issues was what to do with the place once we got it back... we held meetings with former detainees in several different homes... it produced an array of opinions about what should be done: ranging from a park with understated themes... to the more extreme idea of portraying the killings and kidnappings that took place there, with the intermediate view that we weigh options against the possibility of finding funding for each project... until we finally settled on the idea of a park instead of a horror museum. (In Corporación Parque por la Paz Villa Grimaldi 2012b: 8)[5]

The design that was finally awarded the memorial project was based on an X-shaped layout of the space, "since an X or a cross are universal symbols, meaning 'this is wrong and never again', or 'Calvary, death and resurrection'" (Corporación 2012a: 6). This was flanked by a series of pillars, eight metres high, made of glass bricks that diffused a diaphanous light like that of a chapel or funeral parlour. Two sculptures (the Central Courtyard and the Flame) were

---

handling of collective memory that arose in Chile after the inauguration of the Museum of Memory and Human Rights in 2010.

[5] Lucretia Brito, who had been detained in the Cuartel Terranova, held a different opinion of the recovery project: "The women did not agree with so much symbolism at all. We thought that a memorial could not possibly be a villa decorated with lights, trees, and gardens. We thought that some of the more significant elements should be reconstructed, no matter how reminiscent of the horror, since future generations would not understand mere symbols" (00:09:36—00:10:07).

built from scratch using fragments of floor tiles left from the demolition of the original building—illustrating the prisoners' experience, that is, the experience of those who had been blindfolded and had therefore never been able to see more than the floor upon which they trod. Those same fragments were used to produce the signs for the Park (figs. 8 and 9).[6]

During the first phase, a landscaping project of reforestation with indigenous trees was developed alongside the construction of the Birch Tree Patio (*Patio de Abedules*) and the main circumference of the Rose Garden (Jardín de Rosas), where previously there had been an old rose vine belonging to the Villa, around a small pool in whose depths could be read words from Gabriela Mistral's poem, "We were all going to be queens." Between 1997 and 2004, the second phase of implementation of the Park was carried out, and two new elements were introduced. The Wall of Names (Muro de los Nombres), inaugurated on 20 December 1998, presents the names of the 226 people who were executed or seen for the last time at the Cuartel Terranova, conceived as a sculptural project. The mock-ups on a life-size scale of The Cell (La Célula) and The Tower (La Torre) were included. The Cell corresponded to the reconstruction of the so-called Homes of Chile (Casas de Chile), tiny spaces of solitary confinement measuring 70cm x 70cm at their base, and one or two metres in height. They were referred to as "the rabbit hutches", and each had a small door into which the victim had to crawl on his hands and knees. In The Tower (La Torre), there was a torture room with a rack. Some still refer today to this place as "the place of certain death", since most of the people who were detained there remain missing—only twelve have survived.

---

[6] The domestication of the signs can clearly be seen in the differences between the original and the restored designs. The same evolution can be observed in the successive versions of the mock-ups of the Villa Grimaldi/Cuartel Terranova that occupy a prominent place on the site, available for viewing by visitors. To date, three versions have been identified in a progression that starts with a replica of the basic site, colourful and folkloric, and ends with an impeccable model made in a range of muted greys. The aesthetic restraint of these museums' elements reflects the disciplining over the last decades to which the account of events regarding traumatic memory has been subjected (Grass 2016).

MemoSur/MemoSouth

Figs. 8 and 9: The original sign of the Villa Grimaldi Peace Park and after its "restoration" (2008, photography by M. Grass, 27 September 2012)

Campo de la Ribera and Villa Grimaldi

Finally, from 2005 to the present, construction of the Villa Grimaldi Peace Park project has progressed in accordance with its current design. The new entrance was built, the site fenced off and the Velarium (la Velaria) inaugurated when road works began to widen Arrieta Avenue (2006). The Velarium serves as a Life Theatre, a venue for diverse cultural and artistic activities fulfilling community-centred objectives to promote human rights. During the same period, the Quintero Bay Railway (Rieles Bahía de Quinteros) monument was inaugurated, a project undertaken in collaboration with an external organization, consisting of a glass case showing fragments of rails from a railway used to convey to the ocean for disposal the bodies of detained and assassinated victims of the dictatorship. A series of monuments was also built in homage to the militants of various political parties who died at the hands of the dictatorship. Those parties include the Popular Movement for United Action (Movimiento Popular de Acción Unitaria, MAPU), and the Revolutionary Left Movement (Movimiento de Izquierda Revolucionaria, MIR), as well as the leaders of the Communist Party (PC) and the Socialist Party (PS). All the monuments might have been the same size but they displayed great autonomy in terms of design, materials employed and type of landscaping. Along with the aforesaid elements created expressly for the Peace Park, the visitor might also find remnants of the original building: two water fountains, a pool, and a reflecting pool; the poolside locker rooms—now converted into the Memory room; the entrance gate; the great Ombu tree—that was used to torture prisoners; the scaffolding (discovered in 2007) and other ruins of walls and pavements.

The aesthetic tension among the original features (pool, water fountain, staircases that hold archaeological value); the locker rooms refashioned into the Memory Room,[7] those features of Villa Grimaldi that were recreated to scale (The Tower, The Cell), and finally the new artefacts

---

[7] The place was inaugurated in 2004 and designed with the help of relatives of the victims of Villa Grimaldi who remembered the identities and lives of the persons who died or went missing from there. There are sixteen showcases in which photographs and other personal items (spectacles, letters, articles of clothing, and so on) are displayed, and there is a kind of mural on the wall depicting the portraits of the missing detainees.

(signage, mock-ups, memorials) beg a series of questions regarding the coherence between these various forms, and in terms of the interstices that occur between them. The huge variety of materials, aesthetic criteria, and the forms for each element work together to convey the intended content: history is conveyed through mosaic, photography, drawing, architecture, landscaping, and in less frequent form, theatre, movies, literature, and music... Additionally, several disciplines were called upon to give shape to the memorial project, including history, geography, landscaping, architecture, urban studies, forensic anthropology, art, museology, and others. This variety of forms and perspectives has created a Park both complex and eclectic: thirty years of existence have transformed it into a kind of place that overwhelms the senses, complete with the long lists of names of those who were detained and executed in the Cuartel Terranova.[8]

This is how the Peace Park has evolved to this day, where the dynamic multimedia-type representation of relationships among groups of people, facts and dates, and physical sites and remains (Stern 2013) reveals the delicate balance between competing interests in building a memorial. These interests are represented through narratives that vie for control in their attempt to recreate a coherent account of the past. In this "society of narratives" (Olick 2003) the project of a nation-state is built through careful balancing of different memorial narratives whose accounts bring to light and help define important issues of national identity. The narratives allow for a validation of certain experiences, give legitimacy to certain interpretations in preference to others, and offer multiple perspectives on history through the myths and accounts that transmit culture.

---

[8] The Peace Park Corporation also has Oral Archives, instituted in collaboration with the Institute of Communication and Images of the University of Chile (ICEI). It preserves over one hundred audiovisual testimonies on the Cuartel Terranova, including those of former detainees; the Corporation is also working on a Villa Grimaldi Educational Project, whose main goal is to promote a culture of peace through a teaching model that centres around four axes: the links between the past and the present; the promotion of a human-rights culture, the development of thoughtful and critical thinking, and the promotion of critical memory.

Campo de la Ribera and Villa Grimaldi

The Villa Grimaldi Peace Park represents a society's search for meaning. During periods of dictatorial or post-dictatorial rule, memory operates not only as a tool for one group or another, but also as mediation in and of itself (Olick 2011). And to that end, understanding how or why certain accounts of the past persist, or perhaps change, implies a drive to reflect more deeply upon our own recent history and the role that each narrative has played in the complex act of remembering history.

A politics of consensus (Richard 2010) was chosen to manage the history of the Chilean transition back to democracy, a process fraught with tension while the society struggled to return to order. At times, demands for justice for atrocities committed threatened to derail the politics of consensus, and, as we all know, justice was achieved "to the extent possible." This phrase from President Aylwin in his first public message at year's end (31 December 1990) sounds almost timid today, because we tend to look back from the context of the future which we have achieved. Yet justice that comes after a period of conflict in societies is a part of the transition wrought from the vestiges of fear and trauma, within the framework of an extremely precarious social and political order that has been recently restored. In this context, clearly the construction of some and denial of others, and the overall role of the diverse memories which compete for predominance, are mixed up with diverse political objectives: on the one hand, participants in the majority groups benefit from the politics of consensus; and on the other, there are those who struggle against the threat of being forgotten. The narratives of these latter groups are directly related to the violence carried out and therefore generate the most dissension, and are viewed as highly disruptive.[9]

The evolution of Villa Grimaldi from a Clandestine Centre of Detention, Torture, and Extermination into a Peace Park allows for a productive process of diachronic analysis regarding the negotiation of memory. This memorial site, an emblematic place of remembrance for the victims of political

---

[9] Gómez-Barris (2010: 29) indicates that, "Selectively forgetting memories about State violence gives the opportunity for a new governmental regime to rebrand its tarnished image, especially in the neoliberal global arena".

violence, not only in Chile but in all of Latin America and the rest of the world, has not ceased to generate controversy. Opinions are divided and swing between considering the place a tame version of memory (Richard 2001) and the "unofficial site of national atrocity" (Gómez-Barris 2010: 34), offering not only "an antidote against forgetting, but a meaningful historical and present-day location in which communities politically engage their past" (Gómez-Barris 33).[10] Whatever it may be, the uncontested fact remains that, for better or for worse, Villa Grimaldi occupies a symbolic place. The work that has been carried out among the ruins keeps alive a more nuanced version of the recent past than that put forth by specific political groups, whose interests reduce history to a partial version of the facts. Furthermore, the Peace Park fulfils an important role by providing the experience of having been there, "where the facts occurred and those things happened," which has an impact on the visitor's emotions regarding history. For some, the device is eloquently presented via the suggestive form, both allegorical and metaphorical, which permits the visitor a more personal and unconstrained experience of the difficult subject of violence which this site seeks to denounce. For others, the Park is confusing, full of clichés, impenetrable, and hard to read. Whatever the interpretation and beyond the discussion of how effective it is as a memorial, Villa Grimaldi is, in fact, lost to memory. What we have is a representation of memory (Lassara 2007), an installation (Taylor 2011), one that has been built within a complex, interdisciplinary, and multi-medial interplay of features whose elements convey the testimonies of ordinary citizens

---

[10] Gómez-Barris (2010: 27) writes: "public memorials like the Villa Grimaldi Peace Park can be important complements to the incomplete process of transitional justice in nations that have experienced grave human rights violations. Such sites provide significant forms of sociability, which I call 'witness citizenship' (human rights participation, generational transmission, and other forms of civic action) that deepen the reach of democracy, especially in the social spaces where truth commissions and institutional processes have not been able to reach". This serves the process of re-democratization of the country, to the extent that the social groups "reenact the past as exercise of citizenship through symbolic repertoires and through collective narratives" (44).

Campo de la Ribera and Villa Grimaldi

(Gómez-Barris 2010) to the visitors, putting into motion a map of social memory in constant evolution (Richard 2001).

The Villa Grimaldi Peace Park thus becomes a highly complex site, whose development is affected by the progress in mutual understanding achieved by the respective political parties on the right and left as they work to preserve social peace. The project is also affected by the political bent of subsequent governments charged with its implementation. The previous government determined the nature of the Park, which had to develop a narrative in line with the concept of political struggle and violence under the Chilean dictatorship, without promoting the idea of victimhood of those who fought against the oppressive forces. The prevalence of the Park project meant that the most combative dimension of those who died was made invisible, establishing a politics to manage the nation's memory based on a concept of pain and redemption, one adopted readily by the Catholic imagination, allowing for a reinterpretation of the significance of events as sacrificial death on the part of the executed.[14]

The decision was based on two ideas: the first, that the possibility of recapturing the horror of the original site instead of merely promoting human rights brought to the place a more diverse audience (see footnote 13); and the second, that there were several features in which the state violence perpetrated was recreated in its actual proportions, including The Tower, The CORVI houses, and the Chile houses.[11] It is these reconstructions and artistic interventions at the site that allow for the perpetuation of memory and reflection upon the past, projecting forward into a desired identity (Violi 2009). In other words, the construction of the Park by the Chilean government in 2004 was founded on its contribution to the rebuilding of a cohesive society, and this took precedence over keeping the original place intact. The Peace Park is thus not a mere presentation, but a representation and an allegory, and memory then is served by these artificial constructions, and by recreations built upon testimonies of the place which had been demolished to eliminate incriminating evidence.

With this diachronic perspective in mind, the Park

---

[11] The ambiguity of the word *park* is interesting, evoking both consecrated ground (in Chile, many cemeteries are called Parks...) and funpark.

necessarily has oscillated between the roles of accusation and consensus building. Originally, the extent of the crimes was only alluded to in vague terms; at that time, the imperative to preserve social peace through negotiation took precedence.[12] However, with the passing of the years, newer, more explicit evidence has emerged regarding torture and execution: The Railway Monument, The Tower, The Cell, and the audio-guide reveal what had previously been hushed up. At the same time, consensus in society has relaxed its boundaries, and many facts that were denied three decades ago as lies and exaggerations are widely accepted as common knowledge. Allusion and, later, explicit enunciation had both contributed to increasing the expressive means deployed in the battle to conquer the Park. The artistic features function as a pivot between these two desires, to hush up and to speak, due to the symbolic nature of art and its experiential nature in respect of the violent acts that defy description to which it alludes via aesthetic means.

Nevertheless, the capacity of the place to convey what can be said in words (Angenot) about human rights at a certain moment in history, in accordance with a collective imagination which goes beyond the specific events in that specific place, went hand in hand with a cover-up: the project enclosed the Peace Park, confining it within walls. Compared to Campo de la Ribera, the Cuartel Terranova project did not involve neighbours; we do not know what it is they saw or heard. Although it is unlikely that the activities carried out on the site where the offices of the DINA were situated passed unnoticed, testimony concerning it does not figure prominently either in its history or in its reconstruction via memory.

Entering the walls of Villa Grimaldi, portrayed many times in films as an impenetrable barrier, requires going beyond considering it as part of the complex and widespread

---

[12] Richard (2010: 9) sums up well the issue of the edification of memory and transitional justice in Chile, which begins with "the establishment of consensus as the vehicle of national reconciliation articulated by the government of Patricio Aylwin (1990) in the spirit of overcoming the antagonisms of a violent past, and concludes with the inauguration of the Museum of Memory and Human Rights (2010) which represents depicts the institutional culmination of the official narrative of memory by the Chilean transition".

Campo de la Ribera and Villa Grimaldi

system of repression of the dictatorship (fig. 10) to considering its urban context: the events transpired in the midst of a civil society that was nevertheless silent, in a site conveniently located close to the headquarters of the Armed Forces and a small airport, from which the cadavers of the executed were removed. The Villa Grimaldi/Cuartel Terranova/Peace Park is situated on the far side of the San Carlos Canal, a man-made border that creates a barrier on multiple levels: a place beyond the scope of the law, of justice, and of all that is considered human. It also lies beyond social privileges. In 1995, almost twenty years before the historian Gabriel Salazar published his study on Villa Grimaldi, the Chilean novelist Germán Marín (2008: 125-126) had already said these words:

> As I drove along the main avenue in Peñalolén, criss-crossed by bus routes, I realized that the sweet little houses I had passed were now behind me. [...] Beyond the car junkyard arose a shantytown of gloomy, liver-coloured houses—mushroom ghettos, they are still called in this country. One more mole on the face of Santiago, marring the triumphant claims so in fashion of those who wanted to compare Chile to a jaguar, in zoo-like terminology, by those who claimed to represent the reconciliation of different interests. Five or six "kids" and "chicks", using local terminology, as is the narrator's privilege, were sitting on the curb doing nothing but listening to songs by the top rock bands of the moment, on a portable radio. At the end of the next block lay a wooden bridge that crossed the waters of the San Carlos Canal. As I remembered from our records, this bridge had been recognized by some of the victims of the so-called Villa Grimaldi, as they lay on the floor of a vehicle, as the place where they crossed from one side of Santiago over to their deaths.

Conclusion

Our objective has been to establish a relationship between two spaces of memory: one in Chile; the other in Argentina. We have been especially keen to highlight the collective actions that led directly to the transformation of these sites into places of remembrance. In so doing, we considered how the appropriation of the site was the outcome of analysis by

MemoSur/MemoSouth

the local community: "The power of the local, the knitting of relationships among the local practices and their tie to central power, the impact of the framework given by a local interpretation of those facts that are remembered or silenced" (Del Pino & Jelin 2003: Preface).

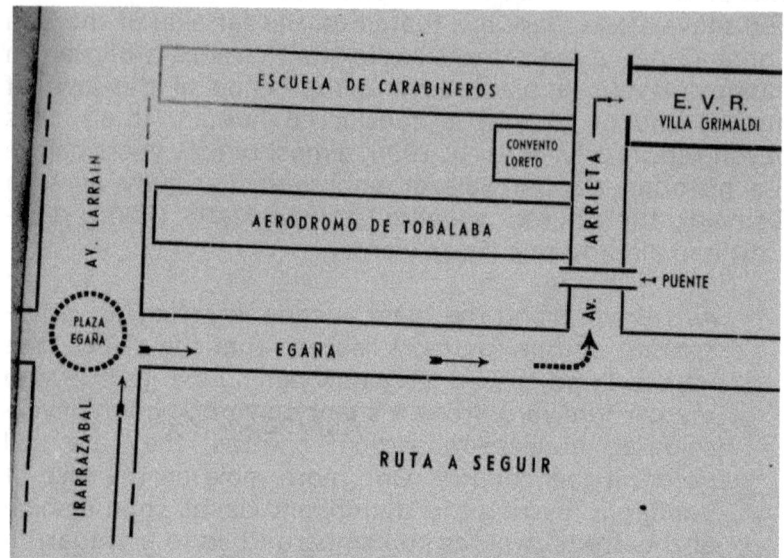

Fig. 10: Map of the Cuartel Terranova (Digital Archive, 38 London Street, Santiago). See:
www.londres38.cl/1934/w3-article-91241.html

It is our understanding that within the frameworks both of the macro-social and the micro-individual, it is pertinent to construct an intermediate interpretation in producing works that represent memory. This happens at the level of the community, of those who were "taken over" as Ricoeur (2013) says, of all the neighbours, of those who lived in the immediate surroundings and who were involved indirectly in the events. This comes as much from the eloquence that arises from the presence of these voices, as from their premeditated absence.

As seen from outside the walls of the clandestine centres, we have established their strategic location for military logistics for the purposes of detention, torture, and extermination and also for the purpose of hiding the crimes from the inhabitants of the city's centre. The fact that they were located at the city's periphery represents a double process of segregation and social discrimination: of those detained, and the violence they suffered, and of the communities that were impoverished and confined to the margins of urban existence. From within the walls of the centres, we have emphasized the layout and purposes of the buildings, the original design, and the events that were carried out according to the changing nature of their functionality therein. At the same time that we present these practices, uses and abuses, we feel it also necessary to reveal the narrative that sought to justify, legalize, and legitimize these acts. In this vein, we consider that these clandestine centres, now places of remembrance, operate as mechanisms as defined by Foucault (1991: 128): "What is included under the name is, in the first place, a group of heterogeneous elements that include language, institutions, architectural installations, regulatory decisions, laws, administrative measures, scientific reports, philosophical propositions, morals, and philanthropy; in sum: the elements of this mechanism pertain as much to what is spoken as to what is not spoken. The mechanism is the network that is established among these elements." The place in society held by these sites, considering their panoptic purpose of controlling those within and without, helps to explain their subsequent repurposing, especially in the case of Campo de la Ribera becoming a school. To carry out discipline, vigilance, and punishment (Foucault 2008), buildings would function indiscriminately as military prisons, clandestine centres of detention, schools, or hospitals, if this were to be officially sanctioned.

With the conversion of these sites into spaces for memory, it becomes necessary to dismantle the disciplinary structure built into the installations, and to modify their purpose in society while at the same time preserving the original design or, as in the case of Villa Grimaldi in Santiago, Chile, recreating those designs. The obvious tension arises between the option of maintaining a true representation of these places as they were during the period in which they functioned as landscapes for dictatorial violence, and the option of creating a didactic or heuristic adaptation, in favour of giving shape to processed memory (Todorov 2008).

This time we have sought to incorporate versions from outside the walls of the centres and the repercussions of their internal dynamic on the community life in those neighbourhoods where they were situated. It follows, then, that the spaces for memory be articulated from the very need of these communities to remember and commemorate victims of the centres that existed in their midst. Communication with neighbours and with groups that process these events through reflection, learning, and artistic creation, facilitates the regeneration of the memory of what happened, and permits an appropriation of the past not only as a truthful account of facts, but more so as a recovery of its true exemplary significance.

Translated by Tessa Too-Kong

References
Angenot, M. (2010). *El discurso social. Los límites históricos de lo pensable y lo decible*. Buenos Aires: Siglo XXI Editores.
Archivo Provincial de la Memoria (2015). Espacio para la memoria Campo de la Ribera. Córdoba. At **www.apm.gov.ar/?q=clr/visitas**.
Baldo, A., Maffini, G. et al. (2011). *La historia que nos parió. Memorias del terrorismo de estado en el barrio*. Córdoba: published by the author.
Brito, L. (n.d.). *Construyendo la memoria*. At **https://vimeo.com/23295998**.
Calderón, G. (2012). *Teatro II. Villa – discurso – beben*. Santiago de Chile: Lom.
Codoceo, F. (2012). Guía urbana de Santiago de Chile. Un paseo por Villa Grimaldi Peace Park. At www.plataformaurbana.cl/archive/2012/11/11/guia-urbana-de-santiago-parque-por-la-paz-villa-grimaldi/, accessed 2 September 2016.
Comisión Nacional sobre la Desaparición de Personas (CONADEP). (1984). *Informe* Nunca Más. At **www.derechoshumanos.net/lesahumanidad/informes/argentina/informe-de-la-conadep-nunca-mas.htm**
Comisión Presidencial Asesora para la Calificación de Detenidos Desaparecidos, Ejecutados Políticos y Víctimas de Prisión Política y Tortura (Comisión Valech). Instituto Nacional de Derechos Humanos. At www.indh.cl/informacion-comision-valech, accessed 2 September 2016.
Corporación Parque por la Paz Villa Grimaldi (2012a).

Encuentro sitios de memoria. Ppt. 14 January.

Corporación Parque por la Paz Villa Grimaldi (2012b). *El boletín*, 6 (April), 1-28.

Demaria, C. (2006). *Semiotica e memoria. Analisi del post-conflito.* Rome: Carocci Editore.

Dowd, A., & Cambra, I. (2015). La ciudad como territorio de la memoria. Una visión a través del arte. *Revista aesthethika*, 51-69, University of Buenos Aires. At www.aesthethika.org/la-ciudad-como-territorio-de-la.

Foucault, M. (1991). *El saber y la verdad* (ed., trans. and prol. J. Varela & F. Álvarez-Uría). Madrid: Ediciones la Piqueta.

Garbero, V., Liponetzky, T., Córdoba, G., & Romero, M. (2012). Las memorias se hacen sonido en el Campo de la Ribera: Reflexiones en torno al programa «Jóvenes y Memoria». *Revista question*, 1(36), Universidad Nacional de la Plata.

Gómez-Barris, M. (2010). Witness citizenship: The place of Villa Grimaldi in Chilean Memory. *Sociological Forum*, 25(1), March, 27-46.

Grass, M. (2016). Parque por la paz Villa Grimaldi: Negociaciones de la memoria puestas en acto. *Nuestra América*, Universidad Fernando Pessoa, special volume 10, pp. 147-160.

Lazzara, M. (2007). *Prismas de la memoria. Narración y trauma en la transición chilena.* Santiago de Chile: Editorial Cuarto Propio.

Marchetti, F. (2010). Algunas notas sueltas (para un debate sobre Campo de la Ribera). *Diario de la memoria*, Comisión y Archivo Provincial de la Memoria. Córdoba. 3(4), 1-24.

Marín, G. (2008). *El palacio de la risa*. Santiago de Chile: Random House Mondadori. (Original publication 1995.)

Muñoz Elgueta, E. (2015). El soporte de la ausencia: Estrategias del arte en la construcción de la memoria en Chile. *Punto de Fuga*, 4 October. (Originally published in 2014.)

Olick, J. (ed.) (2003). *States of memory: Continuities, conflicts, and transformations in national retrospection.* Durham, NC: Duke University Press.

Olick, J., Vinitzky-Seroussi, V., & Levy, D. (2011). *The collective memory reader.* Oxford: Oxford University Press.

Olmo, D. & Salado Puerto, M. (2008). Una fosa común en el interior de Argentina: El cementerio de San Vicente. Equipo argentino de antropología forense. *Revista del museo de antropología*. Córdoba: Universidad Nacional de Córdoba. Facultad de Filosofía y Humanidades. 1(1), 3-12.

Richard, N. (2001). Sitios de la memoria: Vaciamiento del recuerdo. *Revista de crítica cultural*, 23, 11-12.

Richard, N. (2010). *Crítica de la memoria (1990-2010)*. Santiago de Chile: Ediciones Universidad Diego Portales.

Salazar, G. (2013). *Villa Grimaldi (Cuartel Terranova). Historia, testimonio, reflexión*. Santiago de Chile: Lom.

Simo, J. C. (2015). Identifican restos de un desaparecido en el cementerio San Vicente. *La Voz del Interior*. At **www.lavoz.com.ar/politica/identifican-nuevos-restos-de-un-desaparecido-en-el-cementerio-san-vicente**.

Stern, S. (2013). *Memorias en construcción. Los retos del pasado presente en Chile, 1989-2011*. Santiago de Chile: Museo de la Memoria y los Derechos Humanos.

Taylor, D. (2007). Trauma, memoria y performance: Un recorrido por Villa Grimaldi con Pedro Matta. *E-misférica 7.2*. At **http://hemi.nyu.edu/hemi/en/e-misferica-72/taylor**, accessed 2 September 2016.

Todorov, T. (2008). *Los abusos de la memoria* (trans. M. Salazar). Barcelona: Ediciones Paidós Ibérica.

Verón, E. (1993). *La semiosis social. Fragmentos de una teoría de la discursividad*. Barcelona: Editorial Gedisa.

Violi, P. (2009). Ricordare il futuro. I musei della memoria e il loro ruolo nella construziones delle identità culturali. *E/C, Rivista on-line dell'Associazione Italiana di Semiotica*, 1-16.

Violi, P. (2012). Trauma site museums and politics of memory: Tuol Sleng, Villa Grimaldi and the Bologna Ustica museum. *Theory, Culture and Society*, 29(1), 36-75.

Violi, P. (2014). *Paesaggi della memoria. Il trauma, lo spazio, la storia*. Milan: Bompiani.

Tracing Memory: A Semiotic Analysis of the Museum of Córdoba Provincial Memory Archive

Paola Sozzi

The Archivo Provincial de la Memoria (Provincial Memory Archive; from now on: APM) in the Museum of Córdoba has its seat in a lovely building, in the heart of the old town centre. This place for decades housed the Intelligence Department of the Córdoba Police, in the 1970s worked as a secret detention and torture centre, the so-called "D2" (Department 2), and nowadays is a museum and an archive.

This essay aims to produce an analysis, from a semiotic point of view, of this memory site. We shall focus more on the museum of the D2, while Daniele Salerno (in this volume) focuses on a specific section of the archive. The peculiarity of the museum will prove to be that of testifying to the truth of the terrible events that happened here, physically tracing memory through a complex and intertwined spatial system. Therefore, I shall also address a more "theoretical" matter: why and how memory sites use those semiotic objects we call "traces" to tell a story about the past and make it "seem real".

Semiotics and Memory Sites

We can find at least two main traits in the relationship between space and memory (Violi 2014b: 83): on the one hand, space keeps track of the past in the form of material traces or ruins of what once was.[1] On the other hand, when moving in a space we unlock memories of the experiences we had in it, making a memory site quite effective in preserving and transmitting the past. Both these aspects were of utmost importance in the decision to preserve the detention and torture centres in Argentina, as we shall see. Moreover, remembering is a semiotic act: only the meaningful past is remembered (Assmann 1992) and this "meaningfulness" is always constructed through some sort of text. Memory sites are, then, a crucial part of a society's *system of memory* (Demaria 2012; Violi 2014b: 30), that set of objects, practices, texts of different genres which creates

---

[1] On this topic, see Mazzucchelli (2010, 2015); Sozzi (2015); Violi (2009, 2012, 2014a, 2014b, 2015, 2016).

a collective, shared "habit" (Peirce 1998) of interpretation of reality, working as a sort of semiosphere (Lotman 1990) or local encyclopaedia (Eco 1984).

Memorials and monuments then shape past events and our perception of them as history (Violi 2016), so that building a memory site is one of the most effective acts in the construction of collective memory (Mazzucchelli 2010). Especially after moments of social explosion (Lotman 2009), such as traumatic events, the preservation of the "places of trauma" is one of the most common ways to work through what happened, a phase of that "path of trauma" by which an event may become a traumatic collective heritage (Violi 2014b: 63). When approaching a memory site, then, we shall not only consider the past it is linked to, but also the process of its creation, the agency of such memory, the practices that take place in it and its actual reception (Verón 1988, 2013).[2]

From Police Department to Memory Site

The Department of Information of the Córdoba Provincial Police or D2 was a division of the police force created to repress the "common" crime defined as "subversion". Since the 1940s, "subversives", who were considered "dangerous" for the social order for being part of political movements, trade unions, students' associations, or for their religious or sexual orientation, were interrogated and detained there. From 1971 to 1982 almost 20,000 people passed through the D2.

In the early 1970s, due to the national situation, many riots took place in Córdoba (*el Córdobazo,* 1969; *el Viborazo*, 1971; *el Navarrazo*, 1974) and different political movements flourished, some of them supporting the idea of violent revolution. When the Federal Government decided to send some soldiers to "calm" the situation (Raúl Lacabanne, in 1974; Luciano Menéndez and Raúl Telleldín, in 1975), an escalation of violence began: abduction, torture and inhuman detention became common means to extract the information considered essential for the so-called "Counter-

---

[2] As for my methodology, I visited the place many times over five months (February–July 2016), participated in many events, took notes and photographs, observed the visitors and analyzed the texts displayed in the museum.

revolutionary War". First, in 1974–1975, in order to create an atmosphere of terror and confusion aimed at discrediting the political organizations and justifying the planned *coup d'état*, the "subversives" were kidnapped, tortured, killed and then left at the side of the road. From December 1975, prisoners systematically disappeared: after being kidnapped, they had to pass through the D2 to be photographed, recorded, and "interrogated" under torture. Then they would either remain for some time in the department or be sent to one of the other Clandestine Detention Centres organized in town, the biggest being La Ribera and La Perla. Here they were kept alive while ever they were considered of some use, then executed and buried in common graves.

When democracy was restored in 1983, citizens actually started to discover what had happened, while some traces of the military's crimes were coming to light. Some trials took place, but everything was halted a few years later by three different laws. Therefore, the military coup's twentieth anniversary "in 1996, inaugurated a production of 'small memories' and 'local markings' [...] aimed against the various State politics clearly intending to erase and forget" (da Silva Catela 2015: 10, 11). Finally, in 2005, the laws that had stopped the trials were considered unconstitutional and a new phase of trials began, while in the meantime a series of episodes had established "the idea that the ex-CDCs ought to be the nucleus of the *institutionalisation of memories*" (da Silva Catela 2015: 2). For these reasons, "the thirtieth anniversary of the coup, in 2006, was a moment of 'monumental memories' [...], including the creation of institutions such as archives, cultural centres, memorials and sites centring their narratives on State Terrorism" (2). According to this third phase, in March 2006 a provincial law (Ley 9286/2006 or Ley de la Memoria) created in Córdoba a Memory Commission, composed of members of different local human rights associations, the university and a representative of the provincial government. It gave them the buildings of the ex-D2, specifying that they be preserved and turned into a memory site, and established the Provincial Archive, with the power to search for documents relating to the crimes and to collect victims' testimonies. Subsequently, La Perla and La Ribera camps were converted into memory sites and now the three places form a network coordinated by the Commission.[3]

Visiting the Museum: A Brief Analysis

As the map shows (fig. 1), the buildings of the museum comprise three formerly aristocratic houses: the left entrance leads to the offices of the Commission, the right one to the archive and the middle to the museum. Since the design has been changed many times, we shall not consider the architectural structure per se, but rather how it has been re-organized and re-enunciated. The museum is now a continuous trail through different courtyards and rooms (on the map, the rooms with white on black writing are part of it), without signposting to direct the visitors. Only in the case of temporary exhibitions are stickers arranged on the floor.

In order to decide how to intervene in the site, the Commission invited former prisoners to visit it. In fact, there was no particular sign of what happened there, with the exception of the tiniest cell where the prisoners had engraved names and dates. For the survivors, the experience of walking through the space unlocked hidden memories, while their accounts gained reliability due to their correspondence with the features of the place. It was then decided to "rebuild" the place as it was in those years, destroying a wall that had been erected, but leaving a piece of it upright, or avoiding repainting all the walls, since it is probable that these changes were made by the police to make it harder to recognize the place.

The outside of the museum is clearly designed to highlight its presence (fig. 2): three giant fingerprints drawn on transparent plaques are hung on its unrestored walls. They are composed of the names of all the disappeared and killed in the province, as another large red plaque explains. Many other elements make it impossible to pass by without noticing the museum: a national flag, an iron and glass door with the writing "Archivo Provincial de la Memoria", a coloured tile, the completely wide-open museum entrance, or its green door when it is closed. Plus, every Thursday, the day of the Madres de la Plaza de Mayo's weekly parade, pictures of the *desaparecidos* of Córdoba wave in the street,

---

[3] For more information on the Commission and the archive, see **www.apm.gov.ar**.

in ordered lines of faces and names.

With all these features, the street works as an important extension of the museum into urban space. It calls for citizens' attention and creates a contrast between the locked, inaccessible nature of the ex-CDC, where a severe suppression of human rights took place almost silently, and its central location, its public role, its pedagogical mission nowadays.

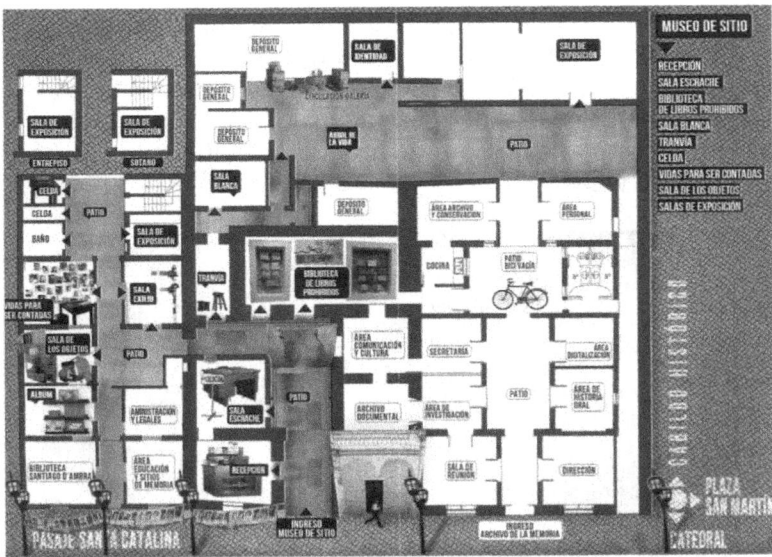

Fig. 1: Map on the last page of the brochure which visitors can collect at the museum entrance

As for the inside of the museum, we may divide it into three different types of space: first, corridors and courtyards; then, rooms with *permanent exhibitions*; finally, empty rooms for *temporary exhibitions*, not defined spaces continuously changing over time. Some of these last rooms were mainly used for torture, but today, following what has been a common solution at many memory sites throughout Argentina, they are completely empty: torture is not represented. Still, the museum hosts temporary artistic exhibitions, as if any other sort of discourse would be inappropriate.

As for the corridors and courtyards (the *patios*), they are not just empty spaces to cross. Many of the victims' memories were unlocked in them: everyone seated on the patio benches, blindfolded, waiting for hours or days to be "interrogated". In those places, seven different transparent plaques are displayed with fragments of the testimonies. Through them, a juxtaposition of the victims' experience and the visitors' experience is created, heightened by a sense of disorientation in the visitors due to the lack of signposting. In addition, the testimonies are written in black handwriting, the sentences in direct speech, using the first person, the present tense and a large number of deictic words. The peculiarity of this discourse is that the speaker becomes the centre of reference: *here* is where the speaker is, *now* when he is talking (Benveniste 1970). The reader has to put himself in that centre of reference too, creating a feeling of proximity with the prisoners based on being exactly *here*, where they were.

Fig. 2: The outside of the museum, Thursday 30 June 2016, with a photographic exhibition on the left.

Fig. 3: One of the patios

Tracing Memory in the Córdoba Provincial Memory Archive

Fig. 4: Patio with cells

We can divide the *permanent exhibition rooms* into two groups: a "photographic" trail and the remaining five rooms. First of all, the photographic trail has diversions throughout the museum at seven different points, each indicated only by a little tile on the floor. In the first one, called "From Negative to Positive" (fig. 5), a case displays some of the boxes in which almost 140,000 pictures were found, mostly mug shots taken by the police between 1964 and 1992. Many texts explain how the images were found, why they are used there, but especially how the images were extracted from the films, creating a sense of the scientific reliability of their content.

The second point, "Focus" (fig. 6), is a room that functioned as a D2 office and that now tries mimetically to represent what it would look like, explaining its history and reproducing some of those pictures that accidentally captured an angle or a detail of the Department. There is also a list of the soldiers who worked there and a collage of images dedicated to the trials. The third and fourth point, "Facing Images" (fig. 7), and a room whose tile is no longer visible, are placed in spaces where prisoners were detained for a long time and where some mug shots were taken. In these rooms we find, respectively, a photographic exposition and two videos made with the photos. In the largest patio we reach the fifth point of the trail, called "Moments of Truth, the Ex-D2 in Pictures". It is composed of a recreated dark room (fig. 8) and an exhibition that reflects on some aspects of the D2 using some photos or "wrong" shots found in the films: the beginning of the repression in 1974, the tortures and the beatings, the organization of the space in the Department (fig. 9). Then, in the same room, point number six, called "Pictures of my Parents", presents two video interviews with children of *desaparecidos* to whom the archive returned pictures of their parents. When the archive was able to identify the people in the photographs, the pictures were returned to them or their relatives, triggering a different kind of emotional reaction, especially because the images show part of the invisible horror they had to face; the very matter upon which the interviews reflect.

The seventh point is composed of a mirror accompanied by a text that lists the different laws that, since 1910, outlined the crimes of subversion investigated by the Department (fig. 10). It encourages visitors to think about "The Construction of the Other", as this stop is called, and to reflect on the very idea of "subversion" as something in relation to our political and cultural schemes. At the end of the trail, we find the Library of Prohibited Books which continues the reflection on the global effects of dictatorship in general, telling of the severe cultural censorship exercised in the 1970s in Argentina, when certain books (which are exhibited), magazines, movies, and so on were banned, burned and confiscated.

Fig. 5: From Negative to Positive

Fig. 6: Focus

Fig. 7: Facing Images

Fig. 8: Moments of Truth 1

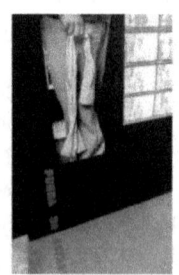

Fig. 9: Moments of Truth 2

Fig. 10: The Construction of the Other

Tracing Memory in the Córdoba Provincial Memory Archive

We may draw some conclusions about this photographic trail. First of all, it is dedicated to the reconstruction of the D2 through images, historical information and some mimetic setups. The images work as another kind of "trace" of the past: in fact, the introductory text of the trail, at the beginning, justifies the fact that they are being exhibited, declaring that "these images unequivocally prove what the testimonies and the survivors had been saying for years [...]. Now, it's not only their testimony, it's the *force of the images* that supports them". Secondly, the trail also works as a reflection on the same act of showing the images, representing the "horror" and dealing with it. The debate on this matter is long and complex (Demaria 2012; Violi 2014b, 2015), but we must consider that these images are an exception in Argentina, since the dictatorship adopted a sort of invisibility strategy that left almost no traces or images of its crimes (Violi 2015). Third, the limit between the intimate, personal space of grief and sorrow collides with the public interest to know what happened. On this trail we find a balanced solution: the pictures of the fifth room only portray survivors, who gave their permission to display them, while at the same time the public is forbidden from taking pictures, "public interest" thereby being set against victims' privacy.

The remaining permanent exhibition rooms are the "Lives to be Told" rooms, the Exile Room and the Identity Room. In the three "Lives to be Told" rooms we find different kinds of object: in the first one (fig. 11), albums of pictures telling the stories of some of the *desaparecidos*; in the second one (fig. 12), many of the victims' personal objects, such as shirts, books, records and much more. The descriptions of the objects and the albums are written by the relatives of the victims: families and friends can ask for the staff's help to compose them or they may simply do it themselves; in any case, they are almost free to write and produce what they want. In the Objects Room we find a plaque with the description of the room penned by the APM, a description that highlights the degree to which these objects are other traces of the event. With their materiality they recall the concreteness of those disappeared bodies, with which they had physical contact.

In the third room, walls are covered with framed

pictures of the victims, smiling, without names or descriptions (fig. 13). As for the three fingerprints on the outside (fig. 2), this room is a sort of memorial, where flowers are laid on the corners of the frames. Even if these two memorials are quite different, they seem to work in a similar way: both of them recover only certain traits of the victim's identity (their name or their face), while they compose the larger figure of The Victim, of the trauma that occurred. It is interesting to note that fingerprints and portraits are chosen as symbols of the memorials dedicated to the memory of those who were illegally killed by the state, while both of them are legal tools used to identify a person.

Fig. 11: The Albums Room   Fig. 12: The Objects Room   Fig. 13: The Pictures Room

As for the Exile Room (fig. 14), it collects the stories of those who left the country or their city. A wall-sized world map represents their main destinations and a notebook in the centre of the room recounts their stories and shows their pictures. As happens at many other points in the museum, a red bookmark reminds the visitors to get in touch with the APM in case they want to add a story to the album.

Fig. 14: The Exile Room

The other permanent exhibition room is the Identity Room (fig. 15). It was put together with the cooperation of the Abuelas of Córdoba, an association comprising grandmothers who are searching for their grandchildren born in captivity and adopted, under false identities, by soldiers' families or friends. On the walls, coloured wallpaper, a few silver silhouettes of toys and frames with pictures of the disappeared mothers. For each of them a white handkerchief, symbol of the Madres and the Abuelas, announces their names, the date of disappearance and the probable date of birth of the child. This room is an invitation to cooperate in the investigation: for this purpose, there is a mailbox and some postcards, each one dedicated to a different mother, giving useful information about her and her child.[4]

Fig. 15: The Identity Room

The peculiarity of this second group of rooms seems to be the recreation of a domestic atmosphere: on the one hand, it invites visitors to stop and feel comfortable; on the other, it depicts the different kinds of victim (the disappeared and the murdered ones, the exiled one, the "stolen children") as normal people. The museum breaks the barrier between

---

[4] For further information on the association of the Abuelas de la Plaza de Mayo and their role in the construction of a particular idea of identity and postmemory, we refer to the contribution of Cristina Demaria in this book. Also the case she analyzes, the direct interpellation of the addressee, proves to be a peculiar trait of the communication and action of the association, as it is here.

domestic space and public space and refuses a "heroic" narration of the victims, proposing a common representation of their lives, with family albums, everyday objects, wallpaper and toys. It underlines the intimacy of their memories while it shares them.[5]

As we can see, the museum is a complex place, with the photographic trail, the rooms dedicated to victims, the corridors and patios, the many different plaques, temporary exhibitions, two "memorials", the street outside, the Library of Prohibited Books and, also, another library on the dictatorship. It is also important to know that the place is often hosting in its rooms and patios many different events: book presentations, artistic exhibitions and performances, historical exhibitions. As Daniele Salerno writes in this volume, it is a "complex enunciative device that assembles different semiotic substances [...] and discursive genres and practices". Therefore, it is almost impossible to find just one Model Visitor[6] for the site, since it addresses at least two categories of people: a general public, citizens not directly involved in the events, and the relatives of the victims, for whom this place became a space for the elaboration of trauma. Moreover, if we consider what story is enunciated here, we may find two different levels: on the one hand, the story of the place; on the other, the many stories of the victims.

It would then be interesting to understand who is telling these stories, who the enunciator of such a place is. Analyzing all the texts and other elements, we may discern a chorus of voices speaking: the voices of the survivors, of the exiled, of the artists who exhibit here, of victims' relatives, of different institutions and associations. Of course, all these voices find a place in the museum because the real enunciator behind them, the Memory Commission, creates a space for them to express themselves freely, in accordance with the remit which the provincial government established.

---

[5] "Human rights organizations restored the humanity of victims and survivors [...] by strongly underplaying their political agency" (Daniele Salerno, in this volume).

[6] The Model Visitor is a theoretical concept from topological semiotics, built around the Model Reader of Eco (1969). The Model Reader is a textual figure, the union of all the interpretative steps that a text prepares for its reader and the necessary knowledge or encyclopaedia that it implies for it to be understood.

Nevertheless, these voices are multiplied and not reduced to one source of truth, since this polyphony is represented by the different styles of the texts and their multiple supports, to the point where the act of telling and sharing seems to be more important than what is told and shared. [7]

Moreover, the visitor is constantly invited to change his role and to speak. The distance between enunciator and addressee, which depends on the type of text and the resulting enunciation strategies, here almost dissolves: first, proximity is created through the space and the use of different kinds of trace, bringing together the visitors' and the victims' experience. Then, a sort of temporal proximity between enunciator and addressee is constructed: the interaction between them is strongly encouraged, making the museum a continuously rewritten text. This site of memory seems a living place that never rests, part of a social process of construction of the past that is still taking place, embracing and embodying what Robin Wagner-Pacifici (2010) calls "the restlessness of the event".[8]

We have noted several times that the way of constructing public memory may be a reaction to the ways in which violence was perpetrated (da Silva Catela 2009, 2015; Salerno 2016; Violi 2015). Since violence annulled victims' identities, names, legal status and rights, the elaboration of memory passes by the restoration of their identities. Since violence invaded many houses, stealing and abducting, and denied its victims one of the most public, yet intimate spaces, the grave, the division between public and private space or grief is almost completely erased. This process seems to be part of that "path of trauma" we mentioned earlier, which leads from the private experience of trauma to a collective traumatic heritage, to the point where it seems possible to define such memory as an "exemplar memory" (Todorov 1995). While a literal memory

---

[7] On the construction of the legitimacy and authority to speak about the dictatorship, we refer to Demaria's and Violi's contributions in this book, both focusing on the specific role of families and direct victims (*los afectados*) in the social discourse of memory, which is now moving to a wider and more shared representation.

[8] On this kind of restless process of memory, see in this book the essay by Lorusso, in which she analyzes the documentary *Habeas corpus*, on the memory of the Chilean dictatorship.

focuses on the individual level and tries to replicate the original event, the exemplar memory does not deny the singularity of the event, but uses it to create a general model for the future, in order to understand new situations with different agents. The individual and collective level of memory represented here or the juxtaposition of private and public seem to move in this direction. Thus, the meta-reflections that many texts propose on the museum itself, on the very act of showing and talking about violence, seem to transform it into a useful tool for public elaboration and debate. The conclusions drawn by Violi in this volume appropriately describe the APM museum:

> The overall meaning of such places is transformed in a stratified and multidirectional way: at the same time sites of memory, witnesses of past traumatic history, places of private mourning, spaces for political actions, they exceed the dimension of simple historical archives or monuments to become affective architectures, archives of feelings.

Finally, we must consider one of the most notable traits of this place: the persistence, exhibition and production of traces.

Tracing Memory/Tracing Memories, or, Why We Believe in Traces

As Carlo Ginzburg (1979) states, one of our ways of building knowledge is the so-called "evidential paradigm": we build theories of the world based on material traces, recollecting them as clues left in space by something past that is no longer present. Charles Sanders Peirce (1998) would say that in these sciences we are using one of our three epistemological schemes: the one based on indices, which allows us to develop hypothetical deductions about the past.

As Peirce explained, a proper index is a rare sign that had some sort of contact with the thing it refers to and, from that contact, retained some characteristic of that thing. These kinds of indices are "tracks" (Eco 1975), like a horse hoof in the mud. But we may also introduce photography into this class, since shapes and colours depend on how the light hits the film. For this mechanism, we "believe" in the pictures shown in the museum: their inner force comes from the knowledge of how they were produced (a lengthy scientific text explains it in detail). More or less the same thing happens with the only other "marks" from the museum: the names engraved in the cells. Even if these signs, like every semiotic object, can be used to lie, we tend to believe in them, seeing them as the result of a process of physical production (Sozzi 2015). Everything passes through the materiality of things: we as bodies perceive a sign, we read that sign as the result of the past presence of another body, hence we feel close to that very body through the materiality that stands in front of us, giving it a stronger sense of "reality".

More often, we use as signs things that do not share any common feature or visible mark with their referent; nevertheless we perceive them as traces, albeit a little less powerful. This depends on another necessary mechanism of the construction of the trace, which of course works also in the previous cases: we perceive something as the trace of an event or a person because we *know* that the event or person had some sort of physical contact with it (Violi, 2014b). We usually get knowledge from that system of memory we mentioned before or, as happens here, the place relays it to the visitor: for example, the descriptions of the objects exhibited link them to the victims, while the plaques in the *patios* describe the former D2. Two different spaces, or objects, thus stand before us: one, the space built by the accounts and texts of the past, which is lost forever; the other, the space we experience with our bodies, which resembles the one in that first, verbal story. Through our physical experience, on the one hand, we make a connection between these two spaces and perceive the entire account as "real"; on the other, we experience a sense of proximity with the event which creates a deep emotional engagement since "the indexicality does not only characterize places, but also, in a way, the actual experience of visiting them" (Violi 2016).

Finally, there is another kind of trace displayed by the museum: the one that is being produced nowadays. Keeping the place open, asking visitors to participate in the archive, always leaving a visitors' book in a room are all means of promoting the continuous inscription of traces. But these kinds of trace move from the present toward the future, writing and rewriting a collective polyphonic story that starts from the past and reaches tomorrow, not only today. The APM museum is an extremely clear example of how traces can be perceived as tools against re-interpretations of the past, as though their physical materiality could guarantee only one version of the facts, "the real one".

References

Assmann, J. (1992). *Das kulturelle Gedächtnis: Schrift, Erinnerung und politische Identität in frühen Hochkulturen*. Monaco: C. H. Beck.

Benveniste, E. (1970). L'appareil formel de l'énonciation. *Langages*, 5(17), 12-18.

da Silva Catela, L. (2009). Lo invisible revelado: El uso de fotografías como (re)presentación de la desaparición de personas en Argentina. In C. Feld & J. Stites Mor (eds.), *El pasado que miramos. Memoria e imagen ante la historia reciente*. Buenos Aires: Paidós.

da Silva Catela, L. (2015). Staged memories: Conflicts and tensions in Argentine public memory sites. *Memory Studies*, 8(I), 9-21.

Demaria, C. (2014). *Il trauma, l'archivio, il testimone. La semiotica, il documentario e la rappresentazione del "reale"*. Bologna: Bononia University Press.

Eco, U. (1979). *Lector in fabula*. Milan: Bompiani.

Eco, U. (1984). *Semiotica e filosofia del linguaggio*. Turin: Einaudi.

Ginzburg, C. (1979). Clues: Roots of a scientific paradigm. *Theory and Society*, 7(3), 273-288.

Lotman, J. M. (2005). On the semiosphere. *Semeiotiké: Sign Systems Studies*, 33(1), 205-229. (Original work published 1990.)

Lotman, J. M. (2009). *Culture and explosion*. Berlin: Mouton de Gruyter.

Mazzucchelli, F. (2010). *Urbicidio. Il senso dei luoghi tra distruzioni e ricostruzioni in ex Jugoslavia*. Bologna: Bononia University Press.

Peirce, C. S. (1998). *The collected papers of Charles Sanders Peirce*. Bristol: Thoemmes Press.

Robles, M. (2010). *La búsqueda. Una entrevista con Charlie Moore*. Córdoba: Ediciones del Pasaje.

Salerno, D. (2016). Políticas del duelo: Perspectivas semióticas. Unpublished paper. Córdoba: Universidad Nacional de Córdoba. 10 March.

Todorov, T. (1995). *Les abus de la mémoire*. Paris: Les Editions Arléa.

Verón, E. (1988). *La semiosis social. Fragmentos de una teoría de la discursividad*. Barcelona: Gedisa.

Verón, E. (2013). *La semiosis social 2. Ideas, momentos, interpretantes*. Buenos Aires: Paidós.

Violi, M. P. (2012). "E' successo proprio qui." Gli ambienti come testimoni: Analisi del caso cileno. *Lexia*, 9-10, 95-132.

Violi, M. P. (2013). Dealing with the past: Politiche della memoria e discorso giuridico: il caso spagnolo. *Versus: Quaderni di studi semiotici*, 116, 31-59.

Violi, M. P. (2014a). Spectacularising trauma: The experientialist visitor of memory museums. In R. Van der Laarse, F. Mazzucchelli, & C. Reijnen (eds.), Special issue of *Versus: Quaderni di studi semiotici*, 119, 51-70.

Violi, M. P. (2014b). *Paesaggi della memoria. Il trauma, lo spazio, la storia*. Milan: Bompiani.

Violi, M. P. (2015). Immagini per ricordare, immagini per agire: Il caso della Guerra Sucia argentina. *Lexia*, 17-18, 619-649.

Violi, M. P. (2016). Traumascape: The case of the 9/11 memorial. *LA+ Interdisciplinary Journal of Landscape and Architecture*, 3, 72-76.

Wagner-Pacifici, R. (2010). Theorizing the restlessness of events. *American Journal of Sociology*, 115(5) (March), 1351-1386.

Live to Tell

Norma Fatala

> The problem for them, for the real killers, is that I never was a policeman. And I lived to tell the tale.
> Carlos R. Moore (Robles 2010)

This essay attempts a sociosemiotic approach to the narratives of survivors of the clandestine centres of detention, torture, and extermination (CCD) that existed in Argentina between 1975 and 1983.[1] The focus of research has been on statements published in "actuality books" (*libros de actualidad*), within the framework of interviews or conversations.[2]

I have referred to the books that make up the corpus as "actuality books" because they are so in many senses; in the first place, because of their very subject. As François Hartog (2007: 234; my translation) says:

> The imprescriptibility "by nature" of crimes against humanity founds a "juridical atemporality" that can be perceived as a form of the past in the present, of a present past, or, still better, as an extension of the present, considering the present proper to the process.

---

[1] Dating the beginning of state terrorism is quite a controversial matter, since it affects political interests (cf. Tcach 2014). The fact is that there are almost 700 forced disappearances reported before the 1976 military coup, involving not only the Armed Forces (the CDD Escuelita de Famaillá, in Tucumán, begins operations in February 1975, in the context of the Operativo Independencia); but also "task groups" formed by policemen and civilians, promoted, protected or tolerated by the state apparatus, which exercised illicit violence in order to terrorize the opposition and the population at large (cf. Robles 2010; Bufano & Teixidó 2015).

[2] Such is the case of *Ese infierno* (That Hell), in which five women (survivors of the ESMA—The Higher Naval School of Mechanics) talk among themselves about their experience in the clandestine camp.

In the second place, every construction of a selective past, as Williams (1997: 137-139) noted many years ago, involves present interests and projects itself into the future.

Last but not least, their actuality is confirmed by the *discursive field* (Angenot 1989: 91-93) in which they are produced. In fact, testimonies contained in the books have already been presented before the courts and human rights organizations; but their (re)production in published materials prefigures a broader public and transforms them into a *production of truth* with polemical implications, designed to affect public opinion about the recent past and, therefore, collective memory.

Nevertheless, these attempts at documenting barbarism are founded on experience and thus become inseparable from the subjective construction of enunciators. The enunciation dispositif (Verón 2004: 173) appears, then, as a document within the document, which offers an entrance into the effects of terror on singular and collective identities.

In order to give a brief report on research involving a very dense corpus and much heartbreaking reading, I shall concentrate on the ethical, subjective and identitarian constructions deployed in/by the narratives.

Telling

According to Mariana Tello (2013), it is common to find in the testimonies of Argentine survivors explicit references to the "unspeakable", "unimaginable" character of concentrationary experience, similar to those present in some classical writings on Nazi camps, such as Primo Levi's or Jorge Semprum's.

Nevertheless, the proliferation of testimonies driven by the reopening of trials for crimes against humanity, as well as the proliferation of statements in published material are indicative of an extended *drive to tell*, usually presented as the fulfillment of an ethical command: survivors must make known the truth about state terrorism, for the sake of those who died. However, the straightforward logic of this obligation is but a starting point in a complex tissue of discourse.

Let us return for a moment to the epigraph, which throws light on the *pathos* that runs through the discourse of many survivors. "The problem for them, for the real killers, is that I never was a policeman. And I lived to tell the tale", says Carlos Raymundo Moore (Robles 2010: 232, my translation), nicknamed Charlie, a prisoner in the much feared Intelligence Department of the Córdoba Police (D2) for six years, from November 1974 until November 1980, when he fled to Brazil, where he wrote, in a few days, a very full declaration which he presented to Amnesty International. His statement was based not just on sheer memory but also on the bits of information, written on small pieces of cigarette paper, which he had been able to get out of prison over the years.

It could be said, then, that the artisanal and risky collection of information gives credibility to the three propositions included in my short quotation, involving the construction of the adversary ("the real killers"), the description of his own position ("I never was a policeman") and the ethical command ("I lived to tell the tale"). Let me add that, after his first months in prison, Moore was considered a traitor by his former comrades, but in his story (in his *autofiction*, as Robin would say)[3] he appears as the freelance operator of a huge counterintelligence scheme that may have saved 60 or 70 lives.[4]

I have chosen this very extreme case because it shows how state terrorism transformed the clichés of political prison in Argentina and triggered new forms of resistance, which rendered fuzzy the clear-cut opposition between the hero and the traitor. It also shows that, after state terrorism, survival required an explanation.

Survival and Suspicion
In terms of the effects of state terrorism on political or social militancy, survival could well apply to a vast number of individuals: those who withdrew into their private lives (internal exiles); those who left the country (external exiles); those who survived prison or clandestine camps. But the dramatic differences, even between the two last cases,

---

[3] In the terms of Régine Robin (1996: 61-2), *autofiction* does not designate a false or invented story, it rather signals the impossibility of (objective) self-narrative.

[4] The operation consisted of implicating as many prisoners as he could in the take-over of the Military Factory at Villa María by the ERP (10 August 1974), in order to have them legalized, since the military planned to stage an "exemplary" trial of that case (cf. Robles 2010; Carreras 2010).

impose particular conditions upon the narrative of the experience.

Although there were many deaths in legal prisons (most of them as the result of shootings disguised as attempted escapes or armed confrontations), their numbers (approximately 130 people, according to Garaño & Pertot (2007)) constitute a reduced proportion of the more than 6,000 political prisoners who occupied the jails from 1974 to 1983.

In the case of forced disappearance, the *returning subjects*, as Calveiro (1998) calls survivors from the clandestine centres, are a small percentage—between five and ten per cent—of those kidnapped.[5]

There are, nevertheless, some differences in situations that should be taken into account. In the first place, the date of *the fall*—that is to say, the date of capture: death was an almost certain fate from the middle of 1975 to the first half of 1977, by which time the political-military organizations—Montoneros and the PRT-ERP—could be said to have been decimated. Afterwards, death became more selective.[6] Casual or unimportant victims of kidnapping could find their way to legal prisons or even to freedom.[7] "Only half of the fifty prisoners that were in La Perla arrived at San Martin [Penitentiary]; the rest were shot", remembers a survivor captured in September 1977 (Mariani & Gómez 2012: 328).[8] Although the figures are shocking, they show the proportional variation in the probabilities of survival.

Nevertheless, the differences underline the status of the long-term survivors, those who were caught in the first

---

[5] Although the official number of forced disappearances—that is to say, of those that were reported—totals about 13,000 victims; real numbers could easily double the figure, considering the fact that many claims were never filed because of material impossibility (some families were decimated), ideological differences, fear or ignorance.

[6] ERP (Ejército Revolucionario del Pueblo [People's Revolutionary Army]) was the armed branch of the PRT (Partido Revolucionario de los Trabajadores [Workers' Revolutionary Party]).

[7] Calveiro (1998: 44-45) includes in this category persons kidnapped because they had witnessed illegal proceedings or were relatives or visitors of military targets.

[8] La Perla (12km from Córdoba city) was the largest CCD outside Buenos Aires. It belonged to the III Army Corps.

stages of state terrorism and outlived their stay in the extermination camps. They were generally put to work on diverse tasks by their captors and thus regained at least the relative possibility of *moving, seeing and hearing*, activities from which the rest of the prisoners were banned. Their living conditions were also better and they were allowed to contact their families and even visit them. Although they were kept under surveillance, they were generally freed long before legal prisoners.

The stigma of collaboration that falls on this group of prisoners depends, then, not only on survival but on this differential treatment. A survivor of the last phase of the dictatorship describes her experience in this way:

> I was questioned by a "broken prisoner" [*un quebrado*]. I know he was a prisoner because I was without the blindfold and I saw him [...]. I understand that the contribution of collaborators to Justice is superior to ours, because they worked with the military files and went about the barracks without a blindfold. However, I consider that terror is one thing—saving your life or the lives of your son and husband—and collaborating with the military another. (Mariani & Gómez 2012: 328)

We can see how many questions are interwoven in such a short paragraph: the proof of a particular collaboration; the general traits that would define a collaborator (moving and seeing) and the subtle line that divides giving information under torture from collaborating.

On the other hand, Moore divides the long-term survivors in La Perla into three groups: those who gave information under torture, those who collaborated doing tasks, and those who changed sides (Robles 2010: 208). Here, the line of treachery isolates those who changed sides, that is to say, those who chose to become one of them, while the rest are considered victims, forced to collaborate by extreme violence, but retaining their status as prisoners.

Now, if we put together the second group—those who collaborated doing tasks—with the superior contribution to justice mentioned in the first quotation, we arrive at the central paradox of the *returning subjects*: survival makes them suspects, but it also transforms them into the only agents who share with the agents of genocide a firsthand knowledge of the clandestine devices of extermination. Their statements, therefore, are the cornerstone of any attempt to achieve "truth and justice", as human rights lawyers understood quite early on. They had to labour, nevertheless, to convince the human rights organizations, mainly composed of relatives of the disappeared, that any expectation of bringing the agents of genocide to justice implied necessarily a symbolic transformation: the *becoming victim* of those up to that point considered traitors.

Knowing

Knowledge seems to be the key to the social reintegration of survivors. But we must look deeper into this harshly acquired competence. If we do, we find that information (collecting, systematizing, communicating data) is at the core of these survivors' trauma, but, at the same time, their only way out of it. In the clandestine camps, they were not only tortured to produce information, but were given the task of analyzing information (for instance, in newspapers) for the military.

On those terms, collecting information against their captors was, as Canetti (1973) would say, the only possible means of *reversal* for human beings subjected to an almost total power. This form of individual resistance gave purpose to survival and helped them regain the human status their torturers had endeavoured to crush: if they had been forced to tell in order to live; they would now, of their own free will, live to tell. Thus, subjection becomes *simulation* and information becomes the gift, the *object of value* which survivors would bring from their descent into hell. However, on the other hand, I must register here some differences that show the multiple nuances of survival. *Simulating* or *acting as if* are recurrent notions in the discourse of survivors, but they frequently refer purely to survival (*Ese infierno* is paradigmatic in this sense). In such cases, the value of information is an afterthought that appears with the return of democracy.

On the other hand, the confluence of simulation and purposeful collection of information anticipates reversal and describes an enunciator that, still in prison, had managed to regain some of his previous competences. In some cases, it is even possible to detect in the statements an undercurrent of self-satisfaction, even superiority, at having outwitted the captors:

The military made a mistake in letting us live. We are the product of their mistakes. They should have killed us all; but they did not do it and now we are stating what really happened.[9]

Los compañeros (The Comrades), a non-fiction novel written by Rolo Diez, a former militant of the PRT, gives yet another twist to the relation information-survival. Towards the end of the book, an exiled survivor receives the visit of a Party intelligence official who even stays the night at their flat. The survivor and his wife are extremely moved by this gesture of confidence and conciliation. The visitor, who is also the narrator, listens to the survivor's story, including his own collaboration, with remarkable equanimity; but the real object of the visit is to learn if the survivor has any information about the existence of a "filter" (a spy) among the members of the Party leadership in Córdoba in the seventies—a real and unsolved question that still provokes arguments (see *Sudestada* 2015).

Narrative Identities
Information, no matter how important, is but a part of the tale. The telling accomplishes other functions, enacting subjects caught in a space-time, producing identities, introducing pathos... In Deleuzean terms, all the properties and qualities of a particular *assemblage* (Deleuze & Guattari 1987: 503-504).

In an article on the incidence of penitentiary treatment upon identitarian constructions of political prisoners and, more precisely, on a classification dreamt up by the last dictatorship which divided "subversive delinquents" into three groups, where "recoverability" was measured in inverse proportion to resistance,[10] Santiago Garaño (2010:

---

[9] Fragment of Piero Di Monti's statement in the trial of Brandalisi et al., quoted in Mariani & Gómez (2012: 98; my translation).

[10] "a) Group 1: (Resistant prisoners)
Negative attitude: they present traits of irrecoverability. Unruly. They have no symptoms of demoralization. They form groups and exercise leadership. They exhibit a strong ideological foundation and a sense of belonging to the SDB [Subversive Delinquents' Bands].
b) Group 2: (Undefined prisoners)
Their attitudes are not clear or cannot be specified. They exhibit

129) concludes that, in legal prisons, differential grouping contributed, basically among the "irrecoverable" prisoners (G1), to the consolidation of group identities, loyalties and comradeship which, after liberation, allowed the construction of a group narrative that, in large measure, determines "what is memorable and how the experience of political prison is to be remembered" (my translation).

I cannot agree with the almost exclusionary productivity which Garaño assigns to penitentiary power, but I share his view about the importance of collective identification in the feedback on resistance and also about the risk implied in considering the narrative of the prison experience of the strongest, "as if it were the same for all political prisoners". Furthermore, I believe it would be even riskier to take the survivors' narrative as the camp experience of all the sequestered, for most of whom self-narration has become impossible.

Both legal and illegal prisoners shared the experience of capture and torture, but the place of detention determined irreparable divergences. According to legal prisoners, death was an ever-present possibility: they could die in torture, they could be "transferred"[11] in order to manufacture an escape shooting, they could be killed as a reprisal for actions carried out by their organizations, or they may simply attract the most brutal punishment from a prison officer.[12] But in

---

doubt. They require more observation and to be subjected to PA [Psychological Action] in order to be defined.
c) Group 3: (Ductile prisoners)
They do not form groups with the resistant prisoners. They tend to collaborate with the PS [Penitentiary Service] staff. They show symptoms of demoralization. Some of them may make public their rejection or disown ideological positions related to the SDB. They are willing to enter into a process of recovery [*recuperación*]" (Special Order N° 13-77 ("Recovery of boarders [*pensionistas*]"). Copy N° 2, Command Zone 1; Buenos Aires, dated July 1977, [p.3]. Personal archive of a former political prisoner, Córdoba, Argentina, in Garaño (2010: 122-3; my translation)).

[11] Taking out prisoners to shoot them or dump them in the sea was euphemistically called "transfer" by the military.
[12] Such is the case of the physician José René Moukarzel, killed on 15 July 1976, in Córdoba's Penitentiary (UP1) (Cf. Garaño & Pertot 2007: 208). Moukarzel's wife, Alicia De Cicco, had been killed in December 1975 in the CDD Campo de La Rivera (Córdoba). According to one of La Perla's survivors, interrogation officer

clandestine centres, devoid of legal restrictions of any kind, death became almost a certainty.

Even the rudimentary legality allowed by a dictatorial regime made a difference in the conditions of captivity. Although there was a perpetual changing of rules, a moving of prisoners from one penitentiary to another, and all manner of difficulties created for them and their families; the legal status meant having a lawyer and, when conditions allowed it, receiving visits, news and packages from relatives, being able to talk to other prisoners, and even maintain collective partisan practices. In their everyday life, legal prisoners were neither blindfolded nor restricted in their mobility by handcuffs, shackles or fetters, as happened in the camps. More important still, even a terrorist state had to account for legal prisoners, but *desaparecidos* had no "entity", as the dictator Jorge Videla said.[13]

In the concentrationary regime, besides information, the prime objective of unlimited torture, for an indefinite time, was the destruction of collective identifications, the breaking up of solidarities and loyalties, the reduction of totally helpless individuals to their own resources, which explains the recurrence of the phrase "each one did what he/she could" in different stories. Survival appears, then, as a rather solitary enterprise, a personal experience ruled by the principle of affection, where no abstraction is possible (see Calveiro 1998: 131)

I have thought very much about the statement of a survivor from La Perla. She says: "The dead have no past, they have memory; I have a past, because I am alive" (Mariani & Gómez 2012: 260; my translation). Inadvertently,

---

Héctor Vergez told them that he had strangled her himself, incensed by the fact that such a beautiful woman would not speak and looked at him with hatred (Liliana Callizo's testimony, *El Diario del Juicio*, 28 May 2012).

[13] "As long as he remains so, the missing person [*desaparecido*] is a mystery. If the man were to appear alive, he would be treated as 'x', if appearance confirmed he was dead, he would count as 'z'; but as long as he is missing, he cannot have a special treatment: a disappeared person has no entity [*entidad*], is neither alive nor dead, is missing. In which case, we cannot do anything." Jorge R. Videla [1979], in *El Día*, 17 May 2013 (my translation).

perhaps, she has distinguished two problematic fields: the production of collective memory and the coming to terms with one's own past, almost along the lines of the opposition social/individual. But dichotomies, we know, are only heuristic tools. Social and individual fields overlap in real life and, in this case, overlap in the figure of the un-returned subjects, the truly disappeared.

From this point of view, it seems necessary to consider survivors' stories on at least two levels of analysis: one dealing with the *expository* sequences of their narrative, basically consisting of *information* about state terrorist methodology and hard data about the victims and victimizers (names, dates, places…) and another dealing with strictly *narrative* components, basically, the configuration of the first-person narrator, his/her pragmatic and cognitive transformations, his/her relation with the other subjects.

The first level, as we have seen, concerns the production of truth, the transmission of an object of value (first-hand knowledge) that, at the same time, reinstates the survivor in the *socius* as a victim of state terrorism.

The second has to do with the basic form of getting to grips with one's own past: the construction of what Ricoeur (1996: 147) calls a *narrative identity*, a dynamic identity that exerts a mediating function between the poles of sameness and ipseity, incorporating discontinuities or variations into permanence in time.

In the discourse of survivors, this operation heals the identitarian breach produced by their concentrationary experience and especially by torture, which frequently evokes a metaphor of death: "There is no coming back from torture", says a survivor; "I died in La Perla", says another (cf. Mariani & Gómez 2012: 248 and 54; my translation). But the implosion of individual identities also implied a loosening of collective identifications and loyalties, overshadowed by guilt. Self-justification, therefore, plays an important role in the discourse of the returning subjects and filters their recollection of their less fortunate comrades. The dead are, in that sense, delivered into the hands of the living.

Causes and Hazards

Among the long-term survivors there is an almost unanimous assertion of the hazardous character of survival. Collaboration, they argue and even exemplify, did not ensure life. Although they admit to a desire to live, the recognition of survival as an option (in the Sartrean sense) appears as a substantial node of the personal trauma that must remain unsaid. It is possible, nevertheless, to assert that there were prisoners who *chose to die* (Actis *et al*. 2001: 157-158).

The discourse of hazardous survival relies for its reality effect on the description of the irrationality and perversion of the agents of genocide, their internal struggles, their paranoia, and their ravings about their power over life and death... But the reasoning has a sophistic angle since, according to the same stories, there is nothing hazardous in the non-survival of those who refused information or collaboration. These cases, nevertheless, are promptly passed over, in order to reinforce the thesis that everybody said something; in which case, resistance consisted in giving false or useless information or retaining as much information as one could.

Since their enunciative stance requires the dismantling of the opposition hero/ traitor, "old" prisoners—including those who write scholarly works—find it hard to recount unbreakable resistance and death.[14] Calveiro arrives at an aporetic solution by shifting suspicion onto the dead:

> Among survivors, there are many who resisted torture and surely that first victory helped them to tolerate the hood, the isolation, the pressures and all they suffered until their liberation. (Calveiro 1998: 74; my translation)

> There are no heroes in a concentration camp.
> The irreducible subject who dies during torture without giving any sort of collaboration is the one who comes closest to that notion, but there are no proofs of that, there is no exhibition of the heroic deed that could be testified to without the shadow of a doubt. Resistance to torture is a solitary representation of the tortured before his/her torturers. (Calveiro 1998: 129; my translation)

---

[14] There are, of course, exceptions to this rule. Some survivors, like Liliana Callizo, include in their testimonies many instances of death brought about by unbroken resistance.

It is easier to find stories of enduring resistance in the testimony of casual victims or even in the statements of repentant military personnel. For instance, former sergeant Víctor Ibáñez recalls the torture and death of a member of the political Buro of the PRT in these words:

> Menna was tortured for months and he never said a thing. I don't know how that man could stand it. They would leave him with the automatic electric prod on, while the interrogators went to have lunch; and not once, but day after day. In the end, he won the respect of the task group [interrogators, torturers]. Anyhow, they "transferred" him like everyone else. (Almirón 1999: Part II, Chap. XVI; my translation)

It can be noted, though, that the sergeant admires the resistance, but does not think it very useful, since it did not lead to survival: an un-paradoxical coincidence with the discourse of some survivors who subtly undervalue stubborn resistance or open confrontation with the military as a lack of the ability to survive.

Them and Us
If torture was designed to alienate the victim from his/her collective political identification, being chosen to collaborate or to do tasks introduced another problematic node: the relationship with the victimizers. The forced coexistence of kidnappers and kidnapped may have brought about a mutual process of "humanization" in the perception of the adversary, as Calveiro (1998: 96-98) puts it; but, according to survivors' stories, it was a process attended by confusion, fear, distrust and simulation. Furthermore, this ambiguous closeness drew a line between the old prisoners and the transitory inhabitants of the extermination centres, which explains why the relationship of long-term survivors to the rest of the prisoners is a disturbing aspect of the narratives.

Separation between chosen and not-chosen prisoners becomes quite evident where there were different living quarters, as in the ESMA. In La Perla, where all prisoners shared the same physical space,[15] there is less talk of the

---

[15] Only in 1978, when there were just five "old" prisoners left, were they taken out of the barracks and allowed to sleep in an

human side of victimizers and more emphasis on the human tragedy. Self-narrative encompasses, then, multiple stories that rescue the absent from anonymity: assassinated teenagers, young mothers separated from their just-born children and "transferred" to death, people who agonized in the camp as the result of torture, people each one knew and loved... Stories that construct a *community of suffering*, an aggregate of individuals not devoid of human solidarity, but deprived of a political horizon by sheer terror. Since militancy and partisan discipline seem to have receded to a past prior to capture and torture, the ethical limit is fixed by the command: if someone gets off, he/she must tell what is happening.

Telling the passion of thousands, after having outlived it, is not, however, an easy task. A legitimizing gesture common to most stories consists of the reference to the survivor's conversations with renowned figures who shared captivity in the camp before being assassinated. Besides the obvious importance of attesting to the presence and fate of political and union leaders in the camp, it could be said that as subjects of the enunciated-enunciation (Greimas), quoted as sources of good-will, support and advice, those leaders become the model or ideal reader (Eco) of the survivors' stories: someone who understands the awful exceptionality of forced disappearance and the extreme conditions it imposes on its victims.

Nevertheless, there are inconsistencies that are difficult to surmount. Principally, as regards the timing of the telling and the (lack of) identification with the non-returned. For instance, some survivors of the ESMA state that they did not attempt to escape or to communicate with the relatives of other prisoners during their outings or even to report the situation to international organizations after being liberated, in order not to harm their *compañeros* (comrades). There is a sort of virtuous reaction against statements presented in Europe as early as 1979 and 1980, oriented, we may presume, *to stopping the practice of forced disappearance* (cf. Actis *et al.* 2001: 183).[16]

---

office (Mariani & Gómez 2012: 182-184).
[16] According to Calveiro (1998: 125), staff prisoners agreed to keep silent about their experience "until the last of them was set free" (my translation).

Compañeros, therefore, cannot refer to the blindfolded, immobilized, anonymous numbers that inhabited Capucha and Capuchita, the quarters of the non-chosen prisoners in the ESMA. They can only refer to other members of staff, the group of recoverable prisoners chosen by navy officers. By semantic displacement, the old word has come to describe an entirely new situation: a collective identification built not around ideological principles but around a new value, unthinkable for the militants they used to be: survival.

Survival takes the place of ideals in the configuration of an unstable community of long-term prisoners. In the first testimonies, it was usual to find criticisms or even accusations regarding other prisoners' behaviour;[17] but the reopening of the trials has brought about an almost corporate defence of the victim status for everyone:

> I do not agree with some survivors' attitudes in La Perla; but I must acknowledge that all of us were victims of the same destructive system. All of us, without exception, entered as victims and left as victims. (Mariani & Gómez 2012: 186; my translation)

> We have to finish once and for all with the arguments among survivors and concentrate on the real victimizers who were the military. (Mariani & Gómez 2012: 257; my translation)

The last quotation, I believe, shows clearly the reasoning that underlies these changes: the possibility of achieving justice (i.e., the conviction of the military) merits forgetting some prisoners' weaknesses. Trials appear, then, as the final confrontation (on a pure symbolic level) of survivors and their injurers on an equal footing, that of citizens. In Verón's (1987) terms, it means the discursive construction of the other as an adversary (a *negative other, a counter-receiver*) and the demonstration of his discourse as absolutely false, but, at the same time, it requires anticipating the *destructive reading* of the opponent:

> Of course the military speak ill of us! They do it to defend themselves. They know we are their main

---

[17] Calveiro (1998: 73-76) attempts a classification of prisoners.

enemies and it's easy to understand that they will do everything to discredit us. (Mariani & Gómez 2012: 126; my translation)

Giving testimony on the perverse workings of state terrorism, it seems, not only accomplishes the ethical command so frequently invoked, but it performs *reversal* as well. Contrary to the pious tendency to circumvent the victim's personal feelings on behalf of abstract justice,[18] I would propose that in crimes against humanity, the intensity of personal feelings gives us the measure of the irreconcilable nature of the crimes.

In the discourse of survivors, especially those who collected evidence against their captors, the wish for reversal (for the opportunity of *telling*) justifies and reinforces the drive for survival.

In Sum

From a juridical and social point of view, survivors' testimonies are invaluable; they belong to the kind of documents that *change history,* even if they are open (as every discourse is) to different and antagonistic (that is to say, political) readings. As regards collective *memory*, I believe their effects are multiple and heterogeneous and will be better assessed in the long term.

As survivors say, they are the memory of genocide and their efforts to bring the military to justice for crimes against humanity—a belated answer to the forty years of struggle of the affected families—may impress on the common doxa the virtues of democracy, but it is difficult to predict the scope of reception since half the population never lived under a military dictatorship and military power is but a shadow of what it used to be.

On the other hand, their fixation on the military was amenable to the administration of memory (and forgetting) operated by Kirchnerist governments, which dated the start of state terrorism to the military coup (24 March 1976),

---

[18] A witness felt moved to explain that in recognizing the agents of genocide he had deliberately disrespected military rank, not as "revenge" but as "vindication" of himself and his dead comrades (Mariani & Gómez 2012: 181).

eliding the responsibility of politicians, union leaders, regular police and para-police organizations for illegal repression long before that time. Collective memory, it seems, does not require a working definition of state terrorism.

Nevertheless, given the present state of discourse, I believe the deeper impact of the survivors' narratives on collective memory may be political, of a negative kind. Survivors proclaim themselves not only the memory of genocide, but also, with scant analysis, the memory of defeat. In order to demonstrate the perversion of the military personnel brought to trial, and to explain their own survival, they produce and reproduce the effects of terror. But in our hedonistic, egotistical times, ruled by self-interest, their survival does not cause moral ripples; while their stories may affect the relatives of disappeared people and a progressive minority, for the general public, torn between clientelism and political disaffection, harassed by economic and labour demands, they just go to prove the unfeasibility of any alternative notion of politics.

References

Actis, M., Aldini, C., Gardella, L., Lewin, M., & Tokar, E. (2001). *Ese infierno. Conversaciones de cinco mujeres sobrevivientes de la ESMA*. Buenos Aires: Sudamericana.

Almirón, F. (1999). *Campo Santo. Los asesinatos del Ejército en Campo de Mayo. Testimonios del ex sargento Víctor Ibáñez*. Buenos Aires: Editorial 21.

Angenot, M. (1989). *1889. Un état du discours social*. Quebec: Le Préambule.

Anon. (2012). Megacausa La Perla, 44th day. *El Diario del Juicio*, 28 May. H.I.J.O.S Córdoba. At **www.eldiariodeljuicio.com.ar/?q=content/día-44-28-05**, accessed 20 October 2015.

Bufano, S. & Teixidó, L. (2015). *Perón y la triple A. Las 20 advertencias a Montoneros*. Buenos Aires: Sudamericana.

Calveiro, P. (1998). *Poder y desaparición. Los campos de concentración en Argentina*. Buenos Aires: Colihue.

Canetti, E. (1973). *Crowds and power*. London: Penguin Books.

Carreras, J. (2010). Madre noche. Algunas consideraciones sobre el libro de Charlie Moore. At **www.juliocarreras.com.ar/charliemoore-libro.html29/11/10**, accessed

20 September 2015.
Deleuze, G. & Guattari, F. (1987). *A thousand plateaus: Capitalism and schizophrenia* (trans. B. Massumi). Minneapolis: University of Minnesota Press.
Diez, R. (2000). *Los compañeros*. La Plata: De la campana.
Garaño, S. & Pertot, W. (2007). *Detenidos-aparecidos. Presas y presos políticos desde Trelew a la dictadura.* Buenos Aires: Biblos.
Garaño, S. (2010). El "tratamiento" penitenciario y su dimensión productiva de identidades entre los presos políticos (1974-1983). *Revista Iberoamericana*, 10(40), 113-130.
Hartog, F. (2007). *Regímenes de historicidad. Presentismo y experiencias del tiempo.* Mexico: Universidad Iberoamericana, Departamento de Historia.
Mariani, A., & Gómez, J. A. (2012). *La Perla. Historia y testimonios de un campo de concentración.* Buenos Aires: Ed. Aguilar.
Montero, H. (2015). ¿Quién traicionó a Santucho? *Sudestada*, 14(136), March-April, 4-17.
Ricoeur, P. (1996). *Sí mismo como otro.* Mexico: Siglo XXI.
Robin, R. (1996). *Identidad, memoria y relato. La imposible narración de sí mismo.* Buenos Aires: Secr. Posgrado Fac. de Ciencias Sociales/CBC.
Robles, M. (2010). *La búsqueda. Una entrevista con Charlie Moore.* Córdoba: Ediciones del pasaje—Comisión y Archivo Provincial de la Memoria.
Tcach, C. (2014). La memoria como cuestión de estado. In *La Voz del Interior*, 23 March.
Tello, M. (2013). Narrar lo "inenarrable", imaginar lo "inimaginable", comprender lo "incomprensible": Aproximaciones a las memorias sobre la experiencia concentracionaria desde una perspectiva antropológica. *Eadaem Ultraque Europa*, 9(14), 211-244.
Verón, E. (1987). La palabra adversativa: Observaciones sobre la enunciación política. In E. Verón, L. Arfuch, M. M. Chirico, *et al.* (eds.), *El discurso político. Lenguajes y acontecimientos.* Buenos Aires: Hachette, pp. 12-26.
Verón, E. (2004). Cuando leer es hacer: La enunciación en la prensa gráfica. *Fragmentos de un tejido.* Barcelona: Gedisa.
Williams, R. (1997). *Marxismo y literatura.* Barcelona: Península/Biblos.

The Closet, the Terror, the Archive: Confession and Testimony in LGBT Memories of Argentine State Terrorism

Daniele Salerno

State terrorism in Argentina forced LGBT people into hiding or into seeking refuge abroad, and their organizations, such as the Frente de Liberación Homosexual (FLH), were dissolved. In the aftermath of the dictatorship, LGBT organizations drew largely on "the playbook used by the Argentine human rights community" (Encarnación 2016: 109), joining the human rights movement and their struggles for memory and identity in the transitional period.

This essay aims to make a contribution to the study of how LGBT people entered the post-dictatorship memory regime (Crenzel 2008), a topic still neglected in the study of the transition to democracy in the Southern Cone. By mixing different discursive practices stemming both from LGBT transnational political practices (e.g. coming out as militant practice) and from post-conflict and transitional cultures (e.g. oral interviews with witnesses and the public display of past atrocities), how do LGBT people construct the memory of state terrorism, join the human rights movement and consequently reposition their subjectivities?

I will analyze a specific textual object: a section of the Archivo de Historia Oral (Oral History Archive) in Córdoba devoted to the memory of sexual repression. What I argue in the analysis is that the memory archive is a complex enunciative device which, through the oral history interview as a genre and as a discursive practice, allows interviewees to reconfigure their own subjectivity. Passing from the police interrogation and the request for truth in confession during the dictatorship to the narration of their lives and the demand for testimony, the interview as an "interrogation of the subject" resignifies the very act of "coming out of the closet" and of disclosing the truth about the self ("I am gay"/"I was born a male") and state terrorism ("I was imprisoned"/"I was abused and mistreated").

The Ex-D2 as Enunciative Device: The *Palabra* between Space and Document

While Paola Sozzi (in this volume) has focused on material traces and images, my contribution will focus on the voices, in the sense of the spoken word in the orality which we can find in the Oral History Archive, part of the Archivo Provincial de la Memoria (Provincial Memory Archive) of Córdoba.

The memory archive is a complex enunciative device (see Violi 2014: 116-118) that assembles different semiotic substances (stones, written documents, voices, pictures, etc.) and discursive genres and practices (the museum, the interview, the archive itself), in accordance with the aims and values listed in the provincial memory law that created the archive: to construct, preserve and transmit the memory of the atrocities that occurred during state terrorism, and to develop methodologies and adequate tools for "keeping it alive" in the struggle against impunity and in support of human rights. The Oral History Area was opened in 2007 and today preserves 100 video recorded interviews with a total of 186 hours of recording. The aim of the oral history archive is also to give voice to victims, victims' relatives, and survivors in order to understand better the use and meanings of the space of the former D2.

The museum, the memory archive and, as we shall see, the interviews reframe the place and the stories that are linked to it, trying to invert their axiology and the meaning of certain practices: from a place of human rights violation to a place for the struggle for human rights; from a place to hide atrocities to a place to disclose and report them; from a place where people's identities and lives were hidden, disarticulated by violence and where some began their path towards *desaparición* (see Violi in this volume) to a place of visibility where the faces, names and stories of the victims are displayed everywhere and where an interview can also function not only as testimony but also as an affirmation of identity, a "right to be, what one is" (see Demaria in this volume). If we read it as a semiosphere, following Juri Lotman, and within a cultural semiotic perspective (Lorusso 2015), we see how this process of resignification and "repolarization" of discursive practices is in action on different discursive levels, informing different practices and semiotic substances.

The oral history archive now brings together

testimonies from different categories of people. As the website says, the interviews are not restricted to political prisoners but also include "trade unionists, students, artists, intellectuals, homosexuals". The political prisoner assumes a central role in the oral archive, which is, however, composed of eleven thematic collections totalling 91 interviews which are currently available and listed on the website.[1]

The setting of the interview includes the interviewee, the interviewer and a cameraman who, although invisible, actively takes part in the construction of the meaning of the interview. The protocol consists of different steps from a first meeting and pre-interview that help to personalize the questions, to the actual recorded interview. The core of this practice is the reconstruction of the biography which the interviewee assembles by him/herself with the help of the questions, linking the past and the present, what happened and the "un-happened" (the disappointment of what might have been, for example unrealized political utopias) and possible futures (projects and dreams). For this reason, each interview always traces the story of the interviewee from childhood and family origins to the present, although some events (in our case the period of the dictatorship) are often emphasized.

The Archive on Sexual Diversity and Repression
As outlined by Violi (2007: 191), the autobiographical life story (and oral) interview can be considered as a discursive genre used for "giving voice" to those categories of people marginalized by official historiography. It has been used in particular for giving voice to the so-called "subaltern" (Passerini 1988), producing works that are today considered a watershed in the way we study and investigate the past (e.g. Portelli 1999). This methodology has also been used for reconstructing the history of LGBT people, the most notable example being the oral history project of the AIDS Coalition to Unleash Power (ACT UP), which collects interviews with the militants of the group that, since 1987, has struggled for recognition of the AIDS crisis.

As Omar Basabe (2014) argues in his review of oral history research on Argentine state terrorism, the life story

---

[1] See **http://apm.gov.ar/apm-historia-oral/**, accessed 28 November 2016.

interview is today an important research practice for shedding light on aspects which (political) history and academic research have marginalized in their accounts of the Southern Cone dictatorships of the twentieth century. *Fiestas, baños y exilios. Los gays porteños en la última dictadura*, by Flavio Rapisardi and Alessandro Modarelli, was one of the works that broke the silence on the conditions of LGBT people during the last dictatorship in Argentina. It was inspired in some way by oral history methodologies, using first-person testimonies of gay people, framed by the authors' analysis.

It is within this theoretical and methodological framework that we approach the section on the repression of sexual diversity during the 1960s and 1970s, part of the oral history archive of Córdoba, consisting to date of three interviews. The aim of the section is to collect and preserve (*rescatar*) "the voices of those people who were condemned and persecuted for having chosen a different sexuality, during the different democratic and repressive periods that happened in our country". Its goal is "to add new elements to discuss the processes of memory construction through the narratives of those who chose and choose a different way of living their sexuality, outside the normative frames culturally imposed by our society".[2]

The way researchers present the archive and structure the interview is symptomatic both of the way they construct the subjectivity of the interviewee as well as of their initial hypothesis. Firstly, researchers position the interviewees as being outside hegemonic social frames, by presenting the conflict in this case as being between society at large and non-normative people. Secondly, temporal and historical boundaries of the "last dictatorship" appear blurred: the repression of sexual diversity does not only involve the period of the last dictatorship, but runs with continuities and fractures through recent Argentine history. As we shall see, these two elements are very important and very peculiar, because they reconfigure the *us (victims) vs them (perpetrators)* axis that is typical of post-dictatorship memory: the military and the repressive apparatus during the dictatorship, on the one hand, and militants and those

---

[2] Text available at **http://apm.gov.ar/apm-historia-oral/**, accessed 28 November 2016.

who were imprisoned, tortured and killed by the military, on the other.

The three interviews, all conducted by Damiana Meca and Pablo Becerra, last between two hours and two hours twenty minutes. What I shall offer in this section is a synthesis of the content of the interviews, while in the next section I shall single out some elements for analysis. To refer to the three interviewees, I shall use their initials: M., H., and D.

M. was interviewed in 2010. Designated as male at birth (given the name Julio César) in 1958 in the province of San Luis, her process of identification as a woman began in childhood and adolescence. In 1976, at the age of 18, M. moved to Buenos Aires where "during the day I was a student and at night I could embody M.". The reaction of her mother was to commit her to a psychiatric hospital where transgender and homosexual people normally received electroshock therapy. M. succeeded in avoiding the treatment and was also exonerated from military service on the basis of the 2H (part of the *edictos policiales* [political edicts] against prostitution that were used for imprisoning gay and transgender people). M. highlights the fact that during this experience what was most striking was to be considered a "sick person" or a "person with disabilities". In Buenos Aires, M. was arrested many times, suffering rituals of degradation, and subjected to what the military called "therapy", i.e. beating (*paliza*, a word that recurs many times in her testimony). Hoping for a better life, M. moved to Córdoba. However, the situation in Córdoba was no different. M. was arrested many times and imprisoned in the D2, where she was also sexually abused. She also remembers her friends, some of them arrested, killed and, one in particular, disappeared. According to M., the return to democracy also marks the birth of *transgéneros* (transgender people) in the public sphere. However, this process was not easy, because of continuities in the repression meted out by the dictatorship and democracy. The event that marked the start of the struggle for rights and recognition was the HIV/AIDS epidemic. M. reflects also on the position that *transgéneros* had in society and in political movements during the dictatorship and also in the transition to democracy. According to M., *transgéneros* were not a "risky group" for the military institution during the dictatorship but were considered "subversive" of public morality. However, out-of-the-closet *transgéneros* and LGBT people were not allowed to take part in political activism.[3] This also happened in the early years of democracy, when discrimination and the impossibility of getting a proper job pushed transgender women into prostitution. The interview ends with an opinion on human rights. M. thinks that, together with the possibility of having a job, human rights dignify people's lives. In order to explain what human rights are for transgender people, M. compares her situation to that of a child with disabilities: "a child with disabilities has an essential right [*derecho esencial*] to education [...] and a particular right [*derecho particular*] to a special needs teacher [*maestra integradora*]. Being transgender, we have all the essential rights but we also have particular rights".

Interviewed in 2010, H. was born in 1950 in the province of Córdoba. He was a primary school teacher and lived in Córdoba and Buenos Aires. He is homosexual and started to dress as a woman in adolescence, calling herself Mara. He was imprisoned twice in the D2. Although he adhered to the Peronist Party, he acknowledges that political militancy was forbidden to LGBT people as such. According to H., the HIV/AIDS epidemic helped construct a community and even "an identity", through the work of prevention (often with the help of the Catholic Church), supporting, caring and mourning. However, interestingly, H. makes a distinction between politics and rights, criticizing those movements or parts of the LGBT movement that "mixed" political ideologies—e.g. adhering to a right-wing or a left-wing party—with claims for rights (which from this perspective should be bipartisan). H. highlights the progress in the recognition and quality of life for LGBT people and the success in deconstructing the stigmas and discrimination which the community and individuals suffered. In particular, he remembers the struggle for the abolition of the law that forbade people born as male from dressing as women, the so-called *ropa indebida* (inappropriate clothes).

---

[3] One of the slogans of the Montoneros was "No somos putos, no somos faloperos: somos soldados de Perón y Montoneros" [We are not fags, we are not druggies: we are soldiers of Perón and Montoneros], epitomizing their homophobia (see Insausti 2015).

D. is a gay man and 50 years old. He was interviewed in 2012. The interview starts outside the D2, the place where gay people used to meet in the 1970s (at the corner of Plaza San Martín and 9 de Julio) and where they were arrested and brought to the D2. D. explains how this normally happened, how they were treated and what they were asked, as well as the practices and codes by which gay people recognized each other in the public space. As emerges from interviews (M. also mentions this aspect), gay and transgender people were considered to be a very important source of information, because they were living clandestinely and were familiar with the dimension of the "night". D. explains that, in the world of the prison, gay people were "the lowest of the low", to the point that "the prison guard and the prisoner allied with one another to humiliate 'this other'". D. pushes his discourse to the point of describing the gay prisoner as *preso de los otros presos* (prisoner of the other prisoners). However, he recognizes that, paradoxically, the disgust that the other men expressed (in particular the military) probably saved them from torture. Echoing M.'s words, D. highlights the fact that he did not talk about his experience for many years (25 years of silence with his family) and only talked about the experience of the prison with other gay men through jokes, never approaching the topic directly, since "by joking we could say things that we could not talk about". However, D. is aware that his silence was not due simply to the impossibility of coming out as gay to his family, or to military repression, but also to a sort of "naturalization of injustice": "no la reconocía como injusticia" [I did not recognize it as injustice], he says. Also in D.'s case, the HIV/AIDS epidemic was a pivotal moment in which people had to come out and LGBT associations started to demand recognition and rights. D. confirms that gay people were treated in the same way after the dictatorship, under the presidency of Alfonsín.

The Double Closet and Disclosure: Memory and Subjectivity in the Oral History Interview

My hypothesis is that the oral history interview, as a discursive practice in the framework of the Provincial Memory Archive, works as an important device, allowing people to reconfigure and (re)construct their subjectivity: a truth-telling performance about the self and state terrorism which also allows for the recovery of political agency.

Above all, this happens at the level of the enunciative frame implied in the discursive practice, which transforms confession into testimony.[4] The three interviews take place in the building where M., H. and D. were interrogated and obliged "to confess" their sexuality and gender deviance, who they were and what they did. The interviewer, at another level, does just the same: asks the interviewees where they are from, who their friends and families are and questions about their sexuality. The situation may appear paradoxical: questions which the interviewees are asked may overlap with the interrogation which they were submitted to during their captivity decades ago in the very same place. D. describes the interrogation and the fact that he had to confess his homosexuality and also "who the homosexuals were, where we partied, where we printed pamphlets, the books we read". The oral history genre changes the meaning of the "interrogation of the subject" and the way in which it affects the construction of subjectivities in discourse.

The interrogation of the subject in the place of his/her captivity reframes this practice and its meaning and, in particular, the act of disclosure. These acts, as Cvetkovich (2003) notes, can dramatically alter their meaning when context, audience, and speaker change. In our case, the oral history interview intersects different discursive practices that have the act of disclosure as a common feature. First of all, the police interrogation in which the authorities ask for the truth, seek confession about sexuality; second, the "coming out of the closet", the act of gay people disclosing the truth about their sexuality; third, the "life story" genre in which a subject reconstructs the truth about his/her life; fourth, history, the reconstruction of the truth about an institution— the state—and the past of a national community from the perspective of an individual.

The oral history interview brings together these acts of disclosure by transforming confession into testimony and consequently producing a series of semantic transformations thanks to an enunciative "reframing" of the disclosure acts

---

[4] There is a long debate on confession, sexuality, and the secret that has as its main reference Michel Foucault's theory of sexuality (1976). See on this Cvetkovich (2003), Kosofsky Sedgwick (1990), Bell (1991), and Radstone (2007). On the archive as confessional in transitional cultures, see also Rogers (2016).

and of the interrogation of the subject. The first transformation is pivotal: to be gay or transgender is transformed from something to be hidden as an illness, source of shame or crime, into something that can be displayed and publicly narrated with dignity. Only this first transformation can open up the possibility of publicly breaking the silence surrounding the other levels and, in particular, surrounding the construction of the memory of state terrorism.

These enunciative shifts make it clear that the LGBT subject was in a sort of double closet. On the one hand, s/he was in the closet as a gay or transgender person. This is particularly evident in the case of D., whose homosexuality was unknown to his family, and in part for M., who had to keep Julio César "alive" during the dictatorship. On the other hand, s/he was in the closet as a victim of the repression instigated by state terrorism. With the return to democracy, LGBT people could not immediately speak of the treatment they had received under the dictatorship: they did not immediately take part in the process of truth-telling and disclosure, the democratic transition and human rights movements. State terror and the secrecy of the clandestine centres that had to be disclosed, along with social homophobia and transphobia in society and the secrecy of the closet acted as if in solidarity, merging into one another.[5]

This explains why these memories are so peculiar and sometimes even uncomfortable for the memory of the human rights movement. While we may consider that the "other", the "persecutor" in the human rights movements' narratives, is mainly the military persecutor and that, temporally, the "end of repression" coincides with the official end of dictatorship, in the three interviews the "other" and the "end" are more blurred and multifaceted.

M., D., and H. agree that the humiliation and repression of LGBT people outlived the dictatorship, in institutions, in the police and in the army, and were a daily occurrence for transgender and gay people. Temporally, this partially disconnects the experience of the dictatorship from the repression of sexual diversity that also continued in democracy.

---

[5] On the relation between secrets, self-disclosure and the epistemology of the closet, see Kosofsky Sedgwick (1990).

The "other", "the perpetrator", is much more multifaceted in these narratives. In different ways, M., D. and H. highlight how as LGBT people their political agency was not recognized by the dissident political movements. Furthermore, as in the case of D., the political prisoner—the central victim-figure in the context of post-dictatorship Argentine memory—may even be represented as perpetrator: the political prisoner and the prison guard might act together to humiliate the LGBT person who was considered an animal or an object. In this sense, the memories of M. and D. may stand at odds in the context of post-dictatorship Argentine memory, as it has been constructed since 1983 (on this see Crenzel 2008).

I want to conclude this brief analysis by looking at how the meaning of being transgender or gay from dictatorship to democracy is re-worked in the narratives. The three interviewees agree they were treated and defined, literally, as animals. On this topic M. says: "Imagine a corral where there are sheep that recognize each other. Because that was how they made us feel. When you take one which you are going to kill and butcher [*matar y carnear*]". The way they arrested LGBT people on the streets is compared to hunting (*cazería*). In the same way that D. uses the sheep as an animal that signifies the way the repression treated homosexuals, H. says how during the dictatorship a man once told him, "my dog deserves more rights than you".

Together with animalization, the other strategy for depriving LGBT people of agency was to define them as sick, affected by an illness. This reference to the discourse of health/illness is very strong in the three interviews and seemed also to have shaped perpetrators' language of violence (for example the act of beating was a sort of "therapy"; see on the language of torture Demaria 2006: 135-156). This discursive feature is also the most difficult to overcome.

At the end of her interview, M. tells how important it was when in the 1990s the World Health Organization declared that homosexuality was a free life choice and not an illness. However, talking about the transgender condition, she compares it to that of a disabled person who deserves human rights as particular rights adapted to his/her condition. The way she compares disability to the transgender condition might appear ambiguous. In fact, during the interview the meaning of "disability" oscillates between the past hegemonic meaning that defined disability as illness and a more recent paradigm that defines disability as a(n existential) condition.[6]

D. says: "medicine catalogued us as sick [...] they locked us away and studied us as a strange insect [*bicho raro*]... well, this means being a victim". However, D. argues that "the struggle for civil rights is condensed around the emergence of AIDS" and that the epidemic played a fundamental role in the construction of community, in the appropriation and claiming of memory and identity ("there were many people that had to say: I have got AIDS and I am gay", another instance of the coming out of the closet discourse) and in the struggle for human rights. In this sense, the AIDS epidemic among gay people played a very complex role. On the one hand, it represented a "real" illness that struck LGBT people just after the return to democracy. Its arrival confirmed and reinforced a stigma. On the other hand, it actually represented the moment, according to all three interviewees, in which LGBT people acquired political agency and were reborn as a community and collective subject. Both M. and H., who collaborate together, find that it was in the work of supporting, caring, mourning and prevention that LGBT people were allowed to recover a collective identity and a political agency, as they were also starting to work through the memory of the dictatorship.

It is on this point of the life stories and of collective history, perhaps the point at which gay people were most vulnerable, that the discourse of human rights plays a fundamental role in "dignifying" the life of LGBT people and in enabling them to recover agency. However, the emergence of the discourse of human rights in the middle of the process of recovering political agency happens in an ambiguous way, according to the narrative of M. and H. On the one hand, as already described, M. goes back to the discourse of illness and health to justify human rights for transgender people. On the other hand, H. highlights the fact that "Nunca mezclé militancia política y lucha por los derechos humanos" [I never mixed political militancy with the struggle for human rights]; it seems that H. separates

---

[6] I thank Elisa A. G. Arfini and Juliet Rogers for helping me to clarify this aspect.

"politics", conceived as confrontation between parties and political constituencies, from the struggle for human rights, conceived as a struggle for dignity and equality that should be politically bipartisan.

Conclusion

The small corpus of interviews from the Córdoba memory archive is exemplary of how the oral history interview, as a discursive practice, can play a role in the rearticulation of memories and subjectivities in the transitional (and post-transitional) process. In particular, I have shown how the interview transforms, on the enunciative level, the practice of "interrogating the subject" from a form of police confession to a form of testimony. The acts of disclosing the truth about the self and about state terrorism are strictly interconnected, mixing the cultural practices of "coming out of the closet" and truth-telling about the past within the frame of the transitional process.

We can single out some peculiarities of the interviews compared to the hegemonic context of the memory of Argentine state terrorism: the polemical dimension (i.e. the identification of the other as perpetrator) is somewhat more blurred. Society at large may appear as perpetrator, without a clear distinction between the elements of the 1970s' conflict. Even the Montoneros and the political prisoner can appear as perpetrators for LGBT people, something that can make these memories uncomfortable. Furthermore, the time-frame of the repression is broadened, extending well beyond the fall of the dictatorship, fixing a temporality that is slightly different from that of the political history of the country. This resegmentation of the historical temporality of the transition in the accounts I have analyzed can be compared to the broadening of "time frames beyond the dictatorship" (Crenzel 2008: 149) but in a different way: although the beginning of the Alfonsín presidency is still a point of discontinuity, it does not appear as strong as it does in the hegemonic accounts.

Finally, in the interviews the subjects reconstruct their own agency. They do so by deconstructing those knowledge and power systems (medicine, law) that defined the gay and transgender person as criminal or sick, denying them any political agency. The interviewees recognize in some parts that they have interiorized such ideologies. For example, D.

speaks of a "naturalization of injustice": he felt like a sick person and that the treatment he received at the hands of the police and the military was natural. However, the reconstruction of political agency and the deconstruction of the systems that defined the LGBT person as sick or criminal appear contradictory in some cases, in particular when the human rights discourse enters the narrative, in a way that is comparable to the role it plays in the hegemonic framework. Human rights organizations restored the humanity of victims and survivors, who were portrayed as immoral and subversive during the dictatorship (which represented itself as a defender of Christian morality and patriotic values), by strongly underplaying their political agency, denying any political connections, and highlighting their individualities and sufferings (Crenzel 2015: 18-19). M. and H. seem to lean towards this strategy. M. used many Christian references to describe "her cross", comparable to Christ's cross, and at the same time compared the condition of a transgender person to the condition of a child with disabilities. H. divides political militancy from the struggle for human rights. So if during the interviews the subjects try to restore their own capacity to act politically, in the end they downplay the reference to political struggle by placing the recognition of human rights on another, perhaps more naturalized, plane, thus neutralizing the potential political and social divisions surrounding the recognition of rights for LGBT people in a society where homophobia and transphobia are still a reality.

References

Basabe, O. (2014). Relato documental en primera persona como sustento de reconstrucción del historia de la Argentina reciente. In L. Benadiba (ed.), *Otras memorias I. Testimonios para la transformación de la realidad*. Buenos Aires: Editorial Maipue, pp. 19-40.

Bell, V. (1991). *Interrogating incest: Feminism, Foucault and the law*. London and New York: Routledge.

Crenzel, E. (2008). *La historia política del Nunca Más. La memoria de las desapariciones en la Argentina*. Buenos Aires: Siglo XXI Editores (English Translation: *Memory of the Argentina disappearances: The political history of Nunca Más*. London and New York: Routledge, 2011).

Crenzel, E. (2015). Toward a history of the memory of political violence and the disappeared in Argentina. In E.

Allier-Montaño & E. Crenzel (eds.), *The struggle for memory in Latin America: Recent history and political violence*. Basingstoke: Palgrave, pp.15-33.

Cvetkovich, A. (2003). *An archive of feelings: Trauma, sexuality, and lesbian public culture*. Durham: Duke University Press.

Demaria, C. (2006). *Semiotica e memoria. Analisi del post-conflitto*. Rome: Carocci.

Encarnación, O. (2016). *Out in the periphery: Latin America's gay rights revolution*. Oxford: Oxford University Press.

Foucault, M. (1976). *Histoire de la sexualité I: La volonté de savoir*. Paris: Gallimard.

Insausti, S. J. (2015). Los cuatrocientos homosexuales desaparecidos: Memorias de la represión estatal a las sexualidades disidentes en Argentina. In D. D'Antonio (ed.), *Deseo y represión. Sexualidad, género y estado en la historia argentina reciente*. Buenos Aires: Imago Mundi, pp. 63-82.

Kosofsky Sedgwick, E. (1990). *Epistemology of the closet*. Los Angeles: University of California Press.

Lorusso, A. M. (2015). *Cultural semiotics: For a cultural perspective*. Basingstoke: Palgrave.

Passerini, L. (1988). *Storia e soggettività. Le fonti orali, la memoria*. Scandicci: La nuova Italia.

Portelli, A. (1999). *L'ordine è già stato eseguito. Roma, le Fosse Ardeatine, la memoria*. Rome: Donzelli.

Radstone, S. (2007). *The sexual politics of time: Confession, nostalgia, memory*. London and New York: Routledge.

Rapisardi, F., & Modarelli, A. (2002). *Fiestas, baños y exilios. Los gays porteños en la última dictadura*. Buenos Aires: Editorial Sudamericana.

Rogers, J. B. (2016). The archive as confessional: The role of video testimony in understanding and remorse. *Journal of Human Rights Practice*, 8(1), 45-61.

Violi, P. (2007). Remembering the future: The construction of gendered identity and diversity in the Balkans. In C. Goh & B. J. McGuirk (eds.), *Happiness and post-conflict*. Nottingham: Critical, Cultural and Communications Press, pp. 189-200.

Violi, P. (2014). *Paesaggi della memoria. Il trauma, lo spazio, la storia*. Milan: Bompiani.

Loathe Thy Neighbour: **State-Led Violence and Popular Involvement in Franco's Spain and Argentina's Last Dictatorship**[1]

Daniel Oviedo Silva

> In order to carry out our work with maximum efficiency, Generalísimo Franco requests your enthusiastic and boundless collaboration. Convinced as he is of your spiritual identification with the cause we are defending, he knows he can count on your support.
> Edict of the Auditing Board of the Occupying Army, Madrid, 30 March 1939

> In making such a transcendent commitment, the Armed Forces issue a resolute call to the whole national community. There is a place for every citizen in this new period. The mission is arduous and urgent, but is undertaken with the absolute conviction that the example will be set from top to bottom and with faith in the future of Argentina.
> Military Junta announcement, 24 March 1976

Introduction

In July 2015 I visited Argentina for the first time. Along with a persistent and annoying jet lag, I carried a heavy suitcase crammed with questions, concerns and echoes accumulated over more than a year of research on accusatory practices in the Spanish Civil War and post-war period. I was haunted by voices and whispers uttered decades ago but seared into

---

[1] This piece has benefited greatly from conversations with Ana Clarisa Agüero, Gabriela Águila, Miriam Grossi, Daniel Lvovich, Jorge Marco, Alberto Martí, José Manuel Rodríguez Amieva and Adam Sharman. Responsibility for any shortcomings remains the author's.

Spain's history. Words that surfaced in the workplace, in neighbourhoods or immediate social circles, flowed up to the authorities and sealed the fate of many. Especially, however, I brought with me the firm—and not so new—belief that the manifold faces of Francoist violence had been partly underpinned by various forms of "ordinary" citizens' collaboration. Such collaboration not only oiled the wheels of repression but also mercilessly shook social and power relations and shaped the boundaries of the new national community. A collaboration, in brief, deeply rooted in intra-community violence and which left the country's body and memory severely scarred.

Intrigued by the relatively little attention that these issues have attracted in Argentine historiography, I crossed an ocean and four decades with my queries to explore their impact on Argentina's last dictatorship. As I visited various cities, I opened my suitcase wide and asked people with very different backgrounds about the possible existence of such forms of popular collaboration with the violence unleashed by the dictatorship. Their reactions and answers were as diverse as the interlocutors. Some made me feel at home by advising me not to stir up the past or to mind my own business. Yet the most common answers highlighted the complicity of part of a company's management or the blood-stained past that tainted institutions such as the Church or the judiciary. Thorny issues revolving around the political, ethical and judicial dimensions of the *quebrados* (the "broken" prisoners) debate were also frequently commented on. Others echoed the accusations levelled by military personnel who, at their trials, have contended that those who were tortured were responsible for catalysing the repression owing to the information they provided. Only a few touched on the more microsocial, community-based side to this phenomenon, pointing out the possible existence of intra-community denunciation in the closest social circles. Others insisted that solidarity networks would have safeguarded this coexistence. Not only has this set of topics often featured in research on Argentina's last dictatorship; it automatically brings to mind some not so different issues that have affected the historical study and memory of Spain's traumatic past as well. It nonetheless also immediately reveals substantial differences between both cases, associated with their particular socio-political contexts and repressive systems, their research agendas and the availability of historical sources or the judicialization of the past.

Despite my persistence, the involvement of "ordinary citizens" in accusatory practices barely featured in the answers I received. And yet there is now enough evidence to state that, even though their extent is still to be determined, these kinds of practice did exist in the period. Analysis of them undoubtedly constitutes one of the most promising lines of research in the field of Argentine political violence. Such matters dovetail neatly both with established lines of inquiry into the repressive apparatus and with the growing interest in social attitudes towards dictatorships, whilst drawing on international debates and the use of primary sources that had barely been explored until now (González Canosa 2011; Lvovich 2016). This essay proposes a brief overview of these issues in the Spanish Civil War and post-war period and in Argentina's last dictatorship. Acknowledging significant differences between the two, the piece discusses whether they share research questions, debates and methods. It assesses, in short, how those echoes that resounded in my suitcase travel and adapt to a new context.

Comparing early Francoism to Argentina's last dictatorship is not innovative in itself. The memory left behind by both systems, their transitions to democracy and transitional justice continue to attract most interest (Barahona de Brito *et al*. 2001; Aguilar 2008; Almqvist & Espósito 2012). Yet in recent years part of this historical research has set out to analyze both dictatorships together, focusing on the periods and some of the topics that concern this essay. The study of issues such as the relationship between dictatorships and society, social attitudes and violent practices has enjoyed considerable dynamism in the historiography of both countries. The appearance of work analyzing both processes has been the result of a fluid exchange of ideas and historians between the two countries and the organization of research projects, conference workshops, panels and publications that have taken on the joint study of Franco's Spain and the Southern Cone military dictatorships (Águila & Alonso 2013; Marco *et al*. 2015;

Míguez 2016a, 2016b).[2] Tellingly, the first studies devoted to accusatory practices in Argentina fall within this field of historical research and have drawn on the international literature that has dealt with these same issues in different European regimes. As a result, these approaches have engaged with ground-breaking research on Nazi Germany, Fascist Italy, Vichy France or Francoist Spain. In this way, they have embraced long-standing debates such as those concerning the way in which denunciation reflects the relationship between state and society as well as the dynamics and motivations that lie beneath these practices or the role they play in repressive systems (González Canosa 2011; Lvovich 2016).[3]

Accusatory practices themselves constitute a subject of historical research often approached through comparative analysis. Denunciation is a phenomenon present in every organized society, which nonetheless takes many different forms in varying contexts (Fitzpatrick & Gellately 1997: 1-2). Research on Nazi Germany that, amongst other things, demonstrated relatively high levels of popular involvement in accusatory practices has been the centre of many of the comparisons (Gellately 1988 & 2001; Johnson 1999). Denunciation can only be fully understood within a given set of social, political and cultural traditions, and comparisons

---

[2] See, for example the workshops organized at the IX Encuentro de Investigadores del Franquismo in 2016, at the XII Congreso de la Asociación de Histórica Contemporánea in 2014 and at the conference De genocidios, holocaustos y exterminios... in 2012. The publication of the journal *Contenciosa* since 2013 and the project Transiciones a la democracia en el sur de Europa y en América Latina: España, Portugal, Argentina y Chile, based at the UAB, are equally good examples. As is Luciano Alonso's (2013) bid to compare these "regressive dictatorships" (*dictaduras regresivas*), through the use of "intermediate concepts" (*categorías intermedias*) and acknowledging "family resemblances" (*parecidos de familia*). Efforts backed by, amongst others, Daniel Lvovich's (2013) analysis of social attitudes.

[3] There is further evidence of direct connections between both states that might well be the centre of future research. Particularly remarkable among these are the presence of Argentine students at the Spanish Escuela del Estado Mayor between 1957 and 1981 (Marco 2013a) and the exchange of military and police personnel between both countries during Argentina's last dictatorship (Albín 2014).

help researchers discover particularities and trace causalities examining different variables. The specific shape of social relations, including solidarity and patronage networks and social conflict, are of great importance in this respect. As are the types of exchange these societies establish with the authorities and whether the latter have the coercive power to force, supervise or channel this collaboration. Comparative analysis may also uncover dissimilarities in military, police or court cultures and how these affect communication between these bodies and the population. For this same reason, the standing legislation and cultural norms that regulate such behaviours can prove decisive. On the other hand, the impact of exceptional circumstances, such as the Spanish Civil War, may influence the dynamics that shape these practices. These are but a few of the elements that an in-depth comparative study might explore. Here, nonetheless, I will simply provide a brief overview of the main features of both cases to assert the need for further research in the Argentine case and the pertinence of comparing the results with those obtained in the study of cases like the Spanish one.[4]

The Argentine Case
The Proceso de Reorganización Nacional (Process of National Reorganization) was accompanied by a high degree of violence—against various social groups—that included a legal side as well as a clandestine one, which has been more widely recognized. The latter included, but was not limited to, abductions, internment in clandestine detention centres, systematic use of torture, physical elimination, the disappearance of thousands of victims, and child-kidnapping. These actions, which were subject to substantial regional and chronological variations, were the result of military plans executed with the assistance of police forces and with the intention of uprooting "subversion" and disciplining society. To narrow it down to the main focus of this work, the literature has shown that intelligence services within different bodies (the "information community") obtained the information that would later on be used to carry out the kidnappings. Part of this information, which proved crucial to

---

[4] Some studies in which comparing different cases has boosted the discussion are Fitzpatrick & Gellately (1997), Gellately (1996), Anderson (2009b), Dunnage (2006 & 2008) and Kalyvas (2006).

sustain the regime's repressive efforts, was obtained through physical and psychological torture conducted in detention centres.[5] Some of the research has focused on these information-gathering techniques and the heated discussions around the various degrees of collaboration of prisoners and *quebrados*. The centrality of such issues to the repressive system, together with their controversial political, ethical, cultural and judicial ramifications, have attracted attention (Longoni 2007; Chababo et al. 2015).

Nevertheless, whilst there is little doubt about the relevance of state terrorism, top-down violence and information-gathering techniques, it is not possible to rule out the existence of denunciations by "ordinary" citizens or the presence of other communication channels with the authorities.[6] Counterinsurgency doctrine, whose influence on the Argentine military is beyond doubt, argued that the population had to be one of the main focuses of military efforts and strategy. According to its teachings, modern warfare entailed a struggle for the hearts and minds of a neutral population, since their support, as essential to insurgency as to counterinsurgency, could well make the difference between success and failure. Among other reasons, this backing was deemed particularly important due to the information the local population could provide the intelligence services with (Galula 1964: 53).[7] Galula (1964: 84-87) described the different phases in counterinsurgency operations and paid close attention to the moments in which the collaboration of the population—whether spontaneous or

---

[5] For a recent summary, see Águila (2013).
[6] Even if the type of repressive system might partly account for accusatory practices being less necessary, common or noticed, there are other possible explanations. On-going problems of accessing relevant archival material or the greater emphasis placed on both the study and the remembrance of clandestine forms of violence are some of them. Furthermore, these practices are distinctly harder to detect for the victims and it is reasonable to assume that the denouncers have no interest whatsoever in airing their past actions (Lorenz 2004: 23).
[7] The School of the Americas' training manuals preferred paid informers "spread throughout society" but also considered the need to obtain information from the local population that would cooperate either "out of free will" or after "persuasion". In that respect, they mention, for example, open systems of information collection such as anonymous statements (SOA 1989).

fostered—could be counted on. Trinquier (2006: 28-31) went further and claimed the need to build a civil structure—in which even he acknowledged totalitarian echoes—that would incorporate part of the population and make it possible, for example, to obtain information about the enemy.[8]

Meanwhile, research on the years 1973-1976 has shown the dissemination and penetration from an early date of discourses that set apart the internal enemy and warned about the danger it embodied (Franco 2012). Suspicion, internal confrontation and denunciation became more common in certain spaces during that period, as evidenced by the internal purge of the Peronist movement (Merele 2015, 2016; Franco 2011). It has also been argued that the military fostered the collaboration of the local population during the manoeuvres of the Operativo Independencia. Oral sources describe how troops encouraged the locals to give up *quién anda de zurdas* ("whoever is a leftie") as well as the different attitudes adopted by the Tucuman population in the face of such situations (Cruz *et al*. 2010). During the dictatorship, the press published announcements in which the authorities attempted to get the population to collaborate in the fight against "subversion" by providing information and by denouncing suspicious characters. Newspapers also had room for press releases in which the authorities thanked the citizens for essential cooperation in successful operations. In this way, the population—and some strategic actors such as letting agencies—were urged to remain vigilant and to identify the enemy, while fear and distrust spread through society (Águila 2008: 243-250; Doval 2006: 236-237). In one such piece—and with a choice of words that brings to mind the Military Junta's announcement after the coup—Paraná's daily *El Diario* called upon youths to give up "subversives" and reminded them that "Every Argentine has a place in this fight. Take yours" (Doval 2010: 8-9). The area of education was one of the spheres in which accusatory practices were more actively encouraged. This included the edition of a manual designed to help teachers identify the enemy as well as the military authorities' direct request for information from management personnel (Doval 2006; Caviglia 2006: 123-135). The regime also launched an

---

[8] For a brief introduction to the military culture of Argentina's armed forces see, for example, Cañón Voirín (2012).

advertising campaign on television, in cinemas and in the print media asking spectators to turn in tax evaders (Carassai 2014: 181-182).[9]

While it is not possible to predict the response of the population to these calls without further research, some authors have pointed out that relatively large sections of Argentine society shared the authority's view that "subversion" had to be nipped in the bud (Vezzetti 2002). It is no surprise that police intelligence services' instructions included encoding and analyzing information from very different sources and of varying degrees of reliability.[10] In fact, it has long been known that complicity and accusatory practices were common in some spheres. The CONADEP report had already indicated that the information used by the Grupos de Tareas (Task Groups) to carry out arrests might also be the result of denunciation and tip-offs.[11] Other sections of the report included testimonies that made abundantly clear the complicity of some companies and part of their personnel in workplace-related repression.[12] These statements have since been backed up by new research (Dicósimo 2013; Verbitsky & Bohoslavsky 2013; Basualdo & Jasinski 2016). Apparently, universities could not escape these sorts of practice either (Águila 2008: 238; Lewis 2002: 148-149). Testimonies show that some workers and students were or claimed to be aware of the identity of the denouncers they shared these spaces with (Caviglia 2006: 139-142, 145-147). Reflections on the impact of the dictatorship often

---

[9] Lvovich (2016) offers a more comprehensive account of the evidence pointing in the direction of accusatory practices in Argentina's later dictatorship. It is also worth noting the existence of other relevant studies that deal with denunciation in more distant (Miglioranza 2014) or close (Rodríguez 2007; Fiorucci 2013) periods.

[10] This is the case, for example, with the *Dirección de Inteligencia de la Policía Provincial de Buenos Aires*. Comisión Provincial por la Memoria. Fondo DIPPBA. División Central de Documentación, Registro y Archivo. The *Dirección Central de Inteligencia* organizational chart includes informers too.

[11] *Informe,* 1.H. Represores y esquemas represivos. Available at **www.desaparecidos.org/arg/conadep/nuncamas/258.html**.

[12] *Informe,* 2.H. Gremialistas. Available at **www.desaparecidos.org/arg/conadep/nuncamas/375.html** and **www.desaparecidos.org/arg/conadep/nuncamas/379.html**.

touch on the devastating effects that denunciation—or at least the widespread distrust and fear generated by the prospect of being denounced—had on social relations (Lorenz 2013: 208-210).

There are just a few studies that have approached accusatory practices in Argentina's last dictatorship drawing on the analysis of primary sources and, unfortunately, so far these have had to rely on small samples. As a result, there is still much we do not know about the scale of the phenomenon, about how this collaboration was channelled, about its relative importance within the repressive system and about some other key variables such as the profiles of those most likely to denounce or be denounced. These studies have nonetheless carried out qualitative analyses that have revealed some of the features of these practices. Most of the accusations analyzed by this research took place in the educational sphere, where individuals, from students to management, filed both horizontal and vertical denunciations. Regarding the everlasting debate about the causes that underlie denunciation, the authors have considered and explored the two most plausible options and their possible combinations: personally motivated or instrumental denunciations and politically motivated accusations. To do so, they have paid close attention to the conflicts that these accusations reflect and the circumstances in which they unfold. Sometimes these accusations offered the possibility of solving longstanding conflicts and grievances that could hardly be recognized as political. In other cases, the denouncers seemed to have been driven by fear to make accusations that would result in others facing a danger they were trying to escape themselves. Not unlike the studies conducted on these same issues in other regimes, researchers have dovetailed with one of the most persisting debates, asking themselves to what extent these practices denote authentic adherence to the state. Research usually shows a wide range of nuances and possibilities, from the manipulation of the system from below to the sincere identification with the principles and aims of the dictatorship (González Canosa 2011; Lvovich 2016).

The Spanish case
Some of these results may, with due caution, be compared with the Spanish case. Denunciation features often in

Spanish literature on political violence during the war and post-war periods and has been the centre of monographic work. Over the last years of the past century, research on Francoist violence experienced a "qualitative leap" (Mir 2001; Rodrigo 2001) that brought to the fore the analysis of forms of violence and social control previously eclipsed by the study of physical elimination. Simultaneously, research on social attitudes towards dictatorships, often mirroring the analysis of other European regimes, has increasingly highlighted the important role played by the population in violence and the effects this participation had on the relationship between state and society (Del Arco *et al.* 2014). The growing interest in the study of denunciation falls within this body of literature and has been further stimulated by the availability of new sources.

Nevertheless, the Spanish case has a crucial distinctive feature that helps explain the intensity, visibility and implications of popular involvement in violence: a bloody three-year civil war. The conflict broke out after a military coup that failed partly due to popular resistance (Aróstegui 2006). The military rebels made systematic use of violence—already anticipated in the insurrectional plans—which allowed them to carry out a political cleansing resulting in some 100,000 victims killed on the rebels' home front during the war and some 40,000-50,000 more in its aftermath (Juliá 2006; Preston 2012). In each phase, the violence drew on the collaboration of different social actors (Marco 2013b). During the first months of the war, the rebellion and the advance of the rebels were assisted by the collaboration on the home front of paramilitary and volunteer groups willing to wipe out political enemies as well as by the information provided by municipal corporations and neighbours (Espinosa Maestre 2007). As the war progressed, the rebel machinery put in place more sophisticated techniques that suited the occupation, cleansing and control of new territories. Notable amongst these was the progressive implementation—especially after February 1937—of military justice, which became the system through which most of the legal repression would be channelled. The various military and police investigation services set out to look for evidence to expedite the prosecution of enemies but the collaboration of the population proved decisive in intensifying the repression. This impetus was directed against a wide range of social groups, including those considered natural enemies before the war by the reactionary coalition that backed the coup and those perceived as liable for prosecution for their behaviour during the conflict (Anderson 2010; Gómez Bravo & Marco 2011).

One such form of collaboration was denouncing fellow citizens before the new authorities. The military rebels were aware of the need to facilitate and force the collaboration of the population to effectively carry out their selective violence. Occupations were followed by announcements that summoned the population to provide information about neighbours who could be liable for prosecution. Many did not need any incentive to come forward and register denunciations. However, the military rebels did not just rely on the good will of the population, especially when it came to big cities, where a more thorough and coercive approach was needed to reach every corner. The edict that opens this study summoned different social groups to appear before the military courts to make statements in which, amongst other questions, they would be asked about their behaviour and that of their neighbours or work colleagues. The parallel purging processes implemented after the occupations followed this same pattern in many cases. Everyone was a suspect, everyone was subject to investigation, and everyone had the chance to single out "the most prominent left-wing members of your department and everything you know about their behaviour".[13] Denunciations usually kick-started investigations and prosecutions during which other accusations could be made and many other people communicated with a system that craved and actively sought information through court statements, endorsement letters and reports filed by public order bodies. The close surveillance exercised by police and parapolice forces and even by immediate social circles added to this atmosphere of suspicion and uncertainty. There is little doubt that in such circumstances assessing the complex relationship between collaboration and coercion and the constraints that individual agency had to face in a situation of intense intracommunity and repressive violence should be considered essential (Anderson 2009a & 2009b, Gómez Bravo & Marco 2011;

---

[13] For an example of these kinds of proceedings, see Archivo General e Histórico de la Defensa de Madrid. 27745 33/7.

Oviedo Silva & Pérez Olivares 2016).

Crucially, research on the Spanish case has been able to better establish the role of accusatory practices in Francoist violence and some of their features thanks to studies that have largely drawn on court sources. There is therefore proof that social involvement was crucial for the functioning of the repressive system and for its scale. Collaboration from below fuelled this violence but the role of the authorities, eager to facilitate and force it, was far from passive. Research has also drawn a link between the prevalence of denunciation and the collapse of previous social relations and the imposition of forms of social control that permeated communities. As in other cases, though, the extent to which these practices expressed allegiance to the regime remains a contested issue, not helped by the complexity which determining the motives that led people to denounce their fellow citizens entails. Records show a number of possible options and combinations that range from the influence of fear and coercion to genuine adherence to the regime but also include revenge and the settling of personal scores as well as various forms of social, personal, family, professional and political conflicts. The profiles of the denouncers are also diverse. Not least in studies devoted to rural areas, research has uncovered neighbourhood, kinship, affinity or patronage-based denunciation networks that cooperated with the authorities.[14] Some authors have highlighted the permeability that existed between citizens and the authorities, suggesting that police information services enlisted some of the denouncers and that the exchange of information was fluid (Anderson & Del Arco 2011). In fact, information services actively recruited civil agents in enemy territory—often before its occupation—in order to get hold of valuable information (Gómez Bravo in press).

The Spanish Civil War and the fearsome Francoist repressive apparatus brought violence to every corner of Spain's social landscape. This violence was largely public and

---

[14] All these issues feature in the literature that has looked into denunciation. See, for example, Mir (2000); Cenarro (2002); Gil Andrés (2006); Anderson (2009a & 2009b); Gómez Bravo & Marco (2011); Melero Vargas (2014); Somoza Cayado (2015); Oviedo Silva & Pérez-Olivares (2016).

participatory and became a crucial element of social cohesion and exclusion, actively contributing to define the boundaries of the new Francoist society. Popular involvement in violence oiled the wheels of repression but also gave tens of thousands of Spaniards the opportunity to delineate where both they and others stood with regard to present and past violent practices and the new social demarcations (Mir 2000: 251-276; Cenarro 2002: 83-84; Gil Andrés 2006: 125-126; Gómez Bravo & Marco 2011: 79-76, 198-200). In short, violence and social involvement in it triggered a redefinition of relations within society and between the state and the citizens. These concerns are also present in Argentine research. Nevertheless, when it comes to accusatory practices and popular involvement in violence, the extent of the collaboration of ordinary citizens, its relevance in the repressive system and its distinctly public nature in the Spanish case seem to surpass these same elements as sketched by the research conducted on Argentina's last dictatorship.

Conclusion

It is no surprise that, given the particularities of each case, comparing accusatory practices results in substantial differences. Civil War and Franco's Spain witnessed a massive, public and highly visible popular participation in violence, encouraged by the state and spurred by social conflict and the civil war, which contributed to shaping new social and community boundaries and political realities. Even though our understanding of these issues in the Argentine case is still very limited, it is reasonable to assume that this participation was not so public or massive and that factors such as the absence of a civil war and the partly secret nature of violence made for a situation that differs significantly from the one lived in Spain. However, both these repressive systems and the manifold forms of popular involvement in violent practices they hosted involve a degree of complexity that goes well beyond the scope of this study. In fact, the Francoist state was underpinned by a systematic and sustained use of violence in which popular participation proved to be decisive but was by no means the only relevant element (Aróstegui 2012; Preston 2012; Anderson & Del Arco 2014).

Meanwhile, given the current state of these lines of

inquiry in the case of Argentina's last dictatorship we cannot yet dismiss the possibility that the incidence of accusatory practices may have been higher than expected. As María Lorena Montero (2016: 389-391) and a number of scholars have suggested (Vezzetti 2002: 180; Águila 2008: 250; Lvovich 2016), in this as well as in other realms of Argentine political violence we might only be seeing the tip of the iceberg. The authorities' calls for cooperation, the precedents of conflict and collaboration, the complicity of some groups and the first studies of primary sources seem to support these claims. The emerging research in this field and the experience of studies devoted to other countries suggest that a more intensive analysis of police records could prove fruitful. Despite the pre-eminence of the clandestine side of repression,[15] there is also evidence to suggest that the analysis of the legal coercive apparatus—not least the judicial system—could also offer opportunities to trace popular collaboration and lead to a better understanding of these issues.[16] This has been the case with regimes in which, as in Francoism, military justice and special jurisdictions became essential. Some authors are also showing that the use of oral sources can yield striking results.[17] As these studies progress, comparing hypotheses, methods and results with those registered for the analysis of different times and places will help assess the incidence and impact of these practices.[18]

It is easy to imagine what the military authorities meant when, after the occupation of Madrid and as part of an edict that decreed the mass appearance of different groups before the new powers, they declared that "Franco requests your enthusiastic and boundless collaboration". Fully understanding the motivations and constraints that explain the behaviour of all social actors involved in violence remains nonetheless a challenge for social historians of

---

[15] For a comparison with Brazil and Chile see Pereira (2010).
[16] Rodríguez (2007) has found denunciation in administrative proceedings involving teachers. See also the proceedings instituted by the Federal Justice quoted by Montero (2016: 390). Scocco (2016) has recently demonstrated that the study of military justice in Argentina offers a number of possibilities.
[17] See the ongoing research of Damián Santos and Cruz et al. (2010).
[18] Maybe starting with not so distant cases, such as the Uruguayan (Demasi 2013: 222).

dictatorships. As does determining the nature of "the place" that Argentina's last dictatorship reserved for "every citizen", what the population's response to violence was, and how the latter impacted on the former. Not unlike my suitcase after wandering through the insides of Ezeiza and Barajas, the questions I carried when I arrived in Buenos Aires returned to Madrid shaken and in need of some degree of upgrade in the light of the answers and silences they had come across. An ocean, several decades, and the peculiarities of the respective historical processes, of ways of looking at the past and of each country's historiographical agenda constituted a jet lag in their own right. Understanding the history of twentieth-century violence, however, can only be achieved by undertaking such expeditions. Some sleepless nights and the occasional headache should not deter us.

References

Águila, G. (2008). *Dictadura, represión y sociedad en Rosario, 1967-1983. Un estudio sobre la represión y los comportamientos y actitudes sociales en dictadura*. Buenos Aires: Prometeo.

Águila, G. (2013). La represión en la historia reciente argentina: Fases, dispositivos y dinámicas regionales. In G. Águila. & L. Alonso (eds.), *Procesos represivos y actitudes sociales. Entre la España franquista y las dictaduras del Cono Sur*. Buenos Aires: Prometeo, pp. 97-122.

Águila, G., & Alonso, L. (eds.) (2013). *Procesos represivos y actitudes sociales. Entre la España franquista y las dictaduras del Cono Sur*. Buenos Aires: Prometeo.

Águila, G., Garaño, S., & Scatizza, P. (eds.) (2016). *Represión estatal y violencia paraestatal en la historia reciente argentina. Nuevos abordajes a 40 años del golpe de Estado.* La Plata: Universidad Nacional de La Plata.

Aguilar, P. (2008). *Políticas de la memoria y memorias de la política. El caso español en perspectiva comparada*. Madrid: Alianza Editorial.

Albín, D. (2014). Torturadores argentinos recibieron cursos en instituciones españolas. *Público* 22-10-2014. Available at **www.publico.es/politica/torturadores-argentinos-recibieron-cursos-instituciones.html**

Almqvist, J., & Esposito, C. (2012). *The role of courts in* transitional justice: Voices from Latin America and Spain. Abingdon: Routledge.

Alonso, L. (2013). Dictaduras regresivas y represiones en Iberoamérica: Trayectorias particulares y posibilidades de comparación. In G. Águila & L. Alonso (eds.), *Procesos represivos y actitudes sociales. Entre la España franquista y las dictaduras del Cono Sur*. Buenos Aires: Prometeo, pp. 43-68.

Anderson, P. (2009a). Grass-roots prosecution and collaboration in Francoist military trials, 1939-1945. *Contemporary European History*, 18.

Anderson, P. (2009b). Singling out victims: Denunciation and collusion in the post-Civil War Francoist repression in Spain, 1939-1945. *European History* Quarterly, 39(1), 7-26.

Anderson, P. (2010). *The Francoist military trials: Terror and complicity, 1939-1945*. New York: Routledge.

Anderson, P., & Del Arco, M. A. (2011). Construyendo la dictadura y castigando a sus enemigos: Represión y apoyos sociales al franquismo. *Historia Social*, 71, 125-141.

Anderson, P., & Del Arco, M. A. (eds.) (2014). *Mass killings and violence in Spain, 1936-1952: Grappling with the past*. New York: Routledge.

Aróstegui, J. (2006). *Por qué el 18 de julio... Y después*. Barcelona: Flor del Viento

Aróstegui, J. (ed.) (2012). *Franco. La represión como sistema*. Barcelona: Flor del Viento.

Barahona de Brito, A., González-Enríquez, C., & Aguilar, P. (eds.) (2001). *The politics of memory: Transitional justice in democratizing societies.* Oxford: Oxford University Press.

Basualdo, V., & Jasinski, A. (2016). La represión a los trabajadores y el movimiento sindical, 1974-1983. In G. Águila, S. Garaño & P. Scatizza (eds.), *Represión estatal y violencia paraestatal en la historia reciente argentina. Nuevos abordajes a 40 años del golpe de Estado.* La Plata: Universidad Nacional de La Plata, pp. 237-268.

Cañón Voirín, J. L. (2012). La guerra revolucionaria en la perspectiva de las FF.AA. argentinas. *Naveg@mérica. Revista electrónica de la Asociación Española de Americanistas*, 9.

Carassai, S (2014). *The Argentine silent majority: Middle

clases, politics, violence and memory in the seventies. Durham & London: Duke University Press.
Caviglia, M. (2006). *Vivir a oscuras. Escenas cotidianas durante la dictadura.* Buenos Aires: Aguilar, Altea, Taurus, Alfaguara.
Cenarro, A. (2002). Matar, vigilar y delatar: La quiebra de la sociedad civil durante la guerra y la posguerra en España (1936-1948). *Historia Social*, 44, 65-86.
Chababo, R., Nardoni, V., Fernández Lamothe, D., & Budassoff, E. (eds.) (2015). *El caso Chomicki*. Rosario & Córdoba: Editorial Municipal de Rosario/Museo de la Memoria.
Cruz, M., Jemio, A. S., Monteros, E., & Pisani, A. (2010). Las prácticas sociales genocidas en el Operativo Independencia en Famaillá, Tucumán: Febrero de 1975-Marzo de 1976. *Primeras Jornadas de Historia Reciende del NOA "Memoria, Fuentes Orales y Ciencias Sociales"*, Universidad Nacional de Tucumán.
Del Arco Blanco, M. A., Fuertes Muñoz, C., Hernández Burgos, C., & Marco, J. (eds.) (2014). *No sólo miedo. Actitudes políticas y opinión popular bajo la dictadura franquista (1936-1977)*. Granada: Comares.
Demasi, C. (2013). Las ambiguas formas de la coexistencia: La sociedad uruguaya frente a la dictadura. In G. Águila. & L. Alonso (eds.), *Procesos represivos y actitudes sociales. Entre la España franquista y las dictaduras del Cono Sur*. Buenos Aires: Prometeo, pp. 221-244.
Dicósimo, D. (2013). Represión estatal, violencia y relaciones laborales durante la última dictadura militar en la argentina. *Contenciosa*, 1.
Doval, D. (2006). La cruzada restauradora en la educación: Uniformizar, descentralizar y moralizar. *Anuario de la Sociedad Argentina de Historia de la Educación*, 7.
Doval, D. (2010). La juventud como blanco. *III Seminario Internacional Políticas de la Memoria. Recordando a Walter Benjamn. Justicia, Historia y Verdad. Escrituras de la Memoria.* Buenos Aires, 28, 29, 30 October 2010.
Dunnage, J. (2006). Policing right-wing dictatorships: Some preliminary comparisons of Fascist Italy, Nazi Germany and Franco's Spain. *Crime, Histoire et Sociétés*, 10(1).
Dunnage, J. (2008). Surveillance and denunciation in fascist Siena, 1927-1943. *European History Quarterly*, 38(2).

Espinosa Maestre, F. (2007). *La columna de la muerte. El avance del Ejército franquista de Sevilla a Badajoz.* Barcelona: Crítica.

Fiorucci, F. (2013). La denuncia bajo el peronismo: El caso del campo escolar. *Latin American Research Review*, 48(1), 3-23.

Fitzpatrick, S., & Gellately, R. (eds.) (1997). *Accusatory practices: Denunciation in Modern European history, 1789-1989.* Chicago: The University of Chicago Press.

Franco, M. (2011). La "depuración" interna del peronismo como parte del proceso de construcción del terror de Estado en la Argentina de la década del 70. *A Contracorriente. Una revista de historia social y literatura de América Latina,* 8(3), 23-54.

Franco, M. (2012). *Un enemigo para la nación. Orden interno, violencia y "subversión", 1973-1976.* Buenos Aires: Fondo de Cultura Económica.

Galula, D. (1964). *Counter-insurgency warfare: Theory and practice.* New York: Frederick A. Praeger.

Gellately, R. (1996). Denunciations in twentieth-century Germany: Aspects of self-policing in the Third Reich and the German Democratic Republic. *The Journal of Modern History*, 68(4), 931-967.

Gellately, R. (1988). The Gestapo and German society: Political denunciation in the Gestapo case files. *The Journal of Modern History*, 60(4), 654-694.

Gellately, R. (2001). *Backing Hitler: Consent and coercion in Nazi Germany.* Oxford: Oxford University Press.

Gil Andrés, C. (2006). Vecinos contra vecinos: La violencia en la retaguardia riojana durante la Guerra Civil. *Historia y Política*, 16, 109-130.

Gómez Bravo, G., & Marco, J. (2011). *La obra del miedo. Violencia y sociedad en la España franquista (1936-1950).* Barcelona: Península.

Gómez Bravo, G. (in press). *Historia social de la represión franquista. Del golpe a la guerra de ocupación (1936-1941).* Madrid: Cátedra.

González Canosa, M. (2011). Consenso y dictadura: Consideraciones analíticas a partir de un legajo policial sobre un conflicto en la ciudad de Lincoln (Provincia de Buenos Aires) durante la última dictadura militar argentina. *Naveg@mérica. Revista electrónica de la Asociación Española de Americanistas*, 7.

Johnson, E. A. (1999). *Nazi terror: the Gestapo, Jews and ordinary Germans*. London: John Murray.
Juliá, S. (ed.) (2006). *Víctimas de la guerra civil*. Madrid: Temas de Hoy.
Kalyvas, S. (2006). *The logic of violence in civil war.* New York: Cambridge University Press.
Longoni, A. (2007). *Traiciones. La figura del traidor en los relatos acerca de los sobrevivientes de la represión.* Buenos Aires: Norma.
Lewis, P. (2002). *Guerrillas and generals: The "Dirty War" in Argentina.* Westport: Praeger.
Lvovich, D. (2013). Actitudes sociales y dictaduras: Las historiografías española y argentina en perspectiva comparada. In G. Águila. & L. Alonso (eds.), *Procesos represivos y actitudes sociales. Entre la España franquista y las dictaduras del Cono Sur*. Buenos Aires: Prometeo, pp. 123-146.
Lvovich, D. (2016). Sospechar, delatar, incriminar: Una aproximación al fenómeno de las denuncias contra el enemigo político en la última dictadura militar argentina. Paper presented to *VIII Jornadas de Trabajo sobre Historia Reciente*. Universidad de Rosario. 9-12 August 2016.
Lorenz, F. (2004). Pensar los setenta desde los trabajadores. *Políticas de la Memoria*, 5, 19-23.
Lorenz, F. (2013). A dejarse de escribir macanas: Huellas de la represión al movimiento obrero argentino. In G. Águila. & L. Alonso (eds.), *Procesos represivos y actitudes sociales. Entre la España franquista y las dictaduras del Cono Sur*. Buenos Aires: Prometeo, pp. 197-220.
Marco, J. (2013a). "Una Corea en pequeño": Contrainsurgencia y represión de la guerrilla en España (1939-1952). *Contenciosa*, 1.
Marco, J. (2013b). Limpieza política en España: Insurrección, guerra civil y posguerra (1936-1953). In G. Águila. & L. Alonso (eds.), *Procesos represivos y actitudes sociales. Entre la España franquista y las dictaduras del Cono Sur*. Buenos Aires: Prometeo, pp. 69-96
Marco, J., Gordim da Silveire, H., & Valim Mansan, J. (eds.) (2015). *Violência e sociedade em ditaduras ibero-americanas no século XX. Argentina, Brasil, Espanha e*

Portugal. Porto Alegre: Pontifícia Universidade Católica do Rio Grande do Sul.

Melero Vargas, M. A. (2014). Alineamiento, indiferencia y formas de resistencia ciudadana ante el nuevo estado franquista en los primeros años del terror, 1936-1945. *Contenciosa*, 3.

Merele, H. (2015). *La "depuración" ideológica del peronismo en el partido de General Sarmiento (1973-1974). Una aproximación a partir del caso de Antonio "Tito" Deleroni*. Masters dissertation. Universidad Nacional General Sarmiento.

Merele, H. (2016). El proceso represivo en los años setenta constitucionales. De la "depuración" interna del peronismo al accionar de las organizaciones paraestatales. In G. Águila, S. Garaño & P. Scatizza (eds.), *Represión estatal y violencia paraestatal en la historia reciente argentina. Nuevos abordajes a 40 años del golpe de Estado.* La Plata: Universidad Nacional de La Plata, pp. 99-123.

Miglioranza, S. (2014). Me han denunciado porque me aborrecen. Poder y delación en tiempos de Rosas (1837-1845). Masters dissertation, Buenos Aires: Universidad Torcuato Di Tella.

Míguez, A. (2016a). *The genocidal genealogy of Francoism: Violence, memory and impunity*. Eastbourne; Chicago: Cañada Blanch Centre & Sussex Academic Press.

Míguez, A. (2016b). *Ni verdugos ni víctimas. Actitudes sociales ante la violencia, del franquismo a la dictadura argentina*. Granada: Comares.

Mir, C. (2000). *Vivir es sobrevivir. Justicia, orden y marginación en la Cataluña rural de posguerra*. Lleida: Milenio.

Mir, C. (2001). El estudio de la represión franquista: Una cuestión sin agotar. *Ayer*, 43, 11-35.

Montero, M. L. (2016). El rol de la "comunidad informativa" en la represión en Bahía Blanca (1975-1977): Prácticas, acuerdos y disputas. In G. Águila, S. Garaño & P. Scatizza (eds.), *Represión estatal y violencia paraestatal en la historia reciente argentina. Nuevos abordajes a 40 años del golpe de Estado.* La Plata: Universidad Nacional de La Plata, pp. 367-394.

Oviedo Silva, D., & Pérez-Olivares, A. (2016). ¿Un tiempo de silencio? Porteros, inquilinos y fomento de la denuncia en el Madrid ocupado. *Studia Historica. Historia Contemporánea*. 34.

Pereira, A. W. (2010). Ditadura e repressão. O autoritarismo e o estado de direito no Brasil, no Chile e na Argentina. São Paulo: Paz e Terra.

Preston, P. (2012). *The Spanish holocaust: Inquisition and extermination in twentieth-century Spain*. London: HarperPress.

Rodrigo, J. (2001). La bibliografía sobre la represión franquista: Hacia el salto cualitativo. *Spagna Contemporánea,* 19, 151-169.

School of the Americas (1989). *Handling of sources*. N.p. Available at **www.soaw.org/about-the-soawhinsec/ soa-manuals/98-soa-manuals-index**

Scocco, M. (2016). Los consejos de guerra militares como práctica de represión política (1956-1983). In G. Águila, S. Garaño & P. Scatizza (eds.), *Represión estatal y violencia paraestatal en la historia reciente argentina. Nuevos abordajes a 40 años del golpe de Estado.* La Plata: Universidad Nacional de La Plata, pp. 207-236.

Somoza Cayado, A. (2015). Delación y violencia en la construcción del nuevo régimen en las sociedades rurales de la provincia de Lugo (1936-1942). In P. Folguera *et al.* (eds.), *Pensar con la historia desde el siglo XXI. XII Congreso de la Asociación de Historia Contemporánea.* Madrid: UAM.

Trinquier, R. (2006). *Modern warfare: A French view of counterinsurgency.* Westport: Praeger Security International.

Verbitsky, H., & Bohoslavsky, J. P. (2013). *Cuentas pendientes. Los cómplices económicos de la dictadura.* Buenos Aires: Siglo XXI.

Vezzetti, H. (2002). *Pasado y presente. Guerra, dictadura y sociedad en la Argentina.* Buenos Aires: Siglo XXI.

Falklands-Malvinas

Traumas, Memories and Identity Processes

María Teresa Dalmasso

Within the framework of a culture that, as Todorov points out, appears to be characterized by the cult of memory, semiotics cannot remain indifferent. Being ourselves trapped in the web of signification, and faced with the task of accounting for the mechanisms of construction, reconstruction—and destruction—of the meaning of the past, we propose to shed some light on certain aspects of these semiotic processes, which are inextricably linked to their socio-historical context.

These polemical signifying productions constitute what we call "discourses of memory". Their political dimension grants them a crucial value in understanding the debates that a society wages in order to impose a vision of itself. These are disputes in which all sorts of strategies tending to the (re)axiologization of the past are deployed from a valuation of the present projected onto the future.

An Argentina Built out of Crises and Traumas

Argentina appears, to a large number of citizens (and particularly to those over 50), to be a country in which the succession of political, economic and social crises continues unabated. The continuity of the crises that occurred in the last decades of the twentieth century and in the first of the twenty-first has left a traumatic effect, whose force actualizes and exalts memories in conflict. These recurrent convulsions interrupt the process of mourning and nurture the trauma with cumulative impotence. Throughout these decades, offset by a few moments of apparent recovery, Argentine society has seen its civil rights violated, has suffered political chaos, and has been subject to repressive violence and economic dispossession. In times such as that of secular inflection, the prolonged succession of failures, bitter misunderstandings and violent antagonisms triggered in its citizens a sense of irreversible decline that plunged them into despair. However, given its persistence throughout history, such a state of mind may come to be viewed as a sort of idiosyncratic tic. To explain this apparent constant, perhaps we would have to consider the confluence of historically more distant factors. We might conjecture that some of the reasons may be rooted in the disappointment stemming from the failure to attain the destiny of greatness pretentiously foretold by the leaders of our country since the beginning of the twentieth century. In this sense, we might assume, taking our cue from Schwab (2015: 54-55), that this unfulfilled prophecy has triggered a kind of destiny-neurosis.

In a history of virtually constant convulsions, it is imperative to address the passional framework that dominates citizens' behaviour. At first glance, one may observe how these passions encourage—especially in times of instability—a sceptical view of the country's present and future possibilities, render difficult the process of mourning, make the trauma more complex, nurture ghosts and, above all, generate profound cracks in the processes of constructing collective identities.

This assessment throws up questions surrounding certain passional traits that seem to contribute to the generation and establishment of a certain identity image in the doxa. Thus, we are induced to reflect upon the signs of melancholy, a passion that seems to occupy a privileged position in the definition of "Argentineness". Without underestimating the effects left by specific crises, we must ask if our difficulty in abandoning the utopia of a successful and thrusting future is not a factor that hinders the process of mourning, in such a way that, disillusioned and self-deprecating, we are stuck in melancholy. This state goes in hand in hand with a tendency to violent reactions, marked by an agonistic bias that makes us inclined to polemics. That is to say, melancholy and anger[1] would seem to be the visible axes of the passional fabric. Both of them, simultaneously or successively, inflame the discursive flow. These two passions may tentatively be understood as variants of frustration, of the impotence brought about by not-being-able-to-do or not-being-able-to-be, which is channelled agonistically and in a non-exclusive way through aggression and/or self-aggression.

Commemorations

We believe we can see a certain relationship between this

---

[1] See Parret (1995: 12-27).

difficult work of mourning, recurrently interrupted, and a sort of compulsion to commemorations (resurrected anniversaries, new monuments and changes in their location, or their replacement, new or recovered museums, rooms dedicated to heroes, with some things removed and others newly included) that increases in times when confrontational obfuscation encourages official revisionism and enflames the civic mood. Paraphrasing Pierre Nora (2008: 175), we might say that, at such times, properly national and civic commemoration sinks into the political.

Thus, at the beginning of this century saturated with anniversaries of a mostly unhappy nature—the twenty-fifth and thirtieth anniversaries of the military coup (2001 and 2006), the twenty-fifth and thirtieth anniversaries of the Malvinas War (2007 and 2012), but also the bicentenary of the May Revolution (2010)—dissidences have exploded, because, as Elizabeth Jelin (2002: 248-250) points out:

> at significant public moments, such as the dates of commemorations, not everybody shares the same memories. Memory refers to the ways in which people construct a sense of the past and how they relate that past to the present in the act of recalling or remembering.

This leads onto the question:

> Are the activities carried out a commemoration of past events or vehicles of present political struggle, akin to electoral propaganda or charges brought against political enemies? (Jelin 2002: 248-250)

Discrepancies become evident in the celebratory modes and accents, in their adherences and in their critical readings, in the moments rescued from oblivion and in those omitted, in the monuments erected and in those moved or suppressed altogether. All these movements prove to be highly revealing of the socio-historical conditions that make them possible.

Memory, Commemorations and the Print Media

Moved by the interest to identify and understand the strategies for the construction of memory/memories deployed in our country over the last decades, as much as their consequences upon the processes of definition of what we would, with due caution, call "national identity", we have embarked upon an exploration of what happens in the intricate discursive web, dwelling with particular interest on moments of commemorative exaltation. This has allowed us to observe transformations and displacements whose relation to different social, political and economic circumstances have caught our attention. At the same time, however, we have detected certain behaviours that appear to stem from an unswerving recidivist tendency.

The present research focuses above all on discourses from the print media, especially opinion pieces, testimonies, chronicles and interviews. The decision to do so responds to the crucial role played by journalistic discourse in the construction of the real (Verón 1987). These public discourses, characterized by their doxastic and persuasive nature, offer and disseminate interpretations of facts that are made possible by a socio-historically determined discursivity which, at the same time, paves the way for such interpretations to be accepted.

We have concentrated particularly on publications that, even if motivated by the same commemorations—specifically, the twenty-fifth and thirtieth anniversaries of the Malvinas War—are the expression of politically antagonistic newspapers. This has allowed us to appreciate both the continuities and the differences, for although in every society discursive interaction guarantees certain constants in the social production of what is considered probable, debatable, plausible (Angenot 1989), social discourse does not impose unique interpretants, but rather is characterized by its openness, contradictions and dynamism.

Malvinas, Memory/Memories and Identities: A Passional Question

In the previous sections, we have alluded to the passions involved in the creation of memory and memories, and to their intricate relationship with the construction of collective identities. While re-reading the pages of the introduction to *Malvinas. El gran relato,* by the Argentine semiologist Lucrecia Escudero, we were particularly struck by a paragraph in which the author recalls the contradictory passions involved in belic encounters. Escudero refers, in particular, to the feelings of a group of intellectuals that would gather together moved by a passional commitment and by the need not to remain on the margins of an unforeseen event that was shaking every fibre of a "territorial identity" internalized at school. In the face of this tragic adventure, which at the expense of innocent victims hastened the demise of the dictatorship that encouraged it, the aim of these intellectuals—which, in my opinion, was not quite fulfilled[2]—was to shed rational light on what was happening. In the words of the author:

> I think this was simply the paradox of the war and the tremendous affective force of the event: the childhood schoolbook where we painted the islands with the national colours and the rationalization of an absurd war which, if won, would perpetuate to infinity the cruel military arrogance. (Escudero 2013: 25)

The scope of the adjective "absurd" applied to the war seems to be restricted to the fact that it favoured the interests of the military, whose power was decaying; but it does not seem to refer to the fact that, given the international context in which the conflict was set, imagining an Argentine victory was equally absurd. This reading calls for a profound reflection upon the need to believe that seemed to dominate society as a whole. A need that, with all its paradoxes, remains present in the discourses of commemoration, and especially in those related to the Bicentenary (Dalmasso 2011a, 2011b, 2014). This perception leads us to focus on what we consider a moving effort to uphold the constructions of national identity that have dominated the social imaginary for most of the twentieth century, and which have been progressively eroded at least since the 1960s. During the most critical periods, this process, along with its contradictions, has sunk Argentines into a confusion from which not even the most lucid intellectuals have been able to escape.

This is related, as we previously pointed out, to a resistance properly to elaborate trauma, which has driven us to ignore our own impotence and to resist a reality that is contrary to our longings. In this respect, Carlos Gamerro, in a quotation harvested by Raquel San Martín (2012: 1-3),

---

[2] On this subject, see Rozitchner (2015).

describes lucidly an Argentine society torn between holding on to the seductions of a promissory image or accepting the one returned to it by the socio-political and economic vicissitudes that inexorably shape daily reality:

> Malvinas is related to an Argentine institutional and everyday discourse of a country that is not where it should be, of a power that declined. Malvinas stands as a symbol of what we lost, of what we imagine we lost or of what we believe we deserve and do not have.

Summarizing what happened in terms of society's mood, Lucrecia Escudero (2013: 30) introduces a key element, specifically the role played by the media: "Argentine society constructed a collective actor of desire, which 'did not want not to believe' and granted a level of trust to a specific discursive genre: the news." In this respect, María Seoane (2007) writes:

> with some exceptions, Argentines entered into a patriotic frenzy encouraged by the government, which included a varied and Felliniesque menu: out of fear or convenience, between official censorship and official propaganda, radio stations and television channels bombarded Argentines and incited them to domestic warmongering, just the climate of support that Galtieri was looking for.

Escudero's work delves into the construction of "The Great Narrative" carried out by the media apparatus. In this respect, she posits that the coherence of a narrative that might satisfy the population's passional expectations was preferred to the accuracy of the information provided. This leads her to question the processes of production and recognition that, once assimilated to the doxa, bestowed verisimilitude on the narrative (Escudero 2013: 27-29).

We can imagine that, at that time, the legitimacy granted to the media as informative enunciators afforded the complicity needed by the will to believe. Discourse, underpinned by a doxa nurtured since school and shared by all, constructed a model destinatee with whom no actual receiver could not not identify.

Traumas, Memories and Identity Processes

Malvinas and their Memories

During the twenty-fifth and thirtieth anniversaries of the war, and above all during the latter, commemorative discourses started to take into account conflicting interpretations of events. In this sense, critical interpretations from certain quarters in respect of the policies pursued by different administrations at different moments started to gain visibility.[3] Reviewing our selection of publications, the most representative of the opposing political positions of late (*Clarín* and *La Nación,* on the one hand, and *Página/12*, on the other), we have been able to observe that, on the former anniversary, one of the salient issues is the difficulty Argentines have in thinking about and putting into words the subject of the war. In this regard, Luis Bruschtein (2007) is clear:

> In truth, the war is rarely brought up, because it is a harsh, insidious, disturbing issue. Extreme positions on one side or another are held by those who prefer not to listen, and opinions are fired off according to mood and humour. Malvinas remains on a symbolic plane. It is a symbol of "the homeland", but also of failure, guilt, shame and deceit.

We can see here a clear synthesis of the contradictions that beset a large part of the citizenry when it recalls the events. We see the possibility of considering the existence of two levels of deceit, one supported by the other. Thus, the sustained deceit carried out by the military, and reinforced by the media's narrative, is irrefutable. However, its efficacy seems rooted in the shared conviction of a territorial identity instilled at school. It is around this issue that a group of intellectuals begins to question whether this construction has not been yet another form of deceit. Naturally, this is a destabilizing, provocative interpretation that triggers significant resistance. The state of political tension makes this questioning assume a somewhat virulent tone in the discursivity of 2012, and become one of the axes of confrontation. In this respect, in a certain sense discouraging these doubts and tribulations, Horacio González (2012) summarizes the situation:

---

[3] In 2007 Néstor Kirchner was in office, and in 2012 his wife, Cristina Férnandez de Kirchner, succeeded him.

The Malvinas War, in 1982, is an event with dates, a beginning and an end, an arc of time that includes proper names, vituperations, exaltations, many deaths, chronicles and novels [...]. These events are all part of Argentine history, implicated in Argentine history, closely tied to what we recognize as the familiar names of an over-historicized concept of the Nation. I say over-historicized, because the name "Malvinas" makes us contemporaries of a history of *longue durée*, fractured many a time, but traversing, with a rare unity, the periods of Rosas, Roca, Yrigoyen, Perón, the military *juntas* and restored democracy.

This generalized belief, unquestioningly shared throughout our history, this rare unity inspired by the Malvinas, persists over time and might explain—as we have already indicated—the difficulty, even among the most lucid groups of intellectuals, of detaching oneself from the passional relation to the islands. The conviction in our rights over the archipelago, an incontestable presupposition for most Argentines, clouded the capacity to take a critical distance from the events at the very moment the war was unfolding. In this respect, León Rozitchner's (2007) implacable accusation is against the citizenry as a whole:

> Malvinas is a key event in our history, wherein a sinister pact that still holds was sealed: the complicity between the majority of its citizens and state terrorism. This union which terror had tied together has still not been broken. For in the "Reconquest of the Malvinas" the totality of its social forces, both right and left, converged.

Some of the questionings that had started to emerge right after the conflagration exploded around the thirtieth anniversary. While there abound objections born of the contradictions inherent in that unfortunate adventure, others emerge, as we have shown, which focus on the criticism of the presuppositions and arguments upheld by the commemorative and celebratory policies pursued by the government in office. Thus does a group of 17 ideologically critical intellectuals dare to question the Malvinas issue as a "national cause" and to review the arguments underpinning that position:

> Three decades have passed since the tragic 1982 military adventure, and we still lack a public critique of the support which society gave to the Malvinas War and which mobilized nearly every sector of the country. Among the reasons for such support, not least was the adherence to the Malvinas-cause, which proclaims the islands an "unredeemed territory", makes of their "recuperation" [MTD: note the use of quotation marks] a question of identity and puts it at the top of our national priorities and of the country's international agenda.[4]

And they indirectly warn the counter-receiver:

> Let us hope that April 2nd and the year 2012 do not lead to the usual escalation of patriotic claims, but rather provide an opportunity for us Argentines—members of the government, leaders and citizens—to reflect, together and without prejudice, on the relation between our own mistakes and our country's failures. (de Ípola *et al.* 2012)

This interpretation, which would allow for the possibility that the islanders had a right to voice their opinion, is opposed not only by those who maintain the deep-rooted position concerning our inalienable rights over the islands, but especially by those who agree with the policies the government adopted on the matter. In such a way that political stance seems to offer one of the keys to understanding an issue that pits the dissident sector against, among others, the group of intellectuals gathered under the

---

[4] A group of 17 intellectuals, constitutionalists and journalists from Argentina who call for a review of government policy on the Malvinas conflict. Under the title "Malvinas, una visión alternativa" (Malvinas: An Alternative Vision), they issued a document that carries the signature of the intellectuals Beatriz Sarlo, Juan José Sebreli, Santiago Kovadloff, Rafael Filippelli, Emilio de Ípola, Vicente Palermo, Marcos Novaro and Eduardo Antón; of the journalists Jorge Lanata, Gustavo Noriega and Pepe Eliaschev; of the historians Luis Alberto Romero and Hilda Sábato; of the constitutionalists Daniel Sabsay, Roberto Gargarella and José Miguel Onaindia, and the former member of the National Congress, Fernando Iglesias.

name Carta Abierta[5] (Open Letter) who support the official position. That antagonism shows clearly in the discourses that contest the arguments of the Group of 17. An example of this is found in an article by Edgardo Mocca, who polemically incorporates his counter-receivers' discourse into his own:

> Outraged by the prominence given to the issue in the political arena, the authors, however, have decided to put it at the centre of their own agenda. That is to say that, given the alleged attempt to malvinize politics, they have accepted the challenge and take it upon themselves to demalvinize it [...]. It is very good to take the islanders' rights into consideration, but political sovereignty is not a subjective right: it is exercised or claimed by national states. And, nowadays, the Malvinas territory is not an independent state. Its government is in the hands of an official appointed by the British state. (Mocca 2012)

Both the difficulty in dealing with this issue, which seems to enforce a conflictive adherence either to nationalism or to anti-nationalism, and the notable direction taken by government policies, are clearly laid out in Raquel San Martín's (2012) article:

> How to join in the claim for sovereignty without being wedded to an extreme nationalism or to the dictatorship that launched the military adventure in 1982? How to critically review the Argentine rights over the islands without being trapped in an anti-nationalist position, now that the government is championing the issue as the new national and popular cause against imperialism?

---

[5] The members of Espacio Carta Abierta made their first public appearance on 13 May 2008, in the City of Buenos Aires, on a panel that gathered together Horacio Verbitsky, Nicolás Casullo, Ricardo Forster and Jaime Sorín, where they presented the first "open letter". Despite its ideological affinity with the political party Frente para la Victoria, the group defines itself as a non-partisan space.

These questions allow us to glimpse the reasons why, at that specific moment, dissident voices were raised, among which those of the group of 17 critical intellectuals stand out.

Heroes or Martyrs?
The heading of this section, which rehearses a question that for all its familiarity has lost none of its vibrancy, was suggested to us by Horacio González's (2012) statement: "It is not the first time that the subject of who are the heroes, and who the martyrs has been discussed in Argentina."

Partly during the twenty-fifth anniversary commemoration, but mostly during the thirtieth, the focus of attention shifted towards the issue of the veterans. We must ask ourselves whether such a shift responds to the intention of avoiding the complexity of a situation doubly contaminated from an ideological standpoint, both by the political circumstances surrounding the war and by the context of the anniversary, or whether it responds, rather, to the will to reinforce the official view of the facts and actors involved in the confrontation. A significant number of the published articles adopt the biographical angle and focus on reconstructing the vicissitudes suffered by ex-combatants of the war, with the additional benefit of inducing the association between the victims of the war and those of the dictatorship. In these chronicles and testimonies, a tragic continuity is traced between the practices deployed by the military during the dictatorship and those used when it came to organizing, conducting and sustaining the war against the United Kingdom. Among the testimonies, we find that of Edgardo Esteban, a veteran, journalist and writer. His narrative provides an insight into the aberrant neglect to which veterans were exposed on their return from the Malvinas, one of whose most dramatic consequences has been the number of post-war victims. The suicides caused by the impossibility of overcoming trauma account for more deaths than those that occurred in combat. The society that had so feverishly encouraged the war now chose denial, perhaps out of guilt or shame. If it was out of shame, we might ask whether it was motivated by its own belligerent impulse, by the deceit to which it was subjected or by the ridicule of the defeat. Erasing the veterans is a way of erasing the war, a war that should never have happened. With bitterness, referring to the veteran's fate, Esteban (2007) reproaches:

> Besides being defeated, we seemed responsible for the defeat which we arrived at by military decision. From then on, there was a tacit agreement to forget the war; we had to endure being hidden and advised to wipe what had happened from our minds, forcing us to keep it to ourselves. For a long time, remaining silent was the preferred option over doing a mea culpa for a war that was lost, and no one wanted to assume responsibility for the defeat.

Here, too, society as a whole is the target of the criticism, for once the patriotic impulse faded before the force of a defeat it had refused to imagine, it superficially closed the episode by adding insult to injury, as the veteran César Maliqueo attests in a newspaper article (Savoia 2012): "In Buenos Aires, when we returned, people were watching the World Cup in Spain." Denial is once again repeated.

As was previously indicated, in the narratives of war references to the mistreatment and unscrupulousness on the part of those of a higher rank dominate. So much so that the comparison between the behaviour displayed by the military during the dictatorship and that displayed towards ordinary soldiers during the war can be found in a significant number of narratives. In them, the ex-combatants are portrayed as the true victims of the conflict. They, however, strive not to be considered mere survivors and claim that what should be highlighted is the extent to which their action was moved by love for their country. Within this framework, opinions are divided in some respects. While some veterans consider that the officers who subjected them to torture during the conflict should be tried, others oppose the idea on the grounds that doing so would be tantamount to making themselves into victims.

During the thirtieth anniversary, many a voice was raised calling for cases to be opened against military personnel who subjected their soldiers to torture. Among them was the voice of H.I.J.O.S.:[6]

---

[6] The name of the group, Hijos e Hijas por la Identidad y la Justicia contra el Olvido y el Silencio (Sons and Daughters for Identity and Justice against Forgetting and Silence), summarizes

> the heads of the Argentine Armed Forces were practitioners of genocide and took to the islands the criminal practices they had deployed in the 500 or so Clandestine Centres of Detention, Torture and Extermination [the CCDTyE, in Spanish] that functioned in our country. Some of these repressors were convicted at the Trials of the Juntas and at the trials taking place at present [...]. These crimes, committed against Argentine soldiers, are crimes against humanity that must not go unpunished. The cause, thus, must go before the courts. (H.I.J.O.S. 2012)

Nevertheless, the proposal to prosecute this latest version of victimizers engendered by the self-proclaimed National Reorganization Process appears to have gone unheard. It is mainly in *Página/12* that the majority of these protests are registered. Mario Wainfeld (2012), for instance, claims:

> The torture perpetrated by the Argentine military during the Malvinas War is not taken to be a crime against humanity by the courts. So decided a ruling at the Court of Appeal [*Cámara de Casación*], the highest instance that has been issued so far. The Supreme Court should analyze this sentence and eventually revoke it, if it would make room for legal actions brought by the victims.

The claims and frustrations testify to the difficulties of mobilizing a society that seems to have deleted the terrible war and its effects from its agenda. In this respect, Federico Lorenz (2012), making particular reference to progressive sectors and human rights organizations, stated:

> its main aims: calling for justice, reconstructing personal history, and reasserting the struggles of their parents and of the 30,000 detained-disappeared, as well as calling for the restitution of the identity of their siblings who were kidnapped. Further, they demand the effective life-long imprisonment of all those responsible for crimes against humanity during the last dictatorship, their accomplices, instigators and beneficiaries.

The thirtieth anniversary of the Malvinas calls for a deep exercise of introspection on the part of those sectors involved in democracy and Human Rights, a taking of responsibility that allows them to fill the unjust gap which a significant majority built between the young ex-soldiers and them.

Memory('s) Games

In our musings we have paid special attention to certain themes which we considered significant for an understanding of the strategies that play a role in the construction of memory and memories, as well as their conditioning and objectives.

One aspect that has interested us and that deserves to be examined at length concerns the variations produced in the discourses of memory according to the political situation. We think there have been certain thematic shifts, accompanied by a polemical element, apparently linked to the positions commentators adopt in relation to government policies at times of increased conflict. On the twenty-fifth anniversary, the emphasis was put on the war itself, on criticism of military actions and on questions surrounding the reasons for the fervent popular support for the war. However, on the thirtieth anniversary—which happened in times of heightened political confrontation—there emerge, on the one hand, dissident discourses referring to the need to review both the legitimacy of the claims over the islands and the policies pursued by the government (which presuppose such legitimacy), and, on the other hand, in sectors closer to the official view, there is the proliferation of veterans' narratives that, portraying themselves as victim-heroes, encourage the prosecution of those who victimized them.

It should be noted that those discourses that involve questioning the doxa, such as those of the Group of 17, presuppose a restricted destinatee, since they require a kind of competence that is only present in certain sectors of society that question belief in a critical spirit. On the other hand, testimonial narratives, chronicles and interviews, which by virtue of their narrative properties incite compassion towards the protagonists of a drama that reactivates memory and facilitates identification, anticipate a destinatee that shares the doxa rooted in school history; that is to say, those who share a belief that furnishes the bedrock of their adherence. At the same time, the equivalence established between military behaviour allegedly predominant during the war and the military's behaviour during the dictatorship constructs a less restricted receiver for, although preferably oriented towards those progressive sectors committed to human rights, when put together with the veterans' narratives of their suffering, they have the potential to make an impact on those sectors of the population who have shown themselves to be moved by such narratives.

The discursive behaviour of the print media on the occasion of the twenty-fifth and thirtieth anniversaries of the Malvinas War allows us to posit that these memory exercises do not escape the conflicts of the day, but rather make them evident. Thus one sees political conflicts and misunderstandings advanced in the demonstration of argumentative strategies aimed at constructing a plausible, convincing version of the past that agrees ideologically with the current positioning of each of the parties.

To conclude, we borrow Claudio A. Jacqueline's (2012) illuminating definition: "Malvinas evokes and means so many things that it is the synthesis of all Argentine paradoxes."

References
Angenot, M. (1989). *1889. Un état du discours social*.
    Québec: Éditions du Préambule.
Bruschtein, L. (2007). Una sociedad presa de los símbolos de
    Malvinas. *Página/12*. At **www.pagina12.com.ar/
    diario/especiales/18-82728-2007-04-02.html**,
    accessed 2 June 2015.
Dalmasso, M. T. (2011a). Semblanzas de la discursividad
    argentina en épocas del Bicentenario. *Bicentenaire des
    Indépendances Amérique Latine Caraïbes.* Paris: IHEAL
    Institut d'Hautes Etudes de l'Amérique Latine, Institut
    Français, CD Rom.
Dalmasso, M. T. (2011b). El Bicentenario. Discurso social e
    identidades. La memoria y el presente. *Actas del V
    Coloquio de Investigadores en Estudios del Discurso y II
    Jornadas Internacionales sobre Discurso e
    Interdisciplina*. Villa María: UNVM. At **www.
    unvm.edu.ar/index.php?mod=cmsjornadas**,

accessed 30 July 2016.

Dalmasso, M. T. (2014). Singularidades del discurso social en torno al Bicentenario. In H. Ponce de la Fuente & M. T. Dalmasso (eds.), *Trayectos teóricos en semiótica*. Santiago de Chile: Universidad de Chile, Facultad de Artes, Escuela de Posgrado, pp. 11-17.

De Ípola, E. *et al*. (2012). Malvinas: una visión alternativa. At **http://lalectoraprovisoria.wordpress.com/ 2012/02/24/el-grupo-de-los-17-sobre-Malvinas**, accessed 5 April 2012.

Escudero, L. (2013). *Malvinas. El gran relato*. Barcelona: Gedisa.

Esteban, E. (2007). Sacar nuestro infierno interior y empezar a curar las heridas. *Página/12*. At **www.pagina12.com.ar/diario/especiales/18-82726-2007-04-02.html**, accessed 3 June 2015.

H.I.J.O.S. (2012). Genocidas: de los centros clandestinos a las Malvinas. *Página/12*. At **www.pagina12.com.ar/diario/elpais/1-190993-2012-04-03.html**, accessed 12 April 2012.

González, H. (2012). Malvinas y el liberalismo. *Página/12*. At **www.pagina12.com.ar/diario/elpais/1-191005-2012-04-03.html**, accessed 10 April 2012.

Jacqueline, C. (2012). Malvinas, la epopeya y el circo. *La Nación, Suplemento Enfoque Especial*, 1 April, p. 2.

Jelin, E. (2002). Los sentidos de la conmemoración. In E. Jelin (ed.), *Las conmemoraciones. Las disputas en las fechas in-felices*. Madrid: Siglo XXI, pp. 245-250.

Lorenz, F. (2012). Malvinas: prejuicios y deudas. *Página/12*. At **www.pagina12.com.ar/diario/ elpais/1-190944-2012-04-02.html**, accessed 12 April 2012.

Mocca, E. (2012). La alarma por la "agitación nacionalista". *Revista Debate*. At **www.espacioiniciativa.com.ar/ ?p=6858**, accessed 15 April 2012.

Nora, P. (2008). *Pierre Nora en Les lieux de mémoire*. Montevideo: Ediciones Trilce.

Parret, H. (1995). *Las pasiones. Ensayo sobre la puesta en discurso de la subjetividad*. Buenos Aires: Edicial.

Rozitchner, L. (2007). Una complicidad de muerte que se mantiene en silencio. *Página 12*. At **www.pagina12. com.ar/diario/especiales/18-82730-2007-04-02.html**, accessed 2 June 2015.

Rozitchner, L. (2015). *Malvinas. De la guerra sucia a la guerra limpia. El punto ciego de la crítica política*. Buenos Aires: Ediciones Biblioteca Nacional.

San Martín, R. (2012). Malvinas, herida abierta. *La Nación, Suplemento Enfoque Especial*, 1 April, pp. 1-3.

Savoia, C. (2012). Honra a los caídos en bici por el sur. *Clarín, Suplemento Especial Malvinas 30 años 30 historias*, 1 April, p. 19.

Schwab, G. (2015). Escribir contra la memoria y el olvido. In S. Mandolesi & M. Alonso (eds.), *Estudios sobre memoria. Perspectivas actuales y nuevos escenarios*. Villa María: Editorial Universitaria Villa María, pp. 53-84.

Seoane, M. (2007). Los argentinos, entre el fervor y la decepción. *Clarín, Suplemento especial*, 1 April. At **edant.clarin.com/diario/2007/04/01/deportes/m-01391499.htm**, accessed 14 April 2015.

Verón, E. (1987). *Construir el acontecimiento.* Buenos Aires: Editorial Gedisa.

Wainfeld, M. (2012). Héroes estaqueados. *Página/12*. At **www.pagina12.com.ar/diario/elpais/1-190942-2012-04-02.html**, accessed 13 June 2012.

More Than 30 Years after the Malvinas: War in Film and on Television

Sandra Savoini

Introduction
In the field of Argentine post-dictatorship cultural production, the number of audiovisual works on the Malvinas War is far from negligible: since 1982, there have been at least 19 documentaries and 15 fiction films. These include a compilation of short films from various directors entitled *Malvinas—30 miradas* (2014), as well as whole series—and single episodes within series—delving into the topic and audiovisual teaching initiatives.[1]

---

[1] A brief mapping identifies the following productions:
Documentaries: *Malvinas, historia de traiciones* (J. Denti, 1983), *Malvinas, alerta roja* (A. Rotondo, 1985), *Malvinas, me deben tres* (C. Giordano, A. Marino, I. Matiasich, A. Alfonso, L. Rueda, J. B. Duizeide, 1992), *Hundan el Belgrano* (F. Urieste, 1996), *Malvinas, historias de dos islas* (D. Alhadeff, 1999), *Vamos ganando* (R. Longo, 2001), *El refugio del olvido* (D. Alhadeff, 2002), *Malvinas, 20 años* (R. Lejtman, 2002), *Malvinas, la lucha continúa* (F. Cola, 2003), *Locos de la bandera* (J. Cardoso, 2005), *No tan nuestras* (R. Longo, 2005), *Estamos ganando, periodismo y censura en la guerra de Malvinas* (R. Persano y E. Ciganda, 2005), *Malvinas, tan lejos, tan cerca* (Lanata, 2007), *Malvinas, la historia que pudo ser* (Cuatro cabezas producciones/Discovery Channel, 2007), *Malvinas, 1982. La guerra desde el aire* (Argentina coproduction for History Channel, 2008), *Desobediencia debida* (V. Reale, 2008), *Huellas en el viento* (S. di Luca, 2008), *Malvinas, 25 años de silencio* (M. Anguelra, 2008), *Malvinas, viajes del Bicentenario* (J. Cardoso, 2010), *Piratas, pastores, inversores* (F. J. Palma, 2010), *14 de junio, lo que nunca se perdió* (D. Circosta, 2011), *1892-1982: dos historias de Malvinas* (P. Walker, 2011), *El héroe del Monte de dos Hermanas* (R. Vila, 2011), *La forma exacta de las islas* (D. Casabé & E. Dieleke, 2012), *Combatientes* (E. Spagniolo, 2013), *Pensar Malvinas* (canal Encuentro), *Malvinas, historia de la usurpación* (canal Encuentro), *Historias debidas IV* (canal Encuentro), *Historias de un país. Argentina siglo XX* (canal Encuentro).
Fictional films: *Los chicos de la guerra* (B. Kamín, 1984), *La deuda interna* (M. Pereira,1988), *Guarisove, los olvidados* (B. Stagnaro, 1995), *El visitante* (J. Olivera, 1999), *Fuckland* (J. L. Márques, 2000), *Los días de junio* (A. Fischerman, 1985), *La deuda interna* (M. Pereira,1988), *El visitante* (H. Olivera, 1999), *El mismo amor,*

The majority of these works appeared between 2003 and 2015, under a presidency that turned the examination of the dictatorship into government policy. This rekindled and promoted the actions of various civil organizations that had already been working on the pursuit of justice and remembrance. Audiovisual production was a consequence of various measures for the construction of memory closely related to other areas of memory production of the time. Visibility was particularly high in the media around the dates of commemoration—April, when it comes to the Malvinas— when programming on state television channels (Encuentro, INCAA TV and TV Pública) focused on paying homage through various television productions, documentaries and fiction films about the war.

By revisiting conceptions of intertextual and interdiscursive relations between memories from the perspective of semiotics and discourse analysis, we shall identify some veins of meaning that run through these audiovisual works in the context of commemorative television programming. Within this framework, we shall be able to understand the way in which the protagonists of history are construed, depending on the hegemonic discourse of each period (Angenot 2010).

This essay is based on the proposal by Courtine (1981), among other discourse analysts, for whom relations of meaning bring into play discursive memories, insofar as as they form a bridge that ties the present to the past experience that is being evoked. It is in this context that the representation of the world and of the individuals living in it is developed. In this way, memories can be understood as historical devices of power-knowledge that produce what can be said and shown from the perspective of particular

---

la misma lluvia (J. Campanella, 1999), *Pozo de Zorro* (M. Mirra, 1999), *Guarisove, los olvidados* (B. Stagnaro, 1995), *1982, estuvimos ahí* (2004), *Iluminados por el fuego* (T. Bauer, 2005), *Palabra por palabra* (E. Cabeza, 2007), *Cartas a Malvinas* (R. Fernández, 2009), *La campana* (2010), *Un cuento chino* (2011), *Malvinas—30 miradas* (30 short films by various directors, 2014), El último, an episode of *Vindica* (E. Crupnicoff, J. Laplace, M. Ardanaz, N. Parodi, 2011), *Combatientes* (J. P. Clemente & T. de las Heras, 2013), *La asombrosa excursión de Zamba en las Islas Malvinas* (canal PakaPaka).

ideologies that permeate different parts of discourse. These memories allow us to understand the way in which the present is built by recovering that which has already been said and seen, given that the production of discourse repeats, transforms or refutes discourses that have already been articulated, contributing to the semiotic construction of reality (Verón 1993).

Time in Memory

The Malvinas War of 1982 was the only Argentine war of the twentieth century. It took a toll of 649 deaths in the arena of operations and over a thousand wounded. Moreover, as estimated by veterans' organizations, it led to the suicide of some 500 soldiers—an estimate, since there are no official data—over the course of the following 30 years. The war was a breaking point not only for foreign policy, but also for domestic policy, as it precipitated the end of the military dictatorship. Malvinas is a proper noun that, after the conflict, became a trope, invoking the concept of war and a particular period in history. It is this traumatic experience, marked by defeat and deception, which has survived over the years as the meaning of that word. This meaning hegemonizes and obstructs other possible ways of understanding that territory.

According to the Real Academia Española, "trauma" comes from the Greek word for wound. Many of its meanings refer to a wound that persists in time.[2] Certain events that disrupt individual or collective experience can become incidents that inflict serious injuries. However, trauma is not the event itself, but the imprint left on the individual. From an individual point of view—although it can be coextensive with a community because certain events that affect a person are partly created out of collective experience—trauma is the result of some sort of violence that goes beyond what is tolerable and persists after the event, especially when it is unresolved because it cannot be seen or articulated. This would be the case of all those who participated in the war in

---

[2] Trauma: "1. Lasting injury produced by a mechanical agent, generally an external one. 2. Emotional shock that causes permanent damage in the unconscious. 3. Feeling or impression which is negative, strong and persistent" (Real Academia Española 2001).

one way or another, the case of Argentine society itself. The cause is a complex range of factors that might be part of what some people call the politics of forgetting, which are also part of memory.

As a consequence, the *process of de-Malvinification* (which took place, at least, in the first two decades after the conflict) resulted in the general effacement of the event from public memory. The only exception was during anniversaries, when it appeared in the form of highly stereotypical figures and focused on the victimization of the young soldiers, categorizing the event as the consequence of an irrational military adventure. The military government invoked nationalistic stereotypes in order to achieve consensus and remain in power, something that proved hard at the time for several reasons, one of them being the serious economic crisis. The paradox is that Malvinas therefore stands at a point of inflection between the dictatorship and democracy. Being a liminary experience, it proved very uncomfortable to think about in the post-dictatorship context.

The film *Los chicos de la guerra*, by Bebe Kamín (1984), is the epitome of this form of representation. It was the first film to deal with the topic, only two years after the conflict, in the context of the emerging democracy of Raúl Alfonsín. As such, it is an obligatory part of commemorative rituals shown on television every year. In the words of R. Guber (2001: 88):

> The movie begins with the image of the end of the war, with young soldiers digging the graves to bury their dead (fellow soldiers with whom they shared the same trenches, nationality and generation). This image summarizes the heart of Kamín's message: dead or alive, those kids were victims of the National Reorganization Process, of a war between the armed forces and their countrymen. The British are nothing but the platform on which the Argentine drama was displayed.

This can be seen, for example, in a sequence where Santiago, one of the protagonists, decides to untie a fellow soldier who had his arms and legs tied to spikes in the ground by his officers for stealing a sheep (a punishment that became a method of torture). After doing so, the soldier is taken to the commander to justify his actions while the other soldiers declare: "Sí, es cierto, nos están cagando de hambre, nos tratan peor que a los enemigos" [It's true. They're starving us to death. They treat us worse than they treat the enemy].

This type of representation was pervasive during the 1980s and 1990s, characterized by the predominance of the victimizing narrative that has already been mentioned. This style created consensus because it worked for Argentine society, for the reasons stated by Lorenz (2011: 55):

> it corresponded both with the image of the young constructed during the transition back to democracy and with the self-exculpatory view which society was trying to build [...] and this context placed the soldiers in the position of victims of their own officers and of the capriciousness of the highest ranks. The analogy was created by Argentine society, which considered itself a victim of its armed forces. The soldiers in the Malvinas were other, younger victims of the dictatorship.

This interpretative framework tends to depoliticize and to create passive individuals who are part of a discourse infused with altruistic values linked to heroism and commitment. At the same time, it helps to erase the role played by the community before, during and after the armed conflict.

This subjective construction is not only present in audiovisual discourses about the war. To a great extent, documentaries and fiction in Argentina in the eighties and nineties on the topic of the dictatorship and the young represent the latter as innocent victims, effacing the ethical and political commitment to processes of collective action and transformation.[3]

In the context of this dominant representation of the armed conflict—or the dismissal of it—Malvinas progressively became a public topic as a result of the demands articulated by certain social actors, such as the veteran or ex-combatant associations (the difference between the terms has political implications and has been the subject of conflicts among the

---

[3] Although they have different styles and epochal characteristics that differentiate them, *La república perdida 2* (Pérez 1986) and *Montoneros, una historia* (Di Tella 1994) are two prime examples of documentaries on the topic.

different associations).⁴ These groups succeeded in getting their proposals strategically adopted by the governmental discourse in this new social context, which led to state policies.

As of 2003, the subject, referred to as the "Malvinas question", began to be reframed and became increasingly more prominent as a result of different actions enforced by the government in a variety of cultural (among other) areas. With it came the proliferation of voices and views, which joined the argument about the imposition of meaning relating to the war and post-war, emphasizing the use of testimonies or narratives from the protagonists' perspective. This can be perceived in different fields and discourses, such as in film and television. The changes in the narrative and articulation strategies of the audiovisual productions (documentaries or fiction) used to tell the stories about the Malvinas entail a transformation in the ways of remembering and, consequently, in the ways in which we interpret the recent past. These strategies show an increasing questioning of the role of society and, particularly, of the Argentine state during the post-war period, which are recurrent topics in the discourses heard over the last decade.

The fictional television drama *Combatientes* (2013)—whose title ("Combatants") focuses on the protagonists, highlighting their active role—is a prime example of this.⁵ This drama highlights the traumatic effects which the experience has had on the lives of a soldier and a young serviceman in the post-war period. These characters embody the failure of a social and individual project with which the survivors cannot deal, bringing them close to death. Like many others, this drama deals with one of the issues that

---

⁴ According to Argentine legislation, a Malvinas ex-combatant is any official, non-commissioned officer or conscript from the Armed and Security Forces who participated in the military actions which took place in the Malvinas theatre of operations (Teatro de Operaciones Malvinas, TOM) and in the South Atlantic theatre of operations (Teatro de Operaciones del Atlántico Sur). This statute's accreditation can only be issued by the Force to which each combatant belonged and endorsed by the Ministry of Defence.

⁵ *Combatientes* was written and directed by Jerónimo Paz Clemente and Tomás de las Heras, and was shown in April 2013 by TV Pública.

marked individuals after the conflict, evidenced by hundreds of suicides that show the difficulties the veterans faced when reintegrating into society during the post-war period.

This television series tells a story that begins in 1982, before the war, introducing five young men drafted to go to the Malvinas: Gustavo, Chapa, Raúl, Facundo and Carlos, who show highly heterogeneous social features and characteristics.[6] One of them is a factory worker, another one is a thief; there is a fearful Jewish singer, a rugby player, a son from a wealthy family and, finally, a designer who dreams of becoming an artist. All these characters, with the exception of Gustavo, show highly stereotypical features and evoke social types of the time, something that seems to be a significant weakness of the show. This may be due to the fact that much of the information about these (mis)adventure partners is tinted by Gustavo's perception and memory, Gustavo being one of the two protagonists (this being one of the narrative strategies, whose aim is revealed in the last episodes of the show). The letter informing them that they are subject to the draft is also received in different ways by each of them: for some, it means an escape from the life they lead; for others, an obligation they have to accept submissively. They are sent to the Malvinas, to the war front, under the command of Lieutenant Augusto López Cabral, a character whose attributes tear down the typical representations of the military leaders of the time (an innovative characteristic of social discourse which had been missing from the public media scene in previous decades). There, they share their everyday lives in a war situation marked by shortages. Finally, towards the end of the conflict, they have to fight the British hand to hand. They are all wounded and four of them die. Gustavo and Lieutenant López Cabral are taken prisoners. On their return, these survivors try to continue with their lives in complete loneliness. On the fifth anniversary of the landing, and in the context of the military coup that took place in Holy Week of 1987 against the democratic government of President Alfonsín, Gustavo tries to contact López Cabral to see if he can help him find his fellow soldiers. Gustavo suffered from memory loss and

---

[6] This television series is the first of its kind, with Malvinas as its topic and, additionally, many elements specific to cinematic language.

could not remember that the other soldiers had died. Although the lieutenant refuses to help him at first, this young serviceman goes looking for Gustavo as a consequence of his insistence and ends up saving him: suicide on the continent is ever-present, in the same way death was on the Malvinas. In spite of this, life goes on for them. In this respect, the narrative in *Combatientes* is encouraging.

The discourse of *Combatientes* shapes protagonists whose identity is defined, among other things, by the limit between reason and insanity. One of the formal devices used to achieve this is temporal (con)fusion as a narrative strategy. Temporal disruptions—achieved mainly by means of flashbacks recalling a selection of what happened on the Malvinas during the war, focused mainly on an internal plane—are interspersed with mental images (dreamlike images play an important role), linked to dreams and fears that allow us to access these individuals' experiences. This framework exacerbates the tension between amnesia and the need to remember in order to know what happened: only accessing the "truth" will allow for the exorcism of the past. Narrative and aesthetic methods are brought together to achieve this purpose.

In this way, the old motif of memory loss—not being able to remember, which is what triggered Gustavo's pursuit in *Combatientes*; not wanting to remember, because it proves unbearable, as is the case of the servicemen in control; and the difficulty of distinguishing between true and false—provides some of the elements that organize the universe of meanings offered to the spectators, and with which we are to re-evaluate what we remember, why we remember it and what for, as well as what we forget, why we forget it and what for.

30 Years, 30 Views of the Malvinas
The movie *Malvinas—30 miradas. Los cortos de nuestras islas* (Malvinas—30 Views: Short Films on Our Islands), a more recent work released in 2014, is made up of 30 short films created by Argentine and other Latin American filmmakers. The piece is a proposal that seeks to contribute to the construction of audiovisual memory, drawing upon multiple aesthetic, narrative and thematic perspectives. It was made by the Centro de Producción e Investigación

Audiovisual (CePIA), part of the Ministry of Culture, together with the Consejo Asesor de la Televisión Digital Terrestre, in cooperation with the National University of Tres de Febrero. This film is part of the commemorative programming of INCAA TV channel and has been displayed in other places with a more limited access.

These 30 short films make up a mosaic where different representations of the Malvinas are outlined and overlap. Many of these narratives are characterized by a parodic style, perhaps because humour—and the distance it creates—is one of the best ways to address fetishes and taboos (Angenot 2010), in an attempt to escape from nationalistic or victimizing discourses. In this case, we will concentrate on the short film *Entrevista* (Interview), by Sergio Bellotti. As its title indicates, this work shows a meeting between a journalist from an opinion-setting magazine of the time and a general who was part of the dictatorship. The following is a fragment of it:

> Periodista: Para ir cerrando, General, ¿no quiere decir un mensaje a los familiares de los soldados muertos en esta guerra?
> General: En todos estos años en los que hemos luchado contra el enemigo interno hemos sido orgullosamente responsables de la tortura, la muerte y desaparición de decenas de miles de argentinos... (Se escuchan balas de fondo) en su gran mayoría jóvenes, incluyendo mujeres embarazadas, casi adolescentes. En comparación, ¿qué son 600 soldados? Incluso algunos de nuestros oficiales los han maltratado y les han hecho pasar hambre, pero siempre hay causas superiores, superiores!
> Periodista: ¡Gracias por su testimonio, General!
> General: No, por favor, usted se lo merece, y salude de mi parte a su editor. Periodista: ¿Quiere agregar algo más?
> General: Mire, si usted quiere un detalle más completo va a tener que esperar un tiempo, unos veinte o treinta años, pero vaya tranquila, su editor va a entender... Veinte, treinta años...
> (Risas) Veinte, treinta años...
> (Se escucha como banda musical la Marcha de

Malvinas)

[Interviewer: To conclude, General, do you want to send a message to the families of those soldiers who died in the war?

General: Throughout the years we spent fighting our internal enemy, we have been proud culprits of the torture, death and disappearance of thousands of Argentines (Bullets can be heard in the background), mainly young ones, including pregnant women who were almost teenagers. In comparison, what are 600 soldiers? Even some of our own officers have mistreated them and starved them, but there is always a greater cause, a greater cause!

Interviewer: Thank you for your testimony, General!

General: No at all, you deserve it. Say hi to your editor for me.

Interviewer: Do you want to add anything else?

General: Look, if you want further details, you're gonna have to wait, some twenty or thirty years, but don't worry about it. Your editor will understand. Twenty or thirty years...

(Laughter) Twenty, thirty years...

(The March of the Malvinas is heard)]

As can be seen, the interview highlights the connivance of certain parts of the press during the dictatorship, the lack of recorded testimonies that can be used as proof of "truth" and the arrogance of power.

However, the film's effect lies in intertextuality. What is said is introduced literally, but from a perspective offered by distance, achieved not only through the passing of time (those necessary 30 years before we can access the details of the events, as the character himself envisaged it), but also as a consequence of the change in the hegemonic discourse. The latter allows for the development of a knowing addressee who shares the values that are being challenged and is capable of recognizing the utterer's stance. At the same time, this addressee recovers the ideological world to which those characters belonged and perceives their attitudes through signs that tend to ridicule or tone down the seriousness of those who embody such values: the journalist steps on excrement on her way in, she asks easy questions and does not realize that there is no cassette in the machine; the photographer takes pointless pictures; the serviceman himself seems to overact, and confidently affirms himself to be a "proud culprit" of the torture, disappearance and death of Argentine citizens, but is obsessed with unimportant details. In this way, we recover utterances that were supposedly delivered in the past by familiar characters, whose literalism states in a straightforward and brutal manner the logic that organized the actions of certain individuals during that period of our history.

In this respect, the narrative is supported by a widely-held view in Argentina nowadays, which equates the victims of state-sponsored terrorism with the soldiers. At the same time, and this is the innovative feature, the fragment quoted above introduces another dimension to this construction of memory, which is the minimization or cancellation of human attributes: "we have been proud culprits of the torture, death and disappearance of thousands of Argentines... In comparison, *what are 600 soldiers?*"

Beyond the struggle over the way the subjects are designated and the semantic field which each of them enables for the interpretation of events (together with the performative consequences this entails), the general's question undermines an identity: what are 600 soldiers? The question, addressed to the journalist (a character who symbolizes and shapes public opinion), is really aimed at society in general, 30 years later, by means of metonymy: what are 600 soldiers (*¿qué son 600 soldados?*)? The interrogative pronoun "qué" (what) opens a statement about people in an objectifying manner. The statement could be reworded as follows: what *thing* are 600 soldiers (*¿qué cosa son 600 soldados?*)? Or, more accurately, given that the statement is about fatalities: what are 600 dead soldiers (*¿qué cosa son 600 soldados muertos?*)? A designation that elides human traits is revealed. This enables an understanding of what happened both during and after the dictatorship from a different perspective. The objectification and the emphasis on the low number of victims ("only" 600) when compared to the other ones mentioned in this narrative—these victims are compared here and in numerous other discourses to the young victims of the dictatorship—demean their existence as a group. The narrative highlights the controversial issues of certain post-war discourses on the Malvinas. Are the deaths of these soldiers important?

Which Lives Matter? Which Lives Can Be Remembered?

The emphasis on the inscription of the subjective in the audiovisual production that has been taking place since 2003 is an attempt to answer these questions, heard in public places, by means of a policy of restoring to the Malvinas soldiers their status as subjects. An example of this reconfiguration can be found in President Cristina Fernández de Kirchner's speech during the commemoration ceremony of the thirtieth anniversary of the war:[7]

> Today, before coming here, I read a phrase from one of the (thousands of) young men who fought in the islands and then became a journalist. He might be around here, Edgardo Esteban. And he was saying [...] that the greatest defeat in a war, or in this war at least, is the truth [...]. I also demand justice for those who have not yet been identified, [which is why last Friday] I sent a letter to the head of the International Red Cross so that he may take the necessary measures and intercede with the United Kingdom to identify those men, Argentine and even British ones, who have not yet been identified, because everyone deserves to have their name written on their tombstone, and every mother has an inalienable right [...] to bury their dead, to get a plaque with their name on it and to cry in front of it.

Justice, truth and memory permeate an address that, decades before, would have been unspeakable in that context. This speech, as do many others in different fields, recognizes the existence of lives whose disappearance is worth honouring through mourning, which is nothing but an exercise of memory, "because if the end of a life produces no pain, it is not a life, it does not qualify as such and it has no value. It does not constitute something that deserves a burial, but rather that which is impossible to bury" (Butler 2006: 61). The recognition of these lives' value, as well as of the value of their deaths, records them in history and gives them a place there.

---

[7] Public speech by C. Fernández de Kirchner on April 2, 2012. Commemoration ceremony of the thirtieth anniversary of the beginning of the Malvinas War, in Usuahia, Tierra del Fuego, Malvinas Islands and Islas del Atlántico Sur, in Argentina.

In this context, then, the numerous audiovisual productions that have brought back the Malvinas War time and again to each one of the presents throughout these three decades could be understood as some sort of collective obituary, honouring the dead and acknowledging the survivors. In the words of Judith Butler (2006: 61), this obituary is "a nation-building action", carrying the marks of the ways in which the past has been remembered in each particular social and historical period.

References

Angenot, M. (2010). *De hegemonía y disidencias*. Córdoba: Universidad Nacional de Córdoba.

Bellotti, S. (2014). Entrevista. *Malvinas—30 miradas. Los cortos de nuestras islas.*

Butler, J. (2006). *Vida precaria. El poder del duelo y la violencia* (trans. F. Rodríguez). Buenos Aires: Paidós.

Courtine, J. (1981). Analyse du discours politique. Le discours communiste adressé aux chrétiens. *Langages,* 62, 9-128. At **www.persee.fr/issue/lgge_0458-726x_1981_num_15_62**, accessed July 3, 2016.

Fernández, C. (2012). Acto por el 30º aniversario de la guerra de Malvinas: Palabras de la Presidenta de la Nación. At **www.casarosada.gob.ar/informacion/archivo/25789**, accessed 2 April 2016.

Guber, R. (2001). *¿Por qué Malvinas? De la causa nacional a la guerra absurda*. Buenos Aires: Fondo de Cultura Económica.

Kamín, B. (1984). *Los chicos de la guerra.* At **https://youtu.be/y95uQDBcOyU**, accessed July 15, 2016.

Lorenz, F. (2011). El malestar de Krímov: Malvinas, los estudios sobre la guerra y la historia reciente argentina. *Estudios,* 25, 47-65. Córdoba: CEA, Universidad Nacional de Córdoba.

Paz Clemente, J., & de las Heras, T. (2013). *Combatientes*. At **www.youtube.com/playlist?list=PLKrigQ85zwZxY3xxVvp_ngh9HaR3IyS3**, accessed 30 July 2016.

Real Academia Española (2001). *Diccionario de la lengua española*, 22nd edn. At **http://lema.rae.es/drae/?val=trauma**, accessed July 10, 2016.

Verón, E. (1993). *La semiosis social. Fragmentos de una teoría de la discursividad*. Barcelona: Gedisa.

Returning: The Journey to the Islands in Contemporary Narratives about the Malvinas

Alicia Vaggione

Owing to its character as a traumatic incident, the Malvinas War[1] remains a historic event to which discourses return time and again to explore, update and negotiate meanings. Surrounded by relentless narratives where literature is central, I choose as my focal point works that consider the journey to the Malvinas as a recurring topic of contemporary narratives. The accounts of the journey persist both in genres of a more testimonial nature (journals and chronicles), and in fictional literature and film. Through them, we can outline a series of questions about war memories. Answers—which are always hypothetical, plastic and versatile in nature—are offered up by each of the respective pieces.

The journey, associated with movement, enables a return to the past through questions about the present. A particular structure of perspective is put into play: that of the travellers who wander in order to interact with the territory that unsettles them. I am interested in the ability of the journey—linked to the movement that defines and constitutes it—to interact with time. In other words, I am interested in the journey's ability to discontinue meanings about the past that have become more or less stagnant, to give way to a new and very necessary perspective derived from the recording of experience.

In this essay, my concern is to study certain aspects of the journey in relation to memory, focusing on the link between bodies and affects, experience and writing, and past and present, as shown in the documentary *La forma exacta*

---

[1] "The Malvinas War is one of the most controversial and difficult chapters in Argentine history. The most important military conflict that the country participated in during the twentieth century [...]. There are different reasons for its complexity. On the one hand, it was a product of the civilian and military dictatorship which, since 1976, had been relying on State-sponsored terrorism. On the other hand, it had the support of a considerable part of society, including some who opposed the military government. At the same time, it was a demand rooted in the history of Argentine thought, as this country's sovereignty claim over the Malvinas Islands is a longstanding one" (Flachsland *et al*. 2014: 95).

de las islas[2] (The Exact Shape of the Islands) (2012) by Edgardo Dieleke and Daniel Casabé, as well as in *Fantasmas de Malvinas. Un libro de viajes* (Malvinas Ghosts: A Book of Journeys) (2008) by Federico Lorenz. Both pieces insist on building a memory made up of multiple ways of reading the war experience and of seeing the island territory located at the end of the world.

La forma exacta de las islas explores the need to get to know the Malvinas by those who write doctoral theses on the topic. The book that emerged from this research, *Islas imaginadas. La guerra de Malvinas en la literatura y el cine argentinos* (Imagined Islands: The Malvinas War in Argentine Literature and Film), was published in 2012, the same year the documentary was released. In the epilogue, we read that Julieta Vitullo (2012: 186), the author, travelled to the islands twice. The aim of the first journey was to write up the conclusions of her research in situ: "What guided the first journey was the idea of seeing with my own eyes that place I had read so much about [...]. I wanted the journey to be not only metaphorical but also physical". The second journey was to be the subject-matter of the documentary. *Fantasmas de Malvinas* also narrates the urgent desire to travel, but, this time, the craving is that of a historian who has focused on investigating the matter in a series of research projects. The book consists of travel chronicles that are largely essayistic in nature.

There seems to be a common concern in these materials. A literary critic and a historian who have investigated the matter of the Malvinas reveal the importance of accessing the islands and recording that experience. What is being narrated in this space "between" the research practice, the writing of it and the experiences of the journey? What meanings does the insular (*lo insular*) acquire? What memories of the territory are updated? What memories of war are drawn upon?

By means of unique paths which I am interested in defining, I consider that these materials—diverging from the canonical traits of the genres of documentary and

---

[2] Film directed by Daniel Casabé and Edgardo Dieleke. Script by the directors and Julieta Vitullo, with the collaboration of Ricardo Piglia.

chronicle[3]—play a role in creating new ways of reading an event whose meanings are never finite. This essay is divided into two parts, one for each piece, and its aim is to assess their features and the questions they raise.

On *La forma exacta de las islas*
The Islands:"The Place Where Everything Happened"

The film *La forma exacta de las islas* is about the journey to the Malvinas, creating journeys within journeys. The film aims to grasp the way in which certain lives are scarred by a particular experience or place. Recording a variety of stories, *La forma exacta* builds multiple ways of viewing the island territory.

The movie offers both images of the islands as they stand now and accounts of the way in which they were seen by travellers and castaways who reached their harbours. It creates an archive of images and sounds: in many scenes, if we focus on listening, it is hard to differentiate the sound of the sea from that of the wind. Be that as it may, we cannot remain indifferent to those physical and perceptible records.

It could be said that the documentary alternates between two times, representing the two journeys of Julieta Vitullo, the protagonist of the film and researcher on fiction in literature and films about the Malvinas. One of the trips took place in 2006, when Julieta's desire to travel to the islands arose. The objective of this impulse to travel is to access the reality of that imagined territory that is part of the fiction she writes about and researches on. The initial proposal, "I am finally on Malvinas. I'm coming to Malvinas to finish my dissertation", was altered by an unexpected event that disrupted the proposed plan. During that week in December 2006 (generally, trips to the Malvinas are that long), Julieta met two Argentine veterans and, instead of writing the end of her thesis, began the production of a film following the travellers' footsteps.

In this material recorded by Julieta's camera, as well as in the veterans' introduction of themselves, they first tell us

---

[3] Current critical opinion challenges the presumption of veracity as a rule specific to these genres. New variations are reflected in order to show hybrids and markers of subjectivity that redefine and invent an event rather than mirror it. María Moreno considers the aforementioned line of inquiry of these genres and, specifically, of the chronicle, as a "writing lab".

their names, Dacio and Carlos, immediately followed by an unforgettable fact of their lives: they were born in 1963. This first trait, encoded in the year of their birth—later materialized when their names were drawn and their luck defined—marks out those young men who were 18 years old at the time of the war. These young men, showing the passing of time on their faces, went back—or should we say "returned"?—to explore the conflict area. In the words of the film: "the place where it all happened".

Returning, the wish to go back, seems to rest on the connection between the ways of assigning meaning to experience, a connection that has never been entirely resolved. Although they outline the possibility that the journey might have beneficial effects to help them move on ("When I go back, I will continue doing my thing, but with a different perspective, I believe. I will think about helping my comrades come over here. I think it is very good for us", says Dacio, looking into the camera), these ways involve a perception of time that is neither linear nor chronological, but rather intensive and purely emotional: "I could make the journey because I knew I was going to look at this with different eyes/with greater life-experience behind me [...]. I had thought about the war a thousand times". On this emotional plane, reinforced by the contact with the territory, a meeting with that which is new is established: "Perhaps the only thing I found that I wasn't expecting was the beauty":

> I don't know. When I come back I'll continue with my stuff/but perhaps with a new perspective and thinking about helping our comrades who want to come back.
> I can tell you that I can analyze this trip because I already did it before I came. In the sense that I knew I was going to look at this with different eyes/with greater life-experience behind me.
> Perhaps the only thing I found that I wasn't expecting was the beauty. (2012)

The beauty that moves Dacio, the hills beneath the sun which he never got to see during the war, is wonderfully captured by the camera countless times during the movie. It captures footage of the beaches, the hills, the streets, the lit homes of Stanley. It captures images of roads that crisscross the islands, accompanied by the sound of the wind.⁴

Carlos, the other veteran, also shares the way in which the trip allows him to see things differently, to shake off a way of thinking about the islands that has remained frozen since the time of the war, in order to appreciate that life went on here as well. The perception of movement is such that, several times during the film, Carlos fantasizes with the idea of staying and settling down there.

The recording carried out by Julieta follows the travellers closely and joins them on their visits, which somehow resemble the typical journeys of veterans exploring the islands: visiting the Darwin Cemetery; finding and identifying the places where they fought, where they lost fellow soldiers or took shelter from the cold and hunger. Julieta's camera records their unsettling, winding, yet precise, search to recognize the places and pay tribute to unforgettable dead comrades with fragile wooden crosses.

Rupture
It is fragments of this film—which registers the unexpected encounter, in 2006, with the veterans and follows their footsteps—that were taken up in November 2010, when Julieta returned accompanied by the two filmmakers who directed the documentary: Daniel Casabé and Edgardo Dieleke. She returned driven by the need to go back to that territory that had marked her life beyond the writing. Well into the film, the viewer finds out that Julieta fell pregnant during the first trip, that she decided to keep the child after she returned to Buenos Aires and that her son, Eliseo, died a few hours after he was born.

This narrative, which revolves around maternity and loss, is reflected in the restrained and frugal gestures of Julieta's face, and introduces an emotional plane where the feminine is highlighted. A turning-point in fiction towards an awareness which, read in the context of war narratives,

---

⁴ Paola Cortés Rocca's (2012) reading pauses to concentrate on images. Critics believe *La forma exacta* steers away from a word-based representation to "offer a visual and perceptive experience of the islands", where the landscape "is not something one thinks of as decoration, but rather as geography that incorporates very different overlapping layers: that of war, love, history, national identities, friendship, eroticism, mourning". Text read during the presentation at Museo Rojas, Buenos Aires, 2012.

where the masculine figure and homosociality prevail, shifts the focus of attention and creates another possible linkage.

It would be possible to read something encoded in Julieta's pain that seems to be related to that of other mothers in its inimitable uniqueness. Linear time disappears once again. One of the images shows Julieta walking around a cemetery while the voice-over narrates how she found a book documenting a plague that ravaged the islands in the 19th century, taking mainly children's lives. The book shows a picture of a mother with her dead son in her arms.

Other images of Julieta in Darwin Cemetery are tinged by a tone governed by loss, as the camera shoots the tombstones on the field, slowly going from one cross to the other so that the viewer can read the names of those killed or notice the names of those missing.

At this point, the documentary establishes a strong connection in which the individual experience of loss, the uniqueness of each life which Derrida speaks about, is related to others. The plague in the 19th century and the Malvinas War seem to outline a common background where death is featured solely as an interruption of lives that had their entire future ahead of them.

In this cancellation of the future, the Mothers of the Plaza de Mayo are called upon through metonymy and as a result of the echo produced by the intensity of the images in the film. As stated by Nora Domínguez (2007: 283), the Mothers barge into the public arena and displace "the representation of a unique mother with one singular son [...] in order to show that the greatest accomplishment of motherhood is reaching out to the group of sons with one embrace or motherly voice, when the place of the mother becomes plural".

A quotation from the writer Carlos Gamerro—part of the theatre version of the novel *Las islas*—gives the documentary its name and, at the same time, acts as an encapsulation of the recorded experience outlined by the movie, focused on the figure of rupture: "Does anyone know how many days the war lasted? Nobody? It isn't true there were survivors. There are two bites torn out of the hearts of every one of us."

Based on the experience of rupture, of something that breaks/cracks and cannot return to its former shape, but rather mutates, acquiring new contours, the movie constructs—with its combination of accounts and experiences—meanings that, time and again, go beyond the personal sphere.

Released 30 years after the Malvinas War, *La forma exacta* gives an account of multiple possible perspectives, this time through images captured by those who were children during the war: the directors and Julieta herself.

On *Fantasmas de Malvinas. Un libro de viajes*
Writing, Travelling and Memory

The book *Fantasmas de Malvinas* is a chronicle that narrates the journey of a historian who travelled to the islands. A disturbing question is posed on the first page: "Can we return to somewhere we have never been before?" Even though it is the first one, the trip is conceptualized as a return and, from page one, invokes a temporality that is not subject to linear chronology, but is connected to that which comes back as a ghost, that which cannot be overridden by memory.

The chronicles open and close with chapters entitled "Luggage". They are entries, similar to those one finds in a personal diary, about the aim of the trip. The first chapter lists a series of elements to be used when recording the experience in writing, as well as garments that will be useful on the trip:

> I have a blank notebook [...], a tentative schedule and a list of questions I have accumulated over the years [...]. I am taking a considerable number of warm garments that are easy to put on and take off because the weather in the Malvinas, like that in the provinces down south, changes all the time. (Lorenz 2008: 27-29)

The comparison between the weather or the landscape on the islands and Patagonia (the province of Tierra del Fuego, mainly) is a consistent characteristic of the text, creating a sense of proximity and even familiarity between the islands and the closest parts of the continent.

Regarding the writing, there is an initial scene that is recalled: that of the child writing letters to the soldiers during the war. This scene,[5] almost elliptically developed—"I who

---

[5] The narration of this initial writing scene and our interest in

wrote them letters every day" (Lorenz 2008: 31)—acts as the beginning of the writing persistence that continued and is now present in the practice of the historian. At the same time, it encodes and encapsulates some central issues: the role of schools during the months of the war (where thousands of letters from the children to the soldiers were written) and the markers of the generation to which the writer belongs.

The journey, as an experience that allows for the encounter with the other and the foreign, results in multiple ways of seeing and looking. The chronicles constitute a chorus of perceptions about the landscapes and the meetings with the islanders and veterans visiting the islands. The chronicles incorporate other voices. Those of the veterans have a central place. They are sometimes mentioned directly ("I don't know what force brought me here, and which now that it brings me here, won't let me go back"), as well as being introduced by the chronicler ("They want to keep promises, close wounds, settle debts and spend a night in their old place. Time stopped for them when the war marked them forever, even though they went on living" [87]).

The chronicle records the marks left by war, written on the lives and memories of the subjects as well as on the materials that are still spread around the islands as footprints of the battles. Examples of this are the parts of a Pucará plane and multiple other objects:

> The islanders dragged it from the place where it crashed in 1982 to the place where it is now. However, more than a vexation, it looked as if someone had delicately arranged it for the purpose of studying it: the wings were spread out, the fuselage was broken [...], the tail was resting on a side, the wounds left by the shots could be seen in different parts of the structure. (85)
> Scattered all over the floor there are remnants

---

reading it as a beginning is related to Sylvia Molloy's study of autobiography in Spanish America. Critics concentrate on a central episode in the lives of the autobiographers they study: the encounter between the self and the book, which highlights the importance which the act of reading itself acquires. This central position can be observed in Lorenz's chronicle of his journey, transferred to the act of writing.

> that represent the life of those men in the pits: wood, blankets, ponchos, rusty irons and telephone cables. (88)

The objects that can be found all over the island, which the chronicler records and photographs, are also footprints or fragments of memory.[6] They are outdoors, worn and preserved at the same time by the cold weather of the islands.[7] They are there, questioning those who find them and are capable of reading them.

I mentioned at the beginning that the chronicles create a non-linear temporality. This means that they build a memory that, far from linear in form, is designed in tiers: "To me, the islands are *successive layers* of locations, places and memories" (my emphasis).

Those Who Stayed
A tone of mourning is present throughout the chronicle. This tone and its meaning are strengthened when visits are made to the places where the dead are buried. The visit to Darwin Cemetery, where the bodies of the fallen Argentine soldiers lie, is the first stop on the historian's trip to the island.

> There is something desolate about Darwin. It might be the wind. [...] There is a cross at each grave, white and glistening due to the rain. At their feet, some of the black plaques display a name, others simply state "Argentine soldier known only to God". There are paths

---

[6] In *Fantasmas de Malvinas*, there are no pictures of the journey. These can be found in other books by the author, as well as in *Pensar Malvinas*.

[7] These objects that are still part of the landscape, probably preserved by the cold weather, invoke the documentary *Nostalgia de la luz* (Nostalgia for Light) by Patricio Guzmán, who took advantage of the Atacama Desert's lack of humidity (which keeps everything unaffected) to search for and read history's footprints: "What *Nostalgia* [...] seems to be highlighting is how there are many pasts within the past. When the connection (between land and sky) is achieved, when the pasts of galaxy time intersect with cave paintings, the signs of nomadic populations and indigenous peoples, the history of nineteenth-century miners, and the history of the prisoners and missing persons of the dictatorship, the documentary turns the desert into a place of revelations" (Boero & Vaggione 2014: 125).

between the crosses, and the grey and black gravel crunches under our feet, as if it was necessary to assert every step. (Lorenz 2008: 35)

The graves of the unknown soldiers are part of a pending debt, waiting for memory to be repaired by history. In his study *Epitafios. El derecho a la muerte escrita* (Epitaphs: The Right to a Written Death), Luis Gusmán (2005: 18) highlights the way in which funerary writing in ancient Greece was regulated by strict legislation that took two rights into account: the right to a written death—knowing who the dead are and where their grave is—and the right to tears as an expression where the threshold prayers act out the sorrow of the bereaved. This is still a pending matter in the politics of memory.

A different chapter states that the cenotaph that commemorates the dead is located in the city of Buenos Aires, in Retiro, across from the Torre gifted by the British community in 1910. Inaugurated in 1990, it includes twenty-five black plaques with the names of fallen soldiers. To Lorenz (2008: 176), the pressures caused by this war are all over this monument, where the only thing that matters is the fact that these men died for their country:[8]

> on the monument, it doesn't matter if the dead were officers who cared about their men or evil beings who meted out the same punishment to their subordinates as they did to the missing [*chupados*] in detention centres. It doesn't matter if the young men who are being commemorated were proud of sacrificing their lives or if they did so cursing.

As we mentioned, Lorenz's book closes with a chapter entitled "Luggage". This takes us to the last scene, in the

---

[8] As we have said, the Malvinas War is a complex episode in recent Argentine history. In her book, Julieta Vitullo (2012: 12), the protagonist of *La forma exacta de las islas*, states the following: "The fact that it was initially supported by the majority of society while the regime behind it was going through its greatest legitimacy crisis, together with the fact that the defeat led to victory (because it opened the path towards the return to democracy), turns this word into something of a blind spot in national history."

Immigration room at the airport, where the travellers have to let go of some objects they will not be able to take with them. A plane made up by the intangible is introduced: memory is that which we carry, that which we take with us:

> Acting as memory smugglers, those who return take with them objects that bring us closer to the islands, which are remote even when we are standing on them.
> The land of positions and of the cemetery.
> Small loafs of peat.
> Rocks in the hills.
> Sand on the beaches.
> Shards, large or small, oxidized and coarse. Outsoles of combat boots, waterbottles.
> The ladies in Customs are polite but categorical:
> —Nothing that can be used to recall the war can leave these islands. [...] It's funny: in that case, we shouldn't be allowed out either. (Lorenz 2008: 18)

To conclude, it is important to highlight that both of the materials addressed reveal the view of those who were children during the Argentine dictatorship. These children were two, three and four years old in the case of Vitullo and the directors of the documentary; and one of them was of school age: Lorenz was finishing primary school when the war took place and he remembers writing letters to the soldiers.

In this sense, both pieces of work show the need of this generation to investigate what happened on the Malvinas through the language of literature, film and history, as well as emotionally, in their relationship to what they show and tell us. Maybe that is the reason behind the journey. The writer Ricardo Piglia (2005: 114) considers that "the journey is a way of creating the experience, in order to write about it later". Both *La forma exacta de las islas* and *Fantasmas* support writing from experience, a type of writing that dives into the complexity of history, producing multiple ways to interpret an event about which we need to keep on thinking.

References

Boero, M. S., & Vaggione, A. (2015). Pasados materiales: Notas sobre el documental *Nostalgia de la luz* de Patricio Guzmán. *Revista digital: Artes, letras y humanidades*, 8

(September), 123-130. At **http://fh.mdp.edu.ar/revistas/index.php/etl/issue/view/72**.

Cortés Rocca, P. (2014). Unpublished text read at the presentation of the film *La forma exacta de las islas*. The Rojas Museum. Buenos Aires.

Casabé, D., & Dieleke, E. (2012). *La forma exacta de las islas*. Audiovisual production.

Derrida, J. (2012). *Espectros de Marx. El estado de la deuda, el trabajo del duelo y la Nueva Internacional,* 5th edn. Madrid: Trotta.

Domínguez, N. (2007). *De dónde vienen los niños. Maternidad y escritura en la cultura argentina*. Rosario: Beatriz Viterbo.

Flachsland, C., Adamoli, C., & Farias, M. (2014). *Pensar Malvinas. Una selección de fuentes documentales, testimoniales, ficcionales y fotográficas para trabajar en el aula*, 3rd edn. Buenos Aires: Ministerio de Educación de la Nación. Audiovisual production.

Gamerro, C. (1998). *Las islas*. Buenos Aires: Simurg.

Gamerro, C. (2011). *Las islas*. Theatrical production, unpublished. Director Alejandro Tantanian.

Gusmán, L. (2005). *Epitafios. El derecho a la muerte escrita*. Buenos Aires: Norma.

Lorenz, F. (2008). *Fantasmas de Malvinas. Un libro de viajes*. Buenos Aires: Eterna Cadencia.

Molloy, S. (1996). *Acto de presencia. La escritura autobiográfica en Hispanoamérica*. Mexico: Fondo de Cultura Económica.

Piglia, R. (2005). *El último lector*. Barcelona: Anagrama.

Vitullo, J. (2012*). Islas imaginadas. La guerra de Malvinas en la literatura y el cine argentinos*. Buenos Aires: Corregidor.

Minefield/Campo Minado:
A Veteran in the Theatre of War

Mike Seear

In late September 2015 I was tipped off that Lola Arias, an internationally-acclaimed Argentine theatre director, was creating the first stage play ever about the 1982 Falklands-Malvinas War. The intriguing aspect of this production was that its cast would only comprise Argentine and British veterans of the war. The opening night would be at the Dome Corn Exchange in Brighton as part of the Brighton Festival (28-29 May 2016). The play would then move to London with performances at the Royal Court Theatre from 2-11 June as part of the biannual London International Festival of Theatre, followed by more in Germany, Greece and Argentina.

Already Lola had interviewed some forty Argentine war veterans and was now in London from 28 September to 4 October to do the same with twenty British candidates. I established a contact with her UK-based assistant, Kate O'Connor, who told me that Lola was very interested to talk to me "about your experience of the conflict as part of the Gurkhas" (I had been the 1st Battalion, 7th Duke of Edinburgh's Own Gurkha Rifles Operations and Training Officer). However, our planned meeting in Buenos Aires the following week, during which I had delivered emergency response training to Aerolíneas Argentinas, the national airline, did not materialize. Back in my Oslo home, I learned that what Lola wanted was a Nepalese Gurkha veteran of the 1982 war to be in the cast.

The importance of such a Gurkha recruitment was obvious. My six visits to Argentina since 2002 had shown me the enduring importance of the war to Argentines, in contrast with the British, who have largely forgotten it following the UK's participation in later conflicts in the Gulf, Balkans, Kosovo, Iraq and Afghanistan. The untruthful myths in Argentina about the Gurkhas in the 1982 war have been perpetuated, as has been highlighted in Bernard McGuirk's book *Falklands-Malvinas: An Unfinished Business* (2007). It includes a vivid review of the one-man show *Gurka/Gurkha*, a schizo-drama created by Argentine playwright Vicente Zito Lema. It was staged at the Sala Calibán, Buenos Aires, in November 1988. Depicting Miguel, an Argentine veteran of the 1982 war who became a patient in the Borda psychiatric hospital because of his Post-Traumatic Stress Disorder (PTSD) and paranoia about the Gurkhas, he alleged that they:

> were giant beasts, with thermal suits, with sharp knives, with infra-red telescopes and laser beam rifles that burned your body, whatever they touched, even stones [...]. The Gurkhas took everything. Even the dead. They built bonfires at night and then ate them. They look like Count Dracula, they get in through the windows, they can fly. I killed several Gurkhas with my knife, and I saw they don't have any blood!

On 25 November I met Lola at the Royal Court Theatre. She had just completed a series of workshops with potential British cast members and explained to me her ambitious aim. The later blurb on the play, posted on the Internet (9 May 2016), elaborated on this:

> I'm interested in investigating what happens with time. In fact, this piece needed time. It needed years. War doesn't interest me, post-war interests me. What matters to me is what happens to a person who went through that experience. What matters to me is what memory has done, what it has erased, what it has transformed. Some have become professional storytellers and my work was and is to undo this in order to show what happened to them.

Lola would not tolerate any external pressure to select the cast. She had a proven set of criteria for such a process. The play would be staged in Buenos Aires at the beginning of November 2016, and to have a Nepalese Gurkha performing there would be a major bonus. But there was no guarantee one would be selected, it being dependent on financial considerations.

Time was also running out for recruiting a Gurkha to *Las islas/The Islands* (the play's original working title). On return to Oslo, I exchanged e-mails with Brigadier David Morgan, who put me in contact with Major Dillikumar Rai (a retired Queens Gurkha Officer and D Company 1982 war veteran). From him was acquired a list of twenty-three

Minefield/Campo Minado

retired 7th Gurkha Rifles Nepalese war veterans. All lived in the UK, but most were still employed. Unavailability therefore reduced prospective candidates to a short list of four. During that Christmas and New Year period, Kate conducted telephone interviews with the candidates. Only Warrant Officer Second Class Sukrim Rai was chosen for a second audition. He was one of my section commanders when I became the A Company Commander post-war. Sukrim was also my second-in-command of our twenty-six-man Company team that ran in the 1983 London Marathon.

The "Marathon Party" before the start of the 17 April 1983 London Marathon, with Sukrim Rai (front row, third from the left) and Mike Seear (rear row, centre)

On 18 February, I received an e-mail from Lola:

> Good news. Sukrim will be part of the play! He is coming to Buenos Aires in the middle of March. I would like you to tell me more about him. Everything you know. He was not so keen on talking about combat situations. But maybe you know more about what he did during the war. We read what's in your book but you might have some more anecdotes or stories.

I did indeed. Some of Sukrim's war experiences were described in my first book *With the Gurkhas in the Falklands:*

A War Journal (Pen & Sword Books, 2003). But Lola needed more information about the Gurkhas in general and Sukrim in particular. The latter sent me more details on his background and participation in the war. Then I wrote a thirteen-page brief and sent it to Lola. By now she had whittled down her final cast choice to six veterans: three Argentine, two British and Sukrim; but the latter had problems in acquiring a visa and did not arrive in Buenos Aires for the planned six weeks of rehearsals until 19 March, four days after the British veterans. The other cast members had participated in some of Lola's workshops for *Minefield* (Spanish: *Campo Minado*). This had become the play's official name: a metaphor for memory, i.e. treacherous terrain that needs to be crossed with care and might prove explosive.

The *Minefield/Campo Minado* cast. Rear row (l. to r.): Gabriel Sagastume, David Jackson, Sukrim Rai and Rubén Otero. Front row (l. to r.): Marcelo Vallejo and Lou Armour

The cast's backgrounds were:

> **Lou Armour** – A Royal Marine Commando Corporal who was captured at Government House, Stanley on 2 April 1982. He is the lead Marine in the iconic "surrender photograph" (below left). Flown back to the UK via Uruguay, Lou volunteered to return to the Islands with 42 Commando and fought at the Battle of Mount Harriet. He left the Marines in 1986 to study politics, sociology and art history at Lancaster

University and then wrote a Ph.D. on the logical grammar of colour concepts. He now teaches boys with ESBD—emotional, social and behavioural difficulties.

David Jackson – A Royal Marine Commando who was the signaller for Brigadier Julian Thompson, Commander of 3 Commando Brigade. David is now a psychologist and leading expert in the social and cultural difficulties faced by war veterans and families. He was an academic advisor to Lord Ashcroft's Veteran transition report and is an advisor to many small veteran charities throughout the UK. In 2010 he completed his Doctor of Education at the University of Bristol, and is an honorary Research Fellow at the University of Exeter.

Marcelo Vallejo – A 6th Infantry Regiment conscript and the aimer for a 120mm mortar located just east of Mount William. After repatriation to Argentina he worked in a tyre-repair shop and then, in 1985, began working for Ford. Eighteen years later he became unemployed because of PTSD and spent three months in a psychiatric hospital. Learning how to swim at the age of forty, Marcelo started running and cycling. He has now participated in five triathlon "ironman" world-series events.

Gabriel Sagastume – A 7th Infantry Regiment conscript who fought in the Battle of Wireless Ridge. Gabriel studied law post-war and entered the judiciary of Buenos Aires in 1985 to become an oral trial attorney. He participated in Malvinas War veterans' organizations, helping fellow veterans with social, financial and work difficulties. He also lectures in schools and universities about the war and has written two books on the subject.

Rubén Otero – An Argentine Navy seaman who was on board the light cruiser ARA *General Belgrano* on 2 May 1982 when she was torpedoed in the South Atlantic by the Royal Navy submarine HMS *Conqueror*, killing 323 of the ship's company. Rubén was rescued after forty-one hours with twenty-one other survivors in a life raft designed for fifteen. Retiring from the Navy, he started his own print shop. In 1997 he joined the Beatles Tribute Band, the *Get Back Trio*, as its drummer. Awarded the best Latin American Beatle

Band Prize, they played in the world-famous Cavern Club at Liverpool in 2005.

Sukrim Rai – A 7th Gurkha Rifles Lance-Corporal who fought in the 1982 war with the Battalion's Recce Platoon. After eighteen years' service he retired from the British Army in 1994, and then served in the Gurkha Reserve Unit in Brunei for ten years. Since then Sukrim has worked for a Ghana gold mine and for security companies in both Iraq and UK.

I established e-mail communication with Lou, who fed me fascinating updates about the rehearsals in Buenos Aires. These were intense, and sometimes understandably fraught with Lola's constant changes. Ideas grew in collaboration with the cast during the next six weeks. In particular, there was an important story about Sukrim that had to be portrayed correctly. It involved the kukri and the Gurkha reputation on the Falklands battlefield spun out of all proportions by the Argentine media and which continues to live a life of its own in Argentina. This had been documented in *With the Gurkhas in the Falklands*, but Sukrim gave me more input just before his departure to Buenos Aires. It involved the surrender of a ten-man Argentine Air Force group tasked with shooting down British aircraft with SAM-7 Strella missiles. Based at Egg Harbour House on the north-west coast of Lafonia, they were captured by a five-man patrol of the Gurkha Recce Platoon on 7 and 8 June. Sukrim was in this patrol. He took three of these Argentines prisoner, including their commander Lieutenant Jaime Ugarte, by the simple expedient of threatening them with his kukri.

Based on this incident, a scene was devised that did not portray Sukrim as a military "Rambo" on a limited conventional war battlefield, but as a "thinking" Gurkha soldier. Lola updated me: "The rehearsals are going great, the British and Argentine veterans are becoming friends and they have fun together. And I'm very happy with how the stories are told."

Lou also informed me about her determination, drive and leadership in the Centre of Experimental Art at the National University of San Martín, where the cast began referring to her as "the Commander-in-Chief". On 16 April Sukrim met a good friend of mine, Dr Eduardo Gerding, the Malvinas War Veterans Medical Coordinator, who briefed

Minefield/Campo Minado

Sukrim about Argentine attitudes to Gurkhas.

Following a Skype conversation with Lola, I asked Eduardo if he could track down Jaime Ugarte. This did not take long, and Sukrim and Jaime (now a retired Brigadier) met in Eduardo's apartment on 29 April. Sukrim described this reconciliation as "really unbelievable after 34 years... I am so happy... I never thought I [would] meet him in my life", while Jaime remarked that "It was a debt I had in my life".

The intense rehearsals in Buenos Aires were nearing their end. On 7 May Lola, via Lou, provided me with more information on the Egg Harbour House scene:

1. The myth. Marcelo reads from an Argentine newspaper that describes the Gurkhas as assassins who cut off the arms and legs of their prisoners. Marcelo was also told this when he was on the Islands and it enraged him. Marcelo said he wanted to fight them, but now that he has met Sukrim he is happy.
2. Egg Harbour House scene (some narration by me, acting and lines from Sukrim and the prisoner).
3. Marcelo, who was on Mount William, tells of how the Gurkhas were meant to attack his position. He says the Gurkhas wanted to attack but the war ended before they could. He then says that instead of meeting Sukrim in battle he met him thirty-four years later in a theatre.

On 14 May Sukrim and I were reunited at the annual 7th Gurkha Rifles Regimental Association Reunion in Aldershot. He was in good form and ready for his theatre debut prior to a final two weeks of rehearsals at Stratford, East London. My peripheral Gurkha support role in this saga was nearly complete. There remained only one thing to do, i.e. see *Minefield/Campo Minado* on Friday 3 June at the Royal Court Theatre.

The stage of the small 380-seat theatre was starkly simple. All necessary props and wardrobes were positioned on-stage with costume changes taking place there as well. It symbolized that the cast would hide nothing from the audience in telling their stories. There would be no language barrier, just as I had frequently experienced none in my meetings with Argentine veterans in their country, where interpreters, of the calibre of such as Eduardo Gerding, had always provided the solution. So it was good that a Spanish and English surtitle translation system would be displayed on three LCD screens above, left and right of the stage. This technology enabled a joint storytelling of the Argentine and British/Gurkha veterans.

Lola employed an impressive battery of techniques to tell the structured story. A large cuboid screen set, which she dubbed as her "time machine", dominated the stage. Resembling the pages of an open book, on these were projected images such as letters, diaries, battlefields, wartime video/film and photographs, newspaper cuttings, magazine publications, toy soldiers, mock-up models, maps, and "close-ups" of the cast.

The latter would adroitly move the cameras. To the left and rear was a drum kit which Rubén would utilize with consummate skill and, to the right, electric guitars which Marcelo, Gabriel and David would play. They all had two decades or more of guitar strumming, but Marcelo only learned to play the bass guitar during rehearsals in Buenos Aires. Their music created an extra dimension. It became a powerful "connector" that further enhanced the on-stage reconciliation between the cast. Their individual memories were brought to life. In effect they were confronting the reality of their trauma by using "on-stage" therapy.

The play moved through the war chronologically. There were seventeen scenes, with titles such as "Going to War", "Waiting", "Jets" and "The Last Day of the War" displayed on the rear video screen. The start depicted the military recruitment of the cast members. For the Argentines this was done by conscription, as the play's text recounted: "In Argentina, military service was obligatory until 1997. Many tried to get out of it by feigning illness". For the British and Sukrim it was done voluntarily: "When I received my green beret I felt it was worth something". And therein lies a major reason for the Argentine eventual defeat: conscripts will fail when matched against professionals on a conventional limited war battlefield.

Humour was present throughout. Laughter was generated, for example, by David's remark that he can still "shit, shower, shave and shampoo" in under three minutes. The message was that the use of black humour provided the

Minefield/Campo Minado

psychological defence mechanism against the battlefield's "fear of the unknown". There was also a realistic sense of an understated "laid-back" attitude in tackling the challenges of war. Panic was never portrayed. It was positive that the audience received such an education in battlefield life, death and survival.

Published by *Gente*, the iconic 2 April 1982 "surrender" image in which Lou is the lead Royal Marine Commando— and a re-enactment (below) on stage performed by Marcelo and Lou

With the remainder of the Royal Marine Commando detachment, Lou Armour was flown out of the Islands on board an Argentine Air Force Hercules C-130 transport aircraft to Montevideo. His chief concern during the flight was of meeting the same fate as those many disappeared in Argentina's "Dirty War", i.e. being pushed out of the aircraft while flying over the sea. Waiting at a hotel in Montevideo for an RAF aircraft, they drowned their sorrows and signed "Margaret Thatcher" on all their bar chits. Lou set the precedent in true Brechtian style by speaking directly to the audience, i.e. breaking the fourth wall. Back in the UK, and after seventy-two hours leave, he volunteered to return to the South Atlantic with 42 Commando.

Marcelo simulating "waiting" on stage with battlefield artefacts laid out. Displayed at the rear is a letter written by Gabriel to his girlfriend (later wife)

Meanwhile Marcelo arrived in the Islands on 15/16 April. He and five other members of his 120mm mortar team dragged their 500 kg "tube" eleven kilometres from "Puerto Argentino" to Mount William's eastern shoulder. There they set up their "base plate" position with another three 120mm mortars of HQ Company, 6th Infantry Regiment to begin a long, torrid wait for the British. Of their sixty days on the Islands, they would be shelled and bombed for forty-five days. Decades later, he revisited the Islands. The battlefields there are like a living museum, and he found some of his equipment, which, on stage, he handled like gold dust. As the lead elements of the British Task Force sail south, the only spoof "political" scene was played with David and Gabriel dressing up as Prime Minister Margaret Thatcher and President of Argentina/Leader of the Military Junta General Leopoldo Galtieri, complete with Spitting Image rubber masks. Interactive and cleverly composed, it had an effective comic dimension. The two leaders' broadcast speeches vividly recalled for this war veteran those extraordinary April days of 1982. Then, against a video screen backdrop from the BBC's "Task Force South" documentary, there featured a Royal Marine Commando party on board the cruise liner SS *Canberra*, otherwise nicknamed as "The Great White Whale". Lou sang from the well-known Cliff Richard song, adapted for the scene, "We're all going on a summer holiday for a month or two—or three or four" and David Jackson (although on board the Amphibious Assault Ship HMS *Fearless*) simulated a drag act, highlighting the fact that many Marine Commandos are not against a bit of cross-dressing. This fun was brutally interrupted by an emergency klaxon for "Action Stations".

Suddenly war had become serious business. The pace increased. The red lighting and smoke blown onto the stage was Rubén's cue to tell his story of the *General Belgrano*'s being torpedoed. Despite being a non-swimmer, he managed to abandon ship, survive in his life raft—accompanied by DIY sound-effects of stick stirred in a bucket of water—and, so frozen that he could not feel his legs, being rescued eventually by the destroyer ARA *Bouchard*. His anger and pain were conveyed by the dinning intensity of his drumming while he shouted out, in monosyllables, a series of words such as "Margaret Thatcher!", "Nuclear submarine!", "323 dead!" as video images of the ship's company shook violently behind him.

Minus Sukrim, the cast united into a rock band whose music constantly disrupted the storytelling in a most evocative way. The deafening acoustics of the three guitars and drums played by these fifty year-olds were appropriate for such a war setting. The initial song "Don't You Want Me?" was followed later by an equally thunderous rendition of the Beatles' song "Get Back", which carried a secondary Argentine message of protest against British ownership of

"Las Malvinas". However, there was little political argument on stage even though differing views on sovereignty popped up briefly towards the end—and no answers as to who was right or wrong. It was about a shared traumatic battlefield experience, combat veteran unity and reconciliation.

Sukrim performed eye-catching solo acts of Nepali culture: such as a gentle kukri dance, singing a Nepali song against an entrancing background of projected falling snowflakes, and reciting a poem. But the Egg Harbour House incident was flawed, with Lou posing as a TV talk-show host with Sukrim and Marcelo. The Gurkha's use of his kukri to capture rather than kill became partially camouflaged in Lou's narrative, which also mentioned the reunion with Ugarte. There were two additional lines of explanation from Sukrim, but no Argentine prisoner appeared. If he had, then this would have provided balance to Lou's surrender at Government House. An alternative cameo re-enactment could have delivered a better-profiled Egg Harbour House message. After later (sold-out) performances that month in London, Braunschweig and Athens, Lou informed me that this scene had evolved positively by adapting a more serious, "BBC tone". The improvement was palpable.

At the performance on 3 June, more DIY sound-effects, such as treading continuously onto small pebbles in a large container, were also employed in the scene with Gabriel as he told his story using toy soldier and model boat and house props of how a small group of starving conscripts acquired much-needed food. One trod on an Argentine mine that blew him into pieces. Body parts were placed in Gabriel's blanket, which, because it was the only one issued to him, he had to continue to use for the rest of the war.

The simplicity of how this and other stories were told is what made them so effective. Lola's imaginative directing reaped a just reward. There were also canned sound-effects: such as the distant roar of jet engines that quickly built into a deafening crescendo from seven incoming Argentine Skyhawk fighter aircraft that bombed 3 Commando Brigade's Main and Tactical HQs. This incident occurred at Bluff Cove Peak on 13 June, it being the only occasion during the land campaign when both HQs were co-located. The attack forced the Tactical HQ's rapid "gravel belly" exit from the target area and into a nearby minefield. Subsequently this HQ's personnel, including David, spent an uncomfortable night in

Minefield/Campo Minado

that most undesirable new location.

My second, and final, negative observation was the continuation of the lopsided "one-way" focus on Argentines killed in action. To the *Belgrano* sinking and mine explosion incident were added two more fatalities. There was a re-enactment of Lou holding a mortally-wounded Argentine officer in his arms on Mount Harriet while they have a conversation in English before the Argentine, played by Rubén, dies. Marcelo had fired his 120mm mortar on Mount Harriet and Lou during 42 Commando's attack there on the night of 11/12 June. But on the morning of 14 June while under heavy shellfire, his section was ordered to withdraw from Mount William. Just afterwards, his best friend, Sergio Azcarate, was hit and killed near him by flying shrapnel. Everything then "went black" for Marcelo during the withdrawal to "Puerto Argentino".

War is about battlefield survival and death on both sides. Acknowledgement of this should have been made in the play. My brief for Lola had included Sukrim's account of his dogged stretcher-bearer efforts following that heart-stopping one-hour Argentine shelling and mortar bombardment of 467 Gurkhas on the north-western slopes of Tumbledown during the night of 13/14 June. Six Gurkhas and two British soldiers were wounded.

Post-war there was closure for the thousands welcoming home the British Task Force in the video clips of *Canberra* arriving at Southampton on 14 July and blown-up photograph of the welcome received by the Gurkhas when marching through the town of Fleet on 9 August. It was not so simple for David, who did not join in the national celebrations. The latter's wife had also left him for someone else. Indeed, divorce is almost the norm for a combat veteran.

After repatriation to Argentina, Marcelo felt "like a rock", devoid of feeling and emotion. Defeat was a lead weight. He and other Argentine war veterans were told they could not talk about their experiences. Later there was debilitating unemployment, drug and drink abuse that drove him to a suicide attempt. His aversion to the English and English films and music was revealed in a gripping simulated on-stage therapy session with Dr David Jackson, who also told Marcelo about his problems with Post-Traumatic Stress Disorder, anxiety, depression and civilian life.

Marcelo (left) and Dr David Jackson in the simulated therapy session during the play. Gabriel (extreme left) and Lou (extreme right) man the projectors

After an uplifting contrast provided by Sukrim's exotic post-war scene in which he dances his way around the world to USA, Hong Kong, Brunei, Iraq, Ghana and UK as a Gurkha soldier and, from 1994, as a civilian, there is another change of atmosphere in the penultimate Scene 16—"Yesterday and Today". In this, Lou courageously tells of personal guilt and shame at his public display of emotion in the 1987 TV documentary film *Falklands War—the Untold Story* relating to the dying Argentine in his arms on Mount Harriet. This prevented him from attending regimental reunions.

The final Scene 17, "Falklands Malvinas", and the play's climax, was a hugely aggressive slow rap cum heavy metal-style song designed for audience shock and awe in its sudden departure from the usual calm, understated story-telling. The effect was all the greater because of this. To the flash of strobe lighting, billowing smoke, crash of drums and cymbals, and ear-splitting electric guitar acoustics, Lou shouted into his microphone many uncomfortable questions to the audience such as: "Would you send your sons and daughters to war?", "Have you ever held a dying man in your arms?", "Have you ever seen anyone die?", "Have you ever seen a man on fire?", "Have you been ignored by your Government", "Would you vote to go to war?"

This inspired cathartic ambush was disliked by some of the twenty-six reviews I found on the Internet afterwards.

Minefield/Campo Minado

One described it as divisive. But their authors could not have experienced war. That final effort was a memorable climax by rightly emphasizing the difference between ex-combatants and all those civilians they had protected. The honesty was "the red thread" that ran throughout the play. And because they were not there at the time, other people cannot tell this story. Only the cast have the right to tell and share it with the audience.

The final scene: "What would you fight for?" "The Queen?", "La Patria?", "Oil?", "Did you go to war?", "Have you ever been to war?", "Have you ever killed anybody?", "Have you?"

Post-performance there was an on-stage forty-five-minute discussion between Lola and her cast. It confirmed a tight bond had been established between them, although she admitted, "There were lots of moments in the rehearsals when I thought the play wouldn't be possible." But Sukrim had no doubt and his remarks were noted by several reviewers of the play, "Thirty-four years ago I was looking to kill them, and they were looking to kill me. That's why I love this project very much. Now we are friends. I love them."

Lou remarked he felt comfortable rehearsing in Buenos Aires but was worried about his performing on home ground. The audience was invited to ask questions, so I could not resist the temptation of being the first to stand up and address Lou directly to allay him of his fears. My labelling the play as "brilliant" and "a demonstration of the power of reconciliation" came from the heart.[1]

Lola had the final word, "The hardest part of this experiment was agreeing what we wanted to say—which doesn't mean we agree. We share feelings because we make a play together, but there is conflict inside this group and the two countries". Forty-eight hours later I sent her my final e-mail:

> I attended the performance of *Minefield* at the Royal Court Theatre on Fri. 3 June. Just wanted to tell you how greatly impressed I was with the play and how well you had put all the different components together. The result was stunning! Many congratulations to you and your cast, and very good luck with all the future performances.

Ten days later she replied:

> Many thanks Mike! I'm so happy with the results of the play. Thanks for your support and collaboration to make this possible.

Watching the play in the circle, I had sat next to two young women and could not stop myself eavesdropping on their conversation. They were university students, and one remarked that her school had never taught her about the 1982 war. There is no excuse for this alarming deficiency, because a huge number of books exist that cover every aspect of the Falklands-Malvinas War. The authors are not just historians, but also those who fought in the South Atlantic during that extraordinary ten-week period. I belong to one of the latter category. My first book was very much a "start-stop-start" process that took twenty-one years to

---

[1] Others have said the following: "Astonishingly moving, sensitive and humane" (*Time Out*/Stewart Pringle); "Work of extraordinary compassion, constructed with a mix of jagged flair and careful intelligence, makes courageous statement" (*Evening Standard*/Henry Hitchings); "A powerful act of remembrance" (*Daily Telegraph*/Dominic Cavendish); "Brings tears to the eyes and the audience to its feet. Tremendous" (*The Times*/Dominic Maxwell); "Extraordinary power and eloquence" (*The Independent*/Paul Taylor); "Sensitive and often moving" (*British Theatre Guide*/Kenneth McKenna).

complete. It was a cathartic effort aimed at structuring my jumbled memory of battlefield trauma. "Structuring" was also a key concept used in Lola's play. *With the Gurkhas in the Falklands: A War Journal* also provided me with a beneficial therapeutic effect, not least in the late 1990s when my life was going through a series of violent upheavals.

My second book, *Hors de Combat: The Falklands-Malvinas Conflict Twenty-Five Years* (CCC Press, 2007), was a co-editorial effort with Diego F. García Quiroga, a former Argentine Naval Special Forces officer and combat veteran of the war who was shot and wounded three times behind Government House, Stanley in the early hours of 2 April 1982. In real life, Corporal Lou Armour had tried to rescue Diego's commander, Lieutenant-Commander Pedro Edgardo Giacchino, who had also been shot together with Diego but later died. This scene involving Lou was tried out in rehearsals for *Minefield/Campo Minado* but later dropped because it was considered too heroic.

Hors de Combat contained an anthology of twenty-one presentations made at a hugely successful two-day "reconciliation" international colloquium held at the University of Nottingham in November 2006 for British and Argentine combat veterans of the war plus a number of other eminent persons. Two years later an enlarged edition, *Hors de Combat: The Falklands-Malvinas Conflict in Retrospect*, was published when I was midway through writing my third book, *Return to Tumbledown: The Falklands-Malvinas War Revisited* (CCC Press, 2012). All this meant that I had been ideally placed for that initial tip-off about *Minefield/Campo Minado*. That war "life event" has been the driving force behind my profession today of designing and delivering crisis management exercises and training for international airlines and other organizations. It also represents a personal war legacy of preparing others to manage the challenges of major crises.

Six months after the Royal Court Theatre performance, I exchanged e-mails with Alicia Castro, the former Argentine Ambassador to the Court of St. James's in London. We had become acquainted by participating in other absorbing University of Nottingham colloquia. During one, the Ambassador and two of her Embassy staff sat three metres away as I made a presentation on the British military imperatives of why the *Belgrano* had to be sunk. Nonetheless she did give me a hug at the colloquium dinner afterwards. In July 2012 Alicia also invited me to the Argentine Embassy in London for a cup of tea and long chat about the issue of "Falklands-Malvinas, Malvinas-Falklands".

In her 2 December 2016 e-mail response to mine, she told me about a *Minefield/Campo Minado* performance she had seen in Buenos Aires the previous day. It was "most interesting and moving", she wrote, "and, of course, it reminded me of the meetings and conversations we had during my mission in the UK". Then Alicia added:

> After the show, I talked to the British veterans and your Gurkha pal Sukrim [...]. I found the story of Lou Armour the most moving. His video showing him as a young Royal Marine crying on TV, painfully remembering an Argentine who died in his arms, asking himself in his last moment what he was fighting for, and mumbling something about Oxford.
>
> "If only he didn't speak English...!" Lou cries.
> This true story, as he recalled later in an open conversation between Lola Arias, "actor" veterans and the public, is the living [Jorge Luis] Borges poem "Juan López and John Ward":
>
>> *He had studied Spanish*
>> *so as to read the Quixote.*
>> *The other professed a love for Conrad, [...]*
>> *[...] They might have been friends, but they saw each other just once,*
>> *face to face, in islands only too well known, and each one was Cain, and*
>> *each one, Abel [...]*
>
> *(The story I tell happened in a time we cannot understand.)*
>
> I can only regret that there are so many wars taking place... The *"time we cannot understand"* goes on and on.
>
> I am looking forward to see you sometime soon.
>
> Fraternalmente,
>
> Alicia.

Staging

Foreign Plays and Repertoire in the Teatro de Ensayo de la Universidad Católica de Chile during the Dictatorship (1973-1989): Constructing a Canonical Interpretation

Andrea Pelegrí Kristić

For several years, Chilean theatrical historiography has studied theatre in the country during the military dictatorship that lasted from 1973 to 1989, the year in which Augusto Pinochet was defeated at the polls by the candidate of the Partidos de la Concertación Democrática, Patricio Aylwin, who took office in March 1990.[1] The most prolific theatre researchers have studied the dramatic, theatrical and aesthetic procedures of the Chilean scene in the period mentioned above. In this context, of particular relevance is what has been written about university theatres, specifically the TEUC (Teatro de Ensayo de la Pontificia Universidad Católica de Chile, founded in 1943 in Santiago).[2]

After the *coup d'état* on 11 September 1973, all spheres of daily life were affected, including the theatre. Censorship, massive layoffs, lack of budget, and repression influenced the choice of plays and repertoires. To continue functioning as normally as possible, one of the main strategies used by institutional theatres—especially the TEUC—was the production of performances of the classic Western canon, mostly in a foreign language, considered of high educational and aesthetic value. This kind of approach allowed them to subvert any censorship on the part of the academic authorities—appointed by the de facto government. From this perspective, theatrical historiography has analyzed the repertoire of TEUC between 1973 and 1989 and has suggested that, as a result of these programming

---

[1] This essay is part of the project Fondecyt Regular N°1141095: *History And Memory Of Recent Chilean Theatre between 1983-1995: A Critical Analysis of the Construction of a Canon and its Exclusions*. The project coordinator is Milena Grass Kleiner. Other project members are: Andrés Kalawski, Nancy Nicholls, Inés Stranger, Mariana Hausdorf and Andrea Pelegrí Kristić.

[2] Nowadays the institution is called Teatro UC, which is why, when referring to it today, I shall use this name. However, when referring to the theatre during the dictatorship period, we shall use its original name at the time, TEUC.

choices, there was a surreptitious but clear determination to speak of the political situation through the voice of authors considered universal. The paradigmatic example of this would be the staging of Pedro Calderón de la Barca's *La vida es sueño* (Life Is a Dream) in 1974. This particular mise en scène has repeatedly been considered as a theatrical milestone against the dictatorship, camouflaged by classical language and Calderón's incontestable authority.

While one of the reasons behind the staging of foreign and/or classical plays was a form of (self-)censorship, and thus a survival stratagem in an extremely hostile political context, I argue that the aura of resistance attributed to some of the programming decisions also corresponds to a later historiographical construction.[3] That does not imply, of course, that these works have not had such an impact. A general examination of the different reviews or chronicles of those years, as well as of the authors who have written on the history of the Chilean theatre in that period, is enough to measure their effect on the audience. But it is necessary to put into perspective later interpretations of those repertoire choices and their meaning, since they are often read as isolated phenomena, without taking into account, for example, TEUC's previous programming decisions, as well as its founders' declaration of principles. In fact, interpretations vary widely according to the context of production.

The present contribution aims to reexamine the repertoire of foreign works—especially in a language other than Spanish, although there are some examples of foreign works from Spain or Latin America—performed at TEUC between 1973 and 1989. I have chosen this particular year because Aylwin assumed the presidency in March 1990. I

---

[3] I use both terms (censorship and self-censorship) because, although a censorship authority per se did not exist at the time, there were several mechanisms to discourage artists from creating new work. At times, the mechanisms were explicitly violent, occasionally even self-inflicted, to avoid any danger or disagreement with the authorities. However, one of the most curious indirect censorship measures was charging a 22% tax on companies deemed harmful or dangerous to the military regime (law Nº 827 in 1974). The decision whether or not to apply the tax was arbitrary, depending on whether the government sponsored the show or considered it had any cultural, artistic or educational value.

have also included all works from 1973—even though the coup was carried out in September—to highlight the radical change between pre- and post-dictatorship repertoires. The choice of this corpus is explained by the large number of classic and/or foreign plays staged during the period in question, for the reasons stated above.[4]

Before exploring the repertoire of foreign texts translated between 1973 and 1989, it is necessary to conduct a brief review of the history of university theatres in Chile, which will make it possible to understand the structure and functioning of these institutions.

The Emergence of University Theatres in Chile: Their Origin and Distinctive Features (1941-1962)[5]

The rise of university theatres in Chile in the early 1940s is the result of a series of social, cultural, artistic and political conditions. First, the succession of Radical Party

---

[4] In general terms, the theoretical framework of this study stems from Translation Studies. It is not a comparative analysis of source and target text. Rather, it is a sociocritical and historical exploration of the choice of a particular foreign repertoire. Plays in translation allow us to understand how the literary and artistic system works in a particular culture: "The theatre, social art, speaks to a group in a specific place and time. It must connect to the community much more than other literary genres, which are indeed perceived in an individual process and rhythm" (Lefebvre 1978: 34). Also, translation is a discursive act in a given society and culture: "Literature in translation constitutes a discursive formation among others, regulated like others. In order to be admitted in the target culture, it had to undergo the same institutional restrictions as the source language literature in its own culture" (Brisset 1990: 25). Thus, the examination of translated plays allows us to understand as well how the discourse of a given society works, and, at the same time, how it relates to foreign literature. Nevertheless, this particular study does not pretend to conduct a comparative analysis of one or more texts with their original, but a corpus of plays. Macro-textual and micro-textual examination will not be relevant in this case, nor their meanings according to later historiographical interpretations. This essay will focus more on the extra-textual factors surrounding the translated texts than on particular translation strategies.

[5] This includes the foundation of the first university theatre, the Teatro Experimental de la Universidad de Chile (TEUCH) in 1941, and the creation of the Teatro de la Universidad de Antofagasta in 1962 (TUA).

governments between 1938 and 1952 (particularly with the arrival of the Frente Popular [Popular Front], commanded by President Pedro Aguirre Cerda), which promoted a government programme to encourage the development of the arts in Chile.

Together with the modernization of the Chilean state and the introduction of the import substitution model that sought to give greater independence to the Chilean economy, the middle classes were consolidated as well. Economic development significantly improved their living conditions, which helped them acquire an increasingly dominant role in the political, social and cultural life of the country. Education became one of the pillars of the radical government of Aguirre Cerda; not in vain was his campaign slogan *gobernar es educar* (to govern is to educate). The middle class became a professionalized and politicized agent.

However, despite the state's interest in promoting artistic development, Juan Andrés Piña (2009: 105) points out that "The Frente Popular [...] lacked an organizational and programmatic cultural policy, and initiatives related to these issues were erratic and often improvised". Thus it was the academic intelligentsia that was in charge of bringing about artistic and cultural progress.

Many scholarly papers published during that period, as well as some chronicles of notable authors of the time, admit that Chilean theatre was in "crisis" at the time. The causes may vary, and cannot be explained solely by the poor quality of the performances or lack of artistic experimentation of the time.[6] There is, in the first place, the economic crisis of 1929, which strongly affects Chile and forces companies to reduce their budget. Secondly, the appearance of cinema with sound, cheaper and with mass appeal, relegates theatre to a secondary place. And finally, "the massification of new genres linked to musical theatre, labelled 'frivolous,' which set aside other kinds of play aspiring to greater depth and creativity" (Piña 2009: 375). This crisis, for Piña at least, not only extended to the mise en scène, but also to Chilean dramaturgy. If some of the most prominent national authors shone in previous decades (Luco Cruchaga, Armando Moock

---

[6] Until then, Chilean theatre, strongly influenced by the model of the Spanish companies of the early twentieth century, had kept its distance from the European theatrical avant-garde.

or Acevedo Hernández), they were less prolific during the 1930s. Furthermore, their works were of a lesser quality (Piña 2009: 386) or could not find "in the procedures and methods of local staging, a space to decipher and communicate their style" (Hurtado 2010a: 28).

However, according to Andrés Kalawski, theatrical historiography has perpetuated this idea of crisis without specifying that such an interpretation comes from the university itself, as well as the playwrights of the period (Kalawski 2015: 105). These texts not only had to compete with the box-office success of "revistas" (reviews) and "variedades" (variety shows) (less text-oriented and more performative), but also with economic precariousness, due to the weak funding of theatre by the Chilean state.

In this context, the future founders of university theatres, who studied diverse degrees, sought to renew the performing arts in Chile. In general terms, they sought to follow the precepts of the European art theatres, with a strong educational component. The influence of the European artistic diaspora that arrived in America because of the World Wars in the thirties is vital to understand the aesthetic objectives behind the programme of these young people (Hurtado 2010b: 17). Foreign actors and playwrights, like Margarita Xirgú or José Ricardo Morales, played a fundamental role—albeit indirectly—in the foundation of the university theatres. Also, many of the foreign works that were performed during that period in Chile inspired the future theatrical models on which university theatres in our country were built. It should be noted, however, that these influences specifically and exclusively had an impact on this group of youngsters, and not on Chilean society as a whole. Indeed:

> It has been repeated as a mantra that the visit of the Jooss ballet [...] and the passage through Chile of Margarita Xirgu [...] were essential for the emergence of university theatres. But to be more precise, it was the tiny group that later formed the university theatres [...] who used to visit the dressing rooms of those professional actors. [...] The professional theatre remained unchanged for a long time. (Kalawski 2015: 107)

Thus, the primary objective of this group of students was to spread and universalize classical and modern plays, as well as some contemporary works that had clear aesthetic and educational value. This repertoire is eminently foreign.

The Foundation of the Teatro de Ensayo de la Pontificia Universidad Católica de Chile in 1943 and its Subsequent Role during the Military Dictatorship

On 17 October 1943, the Teatro de la Universidad Católica (or, later, Teatro de Ensayo de la Universidad Católica) premiered Josep de Valdivieso's *El peregrino* (The Pilgrim), an auto sacramental directed by Pedro Mortheiru. The production premiered at the Teatro Cervantes in Valdivia. Less than a month later, on 2 November, *El peregrino* is produced in Santiago, in Teatro Miraflores. The choice of this text is no minor matter, because the students decided upon a play that largely escaped the usual repertoire of professional theatres at the time. It also involved many challenges. Firstly, the artists' amateurism and scant experience in theatre complicated their task. Secondly, the fact of staging a classic play with no budget made this endeavour even more arduous. To perform these classic texts became in itself an innovative gesture, considering the prevailing taste of the public at the time. Like TEUCH, TEUC pursued the creation of a theatre with high artistic and educational value, unlike the professional theatre of those years.

The beginnings of TEUC were nevertheless not easy, not only because of its actors' lack of training but also because of insufficient resources. Also, the academic authorities were not very convinced of the purity of such an endeavour. Finally, albeit reluctantly, the University handed over a rehearsal room to the company. This paradoxically tense but close relationship between university authorities and the TEUC continued over time. During the first years of TEUC, the repertoire had to be approved by the Dean and other authorities. After 1973, this mechanism of censorship, which had disappeared in the years following its foundation, was put into practice again for obvious reasons.

Politically speaking, TEUC members, unlike those of TEUCH, had less radical positions, sometimes even less defined, closer to Catholic spheres. Fernando Debesa comments on this point: "in that year the political did not exist for us, the political was not our concern" (in Hurtado & Munizaga 1980: 18). The positive aspects of this Catholic

Foreign Plays and Repertoire during the Dictatorship

Church-University relationship were abundantly clear during the dictatorship. The TEUCH was completely dismantled, following the massive intervention by the military throughout the whole Universidad de Chile, the imposition of military authorities, as well as the redundancy of students and staff. In contrast, the Pontificia Universidad Católica de Chile suffered a little less, partly because of the protection from the Vatican, and probably due to its conservative preferences, particularly in certain departments. About this, Grinor Rojo (1983: 129) suggests that:

> because of its status as a private, elitist and, like it or not, Catholic University, the authorities paid less attention to what happened in there than to the Universidad de Chile […]. Subsequently, for the same reasons […] such as […] the continuity and relative sanity of its administration—since their Dean is an Admiral a bit more well-read and a little less stupid than the thick-headed army and air force generals who have been placed in the same position in other institutions of higher education—some of the university work has been able to take place in there.

Thus, although the TEUC underwent many substantial changes during the period, its circumstances were less critical compared to what happened in TEUCH. In fact, its productions during that time received harsh reviews from the critics, although they followed repertoire policies more or less coherent with its previous authorities. Furthermore, the subsequent artistic directors were known to be intolerant towards any attitude considered as dissident; Fernando González, an actor and theatre director, called them even "Mephistophelic" (in Piña 2014: 774). If the military intervention in the TEUCH was entirely evident, the TEUC director during the coup, Eugenio Dittborn, continued to exercise his functions, which "gave assurances of continuity and decency" (Piña 2014: 778). This continuity manifested itself not only in administrative but also artistic terms. Although the financial situation was precarious compared to previous years, they had at least the intention of staging major classics and, in some cases, providing a particular point of view, based on contingency. In this regard, some of the comments or analyses of critics and historians are enlightening:

> Its then president and theatre director Eugenio Dittborn, together with close collaborators such as the directors and actors Raúl Osorio and Héctor Noguera, dedicated themselves to discovering in the works from the [Spanish] Golden Age, the Renaissance, and romanticism, their potential to demand justice and respect for human rights, and to explore the existential, emotional anguish and the dislocation or reaffirmation of the personality of those affected by these violations. Thus, with plays from widely acknowledged authors [...] such as those from Calderón, Lope de Vega, Shakespeare, Molière, Schiller, the TEUC staged many works willing to reflect upon and condemn their current situation, turning this theatre into a referent, deeply connected to the Western libertarian and humanistic culture. (Hurtado 2010c: 19)

Similarly, Juan Andrés Piña (2014: 778) also states:

> Behind the performances of TEUC directors, you could guess there was an aesthetic and even ideological desire to bring to the present those old messages, giving them a new dimension and interpretation. This was the early case of *La vida es sueño* [Life Is a Dream], in 1974, whose mise en scène gave a substantial boost to the yearning for freedom of the protagonist, Segismundo. His desperate monologues, amidst the oppression that the country was living, resonated in a particularly significant way for a part of the public.

What happened with *La vida es sueño* in 1974 is a significant example of this interpretative trend. Even if it is not a translated text—and therefore of less interest for the corpus included in this essay—it inaugurates the hermeneutic construction that has been carried out around the classic repertoire during the period of the military dictatorship in Chile.

Years later, however, to celebrate the fifty-sixth anniversary of its founding, in 2007, Ramón Núñez, actor, director, winner of the National Arts Prize and current professor of the Theatre School at the Universidad Católica, commented on *La vida es sueño*: "a cry for freedom [...]. Half the audience applauded because they thought freedom had ended, and the other because they thought it had been recovered" (in Otondo & Garnham 2007: 7). Like Piña's clarification in the previous quotation, Núñez's remark points to the important issue of the reception of these performances. Considering the nature of the TEUC, it is entirely possible that the public in attendance not only belonged to the leftist opposition but also—and most likely— to the classes that supported, at least initially, the military regime.

Regardless of how the plays were interpreted and the undeniable fact that *La vida es sueño* does actually represent a cry for freedom in an oppressive context, it is important to note that this particular performance becomes the example that later defines a historiographical canon, which nevertheless leaves aside a substantial number of productions that would not enter into such an interpretation: comedies, national productions, children's theatre, or other contemporary foreign works. These exist, however, and it is necessary to refer to them if one is to speak of the totality of a repertoire.

Translated and/or Foreign Works (Spanish Classics) and Adaptations Staged in TEUC between 1973-1989: Some Figures

Bearing in mind that in the decade preceding the military coup, the number of translated plays in performance was minimal compared to the production of Chilean texts, the contrast with the situation of university theatres in 1973, in particular, the TEUC, is quite radical. In fact, of a total of 43 works staged between 1973 and 1989, 17 of them are translations and/or adaptations of non-dramatic texts (stories or novels) from a foreign language. Then, there are six Spanish Golden Age classics (including two different versions of *La vida es sueño*), two works adapted from non-dramatic texts in Spanish, two foreign works in Spanish, a free version of a Chilean playwright based on a foreign short story and finally fifteen Chilean plays.[7]

---

[7] For this essay, I have not considered the productions including students' plays or graduation performances. Also, I include a version of *La vida es sueño* directed by Héctor Noguera (actor and professor at the Theatre School of la Pontificia Universidad

- Translations
- Spanish Golden Age
- Adaptations from other genres, foreign
- Others
- Chilean playwriting
- Foreign playwriting in Spanish
- Adaptations from other genres, Spanish

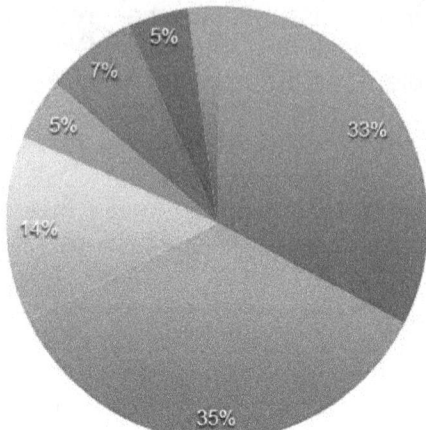

However, contrary to what many historians have affirmed in the past, Chilean theatre does not completely disappear from the repertoire. María de la Luz Hurtado (2010c: 19) is but one example of this trend:

> The drastic change of repertoire implemented in the Teatro de la Universidad Católica could not be more shocking: it goes from virtually 100% of Chilean or Latin American theatre in the decade before 1973, to 100% of classic European theatre.

Certainly, it is clear that from September 1973 to 1978 Chilean playwriting disappears entirely from the billboard. In that year, Egon Wolff's play *Espejismos* (Illusions) opens. Then we have to wait until 1982 to see another Chilean text on stage, also from Wolff, *Parejas de trapo* (Ragged Pairs). The passage between the clear predominance of Chilean playwriting to a foreign repertoire, primarily formed by classic plays, is especially drastic in the year of the coup, for only just a few months before, TEUC was producing two

Católica de Chile) and Erto Pantoja (actor and former student of the same school). It was not performed in the theatre, but on Campus Oriente UC, where the Theatre School is situated.

works by Chilean authors, Antonio Acevedo Hernández's *Almas Perdidas* (Lost Souls), and Fernando Cuadra's *Croniteatro* (Chronitheatre). Acevedo Hernández's play is a social drama written in 1915, and its plot focuses on the Chilean *conventillos* (slum tenements) of the beginning of the century. Cuadra's *Croniteatro* is, as indicated by its subtitle, "an incomplete history of Chilean theatre". The text includes many different scenes from Chilean plays of the past. While both works are Chilean, and more or less contemporary, they cannot be considered as political works, either because of their theme or their style.

A simple review of the previous figures reveals—and here I agree with authors such as Hurtado, Piña and Rojo—that the classic plays from the Spanish Golden Age burst onto the TEUC stage almost explosively, with six productions (but only five plays, for *La vida es sueño* is performed twice, in 1974 and 1988). Even though at the dawn of university theatres works from the Golden Age were chosen for their repertoires, this trend gradually disappeared over time. Thus the contrast with this period is indeed remarkable.

Continuing with the foreign repertoire, we have a meagre 5% for Spanish-speaking playwriting. This figure does not seem surprising, however, since the presence of Latin American theatre in TEUC throughout its history has not been at all significant. Except for the Spanish classics of the Golden Age, as well as other Hispanic canonical writers, such as García Lorca, for example, the presence of Spanish theatre has not been substantial.

As for other texts of the repertoire during the dictatorship, it is also possible to observe a progressive tendency, towards the end of the 1980s, to stage children's plays and adaptations of literary classics (such as *Don Quixote*) or contemporary works (such as Michael Ende's *The Neverending Story*), as well as other textual materials, such as the Declaration of Children's rights (Gerardo Cáceres' *Los niños que no podían ser niños* (The Children Who Couldn't be Children). The same author secured an adaptation of Maeterlink's *The Blue Bird*). If we now turn our attention specifically to translated works, particularly their authors, there are also some revealing facts about the interpretative hypotheses of Chilean theatrical historiography:

- Translations
- Spanish Golden Age
- Adaptations from other genres, foreign
- Others
- Chilean playwriting
- Foreign playwriting in Spanish
- Adaptations from other genres, Spanish

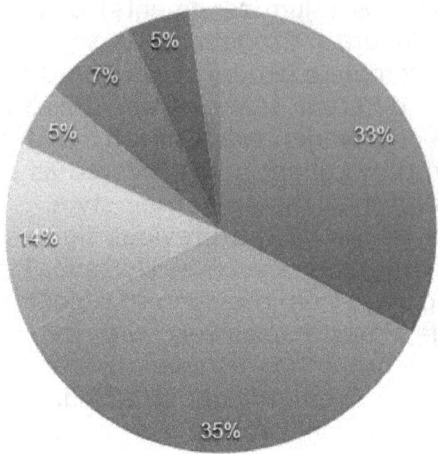

Excluding from this group the texts belonging to the Spanish Golden Age, the fact that the most translated author (with four works) is Molière, a master of comedy, is striking. It should also be mentioned that the French playwright's texts are a clear preference among TEUC's directors. In fact, Molière is one of the most translated authors in that theatre, together with Shakespeare (Grass 2011: 143-146). This predilection is not surprising, since Eugenio Dittborn, TEUC's artistic director from 1954 until his death in 1979, was fond of Molière's work. Indeed, *Las preciosas ridículas* and *Sganarelle* were performed a year after Dittborn's death, as a tribute to his legacy.

The fact that Molière is one of the most translated and performed authors is not a minor issue. It is true that Dittborn contributed to the French author's dominance in the TEUC's repertoire, but it is also important that comedy occupies such a strong place at the time. This is significantly striking if we think that one of the blockbusters and critically acclaimed productions of that time was *Le Bourgeois Gentilhomme*.

The Case of *Le Bourgeois Gentilhomme*: Comedy as a Minor Genre?

What happens with Molière's *Le Bourgeois Gentilhomme*, which premiered in 1975 (one year after the paradigmatic *La vida es sueño*), directed by Eugenio Dittborn, is quite particular with regard to the way theatre historiography in Chile has interpreted the choice of repertoire during the dictatorship. Firstly, because, in spite of its success, the performance is only casually spoken of. In the aforementioned prologue by Hurtado, she acknowledges the fact that Molière is one of the classic authors included in this difficult period's repertoire. And yet, she does not thoroughly explain how Molière's texts manage to speak indirectly of the philosophical or psychic problems in the context of the dictatorship. Nor does she mention this particular play. Piña (2014: 779) himself refers to it, but only to use it as an example of a production "that would assure a good economic return" without neglecting its quality, and which would still provide "another perspective on a classic", unlike what happened in the theatre of the Universidad de Chile. The work then becomes relevant only as a "well-staged" classic play. In fact, financial and critical success is seen as a secondary feature from an artistic point of view.

Besides, all of the studies previously quoted in this essay fail to mention that the work received many prizes, both for Dittborn's stage direction and for Ramón Núñez's performance. His rendition of M. Jourdain aroused the admiration of the critics and the audience, and it is one of the most remembered works of the actor. Another remarkable actress who was in the cast was Ana González, known for her comedy character "La Desideria" and her radio show "Radiotanda".

Thanks to an audiovisual record of the performance produced in 1975 (although slightly adapted to film format), it is possible to have an account of the production, as well as the Spanish translation. Apart from some minor changes in the cast, the costumes, set design, music and artistic direction are almost the same as the original stage version. The UC Chamber Orchestra was in charge of the music. Being a comedy-ballet, with music composed in the seventeenth century by Jean-Baptiste Lully, Dittborn keeps the same scores as the original. There are very few cuts and the target text has very few changes. The French version is written in prose, making the translation process easier, for it is not necessary to make the always difficult decision of translating into Spanish verse.

The acting style, which might be described as a physical comedy, is very elegant and clean (especially the performance of Nuñez, who is constantly making different gestures and physical poses reminiscent of the Commedia dell'Arte). There are a few double entendres (for example, Mr. Jourdain looking divertingly towards the breasts of the Marquise), but these are quite sober and inoffensive. Even though it is a comedy, the play is neither vulgar nor unrefined. Nuñez's performance, which stands out above the others (except perhaps for Ana González's work), has both hilarious moments—especially during the fencing or philosophy lessons—and very sarcastic asides in line with Molière's acid comments on society and the bourgeoisie.

If we take the whole play into consideration, and although there is always a sharp social criticism in any work of Molière's, it is actually hard to find in here any reference to issues occurring in Chile during Pinochet's dictatorship. Of course, this is no reason to undermine the mise en scène's value, which, as critics and historians have suggested, was an excellent performance at the time. Its box-office and critical success, however, help understand why there are not many historiographical analyses of the play when talking about the strategies of institutional re-articulation deployed by TEUC after the coup, or the use of classical texts as a subtle and clever way when referring to the political and social situation in Chile in the 1970s.

Conclusion

It seems, then, that theatre historiography pleads for one official Memory of the period of the military dictatorship (and in the particular case that concerns us here, of TEUC), which, being canonical, becomes automatically selective. It is also doubly canonical because it constructs, on the one hand, a biased repertoire that not only clearly defines which authors are appropriate for the stage, but also what genres may be suitable for performance. And then, on the other hand, it is equally canonical for it determines a single interpretation, a metanarrative that repeats itself in many scholarly studies, as a way of comprehending the repertoire according to its historical context. The brief review of the origins of the university theatres at the beginning of this study is therefore not in vain. Their historical trajectory, and specifically TEUC's, explains very well how the bases of this future historiography are established. The germ of the later canon already manifests itself in the statements of the early founders of TEUC. Since its conception, this institution fought against a Chilean theatre supposedly in crisis which did little avant-gardist experimentation, which needed to import foreign models of playwriting and performance. Thus, it is possible to stage only a particular type of play, to talk about certain topics, and to perform according to some codes belonging to a certain artistic style, and no other. Therefore, with the birth of the university theatres, a noticeable modernization of the Chilean scene as well as the academization of theatre took place.

Nevertheless, this notable improvement automatically creates a number of categories that decide what is valuable in theatre. It is now the scholars who dictate the rules of what is educational and artistic, and what is not; what is experimental and what is commercial (and therefore wrong). If the production is a box-office success, it means it has no artistic merit (and if the play is intended for high school students, it may be even worse). In this regard, Cristián Opazo (2014: 125-126) summarizes very well the attitude of university theatres and academia in general:

> Judging by our scholarly production, historians and critics of Chilean theatre of the twentieth century suffer from agoraphobia, or sudden fear of alien spaces. Indeed, in anthologies and essays, we rarely pay any attention to those theatre stages located on the outskirts of the university campus [...]. This same affliction determines how we develop our history books and theatre criticism: [...]. We sanctify, as unexcelled pupils, those playwrights participating in the "educational missions" of university theatres.

In this triad of non-commercial, non-experimental, artistic theatre, only a few specific styles are relevant. Comedy would not be one of them. Also, it is important to make the distinction between "high comedy" (such as Molière) and all the other shows belonging to the "géneros ínfimos" (minor genres). Thus Molière is included in the canon. But, for this particular historical moment, where artists from all disciplines unite against the regime, it is necessary somehow conveniently to cast light on certain events, performances, plays and authors over others, to find meaning in the history and memory of this place, the TEUC. This does not mean in any way that theatre historiography conceals these performances, much less deplores them. In fact, none of these authors expresses negative opinions about these productions, or questions their artistic quality. Nonetheless, their clear interest in these plays tends to hide the other. What happens with *Le Bourgeois Gentilhomme* is just one example of what also happens with other productions of the repertoire. The case of *El Burgués* is compelling because it was performed at the dawn of the dictatorship, perhaps in one of its most critical and violent moments. And it is thanks to its success that it becomes relevant in the light of its context, and even afterwards, since it is an excellent example of a historiographical trend that is inclined to place comedy in second place, not only during the military dictatorship in Chile.

References

Brisset, A. (1990). *Sociocritque de la traduction. Théâtre et altérité au Québec (1968-1988).* Longueuil: Le Préambule.

Grass, M. (2011). Aproximación a la traducción en el teatro chileno. El Teatro de la Universidad Católica (1943-2007). In A. Pagni, G. Payás & P. Willson (eds.), *Traductores y traducciones en la historia cultural de América Latina.* Mexico D.F: Universidad Nacional Autónoma de México, pp. 129-159.

Hurtado, M. (2010a). Prólogo. *Antología. Un siglo de dramaturgia chilena. Tomo I (1910-1950).* Santiago: Publicaciones Comisión Bicentenario Chile 2010, pp. 11-29.

Hurtado, M. (2010b). Prólogo. *Antología. Un siglo de dramaturgia chilena. Tomo II (1950-1973).* Santiago: Publicaciones Comisión Bicentenario Chile 2010, pp. 11-39.

Hurtado, M. (2010c). Prólogo. *Antología. Un siglo de dramaturgia chilena. Tomo III (1973-1990).* Santiago: Publicaciones Comisión Bicentenario Chile 2010, pp. 11-35.

Hurtado, M., & Munizaga, G. (1980). *Testimonios del teatro. 35 años de teatro en la Universidad Católica.* Santiago: Ediciones Nueva Universidad.

Kalawski, A. (2015). *Falso mutis. Oficio de actor en la "época de oro" del teatro chileno 1910-1947.* Doctoral thesis. Pontificia Universidad Católica de Chile.

Lefebvre, P. (1978). L'adaptation théâtrale au Québec. *Jeu*, 9, 32-47.

Opazo, C. (2014). Pedagogías teatrales en el Chile posautoritario. *A Contracorriente*, 12(1), 125-135.

Otondo, F. & Garnham, J. P. (2007). Los protagonistas de las tablas chilenas. *Visión universitaria*, 167, 6-7.

Piña, J. A. (2009). *Historia del teatro en Chile 1890-1940.* Santiago: RIL editores.

Piña, J. A. (2014). *Historia del teatro en Chile (1941-1990).* Santiago: Taurus.

Rojo, G. (1983). Teatro chileno bajo el fascismo. *Araucaria de Chile*, 22, 123-136.

Rojo, G. (1987/8). Teatro chileno en dos tiempos y un epílogo. In J. L. Gómez-Martínez & F. J. Pinedo (eds.), *Chile. 1968-1988. Los Ensayistas*. Georgia Series on Hispanic Thought nº 22-25. Georgia: Center for Latin American Studies, pp. 207-229.

Chronotopes of Truth and Memory in Post-Coup Chilean Theatre[1]

Andrés Kalawski

> The simultaneous attraction to and fear of the dead, the need continually to rehearse and negotiate the relationship with memory and the past, is nowhere more specifically expressed in human culture than in theatrical performance.
>
> Marvin Carlson

Patricio Aylwin became the president of Chile on 11 March 1990. This was the first elected ruler after over seventeen years of dictatorship. One of the first decisions he made, the same year he came into power, was to create the National Commission for Truth and Reconciliation to investigate violations of human rights by agents of the state or persons subject to its powers between 11 September 1973 and 11 March 1990. The Rettig Report, as it was known, determined that the deaths of 2,296 persons were aggravated homicides. In 2004, the National Commission on Political Confinement and Torture published the Valech Report, which, after its revision in 2011, brought the number of imprisoned and/or tortured during the dictatorship to 40,018, including 3,065 dead and missing persons.

The 1973 military coup and subsequent violation of human rights left Chilean society with cultural trauma (Alexander 2004). Attempts made by means of juridical mechanisms supported by reports published by the Truth and Justice Commission and the National Commission on Political Confinement and Torture have not yet been sufficient to reconstitute the damaged social fabric (Demaria 2006) and the issue of state violence is still controversial in our country. The impossibility of bearing witness prevents the

---

[1] This essay is the end result of Regular Fondecyt Project Nº1141095: *Historia y memoria del teatro chileno reciente entre 1983-1995: análisis crítico de la construcción de un canon y sus exclusiones*, coordinated by Milena Grass Kleiner. Andrés Kalawski, Nancy Nicholls, Inés Stranger, Mariana Hausdorf and Andrea Pelegrí Kristić participated in the project.

construction of a narrative of events indicating what happened, which in turn hampers the formulation of the trauma and organization of the events into an account organized and contextualized in terms of space and time (Agamben 2000). This unspeakable truth pervades many of the texts dealing with missing persons and torture, imbuing these works with a porous and recursive surface, where different types of discourses make their appearance and memory gaps become evident. As Lazzara (2007: 60) indicates:

> Instead of literally representing an event exactly as it took place, memory narratives incorporate the past "in a performance mode", making use of transmission methods that make the experience (or some aspects of the experience) an intelligible material for a specific audience and for a specific reason.

At an aesthetic level, therefore, what would be the "appropriate" language—within the freedom granted by the aesthetic regime of art (Rancière 2001)—to provide an account of what happened in extreme situations such as the disappearance of persons at the hands of government agencies? If the idea is to "present something that is not of the order of presence" (Nancy, in Bertrand 2007: 3), the problem is addressed by articulating "the absence [disappearance]" in "the inescapable presence of a representation" (Bertand 2007: 2).

Research into the participation of the arts, especially theatre, in the denunciation and discursive formulation of violations of human rights during the Chilean dictatorship provides models to approach the study of recent traumatic history. A work of art persists in time like a pulse of its era and demonstrates the events, not as they actually happened, but rather as they are processed by the collective imaginary operating at the time the work was created. In this sense, the study of written post-coup Chilean theatre or plays performed during the dictatorship contribute to social discourse (Angenot 1999), determining what could and could not be said, and even what could be imagined in the midst of terror. It also serves as a device for denouncing what the dictatorial state attempted to silence using all means at its disposal.² Consequently, both dramatic texts and those performed on stage show a past that was not contaminated by the present, or by the future of the past, from a perspective that is presently hard to recover, since we know how subsequent history unfolded (Candau 2006). The Chilean director and playwright Ramón Griffero describes this as follows:

> Therefore [...] you didn't know when it was going to end; which is different from seeing it now. You had no idea if there was going to be a plebiscite, if it was going to exist or be respected, or if the state was going to continue its dictatorial process. Your mind was not the way it is now... this finishes in a certain year, and then comes the election and another president, no. If you had already been through fifteen years, it could be forty years, like Franco.³

Theatre would thus be an X-ray of the collective imaginary of an era, portraying a fictional correlation of what is happening at the level of facts and illustrating a symbolic horizon into which these events are inserted. In addition, considering its public and convivial nature, it would enable the collective and individual integration of narration with affection—two elements that are dissociated in the case of the experience of political violence.

Based on these assumptions, this essay analyzes how missing persons and torture were represented on stage in Chile between 1985 and 2011. Based on the analysis of six productions, I shall attempt to discover if there are recurring aesthetic devices in these plays conditioned by the issue they address. In addition, the diachronic dimension of the study aims to determine whether the establishment by the Rettig Report and the Valech Report of an official truth regarding

---

² In the 1970s, the Association of the Relatives of the Disappeared, formed mainly by women, managed, through hunger strikes, denunciations before international organizations, and street actions, to highlight the existence of the disappeared and, in doing so, provide one of the emblematic memories that characterize Chile under Pinochet and in the transition years, laying bare the struggle between remembering and forgetting (Stern 2013).
³ Interview with Ramón Griffero, Santiago, 16 June 2012.

crimes committed had any consequences on the dramatic writing and the performance of plays produced after these two milestones, to the extent that these reports brought violations of human rights into public space as undeniable realities, shifting the problem of denunciation to the representation of what cannot be represented and the possibility of understanding the past and of seeking justice. Understandably, this unspeakable truth will appear in the artistic creation in a manner designed to avoid censorship and to elaborate the trauma. To track it, a sideways glance will be necessary. A chronotopic approach, which brings together space and time indicators from fiction in order to understand a play, may turn out to be useful, especially if we consider the artistic relationship between a play and its surroundings. The chronotope is "the essential interconnection of time and space relations that have been artistically assimilated into literature [...]. We understand the chronotope as a formal category and as a category of contents in literature" (Bakhtin 1986: 270). If space and time are conditions for existence and thought, these will appear in the play in a creative relationship:

> In the literary artistic chronotope, spatial and temporal signs are fused into a conscious and concrete whole. Time thickens, concentrates and becomes artistically visible; likewise, space strengthens, associates to the movement of time, plot and history. The indications of time are revealed in space, and this is assimilated and measured by time. (Bakhtin 1986: 270)

The chronotopical vision would be our way of going from the indication to the whole of the play, finding temporary and spatial traces throughout the text. It has the advantage of bridging the traditional analysis of dramatic texts and texts that do not adhere to conventional annotation (division into acts or scenes, list of characters, etc.), as well as allowing a dialogue between those who appear in the staging and what the dramatic text proposes.

What Plays Are We Talking About?
Before moving further into the analysis as such, it is necessary to give the general background of each of the productions studied.

Cinema Utopía (Cinema Utopia) (first performed in 1985), written and directed by Ramón Griffero, proposes a very complicated situation. A group of characters from the 1950s attend the old Valencia Cinema to see a science fiction movie. The film shows a young couple who were kidnapped, tortured and went missing during the 1980s and lived in exile in Paris—which is a fictionalization of the events taking place at the time Griffero wrote the play. In theatrical terms, although the set was created by the rows of seats and the movie theatre screen, the movie being shown was not the projection of a film, but was rather performed on a stage in front of the seats, where a curtain was raised and lowered to indicate the start and the end of the movie. Plot development at both the Valencia Cinema and in the futuristic film was articulated in chronological terms.

99 La Morgue (99 The Morgue) (first performed in 1986), also written and directed by Griffero, portrays a fragmented work in terms of plot and is eclectic in terms of acting styles. The main plot line is about a young painter who works as a custodian at La Morgue, where a series of autopsies of bodies recovered from the water are being performed. However, the cause of death was not drowning but rather the physical ill-treatment through torture and murder. At the same time, there are scenes telling the story of three Spanish sisters during colonial times, as well as a fragment where Bernardo O'Higgins and his wife appear. The acting styles have recourse to a certain degree of realism, but also to expressionism. The fact that allusions to these different codes is not reserved to certain scenes but corresponds to different characters is particularly relevant, in that an "expressionist" character can relate to a "realistic" character.

Río Abajo (Thunder River) (first performed in 1995), written and directed by Ramón Griffero, is about a young outcast living on the riverbank of the Mapocho river who gets involved in a drug trafficking network. The set design shows nine spaces in a grid recreating an apartment building where the audience can simultaneously view what is happening in six apartments and in the access hallways. Some of the most important elements in this production, for the purpose of this analysis, are the reference to corpses appearing in the Mapocho river following the military coup, and to secret police agents becoming drug cartel ringleaders, and the final murder of a former CNI agent at the hands of a missing detainee widow.

La Huida (The Escape) (first performed in 2000), written (in 1974) and directed by Andrés Pérez, has a plot that develops on several levels. The main plotline—arranged chronologically—is organized around a "historical myth", transmitted orally from generation to generation, while historiography only with difficulty acknowledges this as a fact and refers to the extermination of homosexuals in the late 1930s during the Carlos Ibáñez del Campo administration.[4] The "period" staging, in which the protagonist, Andrés Pérez himself, a homosexual hiding a young couple that want to escape who is betrayed by his lover, is interrupted by first-person testimonials shared by actors themselves, who speak of their homosexual experiences on an autobiographical register, and by a video showing Andrés Pérez's mother referring to the homophobic murders. In this case the use of video brings multimedia on stage, which is only alluded to in the previous staging by using a veil to construct a filmic characteristic.

Cuerpo (Body) (first performed in 2005), directed by Rodrigo Pérez, was completely created on the stage based on extracts from the Valech Report on Political Confinement and Torture and fragments of the text *Pour Louis de Funès* by Valère Novarina, which refers to the body of the actor as a body subject to violence. Production combines monologues, interaction between actors, dance sequences, the projection of anatomical drawings on the wall and even a dog on stage. In this case there is no intention to construct fiction or a coherent narrative in terms of space or time. The use of multimedia is also evident.

Villa + Discurso (Villa + Discourse) (first performed in 2011), written and directed by Guillermo Calderón, portrays three young girls named Alejandra who have to decide the fate of the ruins of the Cuartel Terranova detention and torture centre, currently known as the Villa Grimaldi Peace Park, since a large donation of money has been received from foreign donors that will allow for the rethinking of what the memorial project should look like. Throughout a long

---

[4] In this case the homosexuals had been thrown into the sea from a ship. Understanding the reference to missing persons during the dictatorship does not require much reflection.

discussion—in chronological order and developed in a single space—, they consider different possibilities, ranging from recreating the torture centre as realistically as possible, to the creation of a white, modern museum—a clear reference to the Museum of Memory and Human Rights inaugurated by Michelle Bachelet in 2010— to the reinstallation of the current Peace Park. Beyond the relationship with architecture present in the discussions regarding aesthetics in respect of the museums of memory and reinforced by the Villa Grimaldi manor house centre stage, a series of situations in both the dialogues and monologues are portrayed in documentary format.

The plays analyzed here are framed in the context of the resurgence of theatre following its total destruction at the start of the dictatorship. We say total destruction because it affected the plays themselves through censorship, and creators through prison, torture, exile and death, and the material possibilities of interaction between the show and the audience concerning circulation restricted in space and time, dissemination channels and financing systems, with the end of public funding, the closure of theatres, theatre institutions and schools.

A slow and difficult re-emergence bordering on a clandestine existence followed this situation:

> During the first stages of the military regime, opposition was expressed by means of highly ritualized cultural performances [...]; theatre productions by some independent theatre companies that still performed. [...] The predominant emotional climate at these shows was tender affection, concern and trust in one's fellow man. The human body became the central concept of this sensitivity. [...] These cultural performances were for a long time used by the opposition in order to maintain contact and to reconstruct a stunted political identity in order to renew contracts and reorganize. (Vidal 1998: 125)

Part of this culture remains when more formalized theatre is reorganized. Reactivation of the theatre stage assumed the obligation of relearning some conventions (an unstudied aspect of seeking refuge in the classics that supposedly enabled producers to avoid censorship while showcasing the political situation) and reinventing others. Therefore, the appearance of unique and closed spaces, perhaps the most persistent legacy of the oldest theatre, reappears burdened by the sense of confinement, immobility and oppression, and not just as a reference to tradition.[5]

Also, the emergence of festive space provided a framework for convivial relations between actors and audience. At the El Trolley theatre, where the company directed by Ramón Griffero performed, the parties that included artistic performances, live music and performances by emerging groups alternated the use of Italian-style theatre space that brought together the same community.[6]

In addition to these factors, the plays that concern us exhibit the typical "detention" that tends to spatialize discourse, in what appears to be a constant element in contemporary theatre (Corvin, in Bobes Naves 1997). There is even causative dramatic action in the most orthodox sense. This multiplies and is simultaneously distributed, for instance in *Río Abajo*, which constantly plays with the comparison of activities carried out in the different appartments.

Thinking about the chronotope of these plays also has a comparative sense, as if we moved from one stage to another. Considering the plays one after the other and putting aside their authorship, we might say that it is possible to divine, if not progress, then certainly a transformation in the relations between theatre, time-space and discourse. All of the productions studied are related to the combination of intimate records and public records. The intimate action in the expression of sexuality, reverie and memory coexists with dialogue, confrontation, inquiry and struggle. None of these plays exclusively portrays public action as a tragedy, and this is not only due to the bourgeois theatre tradition that portrayed urban intimacy or censorship but was unable to portray directly political violence or resistance to it. Here we must see the deliberate efforts of integration into the community space of theatrical reception, the need not to segregate intimate problems as less urgent than public

---

[5] Among many other examples, see *Domingo, Isidro, No sé, Antonio*, Mauricio Pesutic, UC Theatre Faculty, 1984.
[6] Interview with Ramón Griffero, 16 June 2012. Interview with Verónica García Huidobro, 16 June 2012.

problems.

First came *Cinema Utopía*. In Griffero's mirror game, the audience watched as on stage another audience sits in front of another stage—or, more accurately, a movie screen. In a kind of temporary fold, the futuristic fiction of the movie theatre set in the 1980s corresponded to the very moment the "real" spectators were experiencing, those who had purchased their tickets; while the "fake" spectators, the characters created by stage fiction, saw this future from the 1950s. Through the linear organization presenting the scenes in both plotlines—the stories of this group of regular moviegoers versus the Paris exile of a bisexual young man whose former partner has been kidnapped and is now supposedly a missing detainee—, the space-time coordinates are fractured. In a voyeuristic action, we observe the flat reality of exile over the shoulders of the audience at the Valencia Cinema.

In *99 La Morgue*, the space, which is to say the morgue, contains different eras that have been boxed-in and refrigerated like dead bodies (the founding fathers, the mother, the dead). However, this cooled preservation and relative isolation is not enough to stop the passage of time. Connected by Germán and the dead body under his bed, the plot advances and transforms the subjects, especially insisting on the level of degradation, of putrefaction. This corruption affecting the subjects and their actions is unable to change the spatial structure which remains the same, a fact reinforced by the identical way in which historical, mythological or recent past eras are at the disposal of the suffering subject Germán. Therefore, the fish in the fish bowl do not act as the index of the play, but rather as its counterpoint. They remain in a stable and safe environment that is only exposed to external danger once the fish bowl is broken. In contrast, the humans in the play swim in a fishbowl punctured by the stories that invade them.

Hans Ulricht Gumbrecht (2013) has observed that the historicist chronotope installed as hegemonic in the nineteenth century has been joined by another, which he calls "the ever broadening present", which does not replace, but rather alternates and coexists with, the historicist chronotope, corresponding to a daily way of conceiving of time for an occidental culture. In it, the future is not an open horizon of possibilities but rather a horizon of approaching threats. We no longer leave the past behind, and this is not a condition for an open future. Instead, the future is flooded by the past. This is a present amplified by simultaneity. If the most obvious manifestation of this chronotope lies in the hypertrophy of on-line files and the illusion of connectivity provided by telecommunications, an issue that Griffero himself would address years later in *Tus deseos en fragmentos* (Your Desires in Pieces),[7] *99 La Morgue* proposes stagnant spaces that, nevertheless, are unable to separate anything, evidencing the failure of a taxonomic project of modern rationality. In turn, showing connections between the different isolations denounces the discouraging mechanism of dictatorship that set out to "atomize your ideas and [make you] think that yours was your own; that everything had disappeared and that the only one still there was you. Atomized people."[8]

Río Abajo repeats the procedure of stagnant spaces, but, as if reason could contain these, the apartment blocks become the analytical system of human behaviour (through the exhibition of variations of sexual behaviour, of struggles against solitude, of dance, etc.) in an intimate sphere, which is only visible to sociologists or spectators, and this same joy of being able to compare things is reinforced in innocent and coordinated popular music choreography. The strength of this comparison is such that it eventually forces each space to remain identical to itself.

The plot also seems to be divided into the realm of what is public (the street next to the river) and what is private (inside the apartments). When the plot should be private it moves into the public sphere (the girl making a call at a phone booth) just to highlight its pathetic nature and inadequacy.

The institutional space encapsulated at the morgue influenced the subjects. The intimate, private space of the apartment blocks seems to be truly isolated. It is true that the subjects behave consistently in both spheres (the former agent of repression has sordid and violent sexual behaviour), but the plot itself is only transformative, that is to say dramatic, in the purest sense, when it takes place in a public

---

[7] The connection between both plays was suggested by Verónica García Huidobro in an interview, 16 June 2012.
[8] Quoted from an interview with Ramón Griffero.

space. It is where that unfinished business can be resolved, where the widow kills the former agent, where the river flows.

La Huida defines space in a different way. Succession prevails over simultaneity, which only occurs because of the theatre space that contains everything. There is no spatial device to organize the plot, but rather a type of standardization. In this sense, it is a consistent play. The spoken word indicates that the persecution of homosexuals is a constant, and the plot shows this as well, ignorant of the changing times. These twists and turns, regarding the Ibáñez dictatorship, the memory of the Pinochet dictatorship, and the present onstage are best anchored in theatre itself. The theatre becomes the space that contains time, the course of the story shelters records of intimate confessions, which prevail over public actions. What remains is to hide, deceive, flee, bear testimony and reveal identity. The spaces of horror have a purely imaginary texture, those of memory and close relationships, those of affection; these are the only certain elements while the plot moves forward.

The only certain element seems to be the body in *Cuerpo*; or perhaps almost the only element. A play based on the idea of a remnant, but not only as a premise but rather incorporated into the process of staging the play. "It was the same procedure. The actors were summoned and there were three books; there were no texts. We started to extract, put things together and amalgamate into a process of creation".[9] There is no intention for the remnants to lead to a hidden harmony, because that would eliminate the awareness of amalgamation. In contrast, there is deliberate resistance to having language organize the plotline. In *Cuerpo*, the space is a theatre but not an apportioned double theatre, as requested by Barthes (1987), but rather a performance theatre, of the action itself, of embodiment. The violence in this play is not a closed space that engulfs us, as is the case in *99 La Morgue,* or a public political event, as in *Río Abajo*, nor even a feared and imagined space, as in *La Huida*. Violence is in the body, it is unspeakable.

The unspeakable nature of violence, its traumatic quality, is a contemporary analogy. In *Cuerpo*, the spectacularization of failed speech, the inability to come to

---

[9] Interview with Rodrigo Pérez, Santiago, 30 June 2012.

fruition, is the present procedure and the theatre, which take place in a real theatre (including the dog), which constitute the spatial support. However, there is a playful quality that escapes this mere description. There is a hidden procedure that sustains the amalgam without joining it:

> in the play *Cuerpo*, as a procedure, there was an invention, because we always invent and then you forget about it; a context was invented, invented, invented, invented, invented. A context that is not real, acting as a support; which finally creates a huge situation, which is a support so that the texts that must appear, in this case, can arise. What was invented here, the invented context—and the truth is that we spent a long time rehearsing this before adding the words—was that this was a theatre troupe, that was... it was actually from Tierra Amarilla, which had been awarded a FONDART grant; it was a FONDART grant used to attract a star director from Volenmüler, a very modern theatre in Germany; that director they were bringing in was me... I'm very serious, it's true.[10]

The lightness that enables the audience to face horror together with the tradition of misunderstanding that produces and condones horror. Therefore, *Cuerpo*, in addition to its association with performance theatre, with second-generation documentary theatre and the cutting-edge tradition of language breakdown, is associated with the oldest tradition and, if it is not enough to turn the complete theatre into fiction, it does enable flow, complicity on the stage that pays tribute to tradition in the full sense of the word.

Finally, *Villa + Discurso* perhaps presents the most radical position in terms of the relationship between time, fiction and reality. Made up of two plays that converse and mirror each other, the discussion regarding the fate of the Villa Grimaldi Peace Park and the speech by the first female president of Chile, who was kidnapped at Cuartel Terranova, *Villa + Discurso* takes place under the three Aristotelian rules: the unities of action, space and time. These are also organized in strictly chronological order—although the multimedia components of the work might allow for the

---

[10] Quoted from an interview with Rodrigo Pérez.

rethinking of the latter. However, the precept imposed by the director—performing and presenting the production, at least initially, at former detention and torture centres—casts the referential space used to produce the play into the abyss. And vertigo was the result when it was presented at the Villa Grimaldi Peace Park. The discussion which the audience witnesses on stage, using a model of the old manor house as a constant indicator, refers to the space that contains and engulfs spectators, actors, model and the production itself. The audience is not just there, it is part of the document/monument that *Villa + Discurso* presents.

From the Fiction of Violence to the Impossibility of Changing the Past

We have provided a scenario of the flow of a corpus of plays related to the representation of state violence in Chile. Although the violence was triggered by the 1973 military coup, our theatrical production starts in the 1980s. It is no coincidence that we began the analysis with two plays staged just one year apart. The 1980s were not just an era when protests and violence escalated, but also witnessed an important revival of stage activity explicitly portraying the issues of torture and missing persons. Discussion of this issue has not ceased since. But what can we say about the diachronic plays we have chosen, and about their relationship with the everyday knowledge, "public" knowledge if you will, which the people of Chile had regarding violations of human rights in their country? How were these violations represented? How were the missing people represented?

As indicated so far, fragmentation seems commonplace. Saturation has also been a permanent resource that takes different forms and is intertwined with the explicit use of different media or with a sort of reference to them. Perhaps a banality, a blown-up black and white photograph of an identification card as testimony and evidence of the real existence of missing detainees appears time and time again. However, all of these constants show inflections and nuances throughout time.

With almost outrageously concise effort, we can state that, in 1985, the concept of disappearing people could only appear as science fiction, where kidnapping and violence were rarified in "slow motion". In 1986, torture could be briefly and succinctly shown on a stage representing the morgue, where a character stubbornly reported incoherence between the reports submitted by forensics and the real causes of death of the dead people floating in the water. This first stage might correspond to a moment of denunciation, where—in a pre-Rettig Report era—the missing detainees are still "out for a stroll" and therefore the portrayal of violence or the staging of events for public knowledge were on the line. No less important, this was recognition in the confederate space of theatrical conviviality for those who suffered repression.

Something had changed in 1995. *Río Abajo* brought justice on stage. The generation of spectators who saw this play remembers it as political recognition. While amnesty, "justice as far as possible", had left *torturers* and secret police agents free of all punishment, there was a place—even if it was just a theatre stage—where they were avenged. The widow of a missing detainee who shoots the *tira* (an agent of the Policía de Investigaciones) made many people's wishes come true.

In 2000, a gap was opened for intimate space to merge with public space, the time of ancient history with the present day. This time, the status of public debate regarding human rights not only allowed for first-person testimonials, a staged autobiography of experiences of repression during the dictatorship, but also extended the hypothesis that extermination methods used by Pinochet's dictatorship were "old history". Pérez inscribed the recent past into the extended timeline of history in the twentieth century and thereby refused to attribute the invention of missing detainees to the DINA/CNI.

And the Valech Report inaugurated another period. As if the victims had already said it all, as if there were no more words, Pérez leaves *Cuerpo* (the body) on stage at the mercy of violence. Here the experiment is not about the audience understanding physical punishment, but rather experiencing it by modulating their own bodies to mirror the corporeality of the actors and dancers appearing on stage. Short-circuited minds, exhaustion, overflowing energy.

What kind of closure is proposed by *Villa + Discurso*? How far can the state of mind go in the social formulation of the cultural trauma we have experienced? If torture is part of our genetics because we are the children born as a result of our mothers' rape in the detention and torture centres, then there is no way to repair this original birth defect. Reports, interviews, documentaries—the truth seems to have been established for good. There is a knowledge-base regarding the atrocities committed in Chile which nobody could presently deny. Someone might try to diminish these events at best. However, half-truths and justice cannot make what happened go away. Perhaps what remains is to learn to live while looking at ourselves in the mirror to see the faces of our torturers. Today's Chile was born of extreme violence. There is no way to erase the past; the only possibility is to recognize and contain that origin.

References
Agamben, G. (2000). *Lo que queda de Auschwitz*. Valencia: Pretextos.
Alexander, J. et al. (2004). *Cultural trauma and collective identity*. Berkeley: University of California Press.
Angenot, M. (1999). *Interdiscursividades de hegemonías y disidencias*. Córdoba: Universidad Nacional de Córdoba.
Bakhtin, M. (1986). *Problemas literarios y estéticos*. La Habana: Arte y Literatura.
Barthes, R. (1987). El teatro de Baudelaire. In *Ensayos Críticos*. Barcelona: Seix Barral.
Bertrand, D. (2007). L'écriture de expérience extrême. *E/C, rivista dell'Associazione Italiana di Studi Semiotici on-line*. 20 March.
Calderón, G. (2012). *Teatro II. Villa – Discurso – Beben*. Santiago: Lom.
Candau, J. (2006). *Antropología de la memoria*. Buenos Aires: Nueva Visión.
Carlson, M. (2001). *The haunted stage: The theatre as memory machine.* Ann Arbor, MI: University of Michigan Press.
Corvin, M. (1997). Contribución al análisis del espacio escénico en el teatro contemporáneo. In M. C. Bobes Naves (ed.), *Teoría del teatro*. Madrid: Arco Libros, pp. 201-228.
Demaria, C. (2006). *Semiotica y memoria. Analisi del post-conflito*. Rome: Carocci Editore.
Espinoza, V. (2005). Un prólogo en seis fragmentos. In R. Griffero, *Diez obras de fin de siglo*. Santiago: Frontera Sur, pp. 7-26.
García Huidobro, V. (2012). Interview. 16 June.

Griffero, R. (1986). *99 La Morgue*. Mimeographed libretto. Libraries System. Pontificia Universidad Católica de Chile.

Griffero, R. (2005). *Río abajo (Thunder River)*. In *Diez obras de fin de siglo*. Santiago: Frontera Sur.

Griffero, R. (2012). Interview. 16 June.

Gumbrecht, H. U. (2013). Historia y experiencia estética conference. Pontificia Universidad Católica de Chile, Instituto de Historia. 8 May.

Lazzara, M. (2007). *Prismas de la memoria. Narración y trauma en la transición chilena*. Santiago: Cuarto Propio.

Pérez, A. (2000). *La huida*. Mimeographed text.

Pérez, R. (2005). *Cuerpo.* Word file.

Pérez, R. (2012). Interview. 30 June.

Rancière, J. (2001). S'il y a de l'irreprésentable. In J.-L. Nancy (ed.), *L'art et la mémoire des camps. Représenter. Exterminer*. Paris: Seuil, pp. 81-102.

Stern, S. (2013). *Luchando por mentes y corazones. Las batallas de la memoria en el Chile de Pinochet. Volume II, La caja de la memoria del Chile de Pinochet.* Santiago: Ediciones Universidad Diego Portales.

Vidal, H. (1998). *Tres argumentaciones postmodernistas en Chile.* Santiago: Mosquito Comunicaciones.

Claudia Di Girólamo and Rodrigo Pérez's *Aquí están*: Little Resistances in the Context of the Fortieth Anniversary Commemoration of the Military Coup in Chile

María José Contreras Lorenzini

In 2013 Chile commemorated the fortieth anniversary of the military coup that ended Salvador Allende's government and began Augusto Pinochet's dictatorship. Throughout 2013 we witnessed an explosion of practices and discourses revolving around our recent past: a plethora of seminars, talks and academic classes; an abundance of acts and homages took place, while in the field of the arts, theatre plays, films and documentaries were produced and broadcast. Public and private museums featured exhibitions related to the last 40 years. Even TV channels scheduled fiction series and documentaries that had as their backdrop precisely the dictatorship years. As Isabel Piper (2013a: 1018) states, all of a sudden everyone was talking about the dictatorship: "numerous social actors (movements, organizations and institutions) that on this occasion—as if they did not want to be left out of this trend—organized acts, seminars, film series, issues of journals, cultural gatherings, etc., related to the coup and the dictatorship".[1]

In the context of the fortieth anniversary commemoration, one of the most active fields in the production and circulation of practices and discourses on memory was the arts. Creative expressions have played a very important role both during the dictatorship and in the post-dictatorship, managing to articulate the meanings that were marginalized, erased and written out of political and academic discourses (Richard 2008). In the post-dictatorship context, the arts' main role has been one of resistance to official memory, unveiling what has not been said or proposing idiosyncratic and expressive forms to criticize the modes of articulation of hegemonic memory. This critical trend was consolidated in the context of the fortieth anniversary, where, as Caterina Preda (2013: 51) reveals, a series of works of art dealing with memorialization emerged: "Rooted in the dictatorial past [they] raise topics and subjects

---

[1] Unless otherwise indicated, all translations are my own.

associated with that very past, unresolved during democracy."

Fig. 1: José Sosa reading Salvador Allende's last speech. Museo de la Memoria y los Derechos Humanos.

In this effervescent context, the project *Aquí están* (Here They Are) emerges as an interesting practice for several reasons: first, it is an action that articulates the political by using artistic strategies of intervention. *Aquí están* proposes a complex game between levels of production, reception and circulation of memories that stands out among other works presented in the context of the commemoration. The expressive resources that come together in this intervention are multiple and are mutually nourished: *Aquí están* works with testimonial word, visuality and performativity. This marks a big difference from the great majority of the commemorative artistic pieces that worked within strict disciplinary frameworks, following the modes of expression and canons of each artistic discipline (visual arts, theatre, dance, cinema, documentaries, etc.). On the other hand, the intervention has an intergenerational aspect that proposes an ongoing and necessary discussion on how the memory of the dictatorship is transferred to new generations. All in all, the dialogue (or the dispute) between the stage of the Museo de la Memoria and *Aquí están* presents two modalities of the commemorative work: on the

MemoSur/MemoSouth

one hand, the museumification of memory; on the other, the less ambitious but always effective creation of a contextual and local practice of memory.

Aquí están: From Testimonial Word to Visual Representation and Performativity

On 11 September 2013, the artistic intervention *Aquí están* is carried out in the Museo de la Memoria y los Derechos Humanos (Museum of Memory and Human Rights) in Santiago, Chile. The intervention stems from the actress and theatre director Claudia Di Girólamo, who, thinking about the emblematic black and white photographs of the *detenidos desaparecidos* (missing detainees) as a way of representation, wonders:

> what would these people be like if portrayed alive, with hope, with strength, with beliefs. I asked myself what the detained and disappeared would be like if they were to be painted and portrayed by the youngest members of their families, grandchildren and great-grandchildren. And who could tell them what these people were like. I obviously thought about the relatives of the detained and disappeared: mothers, fathers. (Di Girólamo in Insunza 2013)

Fig. 2: The paintings by girls and boys displayed in the forecourt of the Museo de la Memoria y los Derechos Humanos.

Di Girólamo designed a complex device in order to raise and elaborate this "vital" characterization of the detained and disappeared in an artistic way. First, family testimonies were collected; in a second stage, these testimonies were read to the younger members of the families of the detained and disappeared: girls and boys listened to tales about relatives whom they had never met. Then, the kids were asked to paint a portrait based on the stories their elders told them. The pictures turned out to be colourful, vital portraits that included distinctive objects that represented the life experience of the detained and disappeared: "full of colour, sun, the football team they liked, the place they liked to go to" (Di Girólamo, 2013a). The paintings were exhibited in the Museum's forecourt, from 11 to 16 September 2013.

On the evening of 11 September 2013 the project concludes with a final event named *Aquí están* (Here They Are).[2] The event was designed and directed by Di Girólamo in collaboration with the theatre director Rodrigo Pérez, who called on thirty actors and actresses to read the testimoninal narratives to the public at the fortieth commemoration of the Chilean state coup. The testimonies were adapted in order to include also solid data regarding the circumstances of their forced disappearance (Di Girólamo 2013b). That evening, little by little the forecourt begins to fill with people: families, elderly persons, youngsters and kids. The guests sit on the floor, in the bleachers, waiting to see what is going to happen. Suddenly the performers move forward to the centre of the forecourt, where several chairs form a spiral. Each one carries a white handkerchief, a red carnation in their hands and a printed sheet of paper. They sit on the chairs and wait. The court is in complete silence. Gradually the people in the audience leave their position as spectators and advance toward the forecourt to sit in front of some of the actors and actresses, who, paper in hand, read the testimonies provided by relatives of the *detenidos desaparecidos*. The spectators-participants wander around the space, sitting in front of different performers to hear diverse testimonies. This intimate reading of the testimonies runs for a couple of hours, after which some of the artists sit in front of the

---

[2] *Aquí están*. Original idea: Claudia Di Girólamo. Co-direction and dramaturgy: Claudia Di Girólamo and Rodrigo Pérez. Researcher: Ximena Faúndez. Co-researcher: Bárbara Azcárraga. Research assistants: Esteban Olivares, Ignacio García, Manuela Maturana and Diego Urra. Induction and family communication: Raffaella Di Girólamo. Artistic supervisor: Fernanda Di Girólamo. Artistic assistant: Francisco San Martín. Production: Teresita Di Girólamo.

microphone to read the testimonies. The audience listens attentively, silently, emotionally. Toward the end of the afternoon, a renowned national actor, José Sosa, shows up dressed as Salvador Allende, with his distinctive spectacles and a three-coloured sash across his chest. The silence turns sepulchral. Sosa sits in front of the microphone and begins to read the speech which Salvador Allende uttered moments before dying during the bombing of La Moneda Palace. The actors hold their white handkerchiefs high. "¡*Viva Chile! ¡Viva el pueblo! ¡Vivan los trabajadores!*",[3] recites Sosa while dozens of people in the forecourt answer yelling with great spirit: "¡Viva!"

Fig. 3: First phase of *Aquí están*. Testimonial narratives are read. Museo de la Memoria y los Derechos Humanos

Mediations and Translation Processes
It is well known that every testimony is a construction which, as Giorgio Agamben (2002: 153) states, is played out within the borders of what can be expressed: the testimony is only capable of translating the presence of an absence, the impossibility of speech, there where the impossibility comes to life through the possibility of speaking. The translation of an absence is even more axiomatic in the case of the testimonies of the detained and disappeared. When

---

[3] "Long live Chile! Long live the people! Long live the workers!"

testimonies are used in artistic practices, their condition of impossibility is reinforced: the artistic work based on testimonies implies a battle where the experience is subdued to fit the rules both of narrative and of aesthetics, while trying to overcome the situation where the borders between what is real and the textual-artistic simulacrum become blurred.

Generally speaking, artistic manifestations that are based on testimonies work in the awareness of the reality-effect they produce, and try to complicate and question notions such as authenticity, rather than establishing truths (Martin 2013; Forsyth & Mergson 2009). What is at stake in these kinds of piece is not what is "real" but the "reality-effect" they may produce. *Aquí están*, on the contrary, installs itself, in a rather naïve way, on the level of truthfulness, concealing the enunciation tracks and presenting the testimonies as if they were the direct recounting of a reality. On the Museum's web page, *Aquí están* is defined as a testimony rescue (Museo de la Memoria 2013), an idea which Di Girólamo reinforces in different instances. The project promotes the idea that the tribute rescues "the" memory, as if there were just one memory, and as if this could be exhumed and shared in the final performative event. Without any problematization of the categories of reality, authenticity or veracity, *Aquí están* achieves the dissimulation of the number of mediations entailed in a collaborative and collective construction of memories which are arranged from the present and, thus, are plagued by mediations and translation processes.

A first level of mediation is the testimony provided by the adult relatives. The act of the relatives of the disappeared giving testimony not only responded to the translation of personal experience into verbal language, but also to the framework imposed by the creative process itself. Unlike other kinds of testimonies, this narrative was raised with a specific methodology that defined its content, tone and type. First, those testifying were instructed to piece together a tale for the children, focusing on the lives of their loved ones, warning them that they would later be read in front of an audience (Insunza 2013). These instructions constitute a framework that significantly shapes the discourse. Then, the research assistants proceeded to cross-examine the relatives of the detained and disappeared, according to particular guidelines: they would begin with physical appearance and then move on to ask what they liked to do, how they behaved, etc. The relatives spoke while the assistants took notes, performing another undeniable selection of the testimonial material. This form of testimonial compilation implies a high level of mediation which results in a narrative that is a co-construction that emerges from the interaction between the one testifying and the examiner. Far from being a "salvaged" truth, this enunciative framework produces a testimony that is strongly marked by the communicational interaction of the present.

The translation of testimonies into portraits is a further level of mediation, a mediation that could be defined as inter-semiotic, since it translates verbal discourse into a visual configuration. In my opinion, this is one of the merits of the project, because it opens up a whole new perspective by admitting that the children's re-elaboration of memory is not restricted to the verbal. The portrait, like the testimony, is not made in a "free way", but it too responds to a clear framework defined by the authors' view of the piece. For instance, all children use standard materials, and, as Insunza's (2013) video shows, each boy and girl is given a small mannequin that guides the portrait, imposing a mimetic figurative pattern of the human body. The simple act of providing a scale figure of a human body demonstrates that the directors were looking for a certain degree of figurativeness in the portraits that could clearly connect the narrative to the portrait. It is interesting to note that although the majority of the portraits were in fact figurative, some strayed from this framework, proposing more abstract paintings. In a radio interview Di Girólamo assesses the abstract elements as "strange", revealing her expectation of figurativeness. "The portraits are truly beautiful, that is, they are spectacular if they weren't so painful; they are really stunning, full of colours, of sun, with the football team [the detained and disappeared] liked [...] the places they liked to visit, so then we have the representation of the countryside, or the city or the house, or nothing; or, suddenly, there are places that are quite abstract or very strange where they locate them" (Di Girólamo 2013a). The preference for the figurative responds ultimately to the prevalence of narrativity over visuality, and might, I think, be due to the director's theatrical training, which implies in one way or another a strong link with the word.

The aesthetic mediation is confirmed too in the remodelling operation of the testimonies before being read in public. Di Girólamo and Pérez adapt the narratives so as to make them more accessible to the public and to incorporate "known and solid data about their disappearance" (Di Girólamo 2013b). Such mediation requires an unquestionable degree of fictionalization that responds to dramaturgical canons: what is selected, discarded and organized responds to a dramaturgical construction that attempts ultimately to increase the efficacy of the discourse for the audience.

Fig. 4: Reading of the testimonial tales. *Aquí están*. Museo de la Memoria y los Derechos Humanos

In the encounter with the public a new mediation process occurs, which passes by way of the voices, the corporeality and subjectivities of the actors and actresses. The vast majority of the actors and actresses participating in *Aquí están* worked in television and so were well known to the general public. This generates a game of mediations that entails not only the framework imposed by the artistic practice, but also an interaction with mass media, such as television. The public recognition and the fame of the actors and actresses participating in the event cannot but influence the reception of the event, which ceases to be one characterized by the "greatest possible simplicity" (Di Girólamo 2013b) and acquires the tones of a spectacle. But the presence of renowned actors and actresses not only spectacularizes the action, it also facilitates an emotional bond, the affective tuning with the public, as well as the identification processes with the public. Because of the pre-established relationship with the actors and actresses (mediated by television), the narratives resonate with greater familiarity, facilitating the affection of the participant. As affirmed by Fisher-Lichte (2008), mutual interaction in live performances occurs with more promptness and effectiveness when a previous emotional circuit exists. Like an already existent path, this allows the emotional and corporeal bond to be more seamless. The inclusion of well-known television faces in this event subverts its own limitations: the public comes waiting to meet their favourite artists, who use this very influence as a seductive and affective tool in order to ease the communicability of the testimonies.

Fig. 5: Actor Héctor Noguera reads one of the testimonies at the microphone. Museo de la Memoria y los Derechos Humanos

Aquí están therefore proposes a device that is full of mediations, this is the reason why it cannot be considered as the mere rescue of a "forgotten memory", as its promise of veracity claims. It is precisely these translations and aestheticization processes that make *Aquí están* such an interesting intervention. What is highlighted here is precisely the abundance of simultaneous and consecutive layers of mediation that are combined in the mobilization of memories, establishing itself as an emblematic example of the procedures and operations of memorialization in and by the arts.

Girls and Boys as Subjects of Memory

One of the main stakes of *Aquí están* is the transmission of testimonies from the older generations to the younger, creating a dialogue between generations. Di Girólamo herself states, "Each family went through a process of memorization both personal and collective so as to bring their relatives back to life in their everyday things" (Di Girólamo 2013a). The procedure designed by Di Girólamo to generate the narratives, portraits and the final event is articulated around the idea of the transmission of a family memory that is not known or that requires a certain kind of repair.

The concern over the exchange and re-elaboration of memories across generations was established as one of the most recurrent issues in the context of the fortieth anniversary commemoration of the coup. One of the factors that presumably explains the persistence of this issue is the generational turnover that happens over four decades and that allows society to overcome the cultural trauma's latency period. That latency period of cultural trauma is no doubt related to the generational relay: forty years after the coup, the generations born under democracy begin to gain importance, even in the political arena. As Aleida Assmann (2010: 41-42) states:

> Social memory does not change gradually but undergoes a perceptible shift after periods of around 30 years when a new generation enters into offices and takes over public responsibility. Together with its public presence, the new generation will authorize its own vision of history. The change of generations is paramount for the reconstruction of societal memory and the renewal of cultural creativity.

For the first time, and with great insistence, the question of how the younger generations understand the period of the civil military dictatorship (what they know, what their stance on it is and how they link it to the present) arose in different cultural, artistic and academic fields. The question concerning the processes of transmission, activation and mobilization of memories seeks not only to understand how that memory travels through the generations, but also to unveil the current politics of memory, which are reflected in the way the dictatorship period is taught in schools, in the way what is divulged by the media is actually grasped by the boys and girls of today, and how families tackle topics regarding the violent past.

The Museo de la Memoria y los Derechos Humanos was one of the institutions that most enthusiastically echoed the preoccupation with the intergenerational transmission of memories in the context of the fortieth anniversary commemoration of the coup. In fact, almost all the emblematic projects carried out by the Museum in 2013 had young people and children as protagonists. Its director at the time explained the reasons why the Museum embraced that curatorial line:

> Memory cannot remain cloistered in the victims who lived through the traumatic experience, or in their relatives. The transition toward all their contemporaries and from one generation to the next is vital to accept the lessons of that painful past as part of a common body, so as to guarantee the "never again". (Brodsky 2013: 7)

The study of so-called intergenerational (Reyes 2009; Assmann 2010) or trans-generational (Scapusio 2006) memories has established itself as one of the preferred topics in memory studies. Undoubtedly one of the most relevant contributions to the conceptualization of the procedures of memorial transference through generations is the notion of postmemory offered by Marianne Hirsch (1997, 2012). As the author warns, the prefix "post" does not directly point to a temporal gap, but to the effects that the memory elicits: postmemory is that memory that transmits consequences and implications for the present day to the generations that were not direct witnesses of past events. One of the most important theoretical innovations in the notion of postmemory is the idea that the transmission of these

The Little Resistances of Di Girólamo and Pérez's *Aquí están*

experiences is emotionally rooted in the bodies and behaviours of the young; postmemory is, after all, an affective and embodied memory which is transferred beyond the verbal discourse (Hirsch 2012). Hirsch proposes that the mediators of postmemory are the narratives as well as the photographs, the objects and the mediating behaviours that set up a constant process of intertextuality and mutual translation that results in the construction of an indirect, more fragmented memory, which challenges the possibilities of a narrativity that exceeds the scope of words. From this viewpoint, the relationship between postmemory and the past would not be mediated by the witness' narrative, but by the imagination, projection and creation that propel other kinds of semiotic artifacts.

Hirsch's interest in the processes of imagination and cultural performance is extremely useful for analyzing the artistic intervention *Aquí están*, which proposes a device that at almost all levels incorporates postmemorial work. One first phase, the workshop, was organized in order to collect the testimonial narratives of the adults and to provide a creative space for the kids' portraits. The workshop is a protected event (both because of the time devoted to it, and because of the constant psychological advice the participants received) where the older and younger relatives can meet, confront each other and participate together in the posmemorial working through.

Fig. 6. *Aquí están*. Museo de la Memoria y los Derechos Humanos

The workshop succeeds in dislocating the perception of a certain generational uniformity, eradicating the notion of generations as communities in which a common memory exists. The workshop does not consider adults and children as distinct collectivities that need to be confronted, but rather installs an intersubjective and dyadic bridge that allows a collaborative working through for the reconstruction of postmemories.

A second instance of postmemorial reconstruction in *Aquí están* ensues in the final event, where the work carried out in the intimacy of the workshop is displayed in the forecourt before the gaze and presence of the spectators. When the actors and actresses read the narratives to "whoever wants to listen" (Pérez in Insunza 2013), a projection of private stories onto public space takes place, contributing to the creation of a wider postmemory. The anchoring in personal and family stories invests these memories with affects that, when communicated in the public sphere, facilitate processes of identification. As Hirsch (2012: 33) suggests, postmemorial work "strives to reactivate and re-embody more distant political and cultural memorial structures by reinvesting them with resonant individual and familial forms of mediation and aesthetic expression". In this way, postmemory can persist even when all the eyewitnesses and their direct descendants are no longer present. The movement from private to public is also enacted in the performative action itself, which moves from the intimacy of the initial reading, through the declamation of the testimonies at the microphone, and concluding with Salvador Allende's emblematic speech. It is remarkable how the intervention uses precisely the transition from private to public as a vehicle for a more communal and shared cultural memory.

Aquí están accomplishes an outstanding political re-definition of the category of childhood. By envisioning girls and boys as subjects endowed with voice and body, capable of receiving memories, but also with the ability to establish a diachrony with future generations, positioning them as memory subjects. From the very first instances, the project considers the younger generations not only as recipients of memory, but as agents of it. Although in the first instance the adults are the ones who tell the tales which the girls and boys "receive", the work that follows deals precisely with positioning these girls and boys as co-agents of a memory that, rather than being "transmitted", must be reconstructed collaboratively. The generation that did not live through the dictatorship personally becomes, then, a generation that is capable of re-elaborating and mobilizing a memory which they did not experience. It is unusual for children to be called upon as legitimate political subjects in the construction of memories, in this case, postmemory. The younger members of the families that suffered the disappearance of a relative acquire in this context a radical role in the responsibility that the mobilization of memories requires for the future. The children can demand their right to memory and, at the same time, become political subjects responsible for keeping that memory alive.

Micro-resistances against the Museumification of Memory

Aquí están takes place in the Museo de la Memoria, probably the most emblematic place in the construction of a national narrative about the dictatorship. The contrast between the museumification of memory and the commemorative procedures of the artistic intervention *Aquí están* is evident and significant. As Andreas Huyssen (1995: 16) puts it, the museumification of memory is a sort of antidote to the acceleration that characterizes late global capitalism, allowing it to "fulfill a vital anthropologically rooted need under modern conditions: it enables the moderns to negotiate and to articulate a relationship to the past", a trend moved and sustained by mass culture and neoliberalism. Unlike the enshrinement of memory which the Museum exercises, *Aquí están* is played out within the intimacy of inter-subjective interactions. The artistic gesture of Di Girólamo and Pérez echoes the feminist statement that asserts that what is private is political, bringing to a hegemonic space intimate and minimal stories of the victims' relatives that are not always validated as significant memories. As a collaborative aesthetic practice, *Aquí están* proposes an alternative way to activate non-official stories, offering other ways of political commitment. *Aquí están* is ultimately a sort of ritual of acknowledgment, where what is at stake is not the consolidation of a single memory, but the possibility of re-constructing a collective memory that turns out to be fragmentary, unstable, dynamic and multiple. This is accomplished by the construction of a temporality in progress that occurs in the context of the performative gathering. The simultaneous situation of production and reception of memories intensifies collective forms of construction that favour processes of recognition and belonging to the provisional and transient community which this coexistence constructs. *Aquí están* constructs, then, a magnificent game of temporalities that involves all the participants as subjects of memory. When performing this manoeuvre, a responsibility towards the past is transferred between generations but, more important, a responsibility regarding the future that looms as a shared horizon is constructed.

Aquí están is a form of action, collaboration and resistance whose political effectiveness lies in the expansion of the responsibility toward the future. Its range is that of "small scale resistances" (Bal 2011), understood as a micro-resistance that does not operate at the level of greater social structures (like the Museum), but is situated in the intimate and at times minimal space of inter-subjective relationships, where what is relevant is the dialogue, the mutual listening, companionship and solidarity. And that is exactly what *Aquí están* does: as Di Girólamo (in Insunza 2013) said, it made it possible "for the people to connect emotionally with the detained and disappeared and to question, once again: Where are they?"

References

Agamben, G. (2002). *Remnants of Auschwitz: The witness and the archive.* New York: Zone Books.

Assmann, A. (2010). Re-framing memory: Between individual and collective forms of constructing the past. In K. Tilmans, F. van Vree, & J. Winter (eds.), *Performing the past: Memory, history, and identity in Modern Europe.* Amsterdam: Amsterdam University Press.

Bal, M. (2011). Heterochrony in the act: The migratory politics of time. *Thamyris/ Intersecting*, 23, 211-238.

Brodsky, R. (2013). Presentación. In Centro de Estudios de la Niñez OPCION (eds.), *Los ruidos del silencio. Los niños, niñas y adolescentes hablan a cuarenta años del golpe militar en Chile.* Santiago: Lom, p. 5.

Di Girólamo, C. (2013a). Claudia Di Girólamo invitó a

participar de la intervención *Aquí están*. Radio ADN interview, 5 September. At **www.adnradio.cl/ noticias/ sociedad/claudia-di-girolamo-invito-a-participar-de-la-intervencion-conmemoracion-aqui-estan/20130905/nota/ 1964521.aspx**, accessed 22 September 2016.

Di Girólamo, C. (2013b). Claudia Di Girólamo lidera montaje con 30 actores. La Tercera. 47. 6 September. At **http://papeldigital.info/lt/2013/09/06/01/paginas/047.pdf**, accessed 26 September 2016.

Fischer-Lichte, E. (2008). *The transformative power of performance: A new aesthetics*. London: Routledge.

Forsyth, A., & Mergson, C. (2009). *Get real: Documentary theatre past and present.* Basingstoke & New York: Palgrave Macmillan.

Halbwachs, M. (1992). *On collective memory*. Chicago: The University of Chicago Press.

Hirsch, M. (2012). *The generation of postmemory: Writing and visual culture after the Holocaust*. New York: Columbia University Press.

Huyssen, A. (1995). *Twilight memories: Marking time in a culture of amnesia*. London: Routledge.

Insunza, P. (2013). *Aquí están*. Intervención/ conmemoración/11 de septiembre 2013. Video on DVD. Museo de la Memoria y los Derechos Humanos.

Martin, C. (2013). *Theatre of the real*. New York: Palgrave Macmillan.

Museo de la Memoria (2013). Página web Museo de la Memoria. At **http://ww3.museodelamemoria.cl/ exposiciones/aqui-estan/**, accessed 19 September 2016.

Piper Shafir, I. (2013). La conmemoración como búsqueda de sentido. *Pléyade*, 11, 1-11.

Preda, C. (2013). Arte de memorialización 40 años después del golpe de estado. *Tiempo Histórico*, 6, 49-62.

Reyes, M. J. (2009). Generaciones de memoria: Una dialógica conflictiva. *Praxis*, 15, 93-104.

Scapusio, M. (2006). Transgeneracionalidad del daño y memoria. *Revista Reflexión Derechos Humanos y Salud Mental,* 32, 15–19.

Richard, N. (1998). *Residuos y metáforas. Ensayos de crítica cultural sobre el Chile de la transición.* Santiago: Cuarto Propio.

Reinelt, J. (2009). The promise of documentary. In A. Forsyth & C. Megson (eds.), *Get real: Documentary theatre past and present*. Basingstoke: Palgrave Macmillan, pp. 8-21.

Scripts and Projections

Opposition to the Pinochet Regime: Two Movies for Two Kinds of Memory

Anna Maria Lorusso

The object of this short essay will be two films, or rather, a television series and a cinema documentary, telling of the period of the Chilean dictatorship and in particular the activities of a subject that has tried to denounce the crimes and to support the victims: the Vicaria de la Solidaridad. The two texts which I refer to are *Los archivos del cardenal* (The Cardinal's Archives), a television series directed by Nicolás Acuña and Juan Ignacio Sabatini[1] and broadcast in 2011 on the national network Televisión Nacional de Chile, and *Habeas corpus*, made in 2015 and directed by Claudia Barril and Sebastián Moreno.

Of course, they are quite different texts, above all generically—a television series and a documentary made for cinema. But the comparison of the two emerges almost spontaneously from the object that both texts, in a very focused and direct manner, confront: as I said, the Vicaria de la Solidaridad, an organ of the Catholic Church, founded on 1 January 1976, under the guidance of Cardinal Raúl Silva Henríquez, which provided legal support (through lawyers) and social support (through social workers) to the victims of the dictatorship's crimes. Being a very prominent organ in the city of Santiago, and closely linked to the Church hierarchy, it enjoyed a special legitimacy that, therefore, made it difficult for the Pinochet regime (which still defended the values of the Church) to attack head on.

We can therefore say that, in a sense, the two films (hereafter, I shall often call them generically "films", with no difference in terms of genre, channel, etc.) recount "the same memory": that of an institution that carried out the very important work of denunciation, resistance, and support for victims of dictatorship. In so doing, they both refer to the same category: that of the archive—the TV series mentioning

---

[1] I shall take into account only the first season, that of 2011. In 2014, there was a second season, but it did not have the extraordinary success of the first. I shall not enter here into the reasons for the failure; I am simply interested in reflecting on the "phenomenon" which the first season of the series produced.

the archive in the title, the documentary in its development, both visually and verbally (I shall return to this point later). Indeed, one of the most important actions of the Vicaria was the work of recording, certifying and storing cases of violation of fundamental rights by the dictatorship. Moreover, both films focus on certain particularly serious cases: the two specific cases on which the documentary focuses are those that constitute the subject of the first and last episodes of the series (the discovery of the remains of some missing persons in Lonquén, a town near to Isla de Maipo, where in 1973 fifteen men were arrested and disappeared, the discovery of the remains showing for the first time that the arrests had ended in extra-judicial killings; and the case of the Degollados (the Slit Throat Case), which consisted of the murders of three opposition members in 1985, one of whom was a Vicaria lawyer—the main character of the TV series).

There is no doubt, therefore, that there is substantial convergence in the subject-matter of the two films. However, we wonder if they are really recollecting the same memory. Indeed, perhaps it would seem more accurate to say that they refer to the same events, but with different memories, not because there are conflicting versions—on the contrary, they are quite convergent—but because we are faced with very different ways of remembering: a coherent memory in the case of the series versus a multifaceted and plurivocal memory in the case of the documentary; a narrative and "self-consistent" memory in the series versus an impressionistic and broken memory in the case of the documentary; a modelling memory in the series versus a memory in progress in the case of the documentary. The two films—so different from this point of view—seem to belong to two different cultural epochs, but we know that this is not the case because, as I said, only four years separate them, the series dating from 2011 (and maintaining the same characteristics in 2014) and the documentary from 2015. In the following pages, I shall try to reflect on and clarify with the help of semiotics the differences I have briefly mentioned above.

Fiction/Reality
What the two films put into play in a very interesting (and different) way is, first and foremost, the fiction/reality relationship. We could say, simply, that we have a complete

Two Movies for Two Kinds of Memory

mimesis in the first case and an entirely subjective relationship in the second case, but this is not the only issue at stake. Before making a few observations on this point, I shall give some brief descriptive notes on the two texts.

Los archivos del cardenal is developed along the lines of a detective series. The directors explicitly mention in interviews that they found in "Law and Order" a model. Each episode, in fact (there are twelve, in the first season), revolves around a case that is discovered by or reported to the Vicaria. The Vicaria, while lending solidarity to the victims involved, investigates and brings to light the violations of rights by the regime. Part of the Vicaria's intervention is a legal action, led by lawyers, to recognize the existence of an offence, whereas the regime wants to normalize and neutralize kidnappings and murders as cases of missing persons or accidental deaths, and as such not prosecutable.

While this legal and social work goes on, there are also several intimate love stories: the "senior" lawyer, who is the main character, is the husband of an anti-regime journalist who was at one point kidnapped and tortured. Their story is a story of resistance and struggle against the regime, together, but it is also a love story and family story. Indeed, also working in the Vicaria is their daughter, a social worker— a beautiful young girl who at the beginning of the story is engaged to a man that chooses the path of armed struggle, and who then, gradually, gets close to and falls in love with a young lawyer from Santiago high society who has grown up in a powerful family close to the regime and who gradually understands the crimes of the dictatorship and begins working at the Vicaria, beside the "senior" lawyer. We find therefore a real love triangle (the girl with the two alternative models of man: the guerrilla and the more socially acceptable "good guy") which then leads to a happy love story (where the guerrilla is the one who loses).

This blend of sentimental drama and detection is the main quality of the whole series, and certainly one of the reasons for its commercial success: we are faced with a pop product, albeit aimed at political denunciation (which does not spare scenes of violence, torture and cruelty). The combination of its commercial quality and its account of the crimes of the dictatorship (perhaps, never recounted so clearly to such a wide and general audience) has, indeed, produced side effects at the social and political level. For example, the president of the Renovación Nacional party, Carlos Larrain, held an extended political committee meeting in La Moneda to express his party's anger at TVN for broadcasting *Los archivos del cardenal*.

What is interesting, though, and I shall return to it, is that throughout the series there is not a single archive image (despite the title *Los archivos* del cardenal): no traces, no documents, nothing from the "real" reality, even in the background of the television screens that sometimes appear. Everything is reconstructed, in some way, *à l'identique*, as if it were real, respecting—with the highest degree of fidelity—the actual characteristics of the facts, while remaining within fiction.

Completely different is the case of *Habeas corpus*. The documentary is a sequence of witnesses. One by one, we listen to the various protagonists of the work at the Vicaria de la Solidaridad: lawyers, doctors, social workers, framed sitting, more or less half-length, against a homogeneous background. Each one speaks for a few minutes (and then maybe comes back later), releasing his testimony, telling what their work at the Vicaria was, giving the impression more of an I-I dialogue than of a I-him/her dialogue,[2] with someone asking questions. Moments that seem self-conscious, recalling more than "depositions".

Among the interviews, to interrupt the sequence, are two types of visual materials: documentary material (several archival files and documentary photographs of the time, some famous, such as the ones of the Estadio Nacional, others less so) and fictional reconstructions, short animations with toy figures, as pictured on the following page.

We could, therefore, simply say that the series is pure fiction, while the documentary is made of documents and testimony, but it is not only this. The thing that seems most interesting to me is the circuit and the *directionality* of the reality/fiction relationship.

In the first case, the textual level—the filmic state-

---

[2] I am referring to Yuri Lotman's (1977) distinction between communication "systems I-I" and communication "systems I-he". The first are those that function to stabilize an identity; the second are those that create growth of information, and therefore cultural evolution.

ment—is totally distinct from the plane of reality. As I said, there are no documentary images, all the characters have fictitious names; no media (TV, radio) are included to report reality (as is the case with other TV fictions that are certainly related to this, such as *Los 80*, another Chilean TV series broadcast in 2008). Each episode of the series refers to something real and totally recognizable to anyone who lived through those years and the main characters work for an institution that really existed, although everything is transposed onto a fictional plane. The film, however, has such a mimetic force—in the setting, in the historical reconstruction of the facts and its protagonists, in the realism of the torture—and exerts it in such a new way (it is the first time one sees these events with such completeness) as to elevate itself to the *status of document*, and with this "documental force" it returns to reality. We do not, therefore, have a fiction that mixes with reality (as very often happens in contemporary movies and documentaries), but a pure fiction that is so mimetic and so original (and, in this sense, so "foundational") as to become a reference, and in this sense a "document". The level of "referential performance" of *Los archivos* is very strong.

Furthermore, the paths through which the series "merges" with reality are (perhaps not surprisingly) numerous and cannot be neglected. *Los archivos del cardenal* is the core of a series of semiotic productions that together create the *reality effect* of the text. We are faced with the clear case of a "textual galaxy", in which to separate the actual text from the context of circulation and reaction to it would mean to amputate the meaning the text had in Chilean society.

Above all, the film is linked to a site that collects the real cases which the Vicaria worked on. Shortly after the broadcast, two journalists from the Universidad de Chile published a book (*Los archivos del cardenal—Casos reales*) that clearly explains the real cases to which the episodes of the series refer. In this way, real cases and fictional cases begin to go hand in hand, through the website and through the book (and after the completion of the series, the book + DVD box was sold as well). It is very interesting to note the way in which the book presents the work. The goal of the book is "to reconstruct the real cases that inspired each chapter of the TV series, separating fiction from the facts using the tools of investigative journalism [...]. So the public who followed the series will know the stories of the men and women who inspired the characters" (12-13). These cases (I am paraphrasing the same pages of the aforementioned book) were known by a few; the series introduced a dramatization of these events to a wider audience. The book is aimed at those who at the time were not born or have few memories (13).

The book, in fact, comes from the film. It was the film that set in motion the mechanism of shared consciousness. The two journalists want to separate reality and fiction, but to describe real cases they refer, at the beginning of each chapter, to an episode from the film. It is as if the cases themselves have neither readability nor interest for the readers. Before recollecting them, it is always necessary to specify in which episode of the fiction the specific case is. Thus we can say that it is not the fiction that refers to reality, but *the documentation that refers to fiction*.

Moreover, in no way negligible is the event constituted by the last episode. I do not speak in terms of "event" for nothing; the transmission of the last episode represented in fact a genuine shared happening, screened live in the most symbolic and institutional place of Chilean public memory: the Museo de la Memoria y los Derechos Humanos, where someone read out a letter from Estela Ortiz, widow of José Miguel Parada, one of the three actual victims of the macabre Casos Degollados (which is the substance of the last

Two Movies for Two Kinds of Memory

episode), and then, with the credits of the series still running, Manuel García (singer of the soundtrack from the series) with the musician Camilo Salinas and his father Oracio Salinas (director of Inti Illimani) sang "Déjame pasar la vida", the song that closed the series. Therefore, we find in this public event a real collective ritual of participation and *re-enactment*, in which the space (the "theatre" of memory par excellence), the text (the staging of memory par excellence), the participants (in some cases directly and personally linked to those events) work together to create an effect of meaning that is anything but fictional, but rather is clearly a political action, in which the representation becomes a discourse in action, and the past of the film becomes the present in the collective ritual. Again, what happens goes from fiction to reality, and it is the reality that seems to "lean on", find inspiration in, fiction (the last episode of the series).

In our second text, *Habeas corpus*, in contrast, "reality" seems to be at the textual level; there is no separation between the level of historical events and the level of discourse on events. On the contrary: the events assume their force throughout the filmic discourse thanks to the density of witness accounts—which stage autobiographical experience, facts, actions, real people—and to the materiality of documents, represented insistently, almost like a visual leitmotif of the film.

The reality of experience and the evidence of the document, however, are not enough to saturate the filmic discourse on memory; on the contrary, they seem to suspend it, if not confuse it, bringing enunciation to silence (with long, empty sound breaks) or to fiction. It is the fictional element that especially attracts the viewer's attention in the film, representing a very strong heterogeneity with respect to all the effort of *cinéma verité*. The fictional scene with toy figures, with which the film opens, and which often returns (often just after a documentary image), clearly constitutes a suspension of realism, the impossibility of realism in memorial discourse, the unspeakable threshold in the language of reality (and it is no coincidence that these types of image are often placed at the most dramatic moments of the story). There is a constant transition from the document to fantasy.

Therefore, where the first film—certainly more simplistic, more Manichaean and more sentimental—may assume a representative force capable of competing with reality, the second film almost retreats from reality: in the face of its violence, it loses its discursive and expressive power. If in one case the spectator moves from fiction to reality, in the second the movement inscribed in the text seems the reverse: from reality to fiction, or at least: to the suspension of realism.

Two Models of Memory

What *Los archivos del cardenal* offers is clearly a model: a memory model, a framework, a master narrative:

> For a trauma to emerge at the cultural level, it is necessary that a social group draw up a new master narrative, whose solidity outlines the reference framework for the enhancement of the trauma itself, in the present and in the future. (Cati 2013: 124)

Each episode has a precise pattern: it corresponds to a narrative unity in which a case emerges at the beginning that catalyses the energies of the characters working at the Vicaria, produces misery and violence (in each episode, there is in fact a moment of brutality—usually in the middle—in which the emotional involvement of the viewer reaches its peak), is intertwined with personal or family worries and inner conflicts, and eventually is resolved—not because it is cancelled but because it is denounced or taken care of. Each episode thus builds a self-contained micro-story, repeating the same pattern in all the other episodes. Overall, in any case, the series follows a chronological line: it begins with a case from 1973-1975 and ends with a case from 1985, and between one episode and the other a clear evolutionary axis is developed (for example, the passage of the young social worker from one boyfriend to the other—from the guerrilla to the rich lawyer).

At the actantial and actorial level,[3] the dynamic is very stable and defined: the series selects four main protagonists from the Vicaria, the three members of the Pedregal family (the lawyer father, the journalist wife and the social worker daughter) plus the latest boyfriend of the daughter: Ramón Sarmiento. The instance of destination is embodied by the Church (called into question both as abstract institution and as particular actors, such as a priest and a cardinal) and, at a more abstract level, by the ethical consciousness. The polemical axis multiplies the opposing actorial figures: the anti-subject is abstract and invisible (the Regime), but locally, in each episode, the series defines opponents who help the regime to do its job: the torturers, the informers,

---

[3] I am referring to the semiotic narrative theory of Algirdas Greimas (1970).

soldiers of various ranks, the silent connivance of civil society (which is characterized more by a non-doing than by an active doing, but which through its inaction protects the action of the dictatorship). The sanction is always clearly expressed, of course positive but always emotionally dramatic: the work of our players is a good thing, of course, but it is not given and does not end in peace; their work always faces much pain and sometimes fails to save the victims. Particularly significant from this point of view is the end of the first season of the series, based on the Degollados case, where the widow of one of the three victims screams her dissent and her despair.

In this way, the series depicts a highly stable and polarized narrative pattern: there are good people and bad people, defined roles and also defined spaces: the enclosed space of the family (which coincides with that of the Vicaria, with a significant overlap of the place of private solidarity and social solidarity), the dangerous space of the streets, the hidden though common spaces (thus disguised) of torture.

In short, in this series we have memory presenting *exempla*: the cardinal's archives, the archives of the Vicaria, show not only a long string of crimes, but also a long series of counter-measures, the work of those who have risked their lives to oppose the regime. The archive (in the series) is not made of documents but is made of examples. And the exempla, as we know, can be placed in an a-chronic time, are valid forever, have pragmatic features (relevant endeavours) and ethical and passionate features, which are also conceivable in other contexts.

This is why the story of the series is able to offer a model: a script for dictatorship and resistance.

Habeas corpus stages a completely different memory. First of all, we have a plurality of enunciations, with many voices involved in building the framework. The entries do not build, do not follow and do not converge on a clear timeline; progressing by leaps, by specific topics, the linearity of the story is further broken by the insertion of documentary images and fictional images which I have already mentioned.

In this case, the archive is both visually represented (the files that are framed are those that were used to make up the archive) and verbally represented (some witnesses say explicitly that one of the main actions of the Vicaria involved, from the outset, building up documentation of the crimes of the dictatorship, taking note of all the reports which the relatives of the victims or the victims themselves produced).

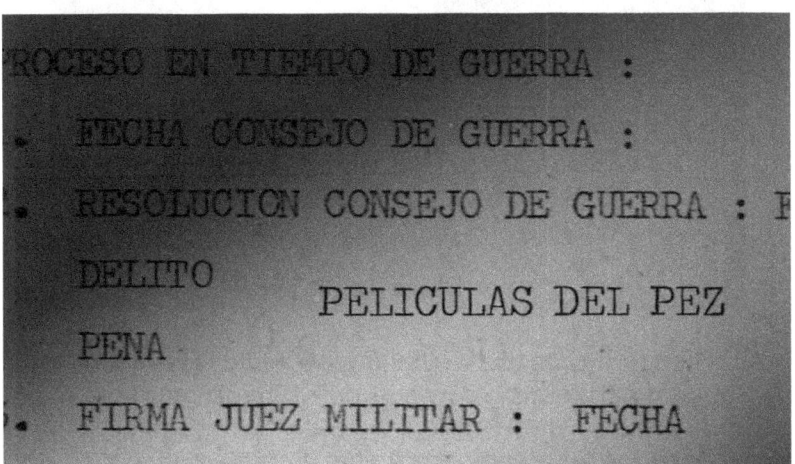

Thus the archive in *Habeas corpus* is *work*, and a cognitive work, not a repository. The movie poster summarizes these elements: a desk, a typewriter (a symbolic picture that comes back very often in the film), a phone, some tracking photos.

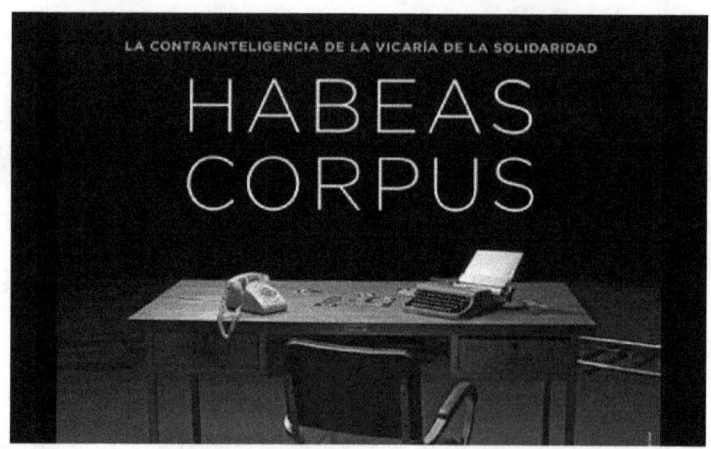

The truth that this archival work builds is not the truth of the criminal detection (made up of investigations, actual actions, raids, interventions), but the truth of lived experience: a testimony truth that is a personal memory. And just as in archival work, the documentary depicts the maximum of fictionalization: current witnesses, on the set of the film, type out the cards of the Vicaria archives, as if today were the past, as if the movie set were the space of the Vicaria. In common, in fact, only the agents: the witnesses are the real workers of the Vicaria.

Faced with this personal memory, the space-time coordinates fade: the stories seem given in an abstract and symbolic space, as in the poster: the time of enunciation (of the witnesses) is intermittent and broken, the enunciation (which witnesses produce) moved to a distant past.

We do not have here, however, the timelessness of the "modelling memory" of *Los archivos*; here we find rather a suspended temporality. We do not have the reduction of events to a scheme, such that the pattern can be abstracted from the space-time in which it is given and moved to other contexts. We find, on the contrary, the suspension of all schemes, a "fog effect" where there is no linear narrative progress, and there are no precise actors, no defined spaces, no precise sanctions.

If *Los archivos* offered us endeavours, *Habeas corpus* provides us with an intense work, with no end and no beginning, an intense activity that—with that typewriter—can go on forever and ever. If *Los archivos* reveals *the episodes* of memory, the other shows rather *its procedures*. One recounts the memory, the other the making of memory.

Almost paradoxically, then, it is *Los archivos*—pop production of popular TV—which cuts deep into Chilean culture, down to the political level, rather than *Habeas corpus*. If the archive, according to Foucault (1969), has a regulatory nature, functional in determining the standards by which the community carves out its knowledge about the past, the series can very well determine this canon, becoming a reference script for Chilean public memory.

Reworking (freely) the suggestions by Aleida Asmann (2010), who opposes the category of *canon* to that of *archive*, we could say that the fiction offers a real canon, selecting items, articulating them in a strong narrative and offering them as a model for subsequent readings of the past. Conversely, the documentary proceeds by accumulation, organizes its sequences by themes rather than by narrative patterns, does not offer an orderly model: provides a sum (an archive) of testimonies and documents.

The canon of *Los archivos* is a canon that refers to the real and returns to the real, as we have seen; it knows how and wants to represent it. It believes in the *referential efficacy of fiction*. The *Habeas corpus* archive, conversely, does not know how and does not claim to represent realistically the real. Each witness proceeds solipsistically through his/her memories, metaphorically at his/her desk. Experience and documentation lead to imagination (as what I call toy figures show well). In the first case, we find a realism that I would define as "dramatic realism", while in the second case we find what Rothberg (2002) calls "traumatic realism": a non-representational and non-referential account, which distrusts the possibilities of the "representation of reality".

Unlike Assman, however, I would not say that the canon of *Los archivos* presents "the past as present", while the *Habeas corpus* archive presents "the past as past". As I said before, in the first case we find a past out of time, an *exempla* gallery that leads to an idea of *historia magistra vitae*. In the second, we find a past rooted in time, a distant time, the subjective time of remembrance that is faced with the limits of speakability, and thus comes to fictional scenes where history, life, days are not present: *not out of time but in the absence of time*, not a gallery of *exempla* but the repetition of some fixed scenes, not *historia magistra vitae* but history as mental experience.

If we were to represent the semantic system that is built around the present/past opposition according to the so-called semiotic square, we would say that the discourse of *Los archivos* has to do realistically with something *not present*, that could happen again; the discourse of *Habeas corpus* has to do with something *not past*, which could continue, at least in the mental and fictional space that is the home of the toy figures or the desk out of time.

Dimension of time

Present	vs	**Past**
Traumatic realism		*Mimetic realism*
Not Past		**Not Present**

Dimension of atemporality

Both texts therefore make memory-building timeless, albeit in one case with a modelling function, and in the other case with an introspective function. In the one case, we are at a tangent to the parable; in the other, to personal recollection. Two highly predictable risks, "easy" risks, when memory is still unstable and far from being history.

References

Assman, A. (2010). Canon and archive. In A. Erll & A. Nünning (eds.), *A companion to cultural memory studies*. Berlin/New York: de Gruyter.

Barrios, L. A., & Mateso-Pérez, J. (2015). Ficción televisiva e historia reciente: El caso de *Los archivos del cardenal*. Paper presented at the XI Jornadas de Sociología de la Universidad de Chile, available online at **http://jornadasdesociologia2015.sociales.uba.ar/wp-content/uploads/ponencias/276.pdf**

Cárdenas, C. (2012). ¿Cómo es representado el pasado reciente chileno en dos modos semióticos?: Reconstrucción de la memoria en *Historia del siglo XX chileno* y *Los archivos del cardenal*. Revista Comunicación, 10(1), 653-665.

Cati, A. (2013). *Immagini della memoria. Teorie e pratiche del ricordo tra testimonianza, genealogia, documentari*. Milan: Mimesis.

Demaria, C. (2012). *Il trauma, l'archivio, il testimone*. Bologna: Bononia University Press.

Foucault, M. (1969). *L'archéologie du savoir*. Paris: Gallimard.

Greimas, A. J. (1987). *On meaning* (trans. F. Collins & P. Perron). Minneapolis: University of Minnesota Press. (Original work published 1970.)

Insunza, A., & Ortega, J. (2011). *Los archivos del cardenal. Casos reales*. Santiago de Chile: Catalonia.

Lotman, Y. (1977). The dynamic model of a semiotic system. *Semiotica*, 21(3/4), 193–210.

Palacios, J. M. (2012). Archivos sin archivo: Sobre el acontecimiento histórico y la imagen de lo real en *Los archivos del Cardenal*. laFuga, 14.

Rothberg, M. (2000). *Traumatic realism: The demands of Holocaust representation*. Minneapolis: University of Minnesota Press.

Monstrosity and the (Re)Creation of Argentine History: An Analysis of *La asombrosa excursión de Zamba*

Sebastián Gastaldi

> I don't believe in monsters, but I do believe that men are responsible for monstrous deeds.
> The Eichmann Show[1]

Introduction

In this study, we are interested in inquiring after exactly what kind of historical memory is legitimized in an audiovisual narrative discourse for children that recreates Argentine history. For this purpose, we have chosen the animated television series *La asombrosa excursión de Zamba* (Zamba's Amazing Trip), broadcast on PAKAPAKA, a public and educational TV channel belonging to the Ministry of Education in Argentina.

From the series, we shall analyze specifically the episode called *La asombrosa excursión de Zamba en la Casa Rosada* (Zamba's Amazing Trip to the Presidential Palace), where the traumatic event of the last military dictatorship in Argentina (1976-1983) is dealt with. The interest in unveiling, from a semiotic perspective, strategies that are part of a "legitimate social memory" is to analyze how meanings are imposed, valuations are configured and narrative identities are constructed in accounts of the Argentine past.

La asombrosa excursión de Zamba on PAKAPAKA

Every discourse is part of an infinite signifying network, a network of multiple connections, not only from the synchronic, but also from the diachronic, point of view. In this way, following Eliseo Verón (1980), every discourse corresponds to or is significantly determined by certain

---

[1] "Dramatisation of the team hoping to televise the trial of Adolf Eichmann, an infamous Nazi responsible for the deaths of millions of Jews. It focuses on Leo Hurwitz, a documentary film-maker and Milton Fruchtman, a producer". At **www.imdb.com/title/ tt4163668/**, accessed 20 August 2016.

grammars and conditions of production/recognition.

Thus, analyzing the marks/traces of a narrative, in relation to its conditions and grammars of production, involves providing clear proof of the ideological dimension of every narrative. "What is ideological is the name given to the system of relations between a certain group of meanings and their conditions of social production" (Verón 1980: 155).

La asombrosa excursión de Zamba is broadcast on PAKAPAKA, the first TV channel for children belonging to the Ministry of Education in Argentina. This channel began regular broadcasting on 9 September 2010 through the Digital Terrestrial Television signal on channel 22 on UHF, and through the Arsat-1 satellite, and is still on the air. The channel, along with other channels such as Encuentro and DXTv, is part of a national policy covering national cultural audiovisual production.[2]

PAKAPAKA is directed at children between two and 12 years of age, and includes short TV programmes, documentaries and cartoons. The channel's remit is that of a TV channel for children with content oriented towards education and entertainment. In that sense, historico-political changes that took place in Argentina between 2003 and 2015 constituted the setting from which it was possible to interpret the emergence of these new types of telling and representing the recent past. In this respect, using an audiovisual language suitable for children, *La asombrosa excursión de Zamba* combines the historical and the pedagogical. As a consequence, the target of these discourses is, to a great extent, individuals who do not know what happened and who are "learning" as Zamba lives his adventures on every trip.

The cartoon recounts Argentine history in different episodes, from the May Revolution of 1810 through to the country's return to democracy in 1983. Referring to the animation's goal, the director and scriptwriter Fernando Salem (2010) states: "There was a very strong commitment to historical accuracy, even a new vision of history that is reflected in the cartoon. Each feature of the historical characters that are depicted has a historical basis."

---

[2] The ten chapters of the series have been distributed to all public schools. Teachers in these schools can also access a set of guidelines for developing activities in the classroom.

The Discursivity of Traumatic Events

To a certain extent, traumatic events obturate, because of their nature, the very possibility of being represented. In order to understand such an impossibility, it is necessary to perceive the relationship and distance between the event and the trauma. Trauma, as an effect, occurs after the event. Trauma is the wound that lasts over time, it is the emotional tremor, the trace that shows, until it has been overcome, an inability to take action.[3]

In respect of trauma, the consequence of a negative event, we are interested in approaching the social dimension, more than the individual one, since "traumatic events not only affect individuals, but also have a destructuring impact on social groups" (Ortega 2011: 9). Therefore, trauma's effects emerge as the destabilization of a state of affairs, and become tangible in the community itself, in its institutions, and in the ties that provide it with cohesion.

Now, as Gabriela Schwab (2015: 61) points out, beyond the set of theories that confirm the non-representability of trauma, "there are forms of violence—holocaust, genocide, torture and rape—that are considered beyond representation". And these are the forms that also demand to be turned into discourse, Schwab declares.

The possibility of turning forms of violence into discourse entails a visibilization of traumatic events, which allows for a positioning in the topography of social discourse, i.e., inside the boundaries of what is thinkable and sayable at a certain historical moment.[4] The place they will have in

---

[3] It would be Sigmund Freud who would strengthen studies on trauma and, together with them, basic psychoanalytic theories. Facundo Ortega (2011: 4) puts it thus: "The idea of trauma only achieves specificity through unconscious formulation and description, which explains the centrality of Sigmund Freud and psychoanalysis for the later evolution of the idea of trauma."

[4] To speak of social discourse in the singular, as a global unit, is to refer "not to that empirical, cacophonous and redundant whole, but to the generic systems, the typical repertoires, the rules for linking together statements that, in a certain society, organize what is sayable—what is narratable and thinkable—and guarantee the division of discursive labour. It is about, then, discovering a global system of regulation, whose nature is not immediately observable, the rules of production and circulation, and likewise a 'framework' for products" (Angenot 2010: 21-22).

global social discourse will be determined by a discursive hegemony that is defined as:

> the synergy resulting from a set of unifying and regulating mechanisms that, in turn, ensure the division of discursive labour and the homogenization of rhetoric, topics and doxa. These mechanisms provide what is said and written with different doses of acceptability, which stratify the different degrees of legitimacy. (Angenot 2010: 36-37)

If social discourse, as Marc Angenot (2010) states, besides possessing the monopoly on representing the world, also presents itself as a fictional conjuration for oblivion and a reconstruction of the past in a "subtle narrative film", the chapter called *La asombrosa excursión de Zamba en la Casa Rosada*[5] allows us to operate analytically on the discursive materiality into which a traumatic event for Argentine society is etched. At the same time, we believe that this discourse belongs to the recreation of a collective memory in relation to history itself, enabling an analysis that allows the identification of legitimacies, assessments and identities that account for our recent past.

The last dictatorship, which begins with the *coup d'état* of 24 March 1976, is the topic developed in the episode. The plot is built around a trip by Zamba (an eight-year-old child from Formosa) and his schoolmates to the Casa Rosada. While students walk through the hall, across the Salón Blanco (the White Hall) (where the presidential sash and baton are presented), one of his schoolmates, El Niño que lo sabe todo (The child who knows it all), is kidnapped by the 1976 military junta.

La República, a statue that represents the republic and which comes to life, informs Zamba that he has to travel back to the past, if he wants his kidnapped friend back. Another temporality opens up in the narrative here. The past he has to travel through is none other than the last military dictatorship in Argentina (1976-1983).

The time travel to reach 1976 entails a trip through what is called the dark ride of the dictatorships. There, other

---

[5] **www.zamba.pakapaka.gob.ar/sitios/zamba/Capitulos/?anio=1976**

Argentine historical dictators are caricatured, tyrants such as Lieutenant General José Felix Uriburu,[6] General Pedro Pablo Ramírez,[7] Lieutenant General Eduardo Lonardi[8] and Lieutenant General Juan Carlos Onganía.[9] Finally, at the time of the 1976-1983 dictatorship, Zamba faces the military junta and demands the return of his disappeared friend. Various incidents happen from then on: Zamba looks for his friend, escapes from the military junta which is chasing him, meets significant Argentine historical characters who would help him, such as the Mothers of the Plaza de Mayo, workers, unionists, students, etc. Finally, Zamba finds his friend and together they demonstrate the power of the people. This triggers the end of the dictatorship and democracy returns to the country. Zamba and his friends return to the present, where they are welcomed again by La República.

After this brief synopsis, we shall now expound the analysis of some relevant aspects of the chapter, in order to reach the goal stated at the beginning of the essay.

The Traumatic Past
Every time period can be interpreted based on its prevailing temperaments or moods. This is what Angenot (2010) calls a component of discursive hegemony, the dominant pathos. How are these passions constructed? They can only be unveiled by the defining traits of the discourse itself.

Zamba's trip back to the last military dictatorship clearly exemplifies a temporality constructed as a period of time that was "the darkest in our country". Before he begins his journey into the past, La República warns Zamba that this will be a very dangerous time of terror, sown by the dictatorship.

The pathos is also represented in the animation lighting. If the present was bright, above all when the students initially walk through the Casa Rosada, the past will be dark, gloomy. Light will only return when democracy returns, represented on Zamba's adventure by a set of ballot boxes that fly, leaving the shadows and confinement they had been subjected to by dictators.

---

[6] Ruled from 6 September 1930 to 20 February 1932.
[7] Ruled from 7 June 1943 to 9 March 1944.
[8] Ruled from 23 September 1955 to 13 November 1955.
[9] Ruled from 29 June 1966 to 8 June 1970.

But not everything in the past happens in an atmosphere of fear and terror. When characters who would help Zamba (the Mothers of the Plaza de Mayo, unionists like Agustín Tosco, artists, workers, etc.) come on stage, the scenery is illuminated again with rainbow colours. The demand for justice, as a dominant emotion of the period, is present. Mothers of the Plaza de Mayo, trade unionists, artists, workers, students, etc. sing: "Es hora de reclamar la democracia, dónde está; preguntar hasta que aparezca; preguntar sin miedo; queremos vivir en libertad y democracia; queremos soñar" [It is time to demand democracy, where is it?; ask until it appears, ask without fear; we want to live in freedom and democracy; we want to dream].

La República

La República is present at the crucial moments of Zamba's trip: at the beginning when she comes alive and at the end when she welcomes him after his adventure. She is seen also in the past, when she is covered in cobwebs, lifeless. Therefore, she is the character who represents, in various ways, two conditions of the Argentine political system, democracy and dictatorship. She is alive during democracy, but dead during dictatorship.

Moreover, La República is the one who knows. She is the one who explains and teaches Zamba what a dictatorship is before he travels to the past. La República: "Es cuando alguien toma el poder sin ser elegido por el pueblo y no respeta el derecho de las personas ni la constitución, ni nada" [It is when someone takes power without being elected by the people and does not respect either people's rights or the constitution, or anything]. In this position adopted by La República we see the activation of one component of the discursive hegemony, ethnocentric egocentrism:

> Hegemony can also be approached as a *pragmatic norm* that defines at its centre a legitimate speaker, who arrogates the right to speak about "otherness", always determined in relation to him/her. [...] Hegemony, then, is an "egocentrism" and an "ethnocentrism". That is to say that it begets that "I" and that "We" who claim for themselves the "right of citizenship". (Angenot 2010: 42)

La República is, consequently, the legitimate speaker authorized to tell and characterize Argentine history. She is the one who can assume the right to speak about what happened and about the main characters involved. She is the one who can judge and classify what happened in the past, the one who warned Zamba she would not be there in 1976.

The Magic Ballot Box

It is the main object in the adventure. It is the device that fits into the characters' universe of meaning and becomes important as a different object throughout the whole episode. If democracy is presented as a fetish, i.e., as what is sacred, the magic ballot box will be the object that represents it. From what the ballot box signifies historically, a new component of discursive hegemony is activated, fetishes:

> The configuration of social discourses is marked by the particularly identifiable presence (like a nova in the middle of a galaxy) of thematic objects represented by the two forms of *sacer*, of the untouchable: fetishes and taboos [...]. It is important to analyze these fetishes and taboos and their degrees of intangibility, because not only are they represented in social discourse, but they are essentially *produced* by it. (Angenot 2010: 41-42)

The magic ballot box is the vehicle that allows Zamba to travel to the past to get his kidnapped friend back. It will be the vehicle that makes it easier for Zamba to travel through the dark ride of the dictatorships.

The magic ballot box is the object that allows Zamba to hide and slip away from the military while they are chasing him. It will be "the only way to get back from a dictatorship", as La República warned him. It is the set of confiscated ballot boxes, the ones that free the country from dictatorship, when the military can no longer hide them.

In this respect, the memory that is legitimized in the configuration of this device in the narrative distinguishes between two universes. The magic ballot box is the limit that separates democracy from dictatorship, the universe that respects and appreciates democracy from the universe that thinks it is completely useless, as the military maintained.

Argentine History in *La asombrosa excursión de Zamba*

Monstrosity

Finally, we get to one of the central aspects that appears on stage in this cartoon.

The military junta is constructed as Zamba's opponent. It kidnaps his friend in the present and takes him back to the period of military repression. General J. R. Videla (Army Commander), General E. E. Massera (Navy Commander) and General O. R. Agosti (Air Force Commander) are the ones who will make it difficult for Zamba to find his schoolmate El Niño que lo sabe todo.

Now, it is necessary here to consider some audiovisual details, in relation to the caricatured configuration of animated characters that represent the military junta. They are caricatured as absolute evil, as monsters. Their physical figures, in combination with their military outfits, suggest something diabolical, phantasmagorical, vampirish, zombie-like and dead. This is particularly seen when Zamba travels through the past dictatorships' "dark ride". Their red eyes represent evil, craziness, in consonance with their metallic voice.

The dictators Zamba has to face have no hands, only claws. At the same time, they are united, as a three-headed and four-legged monster, with a belt that does not allow them to be separated. Is this expressing the internal power disputes inside the coup? General J. R. Videla: "Soy el nuevo presidente y a partir de ahora se hace lo que yo digo, bueno, lo que nosotros decimos" [I'm the new president and from now on you will do what I say, well, what we say].

The monstrosity represented by the military in this animation corresponds to what Michel Foucault (2000: 61) characterizes as the human monster:

> The notion of the monster is essentially a legal notion, in a broad sense, of course, since what defines the monster is the fact that its existence and form is not only a violation of the laws of society, but also a violation of the laws of nature. Its very existence is a breach of the law at both levels. The field in which the monster appears can thus be called a juridico-biological domain. However, the monster emerges within this space as both an extreme and extremely rare phenomenon. The monster is the limit, both the point at which law is overturned and the exception that is

found only in extreme cases. The monster combines the impossible and the forbidden.

In this sense, the dictators would be the ones who "pursue and kill" people, as La República states. Besides, they are the ones who want people to leave the country, the ones who "think differently or stop thinking"; the dictators themselves express this idea in the episode.

It is important to notice that the way these "dictator monsters" get into power is never mentioned in the animation. Although it is mentioned that it was by force, no proper contextualization is forthcoming. Only a caricature of General E. E. Massera announces: "Estamos aquí porque antes había desorden" [We are here because there was chaos before].

Final Remarks
This animation, as a discursive genre, is part of what Omar Calabrese (1994) calls classic taste. The value judgements revealed in this episode, and we can say in the series as a whole, correspond to categorizations and classifications that point towards stable, ordered, officially sanctioned equivalences, i.e., what is beautiful matches the good and the euphoric, while what is ugly matches the bad and the dysphoric. This taste stands opposed to the neo-baroque, which characterizes most of the current widely consumed cartoons, where these distinctions are altered and destabilized.

The elements we have developed in this analysis and which are part of this episode account for two universes that are constructed, respectively. Consequently, a traumatic event, such as the last military dictatorship, is reflected and reconstructed as an opposition between good and evil.

The dominant pathos highlights emotions and moods related to each of these universes. On the side of evil, dictatorship appears related to terror, fear, darkness and horror. On the side of good, we find democracy associated with kindness, light, fight and people's right to demand justice.

In this legitimized memory of the recent past, the ballot box is established as the object that allows us to distinguish between the positions the different characters historically take in relation to it. On the one hand, we see those who confer upon it a positive value, such as La República, Zamba with his schoolmates, and people who help, such as the Mothers of the Plaza de Mayo, trade unionists, workers, students, etc. On the other hand, we see those who give it a negative value, such as the dictators.

In what concerns the construction of the military's identity, they are presented as absolute evil, as monstrous and diabolical. Monstrosity, according to its Greek meaning, refers to what is horrible and fascinating at the same time. It is what generates morbidity or violence. The function of monstrosity in discourse is to crystallize, somehow, the fears of society. The monster, as Jeffrey Cohen (1996) says, is a body that is "pure culture". In this respect, narratives of monstrosity have a great capacity to alter dominant meanings, and also to establish and strengthen hegemonic positions.

From what we have said, a question, not a confirmation, emerges: are dictators not dehumanized and, consequently, positioned by this discursive construct somewhere outside society?

Now, the representation of monstrosity in the discourse of children's cartoons is usually unremarkable in its narrative logic. But *La asombrosa excursión de Zamba* is not just any type of cartoon. It has a pedagogical function. Its narrative is built out of historical events. So, is this construction of monstrosity legitimate, bearing in mind the conditions that the genre itself and its ideal addressee impose on it? We consider it is not.

The dictators' identity construct which social discourse unveils is positioned, notwithstanding certain obvious differences, as the antithesis of Hannah Arendt's theory of the banality of evil. Arendt's thesis is that Adolf Eichmann (Nazi hierarch who lived in Argentina, responsible for devising the "final solution" to kill thousands of Jewish people in the Second World War) is the paradigm of a person who, in spite of not being a monster (even if he was guilty), is a type of bureaucratic-administrative technician who takes a series of chain decisions whose outcome is a monstrous act.

In this respect, and in the context of a traumatic event such as the last dictatorship in Argentina, a discursivization in terms of monstrosity and the logic of a fight between good and evil obturates the discursive complexity of other possible interpretations.

References

Angenot, M. (2010). *El discurso social. Los límites históricos de lo decible y lo pensable*. Buenos Aires: Siglo XXI Editores.

Arendt, H. (1999). *Eichmann en Jerusalén. Un estudio sobre la banalidad del mal*. Barcelona: Lumen.

Calabrese, O. (1994). *La era neobarrroca*. Madrid: Editorial Cátedra.

Cohen, J. J. (1996). Monster culture (seven theses). In J. J. Cohen (ed.), *Monster theory: Reading culture*. Minneapolis: University of Minnesota Press, pp. 3-26

Foucault, M. (2000). *Los anormales*. Buenos Aires: Fondo de Cultura Económica.

Ortega, F. A. (2011). El trauma social como campo de estudios. In F. A. Ortega (ed.), *Trauma, cultura e historia. Reflexiones interdisciplinarias para el nuevo milenio*. Bogotá: Universidad Nacional de Colombia.

Salem, F. (2010). Próceres con menos bronce. At **www.pagina12.com.ar/diario/suplementos/espectaculos/8-17906-2010-05-11.html**, accessed 10 April 2015.

Schwab, G. (2015). Escribir contra la memoria y el olvido. In S. Mandolessi & M. Alonso (eds.), *Estudios sobre memoria. Perspectivas actuales y nuevos escenarios*. Villa María: Eduvim, pp. 53-84.

Verón, E. (1980). *La semiosis social*. Barcelona: Gedisa.

On the Use and Abuse of History in Post-Dictatorship Argentine Documentary

Adam Sharman

> And even if they themselves are late-born—there is a way of living which will make them forget it—coming generations will know them only as first-born.
> Friedrich Nietzsche

Even if we have our suspicions that "memory" will one day become "history", that is, that history is the written record of distant events that were once the stuff of memory, and thus that history and memory have more in common than some are inclined to believe, it is clear that the attention paid to memory in recent times represents a challenge to the notion of history as guardian of the past. Indeed, for some the challenge has been redoubled by "postmemory". Postmemory would seem to be the phenomenon whereby a later generation half-recognizes as another's and half-remembers as its own the experiences of an earlier generation, such that the later generation's connection to the past is mediated by "imaginative investment, projection, and creation" (Hirsch 2012: 5). In post-dictatorship Argentine documentary film-making, postmemory is said to mark a younger generation's "radical break" (Andermann 2012) from an older generation's conventional view of history (and film).[1] The question this study will address is thus simply: is there such a radical generational break in Argentine documentary film?[2] I shall ground my inquiry in an analysis of two films that have a certain "exemplary" status as respective representatives of two kinds, and two generations, of documentary film. Both films deal with the "generation" (their word) of the armed revolutionary groups of the 1970s. The films are David Blaustein's *Cazadores de*

---

[1] Hirsch (2012: 6) says that postmemory "reflects an uneasy oscillation between continuity and rupture".
[2] This essay would not have been possible without the generous material and intellectual support of Guillermo Olivera and, above all, Ximena Triquell.

utopías (Utopia Hunters) (1995), a "classical" documentary (Ranzani 2016) by the generation of the *guerrilla*, and Nicolás Prividera's *M* (2007), a "postmemory" documentary (Andermann 2012) by the generation of the sons and daughters of the armed revolutionaries.

In the two films, personal memory provides the counterpoint to official history. Memory is the testimony of a past existence violently repressed and subsequently subjected to repressive erasure and/or prescriptive forgetting (Connerton 2008). The memory in question is not just individual, but collective. The films record a certain collective memory of the past and are themselves the means to transmit it to new generations, to those who do not remember as such a past they never lived.[3] If the films record the unpleasant truths and suppressed details from the rest of history, they nonetheless exhibit the "liturgical", conservative dimension of remembrance, that is, memory as the ritualistic transmission to future generations of the exemplary path of a (in this case, threatened) group.[4] It is a memory more traditional than *istoria* itself. My point, however, will be that this memory appears not only in Blaustein, where one might expect it, but in Prividera too. Contra Borges, the elders create (the memory of) their sequels.

Where one might therefore expect a real difference to

---

[3] Recalling Plato's distinction between *anamnesis* and *mneme*, Yosef Hayim Yerushalmi (1996: 109, 110) notes that to speak of "a people" remembering a past it never lived is really to say "that a past has been actively transmitted to a present generation" through collective memory. Thus is forged "the *mneme* of the group, the continuum of its memory, which is that of the links in a chain and not that of a silken thread".

[4] According to Yerushalmi, Jewish memory was based on the liturgical transmission of near-mythical events from the Jewish past, the historical detail and accuracy of which were unimportant, since "only those moments out of the past are transmitted that are felt to be formative or exemplary for the *halakhah* [the Hebrew term for path or way] of a people as it is lived in the present; the rest of 'history' falls, one might almost say literally, by the 'wayside'" (113). In contrast, it was modern, critical history ("the faith of fallen Jews") that challenged collective memory, reminding it of unpleasant truths and suppressed details. Yerushalmi's scheme is itself traditional, since history alone (not art, science or documentary film) is critical.

open up between the films is in their view of history (their conception of the nature of history, not just their view of the history of the period). For instance, the classical *Cazadores de utopías* gives off a strong "historical sense", the belief, criticized though not dismissed by Nietzsche (if the generational attack on history is "postmodern", it is, before that, irresistibly Nietzschean), that a culture is the inexorable product of history.[5] But even in the much less conventional *M*, "postmemory" is accompanied by an insistent rationalist historicism that paws at the door of the nation. If memory underpins history (no historian could get under way without the basic neurological capacity to remember), it is doubtless less intuitive that history should in any way underpin memory. But that is what Prividera's film, perhaps despite itself, invites us to contemplate.

History Remembered

> One goes so far, indeed, as to believe that he to whom a moment of the past *means nothing at all* is the proper man to describe it.
>
> Nietzsche

"La recuperación de nuestra memoria no podría ser desapasionada ni imparcial" [The recovery of our memory could be neither dispassionate nor impartial]. Echoing another beginning, that of *La hora de los hornos*, by those other utopians, Solanas and Getino, David Blaustein's *Cazadores de utopías* (1995) begins with the above epigraph, to the sound of rousing music.[6] Followed by a clip of Evita denouncing "foreign capitalism" and by contrived images of

---

[5] For Nietzsche (2001: 64), no one would ever do anything of note without the capacity to shrug off the weight of history. But in such forgetting, i.e. the unhistorical, there is necessarily violence: "the unhistorical [...] is the condition in which one is the least capable of being just; narrow-minded, ungrateful to the past, blind to dangers, deaf to warnings, one is a little living vortex of life in a dead sea of darkness and oblivion: and yet this condition—unhistorical, anti-historical through and through—is the womb not only of the unjust but of every just deed too".

[6] See Sonderéguer (2001) for critical responses to *Cazadores* on its release.

military boots on the march, the film announces that the memory that has been trodden under foot, and that is therefore in need of "recuperation", is that of the "utopia hunters", or Peronist revolutionary left of the 1970s. This is Blaustein's generation (he was born in 1953). One can imagine a different epigraph: "The recovery of our *history* could be neither..." But instead we have *memory*. Where "history" might suggest a residual attachment to official discourse, "memory" announces synecdochically the alternative domain of the witness, more especially of the defeated witness, which is to be granted a dignity at the time denied it by the Argentine state. One of the overriding emotions in *Cazadores* is the simple wish that the story of a "generation" not be so utterly neglected. Some of those interviewed want their experience to be affirmed as a model for the future; many more just want it to be told.[7] In the telling of memory, primacy is not accorded to the classical historian, who claims objective knowledge on the basis of a position external to events, but to the witness, who affirms a truth borne of personal experience and who links it to justice.[8] The recovery of memory, then, has necessarily to

---

[7] Blaustein (in Ranzani 2016) says the film was the result of a generational unease at being treated like nobodies during the Menem years (*el ninguneo de los años de Menem*; the verb *ningunear* means to ignore, ostracize, look down on, treat like dirt; *ninguno* means no one, nobody), which seemed to be "condemning the history of our generation to a story of clandestinity and sewers [*cloaca*]. [...] It is the result of a collective feeling that the story [*historia*] of a generation needed to be told". For Beatriz Sarlo (1997), the armed struggle of the period was a generational matter only up to a point. If the politics of the 1970s required youth (robust, unattached, confident enough of their first steps in the adult world to believe themselves right to destroy it), the "juvenilism" on display was "cultural", fatally flawed by a belief in the messianism of Perón. In other words, it was not necessary to be young to be caught up in a youthful politics.

[8] For Nietzsche (2001: 91), objective history is "the silent work of the dramatist", who himself establishes the unity of the plan in the material: "thus [man] gives expression to his artistic drive—but not to his drive towards truth or justice. Objectivity and justice have nothing to do with one another". He cites Grillparzer: "'What is history but the way in which the spirit of man [...] substitutes something comprehensible for what is incomprehensible; imposes

be passionate and partial. And its resolution into a phenomenon of knowledge, unendingly problematic.⁹

And yet, despite the film's wager on memory and its moving arrangement of memories, *Cazadores* is not antithetical to a traditional view of history. Individual memories are ordered into something resembling a classical historical narrative; here, a reasoned explanation of the actions of the Peronist armed left. The history runs as follows: (1) The need for violence at that moment in history, (2) The *Córdobazo* as the union of workers and students, and the proof that violence was timely, (3) The rise of Third Worldism, indicating that guerrilla militancy chimed with a larger uprising of the oppressed, (4) Perón's blessing for violence, (5) Perón's volte face regarding guerrilla insurgency, and the attempt by López Rega, and then the junta, to destroy the revolutionary left. The film ends its history with recollections of torture and of the pursuit by the state of the pursuers of utopia.¹⁰ Memory in the film is closely linked to a desire for historical explanation, an explanation offered from what Blaustein (in Ranzani 2016), interviewed in 2016 on the re-screening of the film, decribes as the perspective of the national-popular movement.¹¹ If that

---

his concept of purpose from without upon a whole which, if it possesses a purpose, does so only inherently; and assumes the operation of chance where a thousand little causes have been at work. All human beings have at the same time their own individual necessity, so that millions of courses run parallel beside one another in straight or crooked lines, frustrate or advance one another, strive forwards or backwards, and thus assume for one another the character of chance.'"

⁹ "A historical phenomenon, known clearly and completely and resolved into a phenomenon of knowledge, is, for the person who has recognized it, dead" (Nietzsche 2001: 67).

¹⁰ Andrés Di Tella's documentary, *Montoneros—una historia* (1994; first shown in 1998), uses a story about one *Montonera* to tell a history of the *Montoneros* as a whole. The film gives a potted history almost identical to that found in *Cazadores* and its historiographical function is further signalled by the appearance of a real historian, Roberto Baschetti. More so than *Cazadores*, it amasses strange recollections of conflicting emotions, such that the exemplary path to follow is much harder to discern.

¹¹ Jens Andermann (2011: 111) reproduces Gonzalo Aguilar's findings that the memories in question are those of a narrow tranche of the Peronist movement opposed to the central

explanation can be called "Peronist" (there is a moment in the film where Martín Caparrós speaks of Peronism, not as a simple subject, but as the name of a certain collective sentiment), in another sense it can also be called "conventional". History, the film suggests, can be known and explained without too much difficulty. In that same later interview, Blaustein (in Ranzani 2016) says that he asked his interlocutors in the film not to tell the story from the present (to wit: with all the difficulties posed by historical perspective): "No me cuentes la posmodernidad de Fukuyama [...] necesito reconstruir desde aquel presente, no desde la tontería desde el ahora" [Don't give me Fukuyama's postmodernity [...] I need to reconstruct things from the present of that time, not from the stupid idea of the now].

However, despite its form "giving the impression of a single, homogeneous discourse without contradictions" (Andermann 2012: 110), the film contains much that is not linear, objective history, reflections that betray mixed emotions and confused loyalties. It has the critical function Yerushalmi reserves for modern historiography. The foreign viewer, in particular, cannot easily read off the critical function. Unique, singular experiences are codified in a language, Argentine Spanish, which one will not be certain of having understood. Thus, a former guerrilla describes the group's sense of being the "exclusive owners of violence" and of feeling that, with Cámpora-Perón's victory in 1974, the country's future direction was theirs to determine. A trade unionist recalls how some of his number supported the Triple A in its pursuit of the guerrillas. Unwittingly exemplifying O'Donnell's (2002) seminal thesis on the mass praetorianism of Argentine politics and society, a former fighter speaks of the guerrillas sharing a view widely held by the population as a whole: anyone in the Casa Rosada (i.e. the Presidency) apart from "that woman" (meaning, Isabel Perón).

In addition to telling the story of part of a generation, the recollections of experience serve another purpose in *Cazadores*. They are organized in order to preserve "our memory" as legacy. "Vamos a generar compañeros" [We're going to generate compañeros], one speaker says. As we have seen, *Cazadores'* group memory, such as it is, is not medieval-Jewish: the film has a resolutely non-hierarchical attitude towards its subjects, and accurate historical detail matters, including the detail of unflattering contradictions.

Nevertheless, its ending has a liturgical quality. An earlier speaker remarks that while they might want to alter some of the things they did in order to put right certain mistakes, he would not change the "voluntad de transformación", the will to change things. The final voices are less equivocal. One speaks of the invalidity of the "theory of the two demons" that rose to prominence as a way of explaining the period (the idea that there was a moral equivalence between two equally demonic forces, the state and the *guerrilla*, with everyone else as innocent victim).[12] The other demon, he says (the one opposed to the state), is called "need, equality, law, education, health—[...] it's in those kids in the shanty towns who can't study". It is a poignant refusal of the theory's lazy logic.[13] A former guerrilla reflects that his moment of "protagonism" was in his youth and that it now falls to others. "We gambled with the possibility of happiness," he says, as Serrat's "La Montonera" plays over the top, "and now I'm never going to be entirely happy ever; but I think it was worth it". A woman says that they were looking for "a better world"; others (by no means all; some prefer to speak of the "costs") invoke the key word of the film's title: "utopia". But "utopia" and "a better world" are not the same thing: utopia may be a better world, but a better world does not have to be a utopia. As the earlier speaker says, they wanted the kids from the shanty towns to have an education. No utopia here. And yet the man who never mentions utopia utters the utopian "and now I'm never going to be entirely happy ever". Here the critical function divides. Either its object is the man's naiveté—as though revolution *could have* made him eternally happy (no betrayals, no disappointments, no unhappy sacrifices under the "patria socialista")—or, liturgy and legacy duly accepted, its object is the system that prevents the search for utopia. The latter is monumental memory: necessarily recalling the shared ideals of the great battles of the past, while deceiving by analogies.[14]

---

[12] See Crenzel for the theory of the two demons, whose existence qua theory owes more than a little to the fact that commentators refer to it as such.
[13] Blaustein (in Ranzani 2016) says *Cazadores* was a critical response to the theory.
[14] "How violently what is individual in [the past] would have to be forced into a universal mould and all its sharp corners and hard

The Book of History

> —You don't remember anything, do you?
> —No.
> Nicolás Prividera, *M*

A decade on from the first documentary, Argentina has experienced the epoch-defining 2001 crash, a new government has mobilized the state in matters of memory, intellectuals from the generation of the armed revolutionary groups have opened up the debate on their responsibility for what happened in the 1970s, and the children of the *guerrilla* are behind the camera, one product of which is Nicolás Prividera's *M* (2007) (Prividera was born in 1970).[15] I choose *M* for two reasons: first, because of Prividera's importance as a theorist of the new cinema (his meditations gathered together in *El país del cine*), and, second, because of the film's reputation as an instance of "postmemory documentary" (Andermann 2012: 115).

In his excellent study of Argentine cinema, Jens Andermann (2012: 95) traces the emergence of a new type of documentary in which, in Michael Renov's words, "the representation of the historical world is inextricably bound up with self-inscription". Documentary continues to represent history but draws attention to and dramatizes the difficulties posed by any one individual's limited perspective on the world. According to Andermann (95, 107), Renov associates this shift:

> with the shattering of classical-modern documentary's epistemological framework drawn from the social sciences, and based on a belief in the transparency and capacity of optical devices to capture and render "the other" in an objective, unbiased and self-contained fashion. [...] A shift in representations has occurred from the establishing of (juridical, political) truth to its implications in and for the present; that is, a

outlines broken up in the interest of conformity! [...] Monumental history deceives by analogies" (Nietzsche 2001: 69-71).

[15] The key collection on the intellectuals' debate, which dates back to 2004, is del Barco *et al.* (2014). Some of the essays have appeared in translation in the *Journal of Latin American Cultural Studies*, 16(2), 2007.

displacement from historical reconstruction to the act of remembrance, however entangled the one still remains with the other.

It is a generational story:

> a radical break has appeared between the "survivors" tales of the generation of 1960s and 1970s political activists and the "secondary witnessing" or "postmemory" of their children who, at the time of their parents' exile, abduction and assassination, were still in their early infancy and childhood. Postmemory, in Marianne Hirsch's influential formulation, is by no means a state of oblivion "after" or "beyond" memory. Rather, it is particular in that its relation with the object of commemoration—here, the struggles of the 1970s and their violent repression—"is mediated not through recollection but through an imaginative investment and creation". (Andermann 2012: 107)

Like *Cazadores*, Prividera's *M* has recollections from the generation of the *guerrilla*; unlike the earlier film, *M* quite literally turns the camera round to concentrate also on the director, that is, on the younger generation's reception of memories that are not its own but that now become its own. Prividera does not receive these memories as a gift handed down intact, but rather sifts, filters and criticizes them. *M* belongs to the genre of documentary investigation—with its 'phone calls, archive visits, and visits to neighbours, contacts and organizations all sustained by Prividera's sharp, at times barbed, commentary. The film is about the investigation as much as it is about the thing being investigated (his mother's disappearance). However, among the shards of memory, the photographs and the home movies, there is a strange reversal, which one cannot be sure Prividera himself is aware of. For unlike the earlier documentary, here it is the *vox populi* of the older generation that ventures an unusual view of history, while the director falls back on the conventional view.

The history of the period is subordinated in the film to the incomplete story of Prividera's mother, who had probably been involved in guerrilla activities. Prividera criticizes the state for failing to take responsibility (his two principal themes are truth and responsibility) for coordinating the efforts to trace the disappeared. Standing in CONADEP, in the Ministry of Justice, he laments the fact that individuals have to bring their little piece of the puzzle (*rompecabezas*) to the table, rather than the state put it together. His watchword is *cruce* (cross, crossing, intersections). There is no cross-referencing, no cross-checking, no joining the dots to establish the truth (is there a "cruce de datos?" [a database]; "si el cruce no está, es imposible" [if there's no cross-checking, there's no chance]). "No hay plano completo de cómo funcionó" [there's no plan of how the whole thing worked], he laments, everything is "muy parcializado" [very fragmented]. For entirely understandable reasons (he wants to know what became of his mother, not what the meaning of history is), at this point his view of truth is simple enough: if anyone could be bothered to put all the pieces of the jigsaw puzzle together, the result would be the truth of what happened to his mother, Marta Sierra (the "M" of the title). For the director's younger brother, Guido, the whole business is complicated; for the director, who cuts across him, it is not difficult.

It is not difficult for the older Prividera, because he has a classical view of truth, responsibility and justice: we uncover the truth, they take responsibility, and justice is done. Of these, the key is truth. And it is not a difficult truth, since it could be learned in a history class. How come, he laments, the younger generation knows nothing about its country's history? And, later, talking to an older couple who had been ardent Peronist militants: don't you think history could have been different if you'd grasped the significance of the Chile coup of 1973? Didn't people know or talk about the Chilean *desaparecidos* or know anything about what had happened in Uruguay? Later still, he has an encounter, to which we are not privy, with one of the leaders of the Juventud Peronista at the time of his mother's militancy. The encounter has sent a shiver down his spine (the man has told Prividera that his mother had "bad luck": "Mala suerte!", he keeps on repeating, disbelievingly, "As if she'd had an accident. As if she'd been struck by lightning"). Andermann (119-120) discusses the scene at length. Prividera "explicates his and [Albertina] Carri's *political* critique of the survivor generation, while staging in the refracted composition of the shot their impossibility of constructing a stable place of enunciation".[16] Both directors, he argues, are aware of the charges of subjectivity and self-righteousness, but "they counter-attack by exposing—[…] through an aggressive, confrontational interview style, in *M*—the generational abyss motivating these charges". Andermann quotes extensively from Prividera's account of the encounter: the Peronist leader's view that they "fucked up", but that to engage in self-criticism now is to play into the hands of the right; Prividera's view that "being on the Left is to be self-critical. If you're not self-critical, if you're not critical, you're on the Right"; the man's response, that "you're very subjective in your search".

But Andermann stops short of citing what Prividera says next, which is this: "Es increíble como nadie vio eso. O nadie quiso ver" [It's incredible how no one saw this. Or no one wanted to see it]. Prividera continues, facetiously rehearsing the clichéd explanations: "Los vientos de la Historia? Ceguera? Ingenuidad? Estupidez? Un poco de todo" [The winds of History? Blindness? Ingenuousness? Stupidity? A bit of everything]. Earlier in the film, he was left almost as apoplectic by one of his mother's collaborators, who, now suffering from cancer, tells him she has been told not to speak of things that will harm her recovery (in fact, she does take part in the film). You can't just say it's a private matter, they were adults, he rails: "tenían uso de la razón" [they had the use of reason]. *M* may exhibit the tics and traits of postmemory documentary (the hand-held camera, the absence of a narrator, the absence of music, attention to the seemingly insignificant, an apparent scriptless, aleatory quality), but Prividera's stance is a rationalist teleological one. This explains the film's self-righteousness. Why didn't you know? And why didn't you do anything about the situation? Contra Nietzsche (2001: 76), for whom life's judgement is always unjust, "because it has never proceeded out of a pure well of knowledge", Prividera's judgement is the righteous stance of the one who knows how the story ended ("It wasn't difficult") and who cannot understand why rational people did not prevent it from happening. Andermann cites an essay by the director published before

---

[16] Andermann yokes together Albertina Carri, most well known for her lightning-rod documentary *Los rubios* (2003), and Prividera as the flagbearers of "postmemory" documentary.

the release of *M*, arguing that Prividera "goes further in his critique of first-generation memory, reclaiming for his own generation's critique of testimonial discourse the task of recovering historical experience". To which one can only respond: "And even if they themselves are late-born—there is a way of living which will make them forget it—coming generations will know them only as first-born."[17] Prividera, filtered by Andermann: "'The testimonies accumulate—he writes—without helping us to understand better. For some time now, they have ceased to be cathartic [...]. Their multiplication (outside the juridical field) has generated an effect of saturation: a meaningless thicket of experiences of suffering.' There are too many memories but a lack of history, he asserts, in the sense of imposing meaning through the construction of critical distance towards the immediacy of experience: 'How can we write the rest of H/history?'"[18]

But that is not the end of the generational saga, in which the late-born get to sift through, *but also to order*, the rest, the remainder, the remains of history.[19] Things turn out, after all, to be difficult. For *M* has another view of truth, which is to say, of history. This other view comes from the older

---

[17] Nietzsche (2001: 76): "since we are the outcome of earlier generations, we are also the outcome of their aberrations, passions and errors, and indeed of their crimes; it is not possible wholly to free oneself from this chain. If we condemn these aberrations and regard ourselves as free of them, this does not alter the fact that we originate in them. The best we can do is to [...] implant in ourselves a new habit, a new instinct, a second nature, so that our first nature withers away. It is an attempt to give oneself, as it were *a posteriori*, a past in which one would like to originate in opposition to that in which one did originate:— always a dangerous attempt [...]. But here and there a victory is nonetheless achieved, and for the combatants, for those who employ critical history for the sake of life, there is even a noteworthy consolation: that of knowing that this first nature was once a second nature and that every victorious second nature will become a first".

[18] Prividera's essay is called "Restos" (in *El Ojo Mocho* 20 (2006), p.44). *Restos* means "rest", "remainder" but also "remains" (as in mortal remains). Part two of *M* is called *Los restos de la historia* (*The Remains of History*).

[19] Section two of Prividera's *El país del cine* makes the history of Argentine film into a generational *family* saga.

On the Use and Abuse of History in Argentine Documentary

generation. The second half of the film features encounters with people who worked alongside Prividera's mother either at the INTA (the National Institute of Agricultural Technology) or at the adult literacy school. If Prividera's view of truth and history is largely objectivist-teleological, the edited snippets from interviewees hint at a different, discontinuous, relativist view of history. "You see things as they are in a book", one woman says to him, "but history isn't linear"; "it's never total" (*nunca es algo total*). The Peronist couple quizzed about their knowledge (in effect, their ignorance) of the bigger Southern Cone picture of the early 1970s respond to his charge: of course we made mistakes, the woman says, and, yes, we can see that 30 years on; but back then we couldn't.... *M* is not a philosophical treatise, so let us not open up a philosophical discussion on situatedness, the circumscription of the human subject by the material and symbolic order that surrounds it. I wish simply to note the coincidence between these witnesses' insights and a perspectivist philosophical view of truth and history (Nietzsche [2001: 101]: "The human race is a tough and persistent thing and will not permit its progress—forwards or backwards—to be viewed [...] as a whole *at all* by that infinitesimal atom, the individual man"). Another woman (it is always the women) says that at moments of terror you don't know who will betray you—anyone could have betrayed your mother; "there are 20,000 conclusions". She does not, I do not think, mean by this that there is no truth (she says she is more cynical than him and needs only to look into people's eyes to know); she is merely warning against the dangers, despite her own confidence in being able to read people's faces, of taking things at face value: of imagining, for instance (I am extrapolating from her words), that declared political alignments map neatly onto people's actions (it couldn't have been him, he was a Peronist...). At times of terror, you see the worst of humanity, she says. In other words: the only thing that gets in the way of history, truth and memory is people.

Conclusion
M ends on an inconclusive, aleatory note, with images of Prividera's mother from fragments of home movies intercut with images of the director wandering around, agitated and aimless. But this is not before the film has effected a

conclusion of sorts. Part of the epilogue takes us to a ceremony at the INTA at which a plaque to Prividera's mother and others is being unveiled. The camera shows us the inscription: "En memoria a Marta Sierra [...] y a todos los compañeros de INTA encarcelados, desaparecidos y cesanteados, reinvindicamos [sic] la lucha de antes, apoyamos la de ahora, acordamos con la futura. [...] Nunca más!" [In memory of Marta Sierra [...] and of all the imprisoned, disappeared or laid off INTA compañeros, we sallute [sic] the past struggle, support the current fight, agree with the future one. [...] Never again!]. Complete with spelling mistake, which adds poignancy, as if it were needed, the monument is the (necessarily) formulaic commemoration of a life and the no less formulaic transmission of a legacy to the future. The memorial pledges future generations to an unknown future struggle, and appears to be a case of the older generation laying down the law to future ones. *Cazadores*, too, does its share of liturgical legacy-making, using and abusing the word "generation"—part accurate descriptor, part strategic mask of differences within. More surprisingly, after all it has said about its members, *M* receives and seems to want to transmit the older generation's legacy. Prividera leans on the formulaic, but not for all that less heartfelt "what might have been" commonplace. Had his mother and "an entire disappeared generation" lived, he says, another life was possible, as was another nation. The statement must remain a truism, since, in light of his criticisms of the older generation's failure to learn the lessons of history, it is unclear what the otherness of that other life, and of that other nation, would have looked like.

Both films are also commemorations of lives. They record memories, before memory passes into history and history is the only one left to remember. Even if, in the case of *M*, the institutional moment has changed (a government minister responsible for the INTA, and thus directly or indirectly for Prividera's mother's disappearance, is going on trial as the film opens), both films preserve memory as a defence against the evisceration of a life. On one level, then, in neither case can film, as the memory of memory, give up on the traditional history-function, with its attendant values of reason, truth, objectivity. What both films show is that the older generation has an empirical, objectivist view of history *when it is a matter of concrete lives and events*. The older generation knows all too well what happened to the Marta Sierras; it is just that they do not want to, and in many cases cannot, open up a forensic inquiry into what happened. Some are traumatized by having lived the moment, by their responsibility for what happened—and now by being asked, on camera, to recollect. Prividera, from a younger generation, shares this view of history and truth: he simply wants to know what happened to his mother, and he knows someone will have denounced her, someone will have picked her up and someone will have killed her. Memory, history, history, memory: it is a question of truth and justice. On another level, however, *when it is a matter of large historical conjunctures*, at least one member of the younger generation (Prividera) harbours a naïve objectivist historicism, while the older generation has an alternative view of history. Perhaps because the older generation lived the moment without the historical sense. That is to say, members of the generation of the *guerrilla* do not fail, on camera, now, to recollect the moment objectively out of weakness or stupidity, but rather because the historical phenomenon was never *at the time* lived as a simple phenomenon of knowledge, laid out in an instantly graspable, albeit dead, simultaneity. In this instance, it is uncertain that the radicality belongs to postmemory.

References

Andermann, J. (2012). *New Argentine cinema*. London: I. B. Tauris.

Blaustein, D. (1995). *Cazadores de utopías*. Audiovisual production. At **www.youtube.com/watch?v=7vRydH_dAvY.**

Carri, A. (2005). *Los rubios*. Audiovisual production. SBP.

Connerton, P. (2008). Seven types of forgetting. *Memory Studies*, 1, 59-71.

Crenzel, E. (2014). *La historia política del Nunca más. La memoria de las desapariciones en la Argentina*. Buenos Aires: Siglo Veintiuno Editores.

Dandan, A. (2016). De vuelta a los dos demonios. *Página/12*, 12 June. At **www.pagina12.com.ar/diario/elpais/1-301566-2016-06-12.html**, accessed 15 July 2016.

Del Barco, O., Belzagui, P. R., et al. (2014). *No matar*.

Sobre la responsibilidad. Córdoba: Universidad Nacional de Córdoba, Ediciones del Cíclope, Ediciones La Intemperie.

Di Tella, A. (1994). *Montoneros—una historia*. Audiovisual production. At **https://vimeo.com/116316679.**

Hirsch, M. (2012). *The generation of postmemory: Writing and visual culture after the Holocaust*. New York: Columbia University Press.

Nietzsche, F. (2011). On the uses and disadvantages of history for life. In D. Breazeale (ed.), *Untimely meditations/Friedrich Nietzsche* (trans. R. J. Hollingdale). Cambridge: Cambridge University Press, pp. 57-123.

O'Donnell, G. (2002). Modernization and military coups. In G. Nouzeilles & G. Montaldo (eds.), *The Argentine reader: History, culture, politics*. Durham and London: Duke University Press, pp. 399-420.

Prividera, N. (2007). *M*. Audiovisual production. Buenos Aires: Trivial.

Prividera, N. (2014). *El país del cine. Para una historia política del nuevo cine argentino*. Córdoba: Los Ríos Editorial.

Ranzani, O. (2016). Era una historia que tenía que ser contada. *Página/12*, 22 March. At **www.pagina12.com.ar/diario/suplementos/espectaculos/5-38336-2016-03-22.html**, accessed 17 December 2016.

Sarlo, B. (1997). Cuando la política era joven. *Punto de Vista. Cuando la política era joven: Eva Perón, años setenta, democracia, populismo*, 58 (August), 15-19. At **www.ahira.com.ar/revistas/pdv/51/pdv58.pdf**, accessed 21 February 2017.

Sonderéguer, M. (2001). Los relatos sobre el pasado reciente en Argentina: Una política de la memoria. *Iberoamericana*, 1(1), 99-112.

Yerushalmi, Y. H. (1996). *Zakhor: Jewish history and Jewish memory*. Seattle and London: University of Washington Press.

Figurations of Memory in Stories by Children of the Revolutionaries

Pampa Arán

For more than thirty years, the novel has been a major genre in the polyphony of social discourses that addressed the issue of the Argentine dictatorship, restoring a continuously present memory by producing artistic figurations that modify or polemicize with canonical memorials. In previous research, I argued that different novels would be fragmental units of a larger literary chronotope, changing and expanding permanently, but "whose nucleus condenses the social experience of the uncanny" (Arán 2010: 42). Now, I wonder how much of those hidden everyday worlds appears in the current stories by ex-militants' children, where the historical memorial is replaced by subjective memory. Therefore, the object of study I propose to explore is: how a subject who recalls the political behaviour of his parents reconstructs the actors in violent times, and how he interprets their actions and passions, gives meaning to and takes a critical distance from their present; moreover, how he artistically represents that memory construction, from which I would like to rescue the odd significant chronotopic figure.[1]

In the selected novels, the historical, the fictional and the (auto)biographical converge, establishing different conditions of verisimilitude for testimonials that adopt a particular literary form ("autofiction", Alberca 2007). The corpus is composed of novels by Argentine writers living abroad: *El espíritu de mis padres sigue subiendo en la lluvia* (The Spirit of My Parents Continues to Rise up in the Rain) (2011) by Patricio Pron, *Soy un bravo piloto de la nueva China* (I Am a Brave Pilot of the New China) (2011) by Ernesto Semán and *Los pasajeros del Anna C* (The Passengers of the Anna C) (2012) by Laura Alcoba. I detect in them the process of reconstructing a fractured identity and a memory worked out fragmentarily, an "aesthetic of ruins" which "according to Sandra Lorenzano (2001) appears as opposed to the fascist aesthetic of monuments" (Badagnani

---

[1] I use chronotope in the Bakhtinian novelistic sense as a concrete representation of temporalized space that translates some particular metaphorical abstraction of a novel (Arán 2010).

2012).

Pron: The Hole of Memory

In the case of Patricio Pron,[2] I am faced with a novel[3] whose writing emerges as a result of the finding, reading and interpreting of archival documents: newspaper articles, photographs, letters, reports, maps, videos, interviews... documents that are found by the son who has returned from Germany because of the serious illness of his father, Chacho Pron, long time journalist and political militant. During those days of pain in the family home in Rosario, the son unleashes a process of the search for and retrieval of his identity, denied and displaced for a long time, and of his past, linked to the troubled relationship with his father, constituted by fear, rejection and estrangement, and represented in a childhood photo, taken on a mountain in La Rioja next to a chasm (23). That chasm, that emotional and generational distance, is what he will have to overcome as an open question about his own existence.

Narrated in the first person, the novel develops the process of recognition of the narrator and of his father. Although it takes place linearly over a few days, such a process emerges as a detective puzzle, made of fragmentary pieces from experiences and memories. All this magma will be redefined through a moving work of memory, whose development, in my opinion, linearly organizes the novel's structure into four parts: return, research, crisis, discovery. Following this reading which detects a movement of deep descent and a beginning of self-egress, I choose as a recurring chronotopic figure that of the literal and symbolic hole, prison of bodies in different times and spaces: the hole of depression, his father's agony, the hole of Burdisso's crime, Alice's clandestine prison, and all the closed environments over the course of the story (hospital, home, office, museum). Finally, memory is like that deep, enigmatic, dark place to be explored at the expense of the body itself.

[2] Patricio Pron (1975). Romance Philology Ph.D. from the University of Göttingen. He lives in Madrid. Author of an important body of narrative work, praised by critics and translated into several languages.
[3] Pron (2011). Quotations are from this edition; translations by Adam Sharman.

The first part tells of the return of the narrator (we do not know his name) to the country after eight years living in a German city (2000-2008), adrift, rendered dopey by psychiatric drugs consumed daily. At home he experiences mixed feelings, and fuzzy, anachronistic memories that appear as alien.

The second part encloses Aira's heading (55) as a key, because the discovery of a strange folder on his father's desk confronts him with the difficulty of reading and transcribing that file. It is a folder armed with newspaper clippings, photos and maps telling of Alberto Burdisso's disappearance, which had occurred under mysterious circumstances in June of that year in a town where his father's family lived.

Thus, we read about the chronicle of that disappearance and the discovery both of the subsequent crime and of the criminals, which reveals people's sordid background, as well as versions that were woven around the death and its circumstances, because Burdisso had obtained compensation for the disappearance of his sister in Tucumán in 1976, and frequented women with a bad reputation.

The interest his father had shown in the search led him to wonder about the real reasons for that participation in this criminal story, and to think about the symmetry of those searches: his looking for his father and his father looking for someone else, but, who did each of them seek? Who was his father? What had his militancy been like? Why did he associate him with the fear he felt as a child? Is it possible to go back to the past, read other signs and other interpretations?

Questions begin to be answered in the third part, in a visit to the museum hall in a retrospective of the local press. On TV, he watches the video of his father's interview several times.

He begins to assemble the *puzzle* that reminds him of the game he could never complete when he was a child (129), and to make conjectures about his father's motives in his search for Alicia's brother. A collection of photos and notes on the young woman fuels the suspicion that his father had spent decades of guilt for having initiated her into politics and for not being able to get through the thick curtain of fear of those dark days.

He also begins to wonder if his father has left him material to write a novel that he might once have thought of:

> What should the novel which my father had wanted to write look like? Short, made of fragments, with gaps where my father could not or did not want to remember something, full of symmetries—stories repeating themselves [*duplicándose*] over and over again. (135)

And the reader understands the novel they are reading as in a reflecting mirror, whose magma is in this documentary search and in the intimate fractured memory that must be put back together generationally:

> I understood for the first time that all us children of the young people of the 1970s were going to have to shed light on [*dilucidar*] our parents' past as if we were detectives and that what we would find was going to look too much like a detective novel which we would never have wanted to buy. (142)

What genre could narrate this experience? There then follows a metanarrative reflection that runs through the novel about what is true and what is credible, document and fiction, and, finally, the chances of autofiction we are reading (143-44). After the intimate process that unleashes the museum visit, he falls ill, and his feverish dreams of enormous cruelty, death, dehumanization are like a descent into hell: the down hole is reached.

In the last part, the slow recovery of health runs parallel to the recovery of denied memory. He then discovers that fear and threat were present at home due to his parents' political choices in the history of exile and Perón's return, their participation in Guardia de Hierro, their differences with the Montoneros, the group's dispersion after Perón's death, and problems with Isabel and López Rega. His parents are survivors.

Memories start flowing: the conversations with his mother and siblings, the books, the photo album and the awareness of having to tell the story, to honour them, "because what they had done was worthy of being told, because their spirit, not the right and wrong decisions which their parents and their compañeros had taken but their very spirit, would continue to rise up in the rain until it took the heavens [*el cielo*] by storm" (186).

It is a legacy (as Cohen's headline announces), an

ethical order which he owes to the children of the missing, their generation, so that history, open to the future, may be completed by those who dare to keep looking into the hole of memory:

> My father and I among the ruins of a house [...] the two of us looking at the black mouth of the pit [*pozo*] in which lie all the dead of Argentine History, all the defenceless and disadvantaged [*desamparados y desfavorecidos*] and those who died because they tried to oppose a possibly just violence to a profoundly unjust violence and all those killed by the Argentine state, the state that governed a country where only the dead bury the dead. (192)

Pron's novel is a challenge for readers. It is a story of great experimental complexity and diverse registers that develop performatively while the intimate process is narrated, in permanent contrast to the documentary and objectivity. The story goes through different moments, which can cause exhaustion. Initially dark, it is full of difficulties, even visual ones. Its target in a procrastinating and deviant form becomes explicit at the end, even with an epilogue, where the identity of the unnamed narrator appears and is assumed as son and author. The individual experience tirelessly seeks a narrative language with multiple creative resources that force the reader to overcome inertia, and discover meaning also in the form.

Semán: *Soy un bravo piloto de la nueva China*

The novel is organized into five parts and an epilogue.[4] Each part has three chapters with equal titles: The City, The Field, and The Island. For the narrator, they represent different spaces and temporalities: The City is the present in Buenos Aires, when his mother is dying; The Field, the underground place where his father was kidnapped, tortured and murdered in 1978; and The Island, an almost unreal space, which mixes multiple memories and times.

Such chronotopes show a process of imaginary reconfiguration, since the protagonist, Rubén Abdela (in

---

[4] Quotations are from this edition; translations by Adam Sharman.

reality Ernesto Semán),[5] is an adult in the narrative present, and from this present he subjectively rebuilds his family past, his childhood and his past loves, and imagines his father's (in reality Elías Semán's) behaviour as a prisoner with his kidnappers, his torment and death.

The exercise of memory, triggered by his mother's imminent death, is a long process of internal debate to get rid of the resentment towards his father and to understand his struggles and passions. The strength of the novel is to allow the missing to "speak", to understand that past and that biography, generationally so different from that of the son. Besides, I say "speak" because orality and dialogue are central to the novel in a distinctive Argentine and *porteño* register.

As I initially noted, there are three temporalized and interconnected spaces, but the most interesting one is The Island, a literary figure from a long tradition. In this case, it is the representation of individual and family memory, but also of forms of collective memory and a metanarrative place par excellence, where autobiographical fiction is forged and modelled. It is a strange territory, always on the verge of disappearing, surreal, full of signs that are almost indecipherable at first, but that become clearer largely after reading the other novelistic chronotopes, City and Field, which serve as reference anchors.

The Island is reached by an underwater bus that leaves Palermo and arrives at Los Alamos in California, where a boat takes passengers to their destination, providing them with a scanner that reproduces the image on a personal screen. The journey goes into submerged territories, with urban waste and recumbent bodies that are simultaneously the intellectual world of urban planner and geographer Rubén Abdela, and the announcement of the construction of a memory—and a novel—armed with debris, cuts and underground remains to be exhumed in the narrator's present. In this imaginary, chaotic and fragmented space, with uncertain boundaries and unpredictable temporal overlaps, the vicissitudes of the (auto)biography of Ruby

---

[5] Ernesto Semán (Argentina, 1969) lives in the United States and is a doctoral candidate in Latin American history at New York University. Journalist and writer, his fictional work always revolves around history and politics.

(alter ego of the author) are going to be resolved, especially the troubled relationship with his father, a Maoist militant kidnapped and disappeared in 1978, when he was a boy of about eight years of age. His childhood memories, some pictures, and the little plane that his father had brought him from China, are all he retains of the paternal figure for whom he waited for years.

The Island is governed by characters who look like fancy toys: a couple of paper dolls with tails, Rudolf and Rubber Lady, inquisitors of individual memories, whose function is to force the landscape and scenery of memories. If Rudolf occasionally appears as an "eternal witness of an implacable history that unfolds before his eyes" (84), it is because, somehow, they are prisoners on islands created by the conscience of others.

Another thread on The Island is Raquel, Ruby's childhood sweetheart in a deep erotic relationship that has marked him forever, whom he rediscovers in this remote imaginary place and from whom he became separated again. Ruby's inner conflict with the memory of his father is not fully understood unless we analyze the relationship he had with women who marked his life and taught him, each in their own way, the forms of female love, and gave support to his paternal orphanhood: Raquel, his first passion, Clara, today, the foreign wife who will give him a child. And, without doubt, Rosa.

The centre of women's power over Ruby is Rosa, a dying *Yidishe mame*, and the reason why her son has come from the USA, where he lives. She is a hulking woman in her strength and courage and someone to whom Rubén owes his life at least twice: first, by her preventing the abortion which his father had demanded in order not to fall into bourgeois class consciousness against which he was fighting, and, second, by her taking the child to the city to treat a serious infection, when his father had said his son would be cured in the slums where they lived, like other children. To which Rosa replied: "But the children of the slums [*la villa*] don't get cured, idiot. They die, you fucking stupid son of a bitch [*la reputísima madre que te parió*]. If they didn't, why the hell did you come here to set up the clinic" (106-107)?

However, Rosa shines in the unconditional love she had for Abdela, her only partner in life. Rubén cannot understand that his father's unalterable selfishness has not been an obstacle for the love of Rosa Gornstein (in real life Susana Bodner). When Rosa feels her imminent death, she gives her children a box of memories: the famous little airplane, the family photo in the villa, and a long letter (186-193) which Abdela had written to her from Montevideo, when he was going to Cuba in 1961, where he explained what her place as a partner of a revolutionary was. Full of quotations from intellectuals and references to suffering in neighbouring countries, and others around the world, it is a confirmation of his willingness to be a hero to the cause he has embraced. Abdela was then a young thirty-year-old man, and the letter is a document of passion, but also of selfishness and unsubtle authoritarianism.

The reading aloud of such a letter is followed by a rich discussion between the two brothers—Rubén and Agustín—where Rubén tries to interpret his father generationally, against the unmitigated condemnation of the eldest brother. I want to highlight the distance between his mother's acceptance of the demanding conditions imposed by her husband, and the possible reaction which Rubén's current wife would have today: "For a lot less than that, Clara would have left me a nice goodbye note and a free month on a psychiatric ward" (200). I emphasize this because this qualitative leap in gender equality marks an undercurrent of discomfort in the son, and therefore it is not possible to consider the link with his father without taking into account his own bond with women, as I said before.

The ghost of the murdered father (also a significant literary tradition)—the memory of an absent father and of unresolved grief—begins and closes the novel. The ghost of someone real, of whom the novel shows a true picture (185), was a beloved presence in his childhood but left him with the feeling of never being the centre of paternal affection, of being "eternally orphaned and unwanted" (107). An incomprehensible and sometimes hated ghost, he was also admired for his stoicism and revolutionary militancy. Abdela, the Turk (*nom de guerre* of Elías Semán), is the archetype of the communist intellectual of that age, trained in Cuba in the 1960s, who later becomes a worker in a slum in Rosario, where he lives with his family and where he has built a dispensary. He travels to China in 1970 to learn about the Maoist revolution and is kidnapped in 1978. His son (in life and in fiction) recreates the story in different fragmentary flashes, but on The Island he basically recovers him in his martyrdom in the clandestine camp, in the imaginary dialogue with his abductor, full of piety, conviction and strength, evoking the mythical unequal struggle between Christians and Romans.

The ghostly image of the man with the threadbare cloak and signs of torture, who appears hanged in the room at the beginning and at the end of the novel, is an image of a passion and a voluntary suicide, passion diverted to the other, rather than to his own life, with the difference that if at the beginning the ghost unleashes conflicts, he ultimately fades into the light, because Ruben's current maturity allows him to understand his father's suffering for the first time. Then he feels he can leave The Island to which he has come and which he has explored without cowardice. Adult Rubén saves his father symbolically, while—in a parallel story—the kidnapper's son murders his own father (281).

The intimate process of finding the truth behind the memory reaches metaphorical expression in Rubén's stay on The Island, whose topography is constantly changing, dynamic and surreal, unpredictable, and whose centre contains a volcano and a jungle. The paradox is that being the mobile and imaginary construction of a subjectivity, it actually refers to events that took place in collective history. Tumultuous, chaotic and overlapping temporalities gradually order themselves not only to understand the past, but to plan ahead.

Is it possible to reach the truth of memory? Truth and falsehood can be confused when it comes to interpreting the past from personal history (146). However, the author proposes a recovery of individual memories and a rejection of memorials, as in the irony of the *Reconciliation Tour* (262-263) in the manner of Auschwitz which Rudolf proposes, and of everything that might imply flattening or labelling the dimensions of history. It is for this reason that the chronotope of The Island makes sense as a historical truth which does not admit oblivion, but which does not remain in the past as static place. Moreover, finally, it is because The Island contains, in an autobiographical key, the performative gesture of the emergence of the novel we are reading.

Alcoba: Revolutionary Odyssey

The difference between this novel and the ones already

discussed is that the author, Laura Alcoba,[6] daughter of militants, tells of a period in the life of her parents of which she has no memory.

She reconstructs the period when she was born on the basis of the account provided by her parents and some fellow survivors of the utopian adventure that was the trip to Cuba for their training in guerrilla warfare.

At times, Alcoba has referred to this novel as a "salida de la adolescencia [...] una novela de iniciación" [a leaving behind of adolescence... a novel of initiation] (De Núñez 2012). We know that coming-of-age stories are very old and that they are linked to knowledge of the sacred. The archetypical story involves a transformation that embodies the acquisition of knowledge about the identity of the searching subject, the epiphanic discovery of a mission, an existential road map guided by a teacher. It entails suffering, perseverance, humility and, finally, the recognition, the consecrating sanction of the community. In the case of Alcoba's novel, the initiation experience was training in Cuba for the guerrillas undertaken by those who would be her parents, in a group initially formed by five Argentines. However, the vicissitudes narrated in that initiation journey reveal a conflictive process, whose alternatives constitute the novelistic story that takes place from May 1966 to mid-1968.

The narrative is told from an authorial first person who insists on recounting details of reconstructive goldsmithing work, while she works on memoirist material that has been handed down to her orally, but whose reminiscences are often confusing, if not contradictory.[7] That is, there is an intention to show that the craft is hers, but that the material is someone else's, as if an unbridgeable generational gap opened up between the experience of a memory that does not belong to her and her own writing, which aspires to

---

[6] Born in 1968, she has lived in Paris since she was ten. An Arts graduate, she teaches there and publishes in French (Gallimard). The novel discussed here has been translated into Spanish as *Los pasajeros del Anna C* (Edhasa: 2012). All quotations are from this edition; all translations by Adam Sharman.

[7] Adriana Imperatore (2013: 35) states that there is "a kind of oblique autobiographical novel, whose protagonists are the parents who have bequeathed the story, but the quizzical gaze, the questions and the enunciation belong to the perspective of the daughter".

discover some hidden clues in a story full of ambiguities, oversights or disturbing reticence:

> *I no longer know if they do not remember or if they do not want to remember. But, even so, I have managed to gather enough pieces of information. From one conversation to another, I think I can finally make out the thread of a story. The puzzle is beginning to fall into place, although many pieces are still missing... and perhaps will always be missing.* (15; italics in the original)

> A predilection for the secret which an entire generation of revolutionaries cultivated: that is the first hurdle in my way. Discretion and clandestinity. Masters of the art of covering their tracks. At every turn, concealment, imposture and false appearances. We could say that, yes, they managed it. At the end of the day, their memories seem to have been lost almost as much as they would have wanted. But I too know something about this game of codes and masks; and I can try and discover again [*reencontrar*] this story for so long hidden and mute. (13)

The group of idealistic teenagers which Manuel and Soledad, Laura's parents, were part of was initially constituted in La Plata, where they trained clandestinely until they were recruited to Cuba with the exciting asssumption that Che was organizing an expedition to Bolivia. They go on a trip full of adventures (as the return will also be two years later), passing through Paris and Prague before arriving in Havana, where they are received and housed.

The time they live there, which was during the process of the first seven years of the revolution,[8] materializes in Cuba in the space and landscape of the island, so that the chronotope constructed by the novel is that of revolutionary isolation-insulation (*a-islamiento*). If in Semán's novel the island is an imaginary space, the representation of individual, family and collective memory, in the case of Alcoba's novel, the Caribbean island, recovered in two emblematic spaces,

---

[8] The revolutionary process began in 1953 against Fulgencio Batista's regime, but the final victory was in 1959 when Castro's

Havana and the Escambray jungle, is of a realistic *verismo* in its smallest details. However, both the urban landscape and nature are traversed by the time of the revolution, wherein the subjection of the body reigns together with hard discipline, austerity, mistrust, male chauvinism and teachers who behave as prophets and trainers who push human strength to the limit of its endurance. Besides, there is always the almost mythical figure, as if illuminated, of Che, whom they believe to have seen once, and whose death in Bolivia completely changes the plans of Latin American revolutionary expansion. A leader and a heroic prototype without measure, he articulates all young people's actions from the beginning to the end and supports the title of the novel we are reading: on the return trip they discover that Ernesto Guevara had worked on the *Anna C* and read it as a sign: "Somehow we ended up keeping this honourable appointment. For a long time now it was waiting for us here, on this bridge" (280).

The story basically follows the course of the couple, Manuel and Soledad, which consists of—following the idea of the story of initiation—a series of *trials* and moments in which both the personal life of these young people and their group life have exciting achievements or disappointing conflicts. There are three main chapters with subtitles, comprising the three moments of the odyssey: the trip, the Cuban experience, the return trip.

We have identified some situations that are milestones in this process of transformation that has initially been embraced so fervently The first one is: the judgment of El Loco, punished by Cuba for taking five Argentines who are not trained ("El cuartito azul" [The Little Blue Room], 63), which opens with the Argentines' stay on the island and closes with the punishment of the whole group ("Castigados" [Punished], 229). The second one is Manuel and Soledad's separation and the discrimination in the treatment of men and women (work, sexual life, training), which is also understood as part of discipline in a revolutionary culture ("María la O" [Maria O], 121; "El Escambray" [Escambray], 133; "El árbol de mango" [The Mango Tree], 143; "Abismo" [Abyss], 162; "Fuego" [Fire], 154). The third milestone is Che's presence, almost ghostly ("Una visita" [A Visit], 97) but which yet continues to motivate desires and political plans until the tremendous impact of his death ("Un lagarto"

[A Lizard], 204). Another turning point is Soledad's pregnancy and Laura's birth. The latter will have to be registered in another country with a false name and passport to avoid suspicion at the time of the return ("Pasaportes" [Passports], 252).

What continuously gives the story a subjective tinge is a kind of transmutation of the narrator's gaze into the gaze of the character Soledad, a feminine sensitivity, if we may use the term, applied to minute detail and the staging of situations (clothing, food, distractions, gestures), the romantic and faithful bond that never fails to unite the couple and, above all, a sense of frustration between what they went looking for and what they find, which nevertheless conveys an identity and culture conflict, an attitude of distrust on the part of the Cuban leaders of the group towards the Argentines, and the tendency of the latter to anarchic individualism. Ideology has been displaced and acquires trivialized features.

However, if this novel about the trials of life was supposed to end with the consecrating sanction of the community, the group's return to Buenos Aires could not be more tarnished, dressed as they are in those old, outsized Soviet clothes that make the aunts laugh. As Nofal (2014: 283) notes: "Clothes become a disguise, the clothes of others, strange, implausible, removed from the body and space. Old even before being used." The odyssey of these new Ulysses who undertook a learning trip in the hope of achieving heroic stature in the future only arouses the compassionate gaze of family and friends: "the clothes, like the revolution, are too big for our protagonists" (Nofal 2014: 282).

The story does not say if our society was not yet ready or if the revolutionary feat was from the beginning doomed to fail, but the kind of epilogue that closes the novel ("Estelas" [Wakes], 283), with the list of all the dead a few years after they return on the *Anna C*, shows the tragedy of an epic that ended in genocide.

As we saw in Semán's and Pron's novels, the children-authors seek their own identity delving into the reconstruction of their family history, with different documents and oral narratives. In the search, they find a time that is strange for them, and which sometimes reminds them of a painful childhood, and, at other times, as in

Alcoba's novel,[9] of an identity that is unclear from the beginning: a travelling baby whose fake name and place of birth her parents cannot remember even today.

This new passenger of life who today seeks the signs of her novelistic source was also travelling back on the *Anna C*. On that journey, what is biographical and what is autobiographical begin to be (con)fused.

References

Alberca, M. (2007). *El pacto ambiguo. De la novela autobiográfica a la autoficción*. Madrid: Biblioteca Nueva.

Alcoba, L. (2006). *La casa de los conejos*. Buenos Aires: Edhasa.

Alcoba, L. (2012). *Los pasajeros del Anna C*. Buenos Aires: Edhasa.

Arán, P. (2010). Las cronotopías literarias en la concepción bajtiniana: Su pertinencia en el planteo de una investigación sobre narrativa argentina contemporánea. In *Interpelaciones. Hacia una teoría crítica de las escrituras sobre la dictadura y la memoria*. Córdoba: Centro de Estudios Avanzados-Universidad Nacional de Córdoba, pp. 13-30.

Arán, P. (2010). El relato de la dictadura en la novela argentina: Series y variaciones. In *Interpelaciones. Hacia una teoría crítica de las escrituras sobre la dictadura y la memoria*. Córdoba: Centro de Estudios Avanzados-Universidad Nacional de Córdoba, pp. 31-134.

Badagnani, A. (2012). La voz de los hijos en la literatura argentina reciente: Laura Alcoba, Ernesto Semán y Patricio Pron. At **http://patriciopron.blogspot.com.ar/2012/10/la-voz-de-los-hijos-en-la-literatura.html**, accessed 3 March 2016.

De Núñez, A. (2013). Laura Alcoba, la clandestina platense, *Revista Ñ* (5 April 2012).

Imperatore, A. (2013). Una autobiografía oblicua: La memoria clandestina en *Los pasajeros del Anna C*. y *La casa de los conejos* de Laura Alcoba. *Les Ateliers du SAL*, 3, 34-48.

Nofal, R. (2014). La guardarropía revolucionaria en la

---

[9] In a previous novel, *La casa de los conejos* (Edhasa, 2006), Alcoba recreates her childhood in a house that was a clandestine press of the guerrilla organization to which her parents belonged.

novela de Laura Alcoba. *El taco en la brea*. *Revista del Centro de Investigaciones Teórico–literarias* (CEDINTEL), Universidad Nacional del Litoral, 1(1), 277-287.

Pron, P. (2011). *El espíritu de mis padres sigue subiendo en la lluvia*. Barcelona: Random House Mondadori.

Semán, E. (2011). *Soy un bravo piloto de la nueva China*. Buenos Aires: Mondadori.

"Why Did They Take Down the Pictures?":
Conspicuous Absences and "La Historia de Algo Más" in Roberto Bolaño's *Estrella distante*

Rui Gonçalves Miranda

> The photograph is literally an emanation of the referent. Radiations depart from a real body, there, and proceed to touch me, who am here; the duration of the transmission is irrelevant; the photo of the disappeared being will touch me like the deferred rays of a distant star.
> Roland Barthes[1]

In a short journal piece written in 1896, on Lumières' cinematographer, Maxim Gorky famously writes about the impact of the moving images on the screen. Rather than focusing on the sense of estrangement felt by Gorky when faced with the "gray movement of gray shadows, mute and noiseless", I wish to highlight Gorky's brief description of when the images cease to be projected:

> And suddenly—it disappears. Before your eyes there is simply a piece of white canvas in a wide black frame, and it seems there never was anything on it. Someone elicited in your imagination something your eyes supposedly saw,—and that's it. It becomes somehow indefinably unsettling. (Gorky)

Gorky's description functions as the symbol of what Jacques Derrida would come to term the "spectral" effect of the cinematographer, later amplified in and through future artistic (re)inventions of reality in cinema, that invention (*d'après*, supposedly, Louis Lumière) without future. Gorky becomes fixated on the conspicuous absence of the images, or rather, on the effect of these now absent images that cannot be forgotten. It "seems there never was anything on it"; *e pur si muove*, contradicting what the eyes already (supposedly) did not see.

---

[1] All translations are my own, unless otherwise indicated.

Conspicuous Absences in Roberto Bolaño's *Estrella Distante*

The cinematographer marks a watershed moment in the development of technologies of memory, developed to such an extent during the course of the twentieth century that it is now their inexistence before the late nineteenth and twentieth century that seems unreal. As if that were a different time, once upon a time, "era y no era", *in illo tempore*: "In those days there were no cinematographs or phonographs; however, it is implausible and even incredible that no one had experimented with Funes" (Borges 1982: 128). This short, throwaway remark, by the narrator in his remembrance of Funes reveals that one of the many ironies of Jorge Luis Borges' short story of "Funes el memorioso" is that of Funes's prodigious and infallible memory there is no record except for the untrustworthy and often unreliable memory of those who met him: it is a patchy, posthumous memory (to quote a title by Machado de Assis). Funes's existence preceded cinema and the lamented non-existence of technologies such as phonographs and cinematographers, which might produce an external record of his presence, and of the presence of his memory, acts as a reminder of the achievements of new technologies in establishing an archive for future record. Crucially, and in line with Gorky's sense of disquiet when viewing the images captured by the cinematographer, it brings to mind the way in which the "technologies of memory developed during the twentieth century [...] made it increasingly possible for people to take on memories of events not 'naturally' their own" (Landsberg 2004: 19). This possibility is a structural necessity embedded in the *téchnē* (the technology, the technique,...); the "modern possibility of the photograph," notes Derrida—and I would extend this to other technologies of of memory—"joins, in a single system, death and the referent" (Derrida & Stiegler 2002: 114). According to Alison Landsberg (2004: 19), "the technologies of mass culture and the capitalist economy of which they are a part open up a world of images outside a person's lived experience, creating a portable, fluid, and nonessentialist form of memory". In this study, we will be focusing on the ways in which cinema may act both as a mechanism of remembrance and as a technique of projection.

In Roberto Bolaño's *Estrella distante* (Distant Star) the allusions to cinema play a particular role both as background or frame and in creating an effect of disruption in characters' memories. There are two movements that enact this role: on the one hand, the references to cinema highlight narrative devices which convoke cinematic techniques; on the other, allusions to cinema set up projections of presences and events, emphasizing the mediation and artificiality of memory experiences. Cinema is used, both as device and metonymy, to enhance the detective and thriller aspects of the book and to provide an image-based notion of memory: Ruiz-Tagle's is first identified as Carlos Wieder in a photograph of his which Gorda Posadas sees in the paper; Ruiz-Tagle/Wieder photographs his victims before (in poetry workshops) and after torturing and/or executing them—he also sets up an infamous installation/exhibition of said photos; the narrator's description of Wieder's performance of poetry in the sky whilst locked in prison is that of a spectator looking at a screen. Furthermore, Carlos Wieder's ever-elusive presence is traced through photographs throughout the text, he is a visual performer (photography exhibitions, poetry in the air)[2] and, later, a cinematographer in hardcore porn films. This overload of images (and re-imaginings) achieves a disarticulation of the visible as an insight into what is not, and could only very problematically be, represented: torture, violence, repression. Bibiano remarks to Arturo B., reported by the narrator, that Ruiz-Tagle/Wieder's house reminds him of the flat of the Castevets in *Rosemary's Baby*, in the sense that something, "unnameable [*innombrable*]", is missing: "the flat seemed to have been *prepared*, its contents arranged for the eye of the imminent visitor; it was too empty, and there were spaces from which things had obviously been removed [*en donde claramente faltaba algo*]" (Bolaño 2009; 2008d: 17).[3] The absences, so clearly felt and *seen*, together with the fact that Bibiano heard, while in the living room, someone else's hidden presence in an adjacent room, both anticipate and project Wieder's exhibition of

---

[2] See Jennerjahn (2002) and Gamboa Cárdenas (2008) on the artistic acts of Ruiz-Tagle/Wieder and their relation to the (ambiguous morality of) avant-garde movements.

[3] Celina Manzoni (2002: 43, 48) notes the difficulty of what she terms narrating the ineffable—Bibiano's description of Ruiz-Tagle's house and also of the narrator's dream. However, the significance of the reference to *Rosemary's Baby*—which, as we have mentioned, does not appear in *La literatura nazi en América*—and the function of conspicuous absence in the novel is not explored.

photos of his victims (including the Garmendia's sisters, one of whom Bibiano bumped into as he left Ruiz-Tagle's flat) in his bedroom (in a colleague's flat) to fellow military personnel and socialites.

Gorky's above-mentioned insight is revealing because, far from focusing on the effects moving images have when shown, it addresses precisely the lingering effect after the projection has stopped; it focuses on what is clearly missing. Cinema plays also a determining role in the novel (through references and allusions) not because of what it can show but because of the "indefinably unsettling" sensation that persists. The effects of the projection—and in this case what is projected is what text cannot show and that which cinematic (metonymically) and photographic references convoke—are still felt later on, like rays from a distant star (*estrella distante*). It is no accident that *Rosemary's Baby*, namely, the scene of the dream Rosemary had while drugged and violated by Satan, is evoked by the narrator (Arturo B.) to reflect on his role in Chilean and Latin American history as well as his positioning *vis-à-vis* Ruiz-Tagle/Carlos Wieder. B.'s dream (which repeats, albeit with notable differences, Rosemary's dream) is prompted by the resurgence of interest in Wieder when detective Romero enters the scene, ushered in by Bibiano.[4] The sinking ship on which both narrator and Wieder are passengers (albeit very different passengers) provides a powerful visual image, a variation on the recurring image of the youth falling into an abyss (see *Amuleto*; Bolaño 2007: 151-52);[5] the visual image is constructed with reference to, and its power is enhanced by, the scene projected (in both senses of the word) in the supernatural thriller's treatment of Evil lying dormant and emerging in the familiar, a context of banality and proximity (from poetry workshops in Chile to Catalonian seaside coffee shops). The manipulation and exploitation of Rosemary by those in whom

---

[4] The question of the doubles cuts across the text, including when it comes to the initials RB: Roberto Bolaño—Rosemary's Baby...— (see Manzi 2004). See Manzoni (2002) regarding the question of doubles and unfolding in the text.
[5] See Castillo de Berchenko (2005) for a meditation on the "communicating vessels" linking the different writings of Roberto Bolaño (2005) and Grass (2005) for a reflection on Bolaño's "total work". See Lepage (2007) for a comparative take on *Estrella distante*, *Nocturno de Chile* and *Amuleto* in particular.

she trusts—a manipulation which consists largely of denying Rosemary's account, of dismissing as nonsense (effects of tiredness, illness, paranoia) what Rosemary can *see*:

> ROSEMARY (Unhooking her stockings)
> Why did they take down the pictures?
> GUY
> What do you mean?
> ROSEMARY
> Their pictures; they took them down. There are hooks in the wall and clean places. And the one picture that *is* there doesn't fit.
> GUY (Looking at her)
> I didn't notice.

Her husband Guy might not have noticed it then but he will soon *know* what the missing paintings represent and willingly deceive Rosemary. The missing paintings, revealed only at the end of the film, expose the true identity of the Satan worshippers who had been posing as the quirky and unsuspecting Castevets.

Bibiano is reminded of the film, and noticeably of the scene just alluded to, because of the conspicuous absences—and their effects, something like Barthesian and Bolañoan rays from a distant star. In *Estrella distante*, the only reference to distant stars in the text comes very close to the end. References to "stars" throughout the novel are relatively scarce, but significant. Besides the presence in the title and in a William Faulkner epigraph, *estrella* appears twice in the novel: to refer to the twin sisters as the undisputed "stars" of the poetry workshops and to one of Wieder's exhibitions of *escritura aérea* (aerial writing) when Wieder "drew a star, the star of our flag, sparkling and solitary over the sparkling horizon" (Bolaño: 2009).[6] The context in which the above-mentioned reference occurs illustrates the role which cinema plays both as a framing device as well as a disruptive effect; or, in other words, a disarticulation of the visible:

---

[6] As Celina Manzoni notes, in *La literatura nazi en América*, Ramírez Hoffman is referred to as "the most brilliant and enigmatic star" (Manzoni 2002: 44). However, "star" is never applied to Ruiz-Tagle/Wieder in *Estrella distante*.

> As his footfalls grew fainter, I sat there watching the dark shrubs, their tangled branches weaving random designs as they shifted in the wind. Then I lit a cigarette and began to think about trivial matters. Like time. The greenhouse effect. The increasingly distant stars [*las estrellas cada vez más distantes*].
>
> I tried to think of Wieder. I tried to imagine him alone in his flat, an anonymous dwelling, as I pictured it, on the fourth floor of an empty eight-floor building, watching television or sitting in an armchair, drinking, as Romero's shadow glided steadily towards him. I tried to imagine Carlos Wieder, but I couldn't. Or maybe I didn't really want to. (Bolaño 2009)

The decisive action takes place, to use film terminology, off-screen. The growing distance of the stars provides a counterpoint to Wieder's physical proximity at the present time. Romero's steps, which the narrator hears, lead Romero and the narrator to Wieder (whom the narrator met as Ruiz-Tagle and then saw from a distance while in prison, not knowing who he was, in photographs and also searched for behind pseudonyms in literary texts and magazines, behind the camera in pornographic films—before he identified him, at Romero's request). Romero will perform the decisive action; the narrator, while in the last instance refusing to, or acknowledging his inability to, "imaginar" Wieder, will still be able to imagine him (very much through a detective noir lense) in his flat, "an anonymous dwelling, as I pictured it [*que elegí impersonal*]" (Bolaño 2008a: 155). Whether the narrator refuses to imagine or is incapable of imagining Wieder is indicative of the tension between what can and cannot be put into images; Arturo B.'s imagining of the flat as "impersonal", however, refers back to Bibiano's description of the flat of (at that time still) Ruiz-Tagle:

> What did Bibiano say about Ruiz-Tagle's flat? He talked about how bare it was, mostly; he had the feeling it had been *prepared*. He only went there once on his own. He was passing by and, typically, decided to drop in and invite Ruiz-Tagle to go and see a film. He hardly knew the guy, but that didn't stop him. There was a Bergman film showing. I can't remember which one. Bibiano had already been to the flat a couple of times with one or

other of the Garmendia sisters, and on both occasions the visit had been expected, so to speak. Both times, the flat seemed to have been *prepared*, its contents arranged for the eye of the imminent visitor; it was too empty, and there were spaces from which things had obviously been removed. In the letter explaining all this to me (which was written many years later), Bibiano said he felt like Mia Farrow in *Rosemary's Baby*, when she goes into the neighbour's house for the first time with John Cassavettes. What was missing from Ruiz-Tagle's flat was something unnameable (or something that Bibiano, years later, and knowing the full story, or a good part of it at any rate, considered unnameable, but palpably present), as if the host had amputated parts of the interior. Or as if the interior were a kind of Meccano that could be reconstructed to fit the expectations and particularities of each visitor. The impression was even stronger when he visited the flat on his own. This time, of course, Ruiz-Tagle had not been expecting him. He took a long time to open the door. And then he seemed not to recognize his visitor, although Bibiano assured me that he came to the door with a smile and went on smiling through what followed. There was not much light, as Bibiano himself admitted in his letter, so I don't know quite how accurate my friend's account is. In any case, Ruiz-Tagle opened the door, and after a rather incongruous exchange (at first he didn't understand that Bibiano was proposing they go and see a film), he asked him to wait a moment, shut the door, opened it again after a few seconds, and invited him in. The flat was dimly lit. That air was thick with a peculiar odour, as if Ruiz-Tagle had cooked something very pungent the night before, something oily and spicy. For a moment, Bibiano thought he heard a noise in one of the rooms and assumed there was a woman in the flat. (Bolaño 2009: 7)

Cinema provides the framework and the background to the visit. The visit is prompted by the invitation to cine Bergman and ends on Ruiz-Tagle's statement that he does not like Bergman; Bibiano's *a posteriori* evocation, in his retelling to B., of *Rosemary's Baby* further helps frame Ruiz-

Tagle's flat as a film set, "*preparada*" (italics in the original). Bibiano's mention of the noises coming from one of the rooms can be interpreted—if we concede that "the increasingly animated [*cada día más vivo*] ghost of Pierre Menard" (Bolaño 2009; 2008a: 11) is accompanied by another "material ghost", cinema (see Gilberto Perez 1998)—as a literary translation of the importance given to action off-screen/*hors-champ* in cinema. This goes beyond, although does not exclude, Alfred Hitchcock's well-known preference for suggesting rather than showing violent acts in themselves: in "Nana, or the two kinds of space", Noël Burch's (1980: 17-31) comments on the existence of and on the relation between the "two different kinds of space" that constitute "cinematic space" (what happens within the frame and outside the frame) have systematized the complexity and importance of the often overlooked off-screen space. Further consideration of this question has not only increased interest in the importance of the off-screen space for development of story and plot, with an implicit acceptance that what happens off-screen may be as important as what is shown on-screen, but also further pursued the ways in which off-screen space is both constructed and impacts on on-screen space. In film, Gilberto Perez (1998: 137) notes, by appropriating Jacques Derrida, there is no *hors-champ*. A significant (the significant?) action is neither told nor shown to the reader, present in the narrative only negatively through what Bibiano thinks he might have heard and which he frames in cinematic terms by referring to the scene from *Rosemary's Baby* in which Rosemary fatally fails to acknowledge, through the absence of paintings which had been taken off the wall, the horror that will later be revealed. Bibiano's reliability as a narrator is put in question in the extract above and in the preceding paragraph when the narrator introduces Bibiano's account of Ruiz-Tagle's flat:

> Ruiz-Tagle lived on his own, in a flat near the centre of town, with four rooms and the curtains permanently drawn. I never visited this flat, but many years later Bibiano O'Ryan told me about it, no doubt under the influence of the sinister legend that had grown up around Wieder, so I don't know how much to believe and how much to put down to my fellow student's imagination. (Bolaño 2009)

Cinema provides the means by which Bibiano remembers and re-imagines what happened behind closed doors, perhaps influenced by a "sinister legend [*leyenda maldita*]" (Bolaño 2008a: 16) which is no doubt indebted to Carlos Wieder's opening, during the Pinochet regime, of his room so as to exhibit the photos he had taken of his victims. Bibiano can only *imagine* what happened behind the doors in the room in Ruiz-Tagle's flat (whence he believed he heard sound), in light of how the flat had seemed *prepared* (*preparada*) (2008a: 17) and of Wieder's posterior staging of a photographic exhibition of tortured and mutilated women. B.'s imagining of Wieder's flat in Spain as "impersonal" before refusing or accepting the impossibility of "imagining" Wieder, is indebted to Bibiano's cinematic imagination as much as to B.'s, who also has a dream which evokes a scene from *Rosemary's Baby* and will later be commissioned by detective Romero to trace Wieder's presence through publications as well as films in which Wieder participates as R. P. English. Apart from the evident detective noir fiction (be it literature or cinema) traits in the narrative involving Romero, cinema is once again foregrounded when the reader learns that Wieder has become a cinematographer in the porn industry; Wieder will have taken up filming rather than merely photographing his victims. Arturo B.'s playing out in his mind of Wieder's (*hors-champ*) execution by Romero is as much a product of his own imagination as was Bibiano's, equally influenced by Wieder's black legend and noir fiction.

In the end, B.'s stated refusal or inability to imagine Wieder should be read not so much as an act of resignation on B.'s part but rather as a coming to terms with Bibiano's earlier statement that what was missing in Ruiz-Tagle's apartment was "unnameable, but palpably present". This duplicitous status (unnameable but present) does more than confirm the intricate connection between the two spaces, which is blatantly exposed when Wieder opens up his bedroom with the photo exhibition to a host of military personnel, journalists and artists following his aerial writing performance. In B.'s dream, in which it is now up to him to evoke *Rosemary's Baby*, B. feigns no ignorance, offers no excuses and seeks no redemption: a fellow traveller of Wieder on a sinking ship, he did little to stop it from sinking. Neither does Bolaño need to tell or directly show for the reader to know; as Joaquín Manzi (2007: 91-95) has pointed out, Bolaño's works often omit words (*dictatorship*, *torture*, etc) that underlie and condition the entire narrative. Their conspicuous absence, much like the omission of the paintings in *Rosemary's Baby* which Bibiano evokes, is an overwhelming presence; a presence, to paraphrase Bibiano, tangible and, yet, unnamed. *Dictatorship* and *torture* may be absent but are in no way *hors-texte*. The reader can move from work to text, reread and rewrite what is absent (unnameable, yet tangible and present) from the work but overwhelmingly present in the text.

Bibiano and B. are mostly reliable narrators, but they admit to being fallible and are certainly limited by what they (do not) witness. Chris Andrews has called attention to a particular technique of storytelling, which he calls the Piglia-Martínez hypothesis. A short story, according to Piglia in "Tesis sobre el cuento" [Thesis on the Short Story], "always tells two stories [*dos historias*]"; in the classical short story, one story is narrated "in the foreground [*en primer plano*]" and another story is secretly encoded in the gaps of the visible story (Piglia 2000: 17). Andrews concludes that Bolaño belongs to a modern version of the short story, that Bolaño, to use Piglia's words in reference to authors such as Anton Chekhov, Katherine Mansfield, or Ernest Hemingway, "works through [*trabaja*] the tension between the two stories without ever resolving it"; the two stories are told as one (Piglia 2000: 18; see Andrews 2014, chapter 3) and "the most important is never told. The secret story is built on the unsaid [*no dicho*], the implicit [*sobreentendido*] and the allusion" (Piglia 2000: 18). In cinematic terms, it is hard not to think of Burch's above-mentioned "two spaces": (a story) within the frame and (another=the same, since they are told as one) outside the frame, in unresolved tension, in suspension. Two spaces, but, as we have seen, "the *same boat*"; or as Gilberto Perez (1998: 137) puts it: "the out of frame in a film, the *hors-champ*, is not out of text but a construction of the text".

In *Estrella distante*, the stories that are narrated are, in a sense, the stories of spectators, neither perpetrators nor the victims of torture, repression, and murder; victims of the regime, no doubt, but who recognize that the extent of the crimes which they indirectly witness is far more serious and grave than the ones they have suffered. Gorda Posadas,

Bibiano, Arturo B.; through photos, poems, rumours, etc, these narrators are condemned to tracing what happened. The narrations show decorum *vis-à-vis* the unnameable, irrepresentable and, most of all, intransmissible experience of torture and death—which are, in an etymological sense, obscene and are therefore treated outside the frame. In a Heideggerian sense, death is what can be experienced only by oneself: Maurice Blanchot's *récit* "À l'instant de ma mort" is a striking example of the difficulties and the intricateness of the relation between testimony and fiction (see Blanchot & Derrida 2000), which makes the relation between the "real" and what is "represented" (testified, *ergo* textualized and, to some extent, fictionalized) a relation that is far from straightforward. Maurice Blanchot's history of a young man's (*jeune homme*) brush with death in 1944, during WWII facing a firing squad, is picked up fifty years later in the *récit* which ends with a note on the limits of addressing one's own death in 1994, 1944 or ever since, "in abeyance [*toujour en instance*]" (Blanchot & Derrida 2000: 10): "What does it matter. All that remains is the feeling of lightness [*légèreté*] that is death itself or, to put it more precisely, the instant of my death henceforth always in abeyance" (Blanchot & Derrida 2000: 11). The unbearable lightness of... dying. In *Estrella distante*, the instances and instants of death and torture are always narrated from third-person testimony, poems and photographs, as well as limited witnessing (i.e. victims who are named in Wieder's writings in the air and are therefore presumed dead; sounds are overheard; scenes of violence are played out in the minds of characters and readers).

One must therefore supplement the melancholy literary aspects of Bolaño's writing (particularly visible in *Nocturno de Chile* [2008b][7]) with a notion of melancholy in the Freudian sense, a loss that is not fully identified or understood, as opposed to a healthy and conscious work of mourning. Cinema (a tangible presence in the text) thus may act as a device, a technique for "spectral memory" and a magnified work of mourning (Derrida *et al.* 2015: 28). The cinematographer unsettled the nerves during and after

---

[7] H. Ibacache's narrative features a number of references to a tradition and imagery of melancholy: see Aguila (2008), Benmiloud (2007), and Decante-Araya (2007).

projection, because—let us remember Gorky's impressions—it portrays ghosts and it is in itself ghostly when images unnervingly disappear. In an interview, Derrida considers his fascination and outlines his philosophical interest in cinema:

> Cinema thus allows one to cultivate what could be called "grafts" of spectrality; it inscribes traces of ghosts on a general framework, the projected film, which is itself a ghost. It's a captivating phenomenon and, theoretically, this is what would interest me in cinema as object of analysis. Spectral memory, cinema is a magnificent mourning, a magnified work of mourning. And it is ready to let itself be imprinted by all the memories in mourning, that is to say, by the tragic or epic moments of history. (Derrida *et al.* 2015: 27)

The tragic and epic moments of history are precisely what the work *Estrella distante* does not approach directly; they are left in, and to, the dark room (see Fischer 2005). Whether we choose the image of the iceberg or of the two stories, it is hard to argue that historical, tragic, and epic aspects are only known from a distance: as an interpreter of rumours, court proceedings, third-person accounts and confessions; as a bystander in the poetry workshops to the actions of Ruiz-Tagle or in the prison courtyard as an unknowing spectator to (then) Wieder's aerial writing. Ultimately, Bibiano, in Wieder's flat, and B., in his dream, come to terms with the fact that the Wieder's story was the story of something more (*era la historia de algo más*) (Bolaño 2008a: 130). As in Bibiano's reference to that which is unnamed but present, tangible, there is a reference to the supernatural horror thriller:

> When I woke up six hours later, I felt refreshed and ready to go on reading or re-reading (or guessing, depending on the language of the magazine). I was gradually being drawn into the story of Carlos Wieder, which was also the story of something more—exactly what I couldn't tell—but one night I had a dream about it. I dreamt I was travelling in a big wooden boat, a galleon perhaps, crossing the Great Ocean. There was a party on the poop deck and I was there, writing a

poem, or perhaps writing in my diary, and looking at the sea. Then an old man, on a yacht, not the galleon, or standing on a breakwater, started shouting "Tornado! Tornado!" just like the scene from *Rosemary's Baby*, the Polanski film. At that point the galleon began to sink and all the survivors were cast adrift on the sea. I saw Carlos Wieder, clinging to a barrel of brandy. I was clinging to a rotten spar. And only then, as the waves pushed us apart, did I understand that Wieder and I had been travelling in the *same boat*; he may have conspired to sink it, but I had done little or nothing to stop it going down. (Bolaño 2009)

Cinema is not a metaphor, it provides and it acts as a device to frame and dismantle what is (in)visible (behind closed doors, in dark rooms, up in the sky, in photographs), thus configuring a certain spectrality, the materiality of ghosts. Arturo B. presents, as aforementioned, clear reservations regarding Bibiano's account of his uneasy visit to Bibiano when faced with noises coming from behind a closed door. The narration—here lies B.'s circumspection—may have been altered in the light of later revelations once Wieder opens the door (quite literally) on his (not exclusively, but certainly including) actions as Ruiz-Tagle. And yet B.—after being tasked by Romero with the objective of finding Wieder behind his many "heteronyms" and reincarnations—has a dream in which he sees Wieder from a distance in a boat, as in the dream scene of *Rosemary's Baby*, the same film that Bibiano evokes to refer to his sense of uneasiness as he sat in Ruiz-Tagle's flat. B.'s own narrative is itself affected by Bibiano's mode of the account of what is unnamed yet tangible. Derrida approaches this "spectral dimension" in his brief considerations of film's "mode and system of *belief*":

> At the movies, you believe without believing, but this believing without believing remains a believing. On the screen, whether silent or not, one is dealing with apparitions that, as in Plato's cave, the spectator believes, apparitions that are sometimes idolized. Because the spectral dimension is that of neither the living nor the dead, of neither hallucination nor

perception, the modality of believing that relates to it must be analyzed in an absolutely original manner. This particular phenomenology was not possible before the movie camera because this experience of believing is linked to a particular technique, that of cinema. It is historical through and through, with that supplementary aura, that particular memory that lets us project ourselves into films of the past. That is why the experience of seeing a film is so rich. It lets one see new specters appear while remembering (and then projecting them in turn onto the screen) the ghosts haunting films *already* seen. (Derrida *et al.* 2015: 27)

Bibiano and B., picking up on what was mentioned above, are spectators who deal with the many apparitions and disappearances caused by Wieder and others who participate in the ideology, policies, and practices which Wieder comes to incarnate fully. They use cinema to project the spectres (past and future) they cannot name, thus projecting their own spectres. Bibiano and B. evoke a horror film about absolute evil in a banal setting (*Rosemary's Baby*) because they are rather banal spectators of manifestations of evil. They have come face to face with (their own?) death and have been in abeyance (*en instance*) ever since.

Kurt Vonnegut's science fiction/testimony *Slaughterhouse 5, or the Children's Crusade* features a character (Billy Pilgrim) who, not unlike Héctor Oesterheld's Juan Salvo, has become "unstuck in time"—Billy Pilgrim has been abducted by aliens while Juan Salvo fights against them (1957-59; *El Eternauta II* (1976-1977) features a repetition with a political difference; see Sasturain 2010: 176-181). It is the narrator, however, who emerges in the sections of the novel that deal with the firebombing of Dresden by Allied forces in WWII (Wieder, for good measure, uses a WWII Messerschmitt to write in the air) which the narrator/Vonnegut survived as a prisoner of war and labourer involved in the operations in the aftermath of the destruction of the city—Oesterheld, who also become a character in *El Eternauta II*, on the other hand, will be disappeared. The ending of the novel draws on a biblical episode to address the event which the novel has sought to represent (fictionalize and/or give testimony), that of the destruction of Sodom and Gomorrah by divine intervention:

So it goes. Those were vile people in both those cities, as is well known. The world was better off without them. And Lot's wife, of course, was told not to look back where all those people and their homes had been. But she did look back, and I love her for that, because it was so human. So she was turned to a pillar of salt. So it goes. People aren't supposed to look back. I'm certainly not going to do it anymore. I've finished my war book now. The next one I write is going to be fun. This one is a failure, and had to be, since it was written by a pillar of salt. (Vonnegut 2001: 18)

So it goes. Lot's wife's demise, her disobedience and her looking back, is the proof of her humanity. Her confronting of the terror, the image of the destruction, the image of God, is a true witnessing but it comes with a high cost. Can the pillar of salt write? It can, just not—as Slavoj Žižek warned *contre* Adorno's dictum on the possibility of lyrical poetry after Auschwitz (2009: 4)—in realist prose; rather in a science fiction hybrid-genre that can aptly describe the "unreality" of the "real". In the end it is a "war book", as Auxilio puts it in *Amuleto*, about an atrocious crime (*crimen atroz*) (Bolaño 2007: 11).[8]

How, then, can one not be petrified when facing terror? *Toujours en instance*: Arturo B.'s uprooting and wandering in exile—or Juan Stein's and Diogo Soto's—allows him to address a terror that could otherwise be paralyzing. Exile ("cada vez más distantes"...) acts as "una descontinuidad, una brecha en el tiempo en la que sólo resta inventar y narrar, entre el olvido indeseado y la memoria imposible" [a discontinuity, a crack in time in which there is no other option but to invent and narrate, between unwanted oblivion and impossible memory] (Aguilar 2003: 150). Classical mythology, rather than the Bible, can provide a different point of entry; Italo Calvino, in *Lezioni Americane. Sei proposte per il prossimo millennio* (1988) (*Six Memos for the Next Millennium* [1993]), uses myth's "language of images"

---

[8] As Patricia Espinosa (2003: 26) reminds us, "Bolaño embraces the code of the Latin American *neopolicial* [new detective noir], crossing the metaphysical quests of his characters, constantly on the move, with political history, namely that of the Chilean military dictatorship. Nevertheless, with a deliberate sense of humour, he also edges towards parody and the fantastic".

to discuss literature and poetry—a discussion that could enlighten us in ways not to be petrified by the history of horror. In the first note, the text on "lightness" (*leggerezza*; see Blanchot's *légèreté*, above), Calvino refers to the myth of the slaying of the Medusa by Perseus: "To cut off Medusa's head without being turned to stone, Perseus supports himself on the very lightest of things, the winds and the clouds, and fixes his gaze upon what can be revealed only by indirect vision, an image caught in a mirror" (1993: 4). Bolaño addresses the reality of horror/terror—but ultimately opts against and finds protection from (as the mythical hero alluded to by Calvino) a direct vision. References to other visions, reports, photographs and cinematic references frame and reflect (even if negatively) the tangible presence of the horror, even when unnamed and unidentified or unidentifiable. On that depends the force of the text as opposed to the form of the work when facing horror:

> Perseus succeeds in mastering that horrendous face [Medusa's] by keeping it hidden, just as in the first place he vanquished it by viewing it in a mirror. Perseus's strength always lies in a refusal to look directly, but not in a refusal of the reality in which he is fated to live; he carries the reality with him and accepts it as his particular burden. (Calvino 1993: 5)

Estrella distante does not shy away from confronting the "terror", but does so through a game of mirrors, often inverted (Ruiz-Tagle/Carlos Wieder and Arturo B. and Bibiano; Juan Stein and Diogo Soto), heteronyms and doubles (see, for instance, O'Bryen 2015: 29).[9] It does so in a mediated way via references to cinema and photographs (of the criminal, of victims, of Soviet Generals and American writers, the latter admittedly false) and by evoking cinema and photography so as both to frame and disarticulate the (in)visible, revealing a supplement in the Derridian sense, something more and other than what the narrators can see

---

[9] As Patricia Espinosa (2003: 25) puts it, "in both narratives [*Nazi Literature in the Americas* and *Distant Star*], the referent is literaturized, through a sort of fictional mirroring which contributes towards the resituation of horror as a quasi-farcical aestheticization".

or tell—an other history, a second story and a second space, in dark rooms: to use Machado de Assis' formulation, a "memória póstuma" (posthumous as much as prosthetic memory), yet to be revealed... "para memória futura" (for the record). The "literaturización" (literaturization) and farsical aestheticization (Espinosa 2003: 25) emphasizes that *something more* has taken place *hors-champ* but, always already, not *hors-texte*.

The illuminating studies that draw on the reference in the prologue of *Estrella distante* to the ghost of Pierre Menard which animates the expansion of the narrative of the infamous Ramírez Hoffman in *La literatura nazi en las Américas* into the "leyenda maldita" of Carlos Wieder (see O'Bryen 2015; López-Calvo 2015) should be complemented by a study of the other, material ghost which is worked in the narrative only in *Estrella distante*: the phantasms of cinema and photos that, absent in hypotext "Ramírez Hoffman, el infame", play a crucial role in addressing the singularity of that which in the text remains unnamed but is present. The cumulative effect, to the point of disruption, of references, forms, genres and media in Bolaño's fiction avoids petrifying *en instance*.

Roberto Bolaño's fiction is a Menardian rewriting of the (Latin American) tensions between what can be forgotten and what is not/cannot be remembered: what must not be forgotten is what cannot be, strictly speaking, clearly remembered. As Rosemary, in a moment of lucidity as she is violated and possessed by the incarnation of evil, puts it: "This is not a dream. This is happening". There is always "algo más" (something else) beyond what can be simply and clearly represented: that is what is happening. Unnameable but present, tangible, Bibiano—B. would tell us—might add.

References

Aguila, P. (2008). Pobre memoria la mía: Literatura y melancolía en el contexto de la postdictadura chilena. In E. Paz Soldán & G. Faverón Patriau (eds.), *Bolaño salvage*. Barcelona: Candaya, pp. 127-143.

Aguilar, G. (2003). Roberto Bolaño: Entre la historia y la melancolía. In P. Espinosa H. (ed.), *Territorios en fuga. Estudios críticos sobre la obra de Roberto Bolaño*. Santiago: FRASIS, pp.145-51.

Andrews, C. (2014). *Roberto Bolaño's fiction: An expanding universe* [ebook]. New York: Columbia University Press.

Benmiloud, K. (2007). Figures de la mélancolie dans *Nocturno de Chile*. In K. Benmiloud & R. Estève (eds.), *Les Astres noirs de Roberto Bolaño*. Bordeaux: ERSAL/GRIAL-AMERIBER, pp. 109-134.

Blanchot, M., & Derrida, J. (2000). *The instant of my death/Demeure: Fiction and testimony* (trans. E. Rottenberg). Stanford: Stanford University Press.

Bolaño, R. (2007). *Amuleto*, 3rd edn. Barcelona: Anagrama

Bolaño, R. (2008a). *Estrella distante,* 6th edn. Barcelona: Anagrama.

Bolaño, R. (2008b). *Nocturno de Chile*, 6th edn. Barcelona: Anagrama.

Bolaño, R. (2009). *Distant star* (trans. C. Andrews). London: Vintage Books.

Bolaño, R. (2015). *La literatura nazi en América*. Barcelona: Anagrama.

Borges, J. L. (1982*). Ficciones*, 11th edn. Madrid-Buenos Aires: Alianza-Emece.

Burch, N. (1980). *Theory of film practice* (trans. H. R. Lane). New Jersey: Princeton University Press.

Calvino, I. (1988). *Lezioni americane. Sei proposte per il prossimo milennio*. Milan: Garzanti.

Calvino, I. (1993). *Six memos for the next millennium* (trans. P. Creagh). New York: Vintage Books.

Castillo de Berchenko, A. (2005). Roberto Bolaño: Los vasos comunicantes de la escritura. Filiación, poeticidad, intratextualidad. In F. Moreno (ed.), *Roberto Bolaño. Una literatura infinita*. Poitiers: Centre de Recherches Latino-américaines/Archivos Université de Poitiers - CNRS, pp. 41-52.

Decante-Araya, S. (2007). Mémoire et mélancolie dans *Nocturno de Chile*. In K. Benmiloud & R. Estève (eds.), *Les Astres noirs de Roberto Bolaño*. Bordeaux: ERSAL/GRIAL - AMERIBER, pp. 11-32.

Derrida, J., de Baecque, A., & Jousse, T. (2015). Cinema and its ghosts: An interview with Jacques Derrida (trans. P. Kamuf). *Discourse*, 37(1-2), 22-39.

Derrida, J., & Stiegler, B. (2002). *Echographies of television: Filmed interviews* [1996] (trans. J. Bajorek). Cambridge: Polity.

Espinosa, P. (2003). Estudio preliminar. In P. Espinosa H. (ed.), *Territorios en fuga. Estudios críticos sobre la obra* de Roberto Bolaño. Santiago: FRASIS, pp.13-45.

Fischer, M. L. (2008). La memoria de las historias en *Estrella distante* de Roberto Bolaño. In E. Paz Soldán & G. Faverón Patriau (eds.), *Bolaño Salvage*. Barcelona: Candaya, pp. 145-162.

Gamboa Cárdenas, J. (2008). ¿Siameses o dobles? Vanguardia y postmodernismo en *Estrella distante* de Roberto Bolaño. In E. Paz Soldán & G. Faverón Patriau (eds.), *Bolaño Salvage*. Barcelona: Candaya, pp. 211-236.

Gorky, M. (1896). Lumière's cinematograph (trans C. Gilman). At **http://isites.harvard.edu/fs/ docs/icb.topic265838.files/gorky%20lumiere%20 1896.doc**, accessed February 1, 2017.

Gras, D. (2005). Roberto Bolaño y la obra total. In R. González Férriz (ed.), *Jornadas homenaje. Roberto Bolaño (1953-2003)*. Barcelona: ICCI-Casa América a Catalunya, pp. 49-73.

Jennerjahn, I. (2002). Escritos en los cielos y fotografías del infierno. Las "Acciones de arte" de Carlos Ramírez Hoffman, según Roberto Bolaño. *Revista de Crítica Literaria Latinoamericana*, 56, 69-86.

Landsberg, A. (2004). *Prosthetic memory: The transformation of American remembrance in the age of mass culture*. New York: Columbia University Press.

Lepage, C. (2007). Littérature et dictature: Lecture croisée de trois romans de Roberto Bolaño (*Estrella distante - Amuleto - Nocturno de Chile*). In K. Benmiloud & R. Estève (eds.), *Les Astres noirs de Roberto Bolaño*. Bordeaux: ERSAL/ GRIAL - AMERIBER, pp. 67-89.

López-Calvo, I. (2015). Roberto Bolaño's flower war: Memory, melancholy, and Pierre Menard. In I. López-Calvo (ed.), *Roberto Bolaño, a less distant star: Critical essays*. New York: Palgrave MacMillan, pp. 35-64.

Manzi, J. (2004). Mirando caer otra Estrella distante. *Cahiers du Monde Hispanique et Luso-Brèsilien/Caravelle*, 82, 125-141.

Manzi, J. (2007). Dos palabras. In K. Benmiloud & R. Estève (eds.), *Les Astres noirs de Roberto Bolaño*. Bordeaux: ERSAL/ GRIAL - AMERIBER, pp. 91-108.

Manzoni, C. (2002). Narrar lo inefable: El juego del doble y los desplazamientos en *Estrella distante*. In C. Manzoni (ed.), *Roberto Bolaño: La escritura como tauromaquia*.

Buenos Aires: Corregidor, pp. 39-50.
O'Bryen, R. (2015). Writing with the ghost of Pierre Menard: Authorship, responsibility, and justice in Roberto Bolaño's *Distant Star*. In I. López-Calvo (ed.), *Roberto Bolaño, a less distant star: Critical essays*. New York: Palgrave MacMillan, pp. 17-34.
Oesterheld, H. G., & Solano López, F. (2008). *El eternauta*. Buenos Aires: Doedytores.
Perez, G. (1998). *The material ghost: Films and their medium*. Baltimore, MD: Johns Hopkins University Press.
Piglia, R. (2000). Tesis sobre el cuento. *Guaraguao*, 4(11), 17-19.
Sasturain, J. (2010). *El aventurador. Una lectura de Oesterheld*. Buenos Aires: Aquilina.
Vonnegut, K. (1991). *Slaughterhouse 5*. Vintage Books: London.
Zambra, A. (2003). Una novela pendiente. In P. Espinosa H. (ed.), *Territorios en fuga. Estudios críticos sobre la obra de Roberto Bolaño*. Santiago: FRASIS, pp. 255-259.
Žižek, S. (2009). *Violence: Six sideways reflections*. London: Profile.

Notes on Contributors

Pampa Arán is Professor and researcher at the National University of Córdoba, Argentina. She has specialized in literary and historical issues from the perspective of social discourse, as well as in the contributions of different thinkers to this field. Her works are frequently published in national and international journals. Some of her books are: *El fantástico literario. Aportes teóricos* (2000); *Texto/memoria/cultura. El pensamiento de Iuri Lotman* (2005); *Nuevo diccionario de la teoría de Mijaíl Bajtín* (2006). *Interpelaciones. Hacia una teoría crítica de las escrituras sobre la dictadura y la memoria* (2010); *La herencia de Bajtín. Reflexiones y migraciones* (forthcoming).

María José Contreras Lorenzini holds a Ph.D. in Semiotics from the Università di Bologna and is a performance artist. Her work moves between academic research and artistic creation, studying and creatively exploring the relation between the body, memory and performance. As performance artist and theatre director she has worked with testimonies and ethnographic sources, investigating scenic strategies to perform memory. She has conducted research on testimonial theatre and diverse modalities of performing memory through the arts. Her work has been published in Chile, England, Italy, Brazil and Argentina. She is currently Chair of the Ph.D. Programme in Arts at the Pontificia Universidad Católica de Chile.

María Teresa Dalmasso is Professor and researcher at the National University of Córdoba, Argentina. Her research, conducted from a semiotic perspective, has focused on the study of Argentine social discourse during the period beginning with the return to democracy (1983) and continuing until today. Within this framework, her works have been based primarily on the analysis of films, journalistic discourses and political discourses and essays. Some of them have been collected in books and other national and international journals. She is director of the Doctorado en Semiótica at the National University of Córdoba.

Notes on Contributors

Cristina Demaria is Associate Professor in the Department of Philosophy and Communication of the University of Bologna, where she teaches Analysis of Television Languages, Semiotics of Media and Semiotics of Conflict. She is a member of TraMe, the Centre for the Interdisciplinary Study of Cultural Memory and Traumas at the University of Bologna, and has worked extensively on the semiotics of memories and traumas, on gender studies and audiovisual languages. Among her publications: *L'archivio, le immagini e il testimone* (Bologna: BUP, 2012); with M. Daly (eds.), *The Genres of Post-Conflict Testimonies* (Nottingham: CCCP, 2009).

Norma Fatala majored in Spanish Language and Literature; English Language and Literature (FL-UNC) and holds a Ph.D. in Semiotics (CEA-FFyH-UNC). She teaches Spanish in the Faculty of Communication Sciences at the National University of Córdoba, where she also directs the research project Printed Press and Social Discourse: The Place of Sciences and Arts in the Newspaper. Her fields of interest include: Social Discourse (political, economic, journalistic, religious discourses); the printed press; subjects and identities; memory. She has published chapters and articles in books and national and international journals.

Daniel Filmus is a Professor of Sociology at the University of Buenos Aires, a CONICET-CITRA Researcher, and a Mercosur Parlamentarian. He has served as Minister of Education, Science and Technology in Argentina (2003-2007), as a National Senator (2007-2013), and as a Member of the Executive Council of UNESCO (2007-2015). He is the author of *Educar para el mercado* (Buenos Aires, 2017), *Pensar el Kirchnerismo* (Buenos Aires: Editorial Siglo XXI, 2016), *Presidential Voices of Latin America* (London: CCCP, 2015) and *Educar para una sociedad más justa* (Buenos Aires: Editorial Aguilar, Aletea, Taurus, 2012).

Sebastián Gastaldi holds a degree in Social Communication with specialization in Research and Planning from the Department of Social Communication at the National University of Córdoba. He is currently writing a Ph.D. thesis in Semiotics, in the Centre for Advanced Studies and the Faculty of Philosophy and Humanities at the National University of Córdoba. He is Assistant Professor in Semiotics and Interdisciplinary Gender Studies Area and Coordinator of the Social Discourse Programme in the Centre for Advanced Studies, the National University of Córdoba.

Rui Gonçalves Miranda is Assistant Professor in the Department of Spanish, Portuguese and Latin American Studies at the University of Nottingham. His research interests include critical theory, literature, film, post-conflict studies, and the interface between aesthetics and politics. He is currently researching on post-conflict and transoceanic discourses in philosophies, political and cultural products. He has co-edited (with Federica Zullo) *Post-Conflict Reconstructions: Remappings and Reconciliations* (2013) and is the author of *Personal Infinitive: Inflecting Fernando Pessoa* (2017).

Milena Grass Kleiner is a translator and theatre scholar and Professor at the Pontificia Universidad Católica de Chile. She holds an MA in Latin American Studies (Universidad de Chile) and a Ph.D. in Literature (Pontificia Universidad Católica de Chile). Her Spanish translations of English, American, and French plays have been produced by leading Chilean directors and have also been published along with her various translations of books and papers on Chilean history, and theatre studies. Her longstanding work on research methodologies in theatre studies was published in *La investigación de los procesos teatrales. Manual de uso* (2011). In recent years, she has been working on traumatic memory, postmemory, and theatre in post-conflict societies.

Andrés Kalawski is Associate Professor in the Pontificia Universidad Católica de Chile's Faculty of Arts. His research areas include Chilean theatre history and playwriting. He is also a staged and published playwright and currently the artistic director of his University's professional theatre, Teatro UC.

Anna Maria Lorusso is Associate Professor in the Department of Philosophy and Communication at the University of Bologna. She is a member of TraMe, the Centre for the Interdisciplinary Study of Cultural Memory and Traumas at the University of Bologna, and the vice-director of the Italian Association of Semiotic Studies (AISS). Her research interests include cultural semiotics, cultural memory and rhetoric. Among her books: *Cultural Semiotics: For a Cultural Perspective in Semiotics* (New York: Palgrave Macmillan, 2015), *Semiotica della cultura* (Rome and Bari: Laterza, 2010), *Umberto Eco. Temi, problemi e percorsi semiotici* (Rome: Carocci, 2008), *La trama del testo. Problemi, analisi, prospettive semiotiche* (Milan: Bompiani, 2006).

Daniel Oviedo Silva is a Ph.D. candidate at the University of Nottingham exploring social conflict, intra-community violence and accusatory practices in Madrid before, during and after the Spanish Civil War. His research interests include social history, social attitudes towards dictatorships, the history of punitive institutions and urban history. He is a member of the research projects *Madrid 1936-1939: capital, frente, retaguardia y ciudad en guerra* and *El control del delito en la España contemporánea: discursos de seguridad, instituciones punitivas y prácticas de excepcionalidad*. Among his publications: D. Oviedo Silva & A. Pérez-Olivares (eds.), *Madrid, una ciudad en guerra (1936-1948)* (Madrid: 2016), and "Paisaje urbano y mapa de la represión: Carabanchel Bajo 1939-1945", in C. Ortiz García (ed.), *Lugares de represión, paisajes de la memoria: La cárcel de Carabanchel* (Madrid: 2013).

Andrea Pelegrí Kristić is an actress and translator and was Associate Professor at the Pontificia Universidad Católica de Chile from 2013 to 2015, and at the University of Valparaiso in 2013. She is a Ph.D. candidate (Theatre and Spanish Literature) at the Pontificia Universidad Católica de Chile and Paris Ouest Nanterre la Défense. She holds an MA in theatre from the University of Ottawa, Canada. Her thesis, *Approche fonctionaliste de la langue au théâtre. Pour une version chilienne du Chant du Dire-Dire de Daniel Danis*, was nominated for two prizes (the Humanities Award and the Rene Lupien Award). Her research focuses mainly on theatre translation and Translation Studies. She is currently a Regional Managing Editor for France at thetheatretimes.com. She has published scholarly articles on theatre translation in journals from Chile and Canada.

José Manuel Rodríguez Amieva is Ph.D. candidate in Semiotics in the Centre for Advanced Studies, the National University of Córdoba, Argentina. He is a member of the programme Social Discourse and Memory, and part of the Project Memory(ies) in Conflict, Identities and Social Discourse at the same centre. He is also member of the Network of Neighbours of San Vicente, Córdoba. His current studies are focused on the sense of community in this neighbourhood, and the memory of its inhabitants regarding the years of the last Argentine dictatorship.

Daniele Salerno is a post-doctoral research fellow at the University of Bologna. He is a member of the Centre for the Interdisciplinary Study of Cultural Memory and Traumas (TraMe) and of the Interdisciplinary Research Group on Race and Racisms (InteRGRace). He received his doctorate in Semiotics in 2009, with a dissertation on security and terrorism discourses in the "war on terror", published in 2012 (*Terrorismo, sicurezza, post conflitto: Studi semiotici sulla guerra al terrore*, Libreria universitaria). His research interests include cultural semiotics, cultural memory, political discourse, analysis of conflict and media.

Sandra Savoini holds a Ph.D. in Literature (2009) from the National University of Córdoba, Argentina. She is Professor of Semiotics in the Department of Film and Television, School of Arts as well as in the Department of Semiotics, the Centre for Advanced Studies, School of Social Sciences, at the National University of Córdoba. The focus of her investigation and publications is the discourse analysis of the media, as well as of constructions of social identities through discourse. She has published chapters and articles in books and journals.

Mike Seear is a Light Infantry veteran of the Northern Ireland "Troubles" (1971-80) and 7th Duke of Edinburgh's Own Gurkha Rifles combat veteran of the 1982 Falklands-Malvinas War. After twenty-one years' service, he retired from the British Army in 1988 with the rank of Major. Since then he has lived in Norway, initially employed by Scandinavian Airlines as the Security and Emergency Response Manager. Since 2005 he has been a Kenyon International Emergency Services Senior Associate specializing in the design and delivery of highly realistic crisis management exercises to airlines and other organizations. He is the author of *With the Gurkhas in the Falklands: A War Journal* (Barnsley: Pen and Sword Books, 2003), a multiple contributor to, and co-editor of, *Hors de Combat: The Falklands-Malvinas Conflict in Retrospect* (Nottingham: CCCP, 2009), and author of *Return to Tumbledown: The Falklands-Malvinas War Revisited* (Nottingham: CCCP, 2012).

Adam Sharman is Associate Professor in the Department of Spanish, Portuguese and Latin American Studies at the University of Nottingham. He is the author of *Tradition and Modernity in Spanish American Literature: From Darío to Carpentier* (Palgrave Macmillan, 2006) and *Otherwise Engaged: After Hegel and the Philosophy of History* (CCCP, 2013), and co-editor of *1812 Echoes: The Cadiz Constitution in Hispanic History, Culture and Politics* (Cambridge Scholars, 2013). He is currently working on a project called *Moments of Modernity: In Latin America*.

Cecilia Sosa is an Argentine sociologist and cultural journalist. She works as a permanent researcher at CONICET (Institute of Arts and Culture, Universidad Nacional Tres de Febrero, Argentina) and is currently a visiting fellow at the University of Nottingham (UK). She completed her Ph.D. in Drama at Queen Mary, University of London. Her doctoral thesis was awarded the Best Thesis of the Year and published as a book, *Queering Acts of Mourning in the Aftermath of Argentina's Dictatorship* (Tamesis, 2014). She has published extensively on memory and the arts in Argentina, including articles in *Memory Studies*; *Theory, Culture and Society*; *Feminist Theory, Subjectivity*, *Journal of Latin American Cultural Studies*, *Latin American Theatre Review* and *Cultural Studies*.

Paola Sozzi is a Ph.D. candidate in Semiotics at Bologna University, where she also did her Masters. In both these works, she has focused on the semiotic study of places, both on a methodological and analytical level. She is mainly interested in the relationship between spaces and cultures, collective identities, memories, and social processes.

Alicia Vaggione is Professor and researcher at the National University of Córdoba, Argentina. Her research focuses mainly on the relationship between culture, body and illness. She has published a book entitled *Literatura/enfermedad. Escrituras sobre SIDA en América Latina* (2014) and a number of journal articles.

Patrizia Violi is Full Professor of Semiotics at the University of Bologna, Department of Philosophy and Communication, and Coordinator of the Ph.D. Programme in Semiotics. She is the Director of the School of Advanced Studies in the Humanities and the Director of TraMe, the Interdisciplinary Centre for the Study of Memory and Cultural Traumas, at the University of Bologna. Her main areas of research include text analysis, language and gender, and semantic theory, on which theme she has published numerous articles and volumes, amongst others, *Meaning and Experience* (Indiana University Press, 2001). She is currently working on cultural semiotics and traumatic memory, in particular on memorials and memory museums. Her latest book is *Paesaggi della memoria. Il trauma, lo spazio, la storia* (Bompiani 2014), currently being revised for an English translation with Peter Lang.

Index

A

Abuelas, see Grandmothers of the Plaza de Mayo
accusatory, 17, 20, 195, 197-8, 200-3, 206-8, 413
Acevedo Hernández, Antonio, 291
actuality books, 164
Acuña, Nicolás, 333
Adorno, Theodor, 62
aesthetics, 18, 23, 27, 133, 135, 140, 243, 281, 285-6, 288, 299-300, 304, 319, 321, 326-7, 329, 375, 412
afectado/a directo/a (directly affected), 41, 77, 89, 159
affect, 13, 17, 95, 104, 107, 110-11, 165, 179, 199, 238, 350
affective reparation, 93, 97, 101
affective turn, the, 17, 95
Agamben, Giorgio, 299, 312, 318, 328
Alcoba, Laura, 27, 375, 383-5, 388-9
Alfonsín, Raúl, 10, 12, 31, 59, 68, 121, 187, 192, 239, 242
Allende, Salvador, 9, 314-15, 318, 326
Andermann, Jens, 50, 53, 359, 363-4, 366-9, 373
Andrews, Chris, 399
Angenot, Marc, 128, 140, 144, 165, 179, 222, 233, 237, 244, 248, 299, 312, 350-4, 358
anniversary, 12, 21, 24, 97, 100, 149, 225-6, 229-30, 232, 242, 247, 288, 314, 323-4

archive, 14, 16, 19, 47, 80, 82, 86, 90, 102, 144, 147, 150, 154, 161, 171, 181-2, 184, 188, 192, 194, 251, 328, 333, 336, 342-3, 345-7, 367, 391
Arendt, Hannah, 26, 357-8
Argentina, 1-4, 7-10, 12-20, 22, 26, 29-31, 35, 41, 44-5, 49, 51, 53-5, 57, 60-2, 69-73, 75-8, 80-2, 91-4, 96, 99-100, 103-4, 110-11, 115, 117, 119, 141, 146-7, 151, 154-5, 162, 164, 166, 171, 179, 181, 184, 193-8, 201-3, 207-9, 211-13, 215, 219, 227, 229, 236, 240, 246-7, 261, 265-6, 268, 270-1, 273, 348-9, 351, 357, 366, 373-4, 380, 410-11, 414-16
Arias, Lola, 22, 107, 110, 261, 278
Armour, Lou, 264, 270, 277-8
Assmann, Aleida, 13, 79, 91, 147, 162, 323-4, 328
Association of the Relatives of the Disappeared, 9, 300
audiovisual, 21, 67, 83, 136, 236-7, 240-1, 243, 247-8, 293, 348-9, 355, 411
Aylwin, Patricio, 10-11, 137, 140, 281-2, 298

B

Bachelet, Michelle, 11, 24, 304
Bakhtin, Mikhail, 301, 312
Baldo, Alberto José, 123, 144
Barril, Claudia, 333
Belgrano, the, 236, 265, 271, 273, 277
Bellotti, Sergio, 244, 248

417

Bemberg, María Luisa, 10, 29
Blanchot, Maurice, 400, 405, 407
Blaustein, David, 9, 27, 30, 75, 359-3, 365, 373
Bolaño, Roberto, 5, 28, 30, 390-409
Borges, Jorge Luis, 10, 30, 63, 278, 360, 391, 407
Brazil, 7, 166, 208, 410
Brito, Lucretia, 132, 144, 197, 210
Bruschtein, Luis, 225, 233
Bruzzone, Félix, 49, 53, 106
Buenos Aires, 31, 45, 49-51, 53-5, 68, 71-2, 81, 96, 108-11, 144-5, 162-3, 167, 171, 179-80, 185-6, 193-4, 202, 209-15, 228, 230, 234-35, 248, 253, 258, 260-8, 275, 278, 312, 358, 373-4, 379, 387-9, 407, 409, 411
Bullrich, Esteban, 69, 71-2
Butler, Judith, 38, 53, 94, 104, 110, 247-8

C

Cáceres, Gerardo, 291
Calderón de la Barca, Pedro, 282
Calderón, Guillermo, 24, 131, 303
Calveiro, Pilar, 36, 53, 167, 172, 174-7, 179
Calvino, Italo, 404-5, 407
Cambra, Irene, 118-19, 145
Campo de la Ribera, 3, 17, 49, 115-20, 122-3, 125, 128, 140, 143-5
canon, 281, 289, 295-6, 298, 345-6
Carri, Albertina, 98, 104, 106, 110, 368-9, 373
Casabé, Daniel, 22, 236, 250, 253, 260
Castro, Alicia, 277
Catholic Church, 25, 186, 287, 333
censorship, 23, 58-9, 154, 224, 281-2, 286, 301, 304-5
Children for Equality and Justice against Forgetting and Silence (H.I.J.O.S.), 17, 41, 77, 105-6, 230-1, 234
Chile, 1-4, 7-14, 17, 23, 29, 35, 49, 54, 111, 115, 129, 132-3, 136, 138-41, 143-6, 198, 208, 215, 234, 281, 283-8, 290, 293-4, 296-8, 300, 309-10, 312-14, 316, 318, 328-9, 333, 338, 347, 368, 393, 400, 407-8, 410, 412-13
chronicle, 22, 94, 251, 255-7, 377
chronotope, 27, 82, 301, 305-6, 375, 383, 385
cinema, 10, 25, 28, 67, 284, 315, 333, 366, 373, 390-1, 394, 397-8, 401, 403, 405-6
Cixous, Hélène, 99-100
collaboration, 20, 135-6, 168, 170, 174, 195-6, 199-201, 203-5, 207-8, 210, 250, 266, 276, 317, 328
commemoration, 12, 14, 20, 25, 28, 44, 47, 74, 79, 120, 221, 223, 229, 237, 247, 314-15, 317, 323-4, 367, 372
communist, 382
community, 15, 18, 20-1, 38, 40, 47, 51, 56, 64, 78, 97-9, 101-2, 104, 108, 117, 119-20, 122-3, 125, 127-8, 130-31, 135, 142-3, 176-7,

Index

181, 186, 188, 191, 195-6, 199, 207, 238, 240, 258, 283, 305, 328, 345, 350, 384, 387, 413-14

Córdoba, 3, 7, 17-19, 29, 47, 49, 50, 75, 87, 116-18, 120, 123-4, 144-50, 157, 162, 166-7, 170-1, 179-82, 184-6, 192, 211, 248, 312, 374, 388, 410-11, 414, 416

Cortés Rocca, Paola, 253, 260

coup d'état, 8-9, 12-13, 25, 77, 97, 100, 103, 117, 119, 122, 149, 164, 178, 201, 204, 221, 242, 281, 283, 287, 289-90, 294, 298-9, 302, 310, 314, 317, 323-4, 351, 355, 368

Crenzel, Emilio, 12, 30, 54, 181, 190, 192-3, 365, 373

Cuadra, Fernando, 291

D

da Silva Catela, Ludmila, 39, 45, 53, 149, 159, 162

de Ípola, Emilio, 227

Deleuze, Gilles, 13, 95, 110, 170, 180

Demaria, Cristina, 3, 13, 16-17, 39, 42, 53, 73, 77, 91, 145, 147, 155, 157, 159, 162, 182, 190, 194, 298, 312, 347, 411

denunciation, 20, 24, 30, 196, 198, 201-4, 206, 208, 211-12, 299, 301, 311, 333, 335

Derrida, Jacques, 93, 95, 110, 254, 260, 390-1, 397, 400-3, 407

detention centres, 17, 19, 75, 77, 115, 121, 129, 143, 164, 199, 258

dictatorship, 7, 9-13, 15-16, 19-21, 23-6, 28, 36, 42, 53-5, 58-61, 63, 68-9, 74, 76, 78, 84, 92, 99-100, 109, 111, 115, 118-19, 121, 127, 135, 139, 141, 154-5, 158-9, 168, 170, 178, 181, 183-5, 187, 189-93, 196-98, 201-3, 207-9, 223, 228-31, 233, 237-40, 244-6, 249, 257, 259, 281-82, 287-8, 291, 293-4, 296, 298-9, 303-4, 307-8, 311, 314-15, 324, 327, 333, 335, 342-3, 348, 351-4, 356-7, 375, 399, 404, 414

Dieleke, Edgardo, 22, 236, 250, 253, 260

Diez, Rolo, 170

Di Girólamo, Claudia, 4, 25, 314, 316-7, 319-323, 327-9

Dillon, Marta, 16, 94-9, 101-4, 107, 109-10

disappeared, the, 8-11, 14-16, 18-19, 24-5, 27, 29, 35-6, 39, 41-5, 47, 49-51, 53-5, 58, 69, 74-6, 79-80, 83-5, 87, 88, 90, 93, 95, 97, 99, 100-1, 103, 105-8, 111, 117, 119, 123-5, 127-8, 130, 132-3, 135, 149-50, 153, 155, 157, 169, 172-3, 179, 185, 19-4, 202, 231, 242, 254, 257-8, 270, 286, 291, 298-300, 302-3, 306-7, 310-11, 316-20, 328, 334-5, 352, 368, 372, 379-81, 385, 390, 392-4, 396, 398, 403

discourse, 19, 26, 41, 75-8, 128, 151-2, 159, 165, 169, 173-5, 177-9, 187-8, 190-1, 193, 222, 224, 228, 237, 240-3, 245, 283, 299, 305, 319-21, 325, 339, 346,

348, 350-2, 354, 357, 362, 364, 370, 410, 414
Di Tella, Andrés, 363
Dittborn, Eugenio, 287-8, 292-3
documentary, 11, 22, 25-6, 75, 82, 87, 106, 159, 249-51, 253-4, 257, 259, 271, 274, 304, 309, 330, 333-4, 336-7, 339, 342, 344-5, 348, 359-60, 363, 366-7, 369, 378-9
Donda, Victoria, 83, 87
Dowd, Ashley, 118-19, 145
dramaturgical, 321
Druliolle, Vincent, 49-50, 53-4, 111
Due Obedience Law (Ley de Obediencia Debida), 11, 60-1, 100, 121
Duhalde, Eduardo Luis, 12
Dussel, Inés, 62

E

Eco, Umberto, 65, 148, 158, 160, 162, 176, 413
education, 15, 56, 58-61, 64-5, 67, 69-70, 125, 128, 186, 201, 269, 287, 349, 365
Eichmann, Adolf, 26, 348, 357-8
Eng, David, 93, 107, 110
enunciation, 19, 36, 83, 140, 158-9, 165, 174, 176, 181-2, 188-9, 192, 319-20, 339, 345, 369, 384
ERP (People's Revolutionary Army), 166-7
Escudero, Lucrecia, 222-4, 234
ESMA (Higher Naval School of Mechanics), 45-6, 49, 51, 75, 87, 164, 175-7, 179
Espacio Carta Abierta, 228
Esteban, Edgardo, 229, 247
ethics, 17, 93
ex-combatant, 22-3, 229-30, 240-1, 253, 261-2, 265, 271-3, 275, 277, 414
exempla, 25, 342, 346

F

Falklands-Malvinas, 4, 10, 13, 20-2, 30, 59-60, 63-4, 68-9, 217, 221-2, 224-9, 231-51, 254-5, 257-61, 263, 265-6, 272, 274, 276-8, 414
familialism, 42, 77-8
feminist, 13, 17, 96, 107, 109, 327
Fernández de Kirchner, Cristina, 11, 15, 96-98, 225, 247
film, 10, 14, 21-2, 25-6, 67, 82, 106, 160, 239, 241, 243-5, 249, 251-4, 259-60, 268, 274, 293, 302, 306, 314, 337-9, 343-4, 348, 351, 359-64, 366-7, 369-72, 394-5, 397, 399, 401-3, 407, 412
Florencia Escardo Technical College, 126
Fontes, Claudia, 51
forgetting, 15, 21, 57, 60-1, 65-6, 68-70, 137-8, 177-8, 239, 300, 360-1, 373
Foucault, Michel, 143, 145, 188, 193-4, 345, 347, 355, 358
Franco, Francisco, 4, 195, 197, 201, 207-8, 210-12, 300
Frente de Liberación Homosexual, 181
Full Stop Law (Ley de Punto Final), 10, 60-1, 77, 100, 121

Index

G

Gamerro, Carlos, 223, 254, 260
Garaño, Santiago, 167, 170-1, 180, 209-10, 214-15
Gatti, Gabriel, 77, 79, 91
gay, 181, 184-5, 187-92, 194
generation, 13, 25-6, 56, 83, 91, 99, 101, 220, 239, 256, 259, 303, 309, 311, 323-4, 327, 329, 359-60, 362, 364, 366-8, 370-2, 374, 379, 385
Germano, Gustavo, 8, 31
Giorgi, Gabriel, 78, 90-1, 100, 110
Gómez Jacobo, Alejo, 68, 137-8, 145, 167-8, 170, 172-3, 176-8, 180, 205-207, 212, 297
Gómez-Barris, Macarena, 137-8, 145
González, Horacio, 88, 225, 229
Gordon, Avery, 73, 89
Gorky, Maxim, 28, 390-1, 393, 401, 408
grandchildren, 16, 73, 76, 78-80, 82-4, 101, 157, 316
Grandmothers of the Plaza de Mayo, 3, 16, 41-2, 59, 61, 68, 73-84, 86-7, 90-1, 97, 101, 157
Griffero, Ramón, 24, 300, 302, 305-7, 312-13
guerrilla, 9, 27-8, 96, 121, 213, 335, 341, 360, 363-7, 373, 384, 388
Guevara, Ernesto, 386
Gurkha, 22, 261-2, 266-8, 272, 274, 278, 414
Guzmán, Patricio, 11, 257, 259

H

Hall, Stuart, 80, 90-1, 121, 351
Heras, Tomás de las, 237, 241, 248
Hirsch, Marianne, 79, 91, 324-6, 329, 359, 367, 374
homosexual, 185-6, 303
human rights, 11, 17, 20, 24, 41-2, 54, 59-64, 67, 69, 75, 78, 81, 87, 99-100, 108, 115, 117, 119, 121, 124, 130-31, 135, 138-40, 149, 151, 165, 169, 181-2, 186, 189-91, 193, 231, 233, 288, 298-99, 301, 310-11
humour, 23, 105-8, 244, 268, 404
Hurtado, María de la Luz, 285-6, 288, 290-1, 293, 296-7

I

Ibáñez, Víctor, 175, 179
identity, 16, 21, 28, 36, 38, 42, 63, 69, 73-4, 76-88, 90-2, 101, 107, 125, 136, 139, 156-7, 173, 181-2, 186, 191, 194, 202, 220, 222-3, 225, 227, 231, 243, 246, 304, 308, 312, 328, 336, 357, 375-6, 379, 384, 387, 394
imaginary, 24, 89, 223, 299-300, 308, 379-81, 383, 385
index of grandparenthood, 78
Insunza, Pablo, 316, 319-320, 326, 328
intra-bodies, 16, 90

J

Jackson, David, 264-5, 271, 273-4
Jelin, Elizabeth, 41, 54, 76,

142, 221, 234
journey, 22, 84, 249-52, 255-7, 259, 352, 380, 384, 388

K

Kalawski, Andrés, 4, 11, 24, 281, 285, 297-8, 412
Kamín, Bebe, 21, 236, 239, 248
Kirchner, Néstor, 11, 15, 17, 21, 60, 75, 87, 96-100, 104-8, 121, 225, 247

L

La Perla, 149, 167-8, 171-3, 175, 177, 179-80
landscape, 14-15, 17, 22, 43-5, 49, 53, 99, 102, 206, 253, 255, 257, 381, 385
LGBT, 3, 13, 19, 181, 183-4, 186-7, 189-193
literature, 29, 67, 95, 136, 198-199, 204, 206, 249-51, 259, 283, 291, 301, 375, 380, 382, 395, 397-8, 400, 405, 410, 412
Lopérfido, Darío, 68, 108
Lorenz, Federico, 22, 200, 203, 213, 231, 234, 240, 248, 250, 255-6, 258-60
Lotman, Yuri, 148, 162, 182, 336, 347, 410

M

Macri, Mauricio, 12, 16, 67, 69, 82, 97, 108, 111
Madres, see Mothers of the Plaza de Mayo
Marchetti, Florencia, 117, 122, 125-6, 145
Mariani, Ana, 167-8, 170, 172, 173, 176-8, 180
Marín, Germán, 129, 141, 145

media, 14, 55, 67, 92, 125, 202, 224-5, 237, 242, 266, 310, 321, 324, 337, 406, 414
mediation, 25, 107, 137, 319-21, 323, 326, 392
Meek, Alan, 81, 92
memory, 7, 11-29, 35, 40-1, 43-5, 49-51, 53-5, 61-2, 64-7, 69-70, 74-82, 90, 96, 100, 102-3, 106-7, 109, 111, 117, 119, 122, 125, 127-8, 132-3, 136-7, 139-156, 159-66, 172, 178-82, 184, 189-94, 196-7, 210-11, 214, 219, 221-2, 232-3, 237, 239, 242-3, 246-7, 249, 255, 257-9, 262, 264, 277, 296, 298-9, 304-5, 308, 312, 314-15, 319-20, 322-4, 326-9, 333-4, 338-9, 341-2, 344-8, 351, 354, 356, 359-61, 363-4, 366-7, 370-2, 374-6, 378-85, 391-2, 400-1, 403-4, 406-8, 410-16
memory site, 14, 18, 50-1, 53, 117, 147-9, 151, 159, 162
Menem, Carlos, 11, 100, 121, 362
Mercosur, 7, 411
military, the, 8-11, 17, 19-21, 31, 35-6, 40-2, 46, 51, 58-61, 63, 68, 76, 78, 93, 96-8, 100-1, 103, 115, 117, 119, 121-3, 129, 132, 142, 149, 164, 166-71, 175, 177-9, 184-5, 187, 189, 193,196- 201, 204-5, 208, 210, 221, 223, 225-33, 238-42, 249, 266, 268, 277, 281-2, 287-9, 294, 296, 298, 302, 304, 310, 314, 324, 348, 351-2, 354-

Index

7, 362, 374, 393, 398, 404
Mocca, Edgardo, 228, 234
modernization, 8, 284, 295
Molière, 288, 292-5
monstrosity, 26, 355, 357
Montenegro, Victoria, 16, 83, 85-6
Montoneros, 167, 179, 186, 192, 240, 363, 374, 378
Moore, Carlos Raymundo, 162, 164, 166, 168, 179, 180
Morales, Víctor Hugo, 83, 87
Moreno, Sebastián, 333
Mortheiru, Pedro, 286
Mothers of the Plaza de Mayo, 9, 15, 17, 39, 41-2, 44-5, 47, 51, 53-4, 59, 61, 68, 77, 91, 97-8, 100, 105, 111, 150, 157, 254, 352-3, 357
mourning, 13-14, 17, 21, 35, 37-8, 40, 42-4, 47, 49-51, 53-5, 78, 92, 94, 96-8, 102, 104, 106-11, 160, 186, 191, 219-21, 247, 253, 257, 400-1
Munizaga, Giselle, 286, 297
Museum of Memory and Human Rights, 11, 25, 132, 140, 304, 316

N

National Commission on the Disappearance of Persons (CONADEP), 59, 115, 121, 144, 202, 368
National Institute for Agricultural Technology (INTA), 27, 371-2
neighbourhood, 20, 50, 96, 119, 122, 128, 206, 414
Nietzsche, Friedrich, 27, 359, 361-3, 366, 369-71, 374
Nunca más, 10, 12, 30, 59, 71, 372-3
Núñez, Ramón, 288, 293

O

Opazo, Cristián, 295, 297
Otero, Rubén, 130, 264-5

P

PAKAPAKA, 348-9
Parque de la Memoria, Buenos Aires, 50-1
passion, 62, 176, 220, 381-3
Paz Clemente, Jerónimo, 241, 248
Peña, Marcos, 70, 72
Pérez, Andrés, 24, 303
Pérez, Mariana Eva, 106
Pérez, Rodrigo, 4, 24-5, 303, 308-9, 314, 317
Perón, Eva, 9
Peronist, 11, 27, 96, 186, 201, 362-3, 368, 371
photography, 15, 44-5, 47, 49, 132, 134, 136, 153, 160, 343, 377, 392, 398, 400, 405-6
Piaget, Jean, 70, 72
Piglia, Ricardo, 28-9, 31, 250, 259-60, 399, 409
Piña, Juan Andrés, 284, 288
Pinochet, Augusto, 5, 9-10, 13, 23, 115, 129, 281, 294, 300, 308, 311, 313-14, 333, 398
plays, 23-4, 28, 173, 191, 193, 281-3, 285, 288-91, 296, 299-300, 304-5, 307, 309-10, 314, 365, 393-4, 412
Polanski, Roman, 402
politics, 8-11, 13-14, 16-17, 19-21, 35, 40-45, 56-62, 64, 66-7, 69-70, 74-5, 77-9, 81-2, 90-1, 94, 96-7,

MemoSur/MemoSouth

98, 99-100, 104-5, 107-10, 127, 137, 139, 148-9, 178-9, 190-4, 227-9, 232-3, 239-40, 258, 264, 271-2, 282-4, 286, 291, 294, 300, 304-5, 308, 311, 314-15, 323-4, 326, 327-8, 335, 339, 345, 349, 353, 362, 364, 366-8, 371, 374-8, 380, 386, 403-4, 414
post-conflict, 7, 92, 181, 194, 412
post-dictatorship, 7, 10-11, 14, 26, 29, 41, 44, 51, 75, 78, 81-2, 181, 184, 190, 236, 239, 283, 314, 359
postmemory, 25-6, 78-9, 91, 157, 324, 326-27, 329, 359, 361, 366-7, 369, 373-4, 412
Post-Traumatic Stress Disorder (PTSD), 262, 265, 273
press, 20, 94, 201, 206, 212, 222, 233, 245, 377, 388, 411
prisoners, 19-20, 35-6, 130, 133, 135, 149-50, 152-3, 166-8, 170-72, 174-7, 183, 187, 196, 200, 242, 257, 267, 381
Prividera, Nicolás, 27, 360-1, 366-72, 374
Process of National Reorganization, 36, 199
Pron, Patricio, 27, 375-6, 379, 387-9
Provincial Memory Archive, Córdoba, 3, 18-19, 118, 144-5, 147, 150, 180, 182, 187
Puenzo, Luis, 10

Q

queer, 13, 17, 55, 99, 107

R

Rai, Sukrim, 263-4, 266
realism, 25, 302, 337, 339-40, 346-7
Rettig Report, 11, 24, 132, 298, 300, 311
Richard, Cliff, 271
Richard, Nelly, 11, 137-8, 140, 146, 314, 329
ritual, 39, 51, 53, 91, 110, 327, 339
Robin, Régine, 166
Rojo, Grinor, 287
Rozitchner, Alejandro, 70, 72
Rozitchner, León, 226

S

Sabatini, Juan Ignacio, 333
Sagastume, Gabriel, 264-5
Saint Vincent Cemetery, 123-5
San Martín, Raquel, 223, 228
Santiago, 17, 29, 101, 116-17, 129, 141-6, 170, 227, 234, 239, 281, 286, 296-7, 300, 308, 312-13, 316, 328-9, 333, 335, 347, 406, 408-9
Sarlo, Beatriz, 227, 362, 374
schools, 15, 20, 58-61, 65, 67, 69-70, 125, 143, 256, 265, 304, 324, 349
Semán, Ernesto, 27, 375, 379-80, 382, 385, 387-9
semiotics, 15, 22, 40, 43-5, 51, 74, 76, 81-2, 147, 158, 161, 182, 194, 219, 237-8, 320, 325, 334, 337, 341, 346-8, 410-11, 413-16
sexuality, 19, 184, 188-190, 305
Sierra, Marta, 368, 372-3
sociology, 56, 58, 264
Sosa, Cecilia, 3, 7, 13, 15-16,

Index

41, 93, 415
Southern Cone, 7, 14, 29, 54, 101, 111, 181, 184, 197, 371
Spain, 4, 20, 195-97, 206-7, 210-11, 215, 230, 282, 398
Spanish Civil War, 195, 197, 199, 206, 413
Spanish Golden Age, 289, 291-2
state, 8-13, 17, 19-21, 28, 31, 36, 39, 41, 43, 53-4, 56, 59-61, 63-4, 67, 69, 73, 75, 77, 99, 101, 105-6, 108, 110-11, 116-17, 121-2, 125, 127-9, 131, 136, 139, 156, 164-6, 168, 172-3, 176, 178-9, 181-3, 187-9, 192, 197-8, 200, 203-4, 207, 219-20, 225-6, 228, 237, 241, 246, 257, 284-5, 298-300, 310-11, 317, 350, 362-3, 365-67, 379
subversives, 9, 21, 85, 148-9, 201
survivors, 19-20, 36, 43, 77, 132, 150, 155, 158, 164-5, 167-9, 171, 173-9, 182, 193, 230, 241-2, 248, 254, 265, 367, 378, 384, 402

T

Taboada, Marta, 94, 96-7, 100-3
Teatro de Ensayo de la Universidad Católica, 23, 281, 286
technology, 14, 268, 391
television, 14, 21, 25-6, 67, 83, 202, 224, 237, 239, 241-2, 244, 272, 274, 278, 314, 321, 333, 336-8, 345, 348-9, 377, 395, 407
testimony, 19, 51, 83, 125, 140, 155, 172, 175, 178, 181-2, 185, 188, 192, 194, 245, 308, 310, 318-20, 336, 344, 360, 400, 403, 407
theatre, 14, 23-4, 67, 136, 241, 254, 261, 267, 281-95, 299, 302, 304-6, 308-9, 311-12, 314-17, 329-30, 339, 410, 412-13
theatrical historiography, 281, 285, 291
torture, 9, 11-12, 18, 24, 28, 36, 50, 62, 115-18, 120, 123, 125, 129-30, 132-3, 135, 140, 142, 147-8, 151, 164, 168, 171-6, 187, 190, 199, 230-1, 239, 245-6, 299-300, 302, 303-4, 310-11, 335, 337, 342, 350, 363, 383, 392, 399
trace, 37, 44, 85, 115, 124, 155, 159, 161, 199, 208, 350, 368, 398
transgender, 185, 187, 189-92
translation, 30, 45, 78, 88, 90, 100, 164, 166, 170-78, 268, 283, 293, 318-20, 325, 366, 397, 413, 416
trauma, 10, 13-14, 17, 26, 28, 41, 53, 55, 60, 62, 74, 79, 81, 91, 93, 106, 137, 145-6, 148, 156, 158-9, 162-3, 169, 174, 194, 219-20, 223, 229, 238, 248, 268, 277, 298, 301, 311-13, 323, 341, 347, 350, 358, 416

U

United Kingdom, 58, 63, 69, 229, 247
Uruguay, 7, 54, 111, 264, 368
USA, 8, 274, 380-1

V

Valdivieso, Josep de, 286
Valech Report, 9, 11, 24, 115, 144, 298, 300, 303, 311
Vallejo, Marcelo, 264-5
Verón, Eliseo, 124, 146, 148, 163, 165, 177, 180, 222, 235, 238, 248, 348-9, 358
Vicaria de la Solidaridad, 25, 333, 336
Videla, Jorge, 19, 172
video, 80, 82-6, 153, 182, 194, 268, 271, 273, 278, 303, 320, 376-7
Villa Grimaldi (Cuartel Terranova), 3, 17, 24, 115-17, 129-46, 303, 309
violence, 13, 17, 26, 28, 53, 81, 90, 93, 97-9, 105, 107, 110-11, 116, 129, 137-9, 143, 148, 159, 164, 168, 182, 190, 193, 196-7, 199-200, 204-8, 210-11, 213, 219, 238, 298, 300, 303, 305, 308, 310-12, 335, 340-1, 350, 357, 361, 363-4, 379, 392, 400, 413
Violi, Patrizia, 3, 13-14, 35, 49-50, 55, 77, 81, 92, 115, 139, 146-8, 155, 159, 161, 163, 182-3, 194, 416
Vitullo, Julieta, 22, 250-1, 258-260
Vonnegut, Kurt, 403-4, 409

W

war, 13, 20-22, 75, 110, 195, 197, 204, 207, 213, 223, 225-6, 229-33, 237-77, 403-4, 408, 414
Wolff, Egon, 290

Y

Yerushalmi, Yosef Hayim, 60, 72, 360, 364, 374

Z

Zito Lema, Vicente, 261

www.ingramcontent.com/pod-product-compliance
Lightning Source LLC
Chambersburg PA
CBHW060657100426
42735CB00040B/2869